WHITE DOG CAFE COOKBOOK

There's a quaint charm about the lace-curtained dining rooms and bric-a-brac shop
that ramble through the three adjoining Victorian brownstones that make up the White Dog Cafe.
This is a place of seasonal celebrations and culinary experimentation.

—Mimi Sheraton
Condé Nast Traveler

Encountering Kevin von Klause's food at the White Dog Cafe was a rare delight.
My pleasure and excitement were tripled when I learned of Kevin's
and Judy Wicks' commitment to local farmers, inner-city students, and a host of
socially-conscious projects. Their new book offers a refreshing take, not only on cooking,
but on the unique adventure of being a restaurateur.

— James Peterson
Author of *Fish and Shellfish* and *Sauces*

Few restaurants or restaurateurs have used food to encourage community or social changes
and are as committed to these causes as the White Dog Cafe. Judy Wicks and
Kevin von Klause have created a very distinctive restaurant. Having cooked side by side with
Kevin over the years, and eaten his delicious food, I know what a gift these recipes are.

—Nicole Routhier
Author of *Cooking Under Wraps* and *Foods of Vietnam*

Who would have thought that three of my favorite passions—great food, spirited conversation, and
active citizenship—could be integrated into one book? Judy Wicks does it with extraordinary panache.

—Norman Lear
Television writer and producer, Founder of the Business Enterprise Trust

White Dog Cafe

COOKBOOK

**MULTICULTURAL RECIPES AND TALES OF ADVENTURE FROM
PHILADELPHIA'S REVOLUTIONARY RESTAURANT**

by Judy Wicks and Kevin von Klause

with Elizabeth Fitzgerald

RUNNING PRESS
PHILADELPHIA · LONDON

© 1998 Judy Wicks and Kevin von Klause

All rights reserved under the Pan-American and International Copyright Conventions

Printed in the United States

This book may not be reproduced in whole or in part, in any form or by any means, electronic or mechanical, including photocopying, recording, or by any information storage and retrieval system now known or hereafter invented, without written permission from the publisher.

9 8 7 6 5 4 3 2 1
Digit on the right indicates the number of this printing

Library of Congress Cataloging-in-Publication Number 96-69263

ISBN 0-7624-0007-2 paperback
ISBN 0-7624-0306-3 hardcover

Cover design by Ken Newbaker
Illustrations and snapshots by Judy Wicks
Photography for chapter openers © 1998 David Fields
Typography: Bulldog

This book may be ordered by mail from the publisher. Please include $2.50 for postage and handling. *But try your bookstore first!*

Running Press Book Publishers
125 South Twenty-second Street
Philadelphia, Pennsylvania 19103-4399

This book is dedicated to

ORGANIC FAMILY FARMERS

whose stewardship of the land and respect for the lives of farm animals preserves
a way of life that brings us nourishment and good health.

CONTENTS

HOW THE WHITE DOG CAFE GOT ITS NAME 11

ACKNOWLEDGMENTS 13

INTRODUCTION 15
Judy's Story 16
   The Evolution of the Cafe: A Short History 19
   Table for Six Billion: Our Philosophy 21
Kevin's Story 25
   Becoming a Chef 26

CHEF'S NOTE 28

CHAPTER ONE: STARTERS 31
with a tale about Cuba 33

CHAPTER TWO: SOUPS, BISQUES & CHOWDERS 61
with a tale about Vietnam 63

CHAPTER THREE: SALADS, SANDWICHES & LIGHT MEALS 85
with a tale about farming 87

CHAPTER FOUR: MAIN COURSES 113
with a tale about the Soviet Union 117

CHAPTER FIVE: VEGETABLES & SIDE DISHES 183
with a tale about a prison 186

CHAPTER SIX: BRUNCHES & BAKED GOODS 217
with a tale about a neighborhood 219

CHAPTER SEVEN: DESSERTS 243
with a tale about urban youth 245

CHAPTER EIGHT: BASICS 269
with a tale about Nicaragua 272

CHAPTER NINE: SPECIAL OCCASION MENUS & ANNUAL WHITE DOG CAFE EVENTS 299

MORE ABOUT THE WHITE DOG CAFE
Community Programs 311
Resources 312
How To Reach Us 315

INDEX 317

HOW THE WHITE DOG CAFE GOT IT'S NAME

N JUNE OF 1875, MADAME HELENA BLAVATSKY LAY SERIOUSLY ILL WITH AN INJURED leg. On the second floor of her brownstone row house at 3420 Sansom Street in Philadelphia, the doctors urged amputation to save her life, but she would have none of it.

"Fancy my leg going to the spirit land before me," she exclaimed, "and have my obituary read 'gone to meet her leg.' Indeed!" So she shooed off the doctors and cured herself by having a white dog lie across her leg, healing all in no time.

Almost 100 years later, just after moving into that same house, I answered a knock at my door around midnight and found a strange woman who asked, "Is this the home of the great Madame Blavatsky?"

"Who?"

"Is this 3420 Sansom Street?" she asked impatiently.

"Yes, but there's no Madame here."

"No, no, of course not, but would you mind if I came in for a minute, just to see where it was she once lived?"

I swung open the door and she tore around the house, explaining how this was where her bedroom had been, and this her parlor, and oh, how disappointing it was that the rooms had been so altered. Then she was off and I went back to bed, wondering if I had been dreaming. Several months later, I was looking out the window of a bus when I noticed a small message board in the window of an elegant building near Rittenhouse Square that read, "Who was Madame Blavatsky?" I quickly hopped off the bus and ran into the building. The Theosophical Society was celebrating the life of its founder, and I began to learn the story of the remarkable woman who had lived in my house 100 years before.

A Russian noblewoman turned vagabond, Madame Blavatsky had come to the United States to study the philosophy of Native Americans, and during her illness on Sansom Street developed a vision of a world united by a belief in universal brotherhood. After her recovery, she left for New York City to found the Theosophical Society, an organization dedicated to reconciling all nations and religions through a common understanding of ethical truths.

As though fate had brought me to the same house, I discovered my own fundamental belief in the interconnectedness of all life to be at the core of Madame Blavatsky's philosophy. In 1983, I would open a restaurant on the first floor of that house at 3420 Sansom Street and name it for the dog who had saved her. Whether there actually had been a white dog, or the dog was a symbol of the healing powers of faith and good humor, I'll never know. Since dogs for me have always represented the qualities of comfort and fun that I wished for the Cafe, the name suited and I drew the logo to resemble the silhouette of my beloved hound, Newman. He was not a white Lab as most people guess, but the ghost of a tricolored mutt. Some accuse me of creating the White Dog Cafe as a shrine to his memory, and perhaps it's so!

An intellectual and scholar, Madame Blavatsky worked to bring the world together through the study and teaching of ancient truths. With the same goal in mind, I choose a different route—peace through parties!

Over the years, I've developed ways of bringing people together around food with programs such as our international sister restaurant project, Table for Six Billion, Please; the Dance of the Ripe Tomatoes, a festival that we hold the last day of summer to give thanks for our bountiful harvest and to raise awareness of the importance of organic agriculture and humane farming; and our Table Talk series on issues of public concern. When people ask me what I do, I often reply that I use good food to lure innocent customers into social activism. In 1986, I met the person whose irresistible cuisine would make that possible, my chef and business partner Kevin von Klause. I was working at my desk in the same room where Madame Blavatsky was cured by the white dog when I looked up to see a figure dressed all in black, with long cape and bowler hat. I felt as though a magician had entered the room. To my delight, I was soon to discover it was in the kitchen that Kevin performed his magic, and our work together was begun. This book is the story of how Kevin and I have blended flavorful and wholesome cuisine with community building and a sense of fun, to create the White Dog Cafe—a place of good food, good cheer, and good will.

—JUDY WICKS
Founder and proprietor

ACKNOWLEDGMENTS

We thank our publisher Buz Teacher who recognized the character and spirit of the White Dog Cafe and chose to capture it in book form. We thank him for his foresight and confidence in us. We appreciate the work of everyone at Running Press, including Nancy Steele; our able editor Mary McGuire Ruggiero; and our designer Paul Kepple. We also give an extra big thanks to our recipe editor, Mardee Haidin Regan.

We're especially beholden to Elizabeth Fitzgerald, our sous-chef and collaborator, without whose exquisite palate, eloquence, and enthusiasm, this book would not have been possible. For this and much more, we thank her.

We thank all White Dog Cafe employees both past and present each of whom has contributed to the success of the cafe in his or her unique way. In particular we'd like to mention James Barrett, Bill Blake, Mark Bradley, Ami Brown, Tony Burnett, Roland Butler, Frankie Call, Heather Carb, Cindy Carniecki, Anna Chrulkiewicz, Angela Chung, Moises Cruz, Deb DiPaula, Lisa Edwards, Sara Feinstein, Hank Fila, Albert Gotto, Aliza Green, Marge Greenspan, Dan Grimes, Laura Grove, Laura Kaderabek, Carol Kershaw, Sue Ellen Klein, Billy Kline, Goeff Koehn, Anne-Marie Lasher, Scott Lee Lawrence, Rachel Lewis, Yvonne Lighty, Sally Litvinas, Michelle Magee, Lisa Martenson, Deirdre MacDermott, Patricia McGuire, Stefan Nock, Michael O'Halloran, Jenny O'Reilly, Long Pham, Chris Schwam-Piacquadio, Deb Sloan, David Spungeon, Jeffrey Stein, Robert Stokes, Eric Tucker, Bill Webster, John Wicks, Roland Wightman, and Ronald Yeager.

We cannot overestimate the importance of the suppliers who bring us the wonderful ingredients that are where it all begins: Mark and Judy Dornstreich of Branchcreek Farm, Glenn and Karen Brendle of Green Meadow Farm, and Paul Tsakos of Overbrook Farm for our produce; Douglass Newbold of Greystone Farm for our goat cheese; Wendy Born and James Barrett of Metropolitan Bakery for our bread; C.P. Yeatman & Sons for organic mushrooms; Killian's Harvest Green; Philaberry Farm; Alberts Organics; Cornerstone Farm; Paradise Organic; Eberly Poultry; Neshaminy Valley Natural Foods; Mickie Simmons and Sharon Burkhart of New Harmony Coffee; Carol Stoudt of Stoudt Brewery for our private label "Leg Lifter Lager;" Kenwood Vineyard for our private label "Château Chien Blanc Chardonnay;" and Cline Vineyards for our private label "Snaggletooth Red."

We're appreciative of the writers and food critics who have recognized our work and encouraged us onward: Russell Baker, Peter Binzen, David Bollier,

Janet Bukovinsky Teacher, Stephanie Campbell, Michael Cronin, Lisa DePaulo, Gerald Etter, Janet Falon, Fred Ferretti, Stephen Fried, Sam Hughes, Tina Kelly, Marlyn Marter, John Marchese, Jennifer Moore, Rick Nichols, Deborah Scoblionkov, Elaine Tait, Mimi Sheraton, and Jim Quinn.

We thank all of our loyal customers, for whom we work every day to please. As we cook, plan events, or decorate a new dining room, it's their pleased faces we envision and their positive responses that continually encourage us.

—JW & KvK

I'd like to thank my parents, Wanda and Roger, for their unwavering support and belief in me.

—KvK

There are a few people I would like to mention who have inspired my work the most: Alice Waters, who pioneered new American cuisine, generously shares her wisdom, pushes us all toward 100 percent organic, and has the guts to do things like hang a "Stop the War" banner above the entrance to her restaurant, Chez Panisse, during the Gulf War; Ben Cohen, whose ice cream company, Ben & Jerry's, is the world's best example of a values-led business; David Funkhouser and Don Luce, who led me to Nicaragua and Vietnam, and provided me with the international perspective that changed my life; my mom, Betty, who taught me to be of service to others, and my children, Grace and Lawrence, who endured life growing up in a restaurant and turned out just great in spite of it!

—JW

INTRODUCTION

BRINGING PEOPLE TOGETHER AROUND FOOD IS A FAMILY TRADITION. AS FAR back as I can remember, my parents, Jack and Betty, entertained with summer picnics on the patio, holiday gatherings, campfire sings, ladies' luncheons, and their monthly Friday-night Hungry Club, formed in 1947, the year I was born. In Winter Haven, Florida, my grandmother Grace turned her home into a guest house, renting out the bedrooms of her five daughters to put my mother and her sisters through college. Grandma's picture, with Tricksy, her fox terrier, hangs on the dining room wall of the White Dog, along with her business card, which reads "House of the Seven Gables—a good night's rest for every guest. Grace Scott, Proprietress." A cheery, spontaneous woman, she once slept in the bathtub, giving her bed to a weary soldier on his way home during World War II. I remember her most in the kitchen, cooking up big meals for our visiting family, sometimes of fresh fish she had caught in the lake and always with the favorite home-baked sticky buns that she constantly nibbled. My paternal grandmother, Eleanor Wicks, was much more formal though no less social. "Nana" set the perfect table at the many elegant dinner parties she hosted in her big house in Pittsburgh, and it was from her I learned to appreciate the details of good service.

I grew up in Ingomar, a small town north of Pittsburgh. By the time I was twelve I had created numerous business start-ups. With an early interest in design, I began by painting scenes on scraps of wood gathered from construction sites and selling them from my wagon. Before long I began using the larger scraps of wood to build clubhouses in the woods—my greatest childhood passion and a foreshadowing of my future career. Each spring I'd ask for nails and tar paper for my birthday, and would tear down the old shack and build a bigger and more elaborate one every year until I went off to college. I would take great care in creating comfortable places to sit, hanging curtains, and planting flowers around the entrance.

Although most female role models in my town were homemakers, my mother provided much of what I needed to become an entrepreneur by her commitment to community service. A great outdoorswoman, she was the leader of our town's Girl Scout troop and the volunteer director of our summer day camp. She led us on camping and white water canoe trips into the wilds, teaching us how to build a fire and pitch a tent, how to fend for ourselves, and how to work in a group. I watched as she conducted the morning program at camp and organized work assignments for each unit, always with fairness and enthusiasm. Mom planned our family camping trips, which Dad navigated by boat and canoe, to a remote island in Canada. She packed supplies for two weeks and cooked meals for eleven people over the campfire. As it turns out, campfire cooking is the only method I have ever mastered. Rebelling against the 1950s practice of force-feeding home economics to female students, I longed to take wood shop, so I refused to learn to cook and once leaped out the window of the classroom in protest. My mother was concerned that I would not have the skills to feed a family, but she had no cause for worry—living above a restaurant has solved the problem!

After graduating with a degree in English from Lake Erie College, a women's school in Ohio that we affectionately called Lake College for Erie Women, I married my fifth-grade boyfriend, joined VISTA, and went off to live in an Eskimo village in Alaska. In spite of my self-imposed ban on cooking, I learned to make bread and soup, which I consider essential to living and had no other way to get. In the spring of 1970, just after the Kent State killings, the entire Alaska corps was fired by the Nixon Administration for becoming politically active in Eskimo issues and for suggesting that the VISTA program be run by the indigenous community. Suddenly we were un-employed, but back in Ingomar, we found job opportunities unexciting. While visiting a friend at the University of Pennsylvania, we decided to open a store for students. In the fall of 1970, driving a used station wagon packed with suitcases of blue jeans and T-shirts, two dogs, and two white doves, we arrived in Philadelphia. With only $3,000, our stipend from VISTA, we could not afford an apart-ment, so we rented a storefront and moved in. The story of The Free People's Store (which became the national chain

Urban Outfitters) would fill another volume on its own, so I'll skip to the last day, when I left my first business and marriage, went through a red light a block away, and crashed the station wagon. I could-n't turn back after making my getaway, and I needed a job quickly to pay for the repairs. A sympathetic passerby suggested a job as a waitress at a nearby French restaurant where he worked. I took his sug-gestion and began my career in the restaurant business—quite by accident!

As it turned out, I spent the next thirteen years at the restaurant. Moving from waiting tables to run-ning the entire company, I gradually developed a charming, but ill-managed restaurant into a profes-sional and highly successful enterprise with ten times the revenue. That ended when the absentee owner who had promised to formalize our business partnership instead returned to Philadelphia and forced me out of the company. At first I was heart-broken to lose the business I had run as my own for so many years, but I soon realized that the loss pro-vided a great opportunity for something new. On the first floor of my house just down the street from the French restaurant, I had recently started a take-out muffin and coffee shop. Now I turned my full attention to that tiny business, no bigger at first than my childhood clubhouses, and vowed that I would turn it into one of Philadelphia's most successful restaurants. In time it became just that and from my life's most traumatic heartbreak blossomed my greatest love—the White Dog Cafe.

THE EVOLUTION OF THE CAFE:
A SHORT HISTORY

Blue-and-white checked cafe curtains were the first thing I envisioned when I originally thought of the Cafe. I found the fabric, and my baby-sitter, Sita, who later became our first dishwasher, made the curtains, which I hung in the front windows. Everything else was built around the style of the curtains!

With a homey look of old lamps and antique oak furniture, and simple, flavorful food made from high-quality, fresh ingredients, the White Dog began as an old-fashioned kind of place where people gathered to discuss the issues of the day over a cup of coffee and a homemade muffin. Having spent thirteen years eating French cuisine, I now wanted only American food, especially the favorites of childhood—hot fudge sundaes and root beer floats, Mom's marinated beef kabobs, which Dad had grilled over the charcoal, and Nana's strawberry pie.

Call it instinct or luck, but the founding of the White Dog coincided with the surge in popularity of American cuisine that was about to sweep the country, but I was simply doing just what I wanted. Later, when writing my business plan for bank financing, I explained it more scientifically by using John Naisbitt's term from *Megatrends*—"soft touch," an antidote to the cold hardness of the high-tech, computerized culture. While most urban restaurants in the 1980s chose stark modern decor with an aloof atmosphere in tones of gray and mauve and served precious portions on huge plates, I went for more comforting food and the lived-in look, which was literally so since the initial furniture came right out of my home upstairs. When people walked into the Cafe for the first time, they would say, "My, Judy, it's so nice and homey in here—I feel like I'm in your house." It's no wonder!

The White Dog Cafe opened in January of 1983 as a take-out muffin and coffee shop catering largely to the students and professors from the surrounding University of Pennsylvania campus. Our community group had just won a decade-long battle with the university administration to save our row of Victorian brownstones from demolition, and I had finally gained the opportunity to purchase the building that had been my home since 1973. My former husband, Neil Schlosser, an architect whom I had met through our fight to save the block, bought the house next door. We joined the two and opened the Cafe on the first floor. His guidance in construction and design were invaluable over the Cafe's formative years.

As the muffin business held steady, more of a menu was needed to attract a lunch crowd, and there was only one thing I knew how to cook—bread and soup from my Alaska days. So, I began cooking in the evenings in my kitchen upstairs, while my two- and four-year-olds, Lawrence and Grace, tugged at my skirt for attention. I crowded two more used refrigerators into my kitchen and bought a commercial range. Things were getting out of hand, and with increased revenue I was soon able to hire a cook

Original backyard serving area of the White Dog Cafe (1985), which has been converted to a closed-in dining room

to relieve me and expand the menu to include sandwiches. One day from my office at the rear of the shop, I noticed that the take-out line was out the front door. At that time I was also operating a non-profit publishing company that produced community-service resource books. There was a conference table in my office and I asked the research assistant, Wendy Born, who worked on the publishing, if she had ever been a waitress. She had.

"Good," I said, "me, too. So let's open the door and invite that line of customers to sit at the conference table and you and I will wait on them."

Everyone had a jolly good time sitting together around one big table, and it soon grew too crowded. I shoved our desks back into the corners and brought down more tables and chairs from my house. The conference table remains in the same place today, table number 20, and table number 24 is still my old kitchen table. I hired a waitress, and by the next year closed down the publishing business and asked Wendy to become the manager of the Cafe. She accepted and worked with us for seven years, providing stability and grace during the whirlwind and upheaval of rapid growth and change.

First, the Cafe expanded onto the front patio, and then into the second house, where I made a little sitting room, bringing down the rest of my furniture including a couch and coffee table, a piano, and a brass birdcage with two parakeets. I moved our office up to the living room, which had become quite bare. Dish washing soon became a problem. We had no more space in my tiny home kitchen, so I installed a three-bowl sink in the dining room, where the dishwashers merrily conversed with the customers.

Gertrude Redheffer playing the piano at the White Dog Cafe, 1984

What we needed next was more hot food. With no money for a commercial kitchen, I set up a charcoal grill in the back-yard. During my French-restaurant days I had suggested a city-wide promotion of restaurants and visiting cookbook authors. In 1984, this idea became a reality with the launching of The Book & The Cook, an annual event which continues today. Ironically, when the first event was scheduled and I was asked to host a visiting chef for a dinner attended by the mayor, I found myself with no kitchen. Not to be deterred, I invited Bobby Seale as the White Dog's guest cookbook author who grilled his "Radical Ribs" from his *Barbecuing with Bobby* cookbook on our backyard grill. My children were fascinated by his lively chatter as he brewed his secret-potion marinade on the stove in our upstairs kitchen. The aroma filled the whole house until our eyes watered—even when we retreated to our third-floor bedrooms.

That summer the backyard became our most popular dining area. Customers sat on an assortment of lawn furniture and old tables covered with blue-and-white checked tablecloths and decorated with pots of red geraniums, where they enjoyed old family dishes, like Betty's Beef Kabobs and Brother John's Chicken. With no money for advertising, I enlisted Grace and Lawrence to help me pass out flyers on the nearby campus. Afterward, we'd run home and look in the backyard to see if anyone had come. Neil enclosed the yard with a white picket fence and a lovely arbor above, where we grew wisteria and hung the parakeet cage. Undaunted by ensuing cold weather, we enclosed the arbor with plastic and constructed a chimney for the grill. We made it through the fall with many gallons of kerosene for the heaters, but by mid-winter only the chef, wearing a parka and boots, remained outside.

In the early days, the White Dog was a funny kind of place: wait staff went down to the basement and out the back door to pick up their orders; customers were sent upstairs to our living quarters when they asked directions to the restroom; and the night manager deposited the receipts under my pillow while I slept. A new chapter began when my friend Sally loaned us money from the sale of her beach house and we installed a U-shaped oak bar across the front of both houses, placed a grill behind it, and a commercial exhaust system that rose three stories through the house to the roof. Also from the beach house came two lovely Victorian tables, which remain in the dining rooms (numbers 23 and 94).

Loans from family and a small inheritance from Gertrude, an elderly friend who had played the piano for our first few New Year's Eve parties, kept renovations going as we added more seats and kitchen equipment. Our long-sought liquor license finally came through, followed by a loan from the bank. Finally, we bid a fond farewell to our lovely backyard, built an addition with two levels of dining rooms, and installed a fully equipped central kitchen and rest rooms. Finally, we were a "real" restaurant, and the customers who had grown to love us back when the dishwasher was in the dining room, the grill was in the backyard, and the restroom was in my house, stayed and multiplied.

Kevin became executive chef in 1987, bringing his great talent to our kitchen, and by 1993, our tenth birthday year, we were recognized by *Condé Nast Traveler* as "one of the country's Top 50 restaurants worth traveling to visit." Soon after, *Inc.* magazine chose us as one of the best small companies to work for in America, and in 1994 and 1995, I received national awards for combining social vision with successful business. Framed articles and awards now spill out into the hallway from our office, which eventually had to move out of my living room and into one of the five connected row houses that make up the Cafe, and our retail store, The Black Cat, which opened in 1989. The latest addition is Tails, a piano parlor and storytelling salon, which brought our seating capacity to 200. Between "The Dog" and "The Cat," we now employ more than 100 people and enjoy annual sales of more than $4,000,000—much more than could possibly fit under my pillow!

TABLE FOR SIX BILLION:
OUR PHILOSOPHY

The most joyful vision I can imagine is everyone in the world sitting at one big table, sharing in the Earth's abundance and the beauty of each different face. I imagine walking into a restaurant and saying to the maître d', "Table for six billion, please!" This is the name I gave our international sister-restaurant project,

Judy volunteering at Habitat for Humanity during monthly White Dog Cafe Community Service Day

Rev. Leonard Smalls gives a reading during the White Dog Cafe Annual Dinner in Memory of Martin Luther King, Jr.

started in 1987 to promote world understanding through the universal love of eating.

Living with the Eskimos during my VISTA internship in 1969 taught me a lot about inclusiveness.In order to survive the harsh climate, individuals in Alaskan villages depended on the strength of the group and acted in ways that supported the whole rather than profiting at the expense of others. When a man caught his first seal in the spring, his wife would have a seal party for all of the women and divide the meat equally among them. If the family had prospered during the year, other possessions were distributed at the party, such as candy, ribbon, and material for sewing. Accumulating more than your neighbor was not valued. If you admire something an Eskimo has, it is offered to you. Envy does not exist. In sharp contrast, our consumer economy is actually based on creating envy, rewarding greed, and admiring those who accumulate the most. Living with the Eskimos developed my sense of the interconnectedness among all people and with nature, and led to my understanding that what helps one helps all, and what hurts one weakens all.

At first I saw business as a game I didn't want to play. I was offended by the profit-at-any-cost, winner-takes-all value system of corporate America. Drawn to small business entrepreneurship for the personal freedom it provided, I gradually developed my own idea of what business should be. Eventually, I came to the realization that a successful and sustainable economy was not one based on hoarding, but on sharing, not on excluding, but on finding a way for everyone to participate according to his or her individual strengths and interests.

Our international sister-restaurant program uses food as a nonthreatening way to promote understanding among U.S. citizens and countries that have misunderstandings with our government. Many of our travel stories are included in the following chapters, along with recipes Kevin developed from each such culinary adventure. Traveling with our customers to such places as Nicaragua, Vietnam, and Cuba, we have seen the effect of U.S. foreign policy on the lives of others and realize that it is through dialogue and understanding, rather than military confrontation, that we achieve world peace. For me, the trips also provided the opportunity to experience other economic systems, as I continued to struggle with questions about capitalism that began during my days in the Eskimo village. Convinced by my travels and my own experience in business that the free-enterprise system works best in channeling creativity and energy into the workplace, I came to envision a combination of capitalism with concern for the common good expressed in socialist philosophy. I named this hybrid "Capitalism for the Common Good." It allowed me to connect my entrepreneurial energy with my commitment to social change and finally caused me to stop doubting my career in business. The possibilities were endless, and I was filled with great hope and excitement as I created new programs at work for building a more inclusive community around the world and at home.

Realizing that there were cultural misunderstandings right here in Philadelphia, I began a local sister-restaurant program that promotes evenings in various ethnic neighborhoods. We dine at minority owned restaurants and attend cultural events, such as an art opening at the Puerto Rican cultural center or a play at one of America's oldest African-American theaters. Concerned about citizen apathy, I began scheduling dinner and breakfast Table Talks, featuring speakers on issues of public concern to encourage discussion and civic involvement in health-care reform, public education, and environmental protection. On Saturday afternoons, we added talks by and for teens to inspire student activism and discussion among diverse groups of youth. This program led to the founding of our non-profit affiliate, Urban Retrievers, which sponsors the Philadelphia Student Union.

People are brought together in a more personal way during our after-dinner storytelling evenings, where they share tales of marching for civil rights, immigrating from different countries, living with AIDS, fighting in wars, serving in the Peace Corps, doing time in prison, dealing with death, or falling in love. Feeling a need for more direct experience in understanding urban issues, I began running community tours into neighborhoods to meet local activists, combining meals with visits to inner-city wall murals, community gardens, affordable housing sites, child-

Peter Kostmayer, former US Congressman and Director of Zero-Population Growth, giving a talk during Table Talk lecture series at the White Dog Cafe

serving facilities, and a garden project at a state penitentiary. The Native American Thanksgiving Dinner, Noche Latina, and Freedom Seder are among the many multicultural events held annually at the Cafe, as well as birthday dinners in memory of Dr. Martin Luther King, Jr. and Mahatma Gandhi, and a celebration of organic gardening with the Dance of the Ripe Tomatoes each fall.

Inner-city teenagers come to learn the restaurant business throughout the school year as part of our mentoring program, culminating with the Hip Hop, an interracial, intergenerational dinner-dance coordinated by our employee mentors and the students. And days for biking and in-line skating, participating in community service, or taking a senior citizen to lunch dot the calendar published in our quarterly newsletter, "Tales from the White Dog Cafe," which is mailed to 17,000 customers. Next door, The Black Cat, our eclectic gift shop, highlights products that promote a sustainable and inclusive world economy, such as vine boxes made by Brazilian street children, international dolls benefiting a children's fund, and jewelry made from recycled Mardi Gras ball gowns and TV parts by homeless and disabled workers in New Orleans. A book section features writings by our Table Talk speakers with a special section "New Visions for Business," by authors who share a business philosophy of inclusiveness—yes, there are a growing number of us!

The idea of combining business with an agenda for social change was a time-management solution for me. There just aren't enough hours in the day to accomplish social goals separate from business goals.

My energy and attention are focused at work, so I created ways of accomplishing both at once, serving society and making a profit at the same time. There was still a problem, though, in working alone, and I was often discouraged about whether my efforts would really make any difference at all. I also occasionally wondered if I wasn't a bit crazy! Why was mine so different from other businesses I knew?

I have Ben Cohen of Ben & Jerry's to thank for introducing me to a larger business community that operates the way I do. It was his recognition that validated my work and his concepts such as the "double bottom line"—a measure of both profitability and social contribution—that helped me articulate my ideas and gave me the courage to reach further. Through Ben, I became a member of two national organizations, Business for Social Responsibility and Social Venture Network, of whose board I'm now vice chair. I was excited to learn that if I was crazy, at least I was not alone. Joyfully, I joined the ranks of a growing national movement to change the way the world does business from a purely profit-driven model to using business as a vehicle for building a just society. Now I sense there is real hope that the world will someday offer everyone a place at the table. What a great party that will be!   **—JW**

KEVIN'S STORY

GREW UP IN THE PANHANDLE OF TEXAS IN A SMALL TOWN NAMED BORGER, ABOUT forty miles northeast of Amarillo. My relatives were displaced farmers, forced from the land during the Great Depression and the Dust Bowl era. Although they lost their farms, they never lost their frontier spirit or their hankering for tilling the soil or enjoying the bounty of their labor. My mother's parents had a huge garden plot in a vacant lot behind their home, and my father's mother, who lived outside Houston, turned her backyard into a tropical paradise with mango trees, pomegranates, bananas, and her highly praised black roses. They taught their grandchildren how to prepare the soil and sow the seeds, which plants were weeds and which were seedlings, how to water and when to fertilize, and how to know the exact moment to reap the harvest. In the canyons surrounding our town, my grandfather taught the boys how to hunt rabbits, doves, and quail; fish for bass, crappie and catfish; and forage wild plums and grapes, the fruits of cactus, mesquite-tree beans, and yucca flowers for making jams and jellies.

My folks were not solely dependent on supermarkets for the foods they ate and shared. They developed a network of kindred farmers and fruit growers that put out the word when their crops of green beans, black-eyed peas, okra, peaches, melons, apples, onions, and potatoes were ready for harvesting. Sometimes my grandmother was less than thrilled with my grandfather when he would return with bushels of produce that she had to quickly and efficiently preserve in the root cellar, or the deep freezer they kept out in the washhouse, to be consumed later during the cold, windy winter.

Food has always been a fascinating and mysterious subject to me. On Sundays after church the whole family, from twelve to twenty relatives, would gather at my grandparents' house for our weekly Sunday supper. I would sometimes sneak into the kitchen and hide under the table while my mother, grandmother, and aunts prepared the meal. I hid because kids weren't allowed in the kitchen; we might get burned, or stick our dirty little fingers in the pies, or just get underfoot. I would eavesdrop as my mother, Wanda Lee, would ask her mother, Minnie Lee, how she got her chicken so crispy, or how much sugar she put in her cornbread, and why her gravy was so dark and rich. In turn, my grandmother would question her sister, Mabel, about how she got the dumplings for her famous Chicken and Dumplings to be so light and airy, when my grandmother used the same ingredients and hers were heavy and gray. And why did Aunt Olene's piecrusts make them all so jealous? I wanted to know too, and I was amazed because not one of them had a written recipe or used any measuring device that I can recall. Somehow, each in her turn had discovered the how-tos of cooking, and she was eager to share with the others in that warm, aroma-filled kitchen.

Looking back, it was the warmth and sharing of that kitchen that made me fall in love with cooking.

That, and the fact that my mother started working after my youngest sister was born, leaving me to fend for myself. One day after school I came home starving and couldn't find the sweet after-school treat that I craved. While rummaging through the cupboards, I stumbled upon a cookbook with a picture of a big angel food cake with pink frosting; it was the most beautiful thing I had ever seen and I wanted to eat every single pink morsel of it. Every day after school I would climb up to the cupboard, pull out the book, and stare at that pink vision, but I knew that if I wanted the cake, I would have to make it myself. After much trial and error and mess-making I finally succeeded, although it didn't look anything like the picture in the book.

BECOMING A CHEF

That cake was the beginning of my cooking "career," although I never considered cooking a profession. My goal was to become an astronaut, research scientist, or dentist, which I later studied for in college. But all along I continued cooking for my friends and family, garnering many accolades and eventually starting a business as a private cook and caterer. I soon realized that cooking for fun and cooking for a living were very different endeavors. When you cook because you like to, you can allow yourself some error, but when you are paid to prepare meals for special occasions, you've only got one chance, and you'd better know what you're doing.

I decided I wanted some formal training so I attended the Culinary Institute of America. The school offered me the opportunity to learn from some of the finest chefs in the world and make friends with students who shared my passion for food.

After graduation, my roommate, James Barrett (who is today the co-owner of Philadelphia's Metropolitan Bakery along with the White Dog's former managing partner Wendy Smith Born), suggested I come with him to his hometown of Philadelphia where an incredible restaurant "renaissance" was taking place. I blew into town in November 1985 and in December I took a giant step forward in my career, as sous-chef at the esteemed restaurant Apropos, where Executive Chef Aliza Green exposed me to a worldly array of the freshest and finest ingredients a cook could ever dream of and a new cooking style that combined old-world techniques with cutting-edge style. After a year at Apropos I was asked to join the staff of the White Dog Cafe, a place I didn't know existed at the time. I was delighted by the conviviality of the staff and the unpretentious warmth of the antique-filled dining rooms, but my greatest surprise was my introduction to Judy Wicks.

I had never before met anyone like Judy! She was a full-time mother, business person, and community activist who saw something special and good in all people, and who considered life a banquet with a place set for everyone. Judy is someone who believes in fighting for what is right and just, and that all citizens must share in the responsibility of caring for the Earth and all its inhabitants—and that businesses, in particular, can be both successful and responsible. This philosophy of running a business was completely foreign to me. I was also struck by Judy's intuition about her coworkers. By drawing out of them their unique qualities—qualities they often didn't know they had—and nurturing their confidence, she encouraged them to grow and flourish while at the Cafe, and to continue doing so long after they had left to seek adventures of their own.

She certainly showed her trust and intuition when she turned over the kitchen of the White Dog Cafe to me, a relatively unknown and unproven chef. It was her belief in me, along with a tremendously talented staff, that gave me the confidence to use my own intuition and imagination in creating the unique variety of foods that people now associate with our cafe.

My father, Roger, is a professional magician who taught me to believe in magic. Perhaps that's why, when asked to describe or explain the cuisine I've created at the White Dog Cafe, I experience some discomfort in finding a label that fits or a way to categorize what I do. There is an element of alchemy in cooking, a certain magic that can't be notated or codified, an innate sense for specific tastes, textures, and combinations of ingredients that can be savored in the mind without having to taste them with your tongue. My hope is that, with this book, you will learn to develop and trust your inner-chef's voice. Use the recipes here as a guide, not as a textbook, to create some magic of your own.

WHEN I FIRST STARTED COOKING IN PHILADELPHIA I WAS INTRODUCED TO Mark and Judy Dornstreich who grow some of the most gorgeous organic produce I had ever seen at Branchcreek Farm in Perkasie, Pennsylvania. The days when Mark or Judy delivered their harvest were looked upon with great anticipation. All of the busy cooks stopped to admire and sample what they'd brought: painstakingly nurtured baby squash with blossoms still attached, a galaxy of edible flowers, bouquets of freshly cut herbs, miniature head lettuces, tiny pear tomatoes, and unique heirloom varieties of peppers and eggplants. Their stunning produce turned me on to using organic fruits and vegetables long before it became a national trend.

Today, we purchase produce from other local farms and cooperatives as well. These farmers produce the ingredients needed to make the delicious wholesome food our customers have come to love and expect. Without question they are the secret behind our success. We choose to use these ingredients not only to ensure a great meal but also to support the organic farmers from our region. Doing this is good for our bodies, the local economy, the land around us, and the planet at large. In the White Dog Cafe kitchen, I try to excite people about the promise and pleasure of cooking with organic ingredients by serving fabulous food that is raised in a sane manner, by people I know.

Starting with the best ingredients, what else does it take to make good food? Here are the four main ingredients:

BALANCING TASTES

I never like hearing the word "too," as in "too salty," "too sweet," "too tart," or "too spicy" coming from the dining room—or the kitchen. Therefore balance is the most essential ingredient in all of our cooking at the White Dog Cafe. The pleasing combinations of savory, sweet, sour, and bitter flavors along with differing temperatures and textures produces the dishes that we are proud to serve our guests. This balance is achieved by an understanding of how ingredients themselves taste and how they may taste when married to one another. It is finding this balance that makes a great cook and learning to balance flavors comes about through experience, experimentation, and tasting, tasting, tasting. Tasting while you cook is very important. The only way to make good food is to taste it. Taste it along the way, taste it when it is finished, and then balance the taste to suit your personal palate.

ORGANIZATION

Read recipes through in their entirety and prepare all of the ingredients before you begin cooking. Being organized is a prelude to becoming a confident cook. Organization allows you the time to experience the process of cooking. It is only through listening to the sounds, paying attention to the smells, and watching the transformations that occur as you combine ingredients that you can understand and think intelligently about what you are doing.

EQUIPMENT

You don't need a lot of fancy equipment to prepare most of the food in this book. The most essential tools are a good sharp knife and a cutting board. Then, a food processor, citrus zester, pepper grinder, box grater, whisk, fine mesh strainer, measuring cups and spoons, and some standard nonreactive pots, pans, and baking dishes should do the trick. The group that we call "nonreactive" includes those made from any metal that doesn't react with foods—stainless steel, lined copper, anodized aluminum, nonstick-coated aluminum, enameled cast iron, or glass. Raw aluminum reacts with acids and bases—tomatoes, wine, citrus juices, egg yolks, and vinegar—and can adversely change the flavor and color of what you're preparing.

Other items that are helpful include an electric mixer, charcoal grill, meat thermometer, salad spinner, large stockpot, roller-type pasta machine, kitchen timer, and scale.

CHAPTER ONE

STARTERS

STARTERS

Tortilla Floridita: A Cuban Tale 33

Tortilla Floridita 36

Roasted Eggplant–Chèvre Mousse 38

Roasted Beets and Gorgonzola with Orange-Rosemary Vinaigrette 39

Smoked Salmon "Party Hats" with Caviar Confetti 40

Oysters Stewed in Thyme Cream with Thyme Croutons 41

Baked Shrimp and Pork Spring Rolls with Apricot–Pickled Ginger Dipping Sauce 42

Flaky Crab, Shrimp, and Asparagus Strudel 44

Braised Wild Mushrooms Under Herb-printed Pasta 46

Pear and Walnut Tart with Red Grape Compote and Stilton 48

Sherried Lobster and Shrimp Crêpes 50

Chili- and Corn-crusted Calamari with Tangy Citrus Aïoli 52

Warm Shellfish and Asian Vegetables with Spicy Ginger-Lime Dressing 53

Lemon- and Pepper-grilled Calamari with Roasted Pepper–Balsamic Dressing 54

Marinated Goat Cheese with Fresh Tomatoes 55

Braised Fennel with Fresh Mozzarella and Sun-dried Tomato Vinaigrette 56

Broiled Black Mission Figs with Prosciutto, Fontina, and Sage Phyllo Flutes 57

Asian Barbecued Ribs with Gingered Snow Pea–Cabbage Slaw 58

Basil-dressed Melon and Prosciutto with Black Pepper–Orange Mascarpone 59

TORTILLA FLORIDITA: A CUBAN TALE

T WAS PITCH-BLACK IN THE WALK-IN REFRIGERATOR AT RESTAURANTE FLORIDITA, once a favorite haunt of Hemingway's in Havana, Cuba, and now a sister restaurant to the White Dog Cafe. The power was off during one of the frequent blackouts engineered to save energy on an island crippled by the ever-tightening U.S. embargo. Along with eighteen of our customers, Kevin and I had come on a week-long trip sponsored by the Cafe and led by Medea Benjamin of Global Exchange (a non-profit organization based in San Francisco) to find out how our government's policy was affecting the lives of Cubans, as well as to enjoy the cultural delights of the island.

A free-enterprise enthusiast, I'd sworn never to have a state-owned sister restaurant, but curiosity got the better of me. It was 1993, just after the fall of the Soviet Union, and this might have been our last chance to experience a system where every tomato, fork, and toilet plunger was purchased through central planning. Even in Cuba, things were changing as the government, though determined to prevent rampant consumerism and preserve the victories of the revolution, cautiously began opening the economy.

Tonight would be the grand finale dinner. La Floridita's Chef Clemente Harewood was preparing his famous stuffed lobster dish, and Kevin was creating a first course from what could be found in the walk-in. Our anxiety was rising as our hope for fresh ingredients diminished. On the trip we had learned of the food shortage in Cuba, precipitated originally by a dependency on U.S. products while all tillable soil was used for exported crops like sugar and tobacco. After the revolution, the United States imposed an economic embargo to punish Castro, who made the mistake of transferring Cuba's dependency from the United States to the Soviet Union, rather than developing self-sufficiency. Now Cuba had again lost its major trading partner and was desperately trying to diversify its economy to become self-sufficient. It was a race against

Kevin preparing "Tortilla Floridita" with Floridita's sous-chef and maitre d' looking on

Several White Dog Cafe patrons dining at sister restaurant in Havana

time to increase food production enough to feed the population before supplies ran out. Everyone in Cuba, including the employees of La Floridita, takes his or her turn in the fields. While at home we see only those fleeing in boats of opportunity, here I found an indomitable spirit of dignity and hope and a willingness to tolerate authoritarianism and economic hardship rather than surrender to external domination and return to a dependent economic system that had once enslaved the Cuban people.

While the rest of our group enjoyed the unspoiled beach at nearby Valedero, Kevin and I groped through the dark walk-in with dimming flashlights, searching for food. We stumbled over a cardboard box that looked promising until we found it contained only a couple of rotten potatoes. Finally, we emerged clutching a few precious tomatoes, peppers, onions, and a large tubular vegetable called boniato. The kitchen was spacious and immaculate with white tile walls rising up to a high ceiling with a beautiful, big skylight that bathed the kitchen with a precious commodity—light. The staff was dressed in whites and the chefs wore traditional tall chef hats or toques. Clemente's was bright red with a matching kerchief, the same color as Kevin's baseball cap. They were ready to be of assistance, but spoke no English—and we spoke little Spanish. We said *"¡Hola!"* and everyone smiled and shook hands.

Kevin approached the boniato with curiosity. It's similar to a sweet potato, but much larger. In his usual manner of cooking, he wanted to do something that was familiar to the guests, but with a new twist. Boniato dumplings perhaps! He set to work cooking the vegetable, then mashing it by hand—the electric mixer sat useless without power. Next, he added free-range eggs with the most beautiful bright-yellow yolks, a result of never ingesting chemical feed. Green philosophy had developed out of scarcity in Cuba but had taken hold as a national mission. You will never see garbage dumps as clean and efficient as those in Cuba. Crops are grown organically, bicycles fill the streets, and herbal medicine is taught in every high school. Even a paper substitute, *kenaf,* is grown in order to save trees.

Kevin added flour and more eggs to the mashed boniato to form the dumplings. Mashing and kneading, adding more flour, then more eggs—nothing seemed to achieve the right consistency. Instead, the gummy mixture stuck persistently to his hands, refusing the shape of a dumpling.

The dinner hour was all too rapidly nearing. We were expecting about forty guests, including some local opera stars and officials whose permission I had sought to hold the event in this state-run enterprise.

The La Floridita sous-chef watched with puzzlement.

Under his cap, Kevin's face lit with a new idea. He grabbed a rolling pin and flattened the mixture. The kitchen staff looked on with great interest as he broke off pieces and formed them into pancakes.

"Tortilla," he explained.

They smiled and nodded, understanding nothing. This wasn't Mexico.

Judy sampling the food of Restaurante Floridita's chef

Spotting a nice big griddle, Kevin put on the tortilla. After it had browned, he broke off a piece and we apprehensively tasted a bite. Delicious! With the flavor of roasted chestnuts. Success at last! Now Kevin put the staff to work, "*Mas, mas,*" he said as they eagerly patted out the tortillas and put them on the griddle.

Clemente presented Kevin with some lovely shrimp, and things were really looking up. Kevin chopped the tomatoes, onions, and peppers, and added black beans, capers, and olives from the pantry. As the staff lined up to watch, he placed the tortilla on a dinner plate, spooned out the tomato mixture, which formed a bed for the shrimp, and topped it with a dollop of herbed mayonnaise made from those beautiful eggs.

"Tortilla Floridita," he announced.

Everyone smiled with great satisfaction. *"Vive la Tortilla Floridita! Vive la Revolucion!"*

—JW

Tortilla Floridita {Serves 4}

While visiting Havana, Cuba, Judy and I learned to cook boniato, a vegetable similar in appearance to the sweet potato but with a more golden flesh and a flavor reminiscent of chestnuts. In Philadelphia boniatos can be elusive, so we often substitute sweet potatoes in the tortilla recipe, but keep the remaining ingredients in this dish true to the Cuban kitchen. Don't be daunted by preparing the tortillas; they are as easy to make as mud pies. Picadillo (from the Spanish word pica, meaning "to cut into small pieces") is a type of hash consisting of ground beef, olives, capers, and raisins that's found in most Spanish-speaking countries. Our version uses chopped shrimp and black beans in place of the ground beef.

TORTILLAS

1 cup mashed boiled sweet potato

1 cup all-purpose flour

¼ teaspoon ground allspice

1 teaspoon chili powder

½ teaspoon salt

½ teaspoon freshly ground black pepper

Vegetable oil

PICADILLO

2 tablespoons extra-virgin olive oil

½ cup minced white onion

1 green bell pepper, diced

1 tablespoon minced garlic

1 Scotch bonnet chile (see note below), or 2 jalapeño peppers, seeded and finely minced

½ teaspoon chili powder

½ cup golden raisins

1 cup diced tomatoes

1 tablespoon rice wine vinegar

½ cup water

8 ounces raw shrimp, peeled, deveined, and coarsely chopped

1 cup cooked black beans (see page 215)

1. Prepare the tortillas: In a food processor, combine the sweet potato, flour, allspice, chili powder, salt, and pepper. Process until the dough pulls away from the sides of the bowl and begins to form a ball, about 30 seconds. (The dough can be made 1 day in advance, wrapped in plastic, and kept refrigerated. Bring to room temperature before shaping the tortillas.)

2. The dough will be very sticky, so flour your hands and the work surface well. Divide the dough into 4 equal pieces; shape each piece into a ball. Using your hands or a floured rolling pin, flatten each ball into a 6-inch round, about ¼ inch thick.

3. Heat a few drops of vegetable oil in a nonstick skillet placed over medium-high heat. Cook the tortillas, one at a time, until lightly toasted, about 1 minute on each side. Stack the tortillas between sheets of waxed paper until needed. (You can make the tortillas in advance and rewarm them in the same skillet just before serving; doing this will give them a great toasted taste and a crunchier texture.)

4. Prepare the Picadillo: In a large, nonreactive sauté pan set over medium-high heat, heat the olive oil until it ripples. Add the onion and sauté for 3 minutes. Add the bell pepper and cook for 2 minutes. Add the garlic, Scotch bonnet, and chili powder, and cook for 2 minutes more. Stir in the raisins, tomatoes, vinegar, and the water; cook for 1 minute. Stir in the shrimp, beans, olives, capers,

USING SCOTCH BONNET CHILES

Scotch bonnet chiles (also known as habañero chiles) are the hottest chiles in the world, so be careful when working with them. Wear gloves and be careful not to touch your face! If Scotch bonnet peppers aren't available, substitute your favorite hot chili or Tabasco sauce, but you'll be missing out on the intoxicating perfume of the Scotch bonnet, which reminds us of vanilla and tropical flowers.

{continued}

½ cup sliced pimiento-stuffed green olives

1 tablespoon drained capers

1 teaspoon caper brine

1 teaspoon salt

½ teaspoon sugar

1 ripe avocado (preferably Haas), peeled and diced

1 tablespoon chopped fresh cilantro leaves and stems

caper brine, salt, and sugar; cook until the shrimp are just cooked through, 3 to 4 minutes. Stir in the avocado and cilantro.

5. To serve, place 1 warm tortilla on each plate. Top with a mound of the picadillo filling. If desired, top with a dollop of sour cream flavored with saffron and toasted cumin.

OTHER WAYS TO DO IT

The picadillo is also delicious wrapped up in a flour tortilla or served over steamed white rice aside sautéed greens.

Roasted Eggplant–Chèvre Mousse {Makes about 4 cups}

We serve this mousse with our Spicy Pita Crisps as an hors d'oeuvre on cocktail buffets, with lemon-dressed greens as a light first course, or as an integral part of a vegetarian feast. Alone, the mousse is a terrific sandwich spread, filling for stuffed tomatoes, or sauce for a bowl of hot pasta.

---

1 large eggplant (1½ to 2 pounds)

Olive oil, for coating

1 head of garlic, roasted (see note below), the pulp squeezed from the cloves

1 red bell pepper, roasted (see note, page 140), peeled, seeded, and finely diced

4 ounces unaged chèvre

1 scallion, thinly sliced

2 tablespoons chopped fresh basil leaves

2 tablespoons chopped fresh cilantro leaves and stems

Juice of ½ lemon

2 teaspoons red wine vinegar

½ teaspoon ground cumin

¼ teaspoon salt

¼ teaspoon freshly ground black pepper

1. Preheat the oven to 450°F.

2. Halve the eggplant lengthwise and rub the flesh with a little of the olive oil. Place the halves, cut sides down, on a baking sheet. Roast until very soft, about 20 minutes. Remove and let cool to room temperature.

3. Scrape the eggplant pulp out of the skin with a large spoon. Discard the skin; very finely chop the pulp. Combine the eggplant pulp, garlic pulp, roasted bell pepper, cheese, scallion, basil, cilantro, lemon juice, vinegar, cumin, salt, and pepper in a large mixing bowl. Mash together with a fork until well combined. Taste for seasoning; depending upon the how tangy the chèvre is, you might desire more salt or vinegar.

4. Serve at room temperature with Spicy Pita Crisps (page 284), or cover and refrigerate for up to 4 days. If refrigerated, bring to room temperature before serving.

ROASTING GARLIC

Roasting garlic makes its pungent cloves sweet and mellow—perfect for topping grilled chicken and steak. Combined with olive oil or butter, it's a great spread for toasted breads, mashed or baked potatoes, or broiled tomatoes sprinkled with parmesan cheese. For one whole head of garlic, preheat the oven to 375°F. Cut the top off of the head of garlic, exposing the cloves. Rub the head with a little olive oil and wrap in foil. Roast in the oven until the cloves are completely soft, about 30 minutes. When cool, squeeze the softened garlic pulp from its skin; it will have a pastelike consistency. Use immediately.

Roasted Beets and Gorgonzola with Orange-Rosemary Vinaigrette {Serves 4}

If you like beets—and from what we see at the White Dog Cafe many people do—you will love this sweet-tart starter. The combination of flavors and textures can't be beat (no pun intended). When peeling the roasted beets, be sure to wear gloves or rub the still-slightly-warm beets with an old, clean dish towel so the skins will slip off without coloring your hands. The beets and the vinaigrette can be prepared 1 day in advance if you wish and will stay fresh-tasting for several more days in the refrigerator.

2 large red beets (about 12 ounces, total)

1 bunch watercress or young spinach
   leaves, washed, dried, and stemmed

ORANGE-ROSEMARY VINAIGRETTE

1 cup fresh orange juice

$\frac{1}{2}$ teaspoon minced orange zest

1 teaspoon chopped fresh rosemary leaves

1 teaspoon minced shallots

2 teaspoons Champagne vinegar

$\frac{1}{4}$ teaspoon sugar (optional, depending on
   the sweetness of the orange juice)

1 teaspoon olive oil

Pinch of salt

Pinch of freshly ground black pepper

4 ounces Gorgonzola, crumbled

$\frac{1}{4}$ cup pine nuts or walnuts, toasted
   (see note, page 144)

Freshly ground black pepper

1. Prepare the beets: Preheat the oven to 400°F.

2. Place the beets in a deep nonreactive baking dish and add 1 inch of water. Tightly cover the dish with foil. Bake for 45 minutes or until the beets are tender enough to be pierced with a fork. Remove the foil and let the beets cool to room temperature.

3. Prepare the Orange-Rosemary Vinaigrette: Whisk together all of the ingredients in a large bowl. Set aside at room temperature for at least 30 minutes to allow the flavors to meld; cover and refrigerate for up to 1 week.

4. Rub off the beet skins with an old kitchen towel or peel with a paring knife. Cut the beets into $\frac{1}{2}$-inch-thick slices.

5. To serve, arrange some of the watercress on each chilled salad plate. Top with one-fourth of the beets; spoon some of the vinaigrette over the beets, letting a bit of it pool on the plate. Crumble the Gorgonzola over the beets. Sprinkle with the toasted nuts and a grind of black pepper.

OTHER WAYS TO DO IT

In a variation we like to serve, we substitute shaved fennel for the greens and pitted sliced kalamata olives for the Gorgonzola, a hit with all of our vegetarian friends.

ABOUT GORGONZOLA

Gorgonzola, one of Italy's great cheeses, has been made in the town of Gorgonzola since the year 879. The village was once a resting stop for large herds of cows heading home after spending the summer grazing high in the mountains. During their respite, the cows gave lots of milk that the villagers used to make cheese. They put the cheese to age in the cool, mold-infected grottos nearby, and it emerged a few months later with beautiful blue veins. Today Gorgonzola is made in a much more commercial manner; however its strong pungent flavor and buttery texture remain unsurpassed. Although Italians traditionally don't put Gorgonzola in salads or dressings, we can't resist.

Smoked Salmon "Party Hats" with Caviar Confetti {Serves 4}

This makes a festive and elegant first course or an excellent hors d'oeuvre with Champagne and caviar before dinner. Everything can be prepared a day in advance and assembled just before serving. Pre-sliced smoked salmon is very thinly and uniformly cut; we recommend using it to save yourself time and effort.

CAPER CREAM CHEESE

4 ounces cream cheese, at room
  temperature

2 tablespoons milk

3 tablespoons drained capers, rinsed and
  squeezed dry

1 tablespoon minced fresh chives

1/2 teaspoon freshly ground black pepper

PICKLED ONIONS

1/2 cup Champagne vinegar

2 tablespoons sugar

1/4 teaspoon freshly ground black pepper

2 tablespoons chopped fresh dill

1 red onion, sliced into very thin rings

BRIOCHE ROUNDS

2 to 4 thin slices Brioche (page 238) or
  other bread

8 thin slices smoked salmon
  (about 8 ounces)

1 ounce salmon caviar (optional)

Capers, sliced radishes, diced cucumbers,
  and baby greens, for garnishes

8 sprigs fresh dill

1. Prepare the cream cheese: Combine the cheese and milk in a small bowl and stir together with a fork until creamy. Stir in the capers, chives, and pepper. (This will keep for up to 1 week in the refrigerator.)

2. Prepare the onions: Whisk together the vinegar, sugar, pepper, and dill in a small bowl. Add the rings of onion and toss to moisten. Set aside at room temperature for at least 1 hour or up to 6 hours. Cover and refrigerate for up to 1 week.

3. Prepare the brioche rounds: Preheat the oven to 350°F.

4. With a 2-inch round biscuit cutter, cut out 8 rounds of bread; place on a baking sheet. Toast in the oven until crisp and the tops are golden, 6 to 8 minutes. (Let cool and store in an airtight container for up to 2 days.)

5. Assemble the hats: Arrange the salmon slices on a work surface. Each piece should resemble a rectangle made up of 1 long straight side, 1 long irregular side, and 2 shorter sides. Arrange each slice of salmon so that 1 of the short edges is facing you.

6. Spread 2 teaspoons of the capered cream cheese on that short end and top with a few Pickled Onions. Roll up each piece from the short end, pinching the long, irregular side tighter, so that you form a cone shape. Cover and refrigerate for at least 1 hour or up to overnight.

7. To serve, stand each cone, pointed end up, on a toasted brioche round. Arrange 2 party hats on each of 4 chilled salad plates. Sprinkle with the caviar and garnishes and stick a sprig of fresh dill into the top of each "hat" to create a feathery flourish.

BUYING CAVIAR

If you want to splurge, buy the best caviar you can find; we use salmon caviar because it is delicious and practical, and its brilliant orange-red pearls are glorious to behold.

Oysters Stewed in Thyme Cream with Thyme Croutons {Serves 4}

This opulent stew of oysters plumped in a silken thyme cream is served with tiny thyme-scented croutons. It is an elegant dish for special occasions; we serve it on Valentine's Day followed by Roasted Cornish Hens with White Truffle Jus (page 128) or Pan-Roasted Salmon with Oyster Mushrooms (page 164). We buy our oysters already shucked. When purchasing them look for shucked oysters that are plump, have a sweet smell, and are packed in oyster liquor that is clear.

2 cups heavy cream

1 cup whole milk

2 sprigs fresh thyme plus 2 tablespoons minced fresh thyme leaves

5 black peppercorns

1 bay leaf

1 whole clove

1 cup Thyme Croutons (page 282)

2 slices smoked bacon, finely diced

2 tablespoons minced leek or onion

1 small carrot, finely diced

1 small celery rib, finely diced

2 dozen freshly shucked oysters

1 teaspoon *nam pla* (Thai fish sauce, available in Asian markets and specialty food stores; see note, page 95)

Freshly ground black pepper

1. Combine the cream, milk, sprigs of thyme, peppercorns, bay leaf, and clove in a heavy-bottomed saucepan set over medium heat. Simmer until reduced to 2 cups, about 15 minutes.

2. Meanwhile, prepare the Thyme Croutons.

3. Strain the cream mixture through a sieve; reserve the reduced cream. (The cream can be prepared up to 2 days in advance and kept refrigerated.)

4. Cook the bacon in a saucepan set over low heat until it is crisp and has rendered most of its fat, about 5 to 7 minutes. Add the leek, carrot, and celery and sauté until just tender, about 3 minutes.

5. Add the oysters and toss; then add the reduced cream. Slowly warm the mixture to a simmer and stew the oysters until their edges curl, about 2 minutes. Season with the *nam pla*, black pepper to taste, and the 2 tablespoons minced thyme.

6. To serve, divide among 4 warmed bowls and top with the Thyme Croutons.

BUYING OYSTERS

We buy our oysters already shucked. When purchasing them, look for oysters that are plump, have a sweet smell, and are packed in clear oyster liquor. Oysters vary in their salt content, so wait to add the fish sauce to this stew until after the oysters have had a chance to release their liquid and flavor the Thyme Cream.

Baked Shrimp and Pork Spring Rolls with Apricot–Pickled Ginger Dipping Sauce {Makes 15}

These light crispy rolls enclose a traditional spring roll filling in an unconventional wrap of store-bought phyllo dough. They're everything a spring roll should be—flavorful, fragrant, and crunchy—yet because they're baked and not fried, they're not greasy.

1 cup Spicy Asian Marinade (page 289)

5 ounces boneless pork, trimmed and minced

5 ounces shrimp, peeled, deveined, and minced

4 tablespoons vegetable oil

1 tablespoon minced garlic

1 tablespoon minced fresh ginger

3 scallions, thinly sliced

4 ounces shiitake mushrooms, stems removed, thinly sliced (about 1$\frac{1}{2}$ cups)

3 cups shredded white cabbage (about $\frac{3}{4}$ pound)

1 cup grated carrot

1 cup grated daikon (or green apple)

1 cup thinly sliced snow peas

$\frac{1}{4}$ cup dry sherry

3 tablespoons soy sauce

2 teaspoons Asian sesame oil

$\frac{1}{2}$ teaspoon freshly ground black pepper

$\frac{1}{2}$ teaspoon salt

1 cup bean sprouts

2 tablespoons chopped fresh cilantro leaves and stems

2 tablespoons chopped fresh basil leaves

ROLLS

2 tablespoons vegetable oil

1 tablespoon roasted peanut oil (available in Asian markets and specialty food stores) or 1 teaspoon sesame oil plus 2 teaspoons vegetable oil

1 package (1 pound) frozen phyllo dough, thawed

1. Prepare the Spicy Asian Marinade. Add the minced pork and shrimp, and toss to coat well. Cover and marinate at room temperature for 30 minutes.

2. Remove the pork and shrimp from the marinade and set aside. Discard the marinade.

3. Heat 2 tablespoons of the vegetable oil in a wok or nonstick skillet placed over medium heat. Add the garlic, ginger, and scallions and stir-fry for 2 minutes; do not let the garlic brown. Add the mushrooms and stir-fry until the mushrooms start to soften, 3 to 4 minutes.

4. Increase the heat to high and add the cabbage, carrot, daikon, and snow peas. Toss and flip the vegetables until just crisp-tender, about 4 minutes. Add the sherry and 1 tablespoon of the soy sauce and cook, tossing, until the liquids evaporate. Remove the cooked vegetables and set aside.

5. Wipe out the wok with a paper towel. Pour in the remaining 2 tablespoons oil and set over high heat until the oil ripples. Add the minced pork and shrimp and stir-fry until just cooked through, about 3 minutes. Remove from the heat. Add the reserved vegetables; stir in the sesame oil, the remaining 2 tablespoons soy sauce, the pepper, and the salt. Toss to combine. Spread the mixture over a baking sheet to cool to room temperature.

6. When the mixture is cool, add the bean sprouts, cilantro, and basil; toss to combine.

7. Preheat the oven to 400°F.

8. Assemble the rolls: Whisk together the vegetable and roasted peanut oils in a small bowl.Work with 1 sheet of phyllo at a time; keep the remaining sheets covered with a damp towel to prevent their drying out. Place 1 sheet of phyllo on a work surface with a

{continued}

APRICOT–PICKLED GINGER DIPPING SAUCE

$^1/_4$ **cup apricot preserves**

$^1/_4$ **cup extra-strong Dijon mustard**

2 tablespoons unseasoned rice wine vinegar (available at Asian markets)

2 tablespoons minced pickled ginger (see note, page 71)

2 tablespoons water

1 teaspoon soy sauce

long side toward you. Lightly brush the entire sheet with some of the oil. Lay another sheet on top and brush it with oil. Using a sharp knife, cut the sheets vertically into 3 equal rectangles.

9. Spoon $^1/_3$ cup of the filling along the bottom edge of each rectangle, leaving a $^1/_2$-inch border at the bottom and on each side. Fold up the bottom border and fold in the sides over the filling. Begin rolling the phyllo into a tight cylinder. Place the roll, seam side down, on a nonstick baking sheet. Repeat the process until all of the filling is used. (Any unused phyllo can be rewrapped and stored in the refrigerator for another use.)

10. Prepare the dipping sauce: Combine all of the ingredients in a small bowl. Whisk to combine. Serve at once or cover and refrigerate for up to 1 month. Serve chilled or at room temperature.

11. Brush the tops of the rolls with the remaining oil. Bake until golden and crisp, about 12 minutes. Serve immediately, with the Apricot–Pickled Ginger Dipping Sauce.

Flaky Crab, Shrimp, and Asparagus Strudel {Serves 6}

Summer's flourish of fresh bright flavors is captured in this crisp pastry filled with crab, asparagus, corn, and garden herbs. We serve it on a pool of Creamy Basil Sauce (page 293) and inevitably can never make enough to please all of our guests. Serve the strudels as an appetizer or aside a green salad for a light lunch. To be sure that the phyllo dough is fully thawed, leave it in the refrigerator for at least 8 hours or overnight.

2 cups Creamy Basil Sauce (page 293),
 for serving

FILLING

8 ounces jumbo lump crabmeat, picked over

8 ounces rock shrimp or gulf shrimp,
 peeled, deveined, and coarsely chopped

8 ounces asparagus, blanched and cooled,
 tips reserved and stalks sliced into
 $\frac{1}{4}$-inch coins

8 ounces ($1\frac{3}{4}$ cups) fresh or frozen corn,
 blanched and cooled

1 tablespoon chopped fresh dill

1 tablespoon chopped fresh tarragon leaves

1 tablespoon chopped fresh marjoram leaves

1 bunch scallions, thinly sliced

2 eggs, lightly beaten

1 tablespoon *nam pla* (Thai fish sauce,
 available in Asian markets and specialty
 food stores; see note, page 95)

1 teaspoon Tabasco sauce

STRUDEL

1 package (1 pound) frozen phyllo dough,
 thawed

1 cup olive oil

$\frac{1}{2}$ cup toasted fine bread crumbs

1 plum tomato, seeded and cut into $\frac{1}{4}$-inch
 dice, for garnish

6 basil sprigs, for garnish

1. Prepare the Creamy Basil Sauce.

2. Prepare the strudel filling: Combine the crabmeat, shrimp, asparagus coins, corn, dill, tarragon, marjoram, and scallions in a medium bowl.

3. In a smaller bowl, beat the eggs with the *nam pla* and Tabasco. Pour over the crab mixture and mix well to combine. Cover and refrigerate until needed.

4. Preheat the oven to 375°F. Lightly butter a large baking sheet.

5. Assemble the strudel: Work with 1 sheet of phyllo at a time, keeping the remaining sheets covered with a damp towel to prevent their drying out. Working quickly, place 1 sheet of phyllo on a work surface with a long side toward you. Lightly brush the entire sheet with some of the oil. Sprinkle lightly with some of the bread crumbs. Repeat this 2 more times, making a total of 3 layers. With a sharp knife, cut the stack of phyllo sheets vertically in half, forming 2 rectangular stacks.

6. Using $\frac{2}{3}$ cup of the filling for each strudel, spoon the filling along the bottom edge of each rectangle, leaving a 1-inch border at the bottom and each side. Fold up the dough at the bottom and fold in the sides over the filling. Begin rolling the phyllo into a tight cylinder. Place each roll, seam side down, on the baking sheet, spacing them 1 inch apart. Repeat the process making a total of 6 strudels. (Any unused phyllo can be rewrapped and stored in the refrigerator for another use.)

USING PHYLLO DOUGH

Phyllo is widely available in the frozen foods section of supermarkets. It must be thawed before using, and we find that placing it in the refrigerator overnight is the best method. When thawed, carefully unroll it and then keep a towel over the dough so that its many layers don't dry out and become brittle and difficult to work with.

{continued}

7. Brush the tops of the strudels with some of the remaining oil. Bake until crisp and golden brown, about 15 minutes.

8. To serve, cut each strudel in half lengthwise on the diagonal. Pour a pool of the Creamy Basil Sauce on each of 6 salad plates. Place the 2 halves on a plate and garnish with the reserved asparagus tips, some of the chopped tomato, and a basil sprig.

OTHER WAYS TO DO IT
You can substitute roughly chopped lobster or scallops for either the crab or the shrimp, if desired.

Braised Wild Mushrooms Under Herb-printed Pasta {Serves 4}

Fortunately for us, Kennett Square, Pennsylvania (known as the Mushroom Capital of America) is only a stone's throw from Philadelphia. Wild mushrooms are becoming more readily available in better supermarkets nation-wide. If you can't find the mushrooms listed below, purchase the same quantity of the freshest mushrooms available, organic if possible. Mushrooms can become indistinguishable during the cooking process, so we've tried to preserve their beauty and integrity by lightly braising them with aromatic white truffle oil. The herb-printed pasta sheet is visually stunning and yet quite simple to make. If you have a manual pasta machine, taking the time to use it for this dish is more than worth the effort.

1 cup dried porcini (or other type of dried wild mushroom)

3 cups water

¼ cup extra-virgin olive oil

1 medium leek, trimmed and split lengthwise, washed well, the white and light green parts thinly sliced

1 tablespoon plus 1 teaspoon minced garlic

¼ pounds (about 8 cups) mixed fresh wild mushrooms (such as chanterelle, shiitake, oyster, or cèpes), cleaned and cut into bite-size pieces

1 tablespoon fresh thyme leaves

2 tablespoons dry Marsala

2 tablespoons soy sauce

2 teaspoons white truffle oil

½ teaspoon freshly ground black pepper

1 pound Food Processor Pasta Dough (page 281)

½ cup mixed fresh herb leaves (such as dill, tarragon, and chervil)

½ cup grated Pecorino Romano

Crispy Fried Leeks (see page 155)

1. Combine the dried mushrooms with the water in a small saucepan. Bring to a boil over medium-high heat. Remove the pan from the heat and set aside for about 10 minutes. Strain the liquid into a clear container and let stand for 5 minutes to allow any sand and sediment to collect at the bottom. Pour off the liquid and reserve; save the rehydrated mushrooms for another use (see note below).

2. Meanwhile, heat the olive oil in a large, nonreactive saucepan over low heat. Add the leek and cook until translucent, about 5 minutes. Add the garlic and cook for 2 minutes more. Increase the heat to medium and add the fresh wild mushrooms and thyme. Cook, stirring frequently, until the mushrooms begin to release their juices, 5 to 8 minutes. Add the reserved dried mushroom liquid, the Marsala, and soy sauce and simmer until the mushrooms are thoroughly cooked, about 1 minute more. Sprinkle on the white truffle oil and black pepper. Cover and set aside.

3. Bring a large pot of salted water to a boil. Meanwhile, cut the pasta dough into 2 equal pieces. Roll out each piece as thin as possible. Lay 1 sheet out on a work surface and evenly place herb leaves over it, making sure the herbs don't overlap. Top with the other sheet of pasta. Gently press the sheets together with your

USING DRIED WILD MUSHROOMS

We use dried mushrooms in this recipe to produce a flavorful liquor for braising fresh wild mushrooms. Unlike their fresh counterparts, which can sometimes be difficult to track down, dried wild mushrooms are widely available year round. Texture-wise they aren't really a good substitute for fresh wild mushrooms in most recipes, but they do have great flavor and can make an interesting addition to soups, stews, and risotto—and they do work in a pinch if there are no fresh mushrooms to be found.

(continued)

hands. Set the rollers of your pasta machine at a narrow thickness; run the dough through. Process the dough through progressively smaller settings until it's about $\frac{1}{16}$-inch thick.

4. Using a pastry wheel with a fluted edge, cut the pasta sheets into four 5-inch rectangles; trim any ragged edges. Dust the sheets with flour.

5. Add the pasta sheets to the boiling water and cook until al dente—tender but still firm to the bite, about 5 to 7 minutes. Drain well.

6. To serve, divide the mushroom filling among 4 bowls. Sprinkle each bowl with 2 tablespoons of the grated cheese. Top each with a sheet of the hot herb-printed pasta. Drizzle with a little more white truffle oil and top with the Crispy Fried Leeks.

OTHER WAYS TO DO IT
The pasta can be cooked ahead of time and then shocked in ice water. Lightly oil the pasta sheets and layer them between individual pieces of plastic wrap; store in the refrigerator for up to 1 day. Reheat briefly, about 30 seconds, in boiling water before serving.

Pear and Walnut Tart with Red Grape Compote and Stilton {Serves 8}

Embraced by a flaky crust and filled with pears and walnuts, this savory seasonal tart is terrific served with creamy Stilton and a tangy compote of grapes. Although we offer it as a starter, the combination of nuts, fruit, cheese, and port in this dish make it a natural dessert as well.

TART

2 tablespoons unsalted butter

1 leek, trimmed and split lengthwise, washed well, the white and green parts thinly sliced

1 tablespoon chopped fresh thyme leaves

2 tablespoons brandy

Salt and freshly ground black pepper

28 ounces Basic Pie Dough (page 280)

3 ripe pears

¼ cup chopped toasted walnuts (see note, page 144)

1 tablespoon walnut oil

1 egg yolk

1 tablespoon water

RED GRAPE COMPOTE

1½ pounds seedless red grapes, stems removed (about 4 cups)

1 cup ruby port

2 tablespoons red wine vinegar

10 black peppercorns

2 whole cloves

1 bay leaf

1 tablespoon cornstarch

2 tablespoons cold water

8 ounces Stilton cheese, cut into 8 wedges, for serving

1. Preheat the oven to 475°F.

2. Prepare the tart: Melt the butter in a sauté pan over medium heat. Add the leeks and cook until translucent, about 5 minutes. Add the thyme and brandy and cook for 1 minute. Season with salt and pepper to taste. Remove and let cool to room temperature.

3. Meanwhile, on a floured surface, roll out the basic pie dough into a 15-inch circle, about ⅛-inch thick. Carefully fold the dough in half and half again into a triangular shape. Transfer it to a large baking sheet lined with parchment; unfold into a circle (it's okay if the dough hangs over the edges).

4. Slice the pears lengthwise in half; scoop out the cores. Place each half, cut side down, on a work surface and cut lengthwise into ¼-inch-thick slices.

5. Spread out the cooled leek mixture evenly into a 10-inch circle in the center of the pie dough, leaving the outer 5 inches exposed. Starting in the very center, fan out the pear slices in 2 tightly packed concentric circles, slightly overlapping the first circle with the second.

6. Sprinkle the pears with the walnuts and drizzle with the walnut oil. Whisk together the egg yolk and water; brush the exposed dough with the egg wash. Fold the edges of the dough up over the pears in a pleated fashion. Brush this dough with the remaining egg wash.

COOKING WITH PORT WINE

Port is a rich, sweet, fortified wine from Portugal that is generally served as an after-dinner drink. There are two basic types, ruby and tawny, however there is much variety in quality and price with some of the best ports being aged for up to fifty years. The port we use in cooking is inexpensive American-made ruby port that's available in any liquor store. Save your vintage port for sipping!

{continued}

7. Bake the tart for 10 minutes. Reduce the oven temperature to 350°F and bake for 45 minutes more, or until the pastry is golden and the pears are cooked through.

8. While the tart bakes, make the Red Grape Compote: In a heavy nonreactive saucepan, combine the grapes, port, vinegar, peppercorns, cloves, and bay leaf. Bring the mixture to a boil. Reduce the heat to low and simmer until the grape skins split and begin to come off, 5 to 10 minutes. Remove from the heat and strain the sauce into a smaller nonreactive pot. Reserve the cooked grapes; discard the skins and spices.

9. Stir together the cornstarch and water until smooth. Add to the strained sauce and stir constantly over high heat until the mixture thickens and comes to a boil. Stir in the reserved grapes. Remove from the heat.

10. To serve, cut the warm tart into 8 wedges. Top each wedge with a spoonful of the compote. Place a wedge of Stilton alongside each tart.

SELECTING PERFECT PEARS

If you can get them, we recommend our favorite pears, organic Magnuss pears or the tiny, native Pennsylvanian Seckel pears—but any firm ripe pear will do. You can tell a pear is ripe if it yields to gentle pressure from the tip of your thumb.

Sherried Lobster and Shrimp Crêpes {Serves 8}

We serve these crêpes as a first course every year at our July 14th Bastille Day celebration. The delicate crêpes, wrapped around a cool and succulent seafood salad, are always a hit on a hot summer day. Although appearing opulent, these crêpes are deceptive—just one lobster and half a pound of shrimp will satisfy all, sans revolution. We cook live lobsters (see note below) when making this salad, but frozen lobster tails work well, too.

CRÊPE BATTER

1 cup all-purpose flour

¼ teaspoon salt

¾ cup milk

¾ cup water

3 eggs

4 tablespoons unsalted butter, melted

2 tablespoons minced fresh chives

SEAFOOD SALAD

1 tablespoon olive oil

8 ounces shrimp, peeled and deveined

¼ cup plus 1 teaspoon dry sherry

Salt

½ cup Homemade Mayonnaise (page 287), or store-bought

1½ teaspoons sherry vinegar

2 scallions, thinly sliced

2 tablespoons minced fresh chervil leaves and stems

⅛ teaspoon cayenne pepper

1½ cups cooked, diced lobster meat (see note below)

1 small cucumber peeled, seeded, salted, and diced (see note page 298)

2 plum tomatoes, seeded and cut into ¼-inch dice

Avocado Mousse (page 296), for serving

1. Make the crêpe batter: Sift together the flour and salt into a bowl. Slowly whisk in the milk and water to form a smooth batter. Whisk in the eggs and 3 tablespoons of the melted butter. Strain the batter through a sieve to remove any lumps. Set aside for at least 10 minutes and up to 30 minutes. Add the chives.

2. Heat a few drops of the remaining 1 tablespoon of melted butter in a 6-inch nonstick skillet set over medium-high heat. Pour a generous 2 tablespoons of batter into the center of the pan and tilt it in all directions to lightly and evenly coat the bottom of the pan. Cook the crêpes until the underside is browned, about 1 minute. Using a rubber spatula or your fingers, turn over the crêpe and brown the other side. Remove to a rack or baking sheet to cool. Repeat with the remaining butter and batter; you'll need 16 crêpes. When cool, use immediately or stack the crêpes between squares of waxed paper. Refrigerate for up to 2 days.

3. Make the seafood salad: Heat the oil in a nonreactive sauté pan set over high heat until it ripples. Add the shrimp and sauté until just cooked through, about 3 minutes. Add ¼ cup of the sherry and cook until it evaporates, about 1 minute. Season with a pinch of salt. Set aside to cool to room temperature. Dice the seafood and reserve.

4. In a large mixing bowl, whisk together the mayonnaise, vinegar, scallions, chervil, cayenne, and the remaining 1 teaspoon dry sherry. Add the lobster, shrimp, cucumber, and tomatoes, and mix well. Use immediately or cover and refrigerate for up to 2 days.

COOKING LIVE LOBSTERS

Bring a large pot of salted water to a rolling boil. Plunge the lobster headfirst into it. When the water returns to a boil, cook for 12 minutes. Remove the lobster and shock in ice water to stop the cooking process. When cool enough to handle, grasp the tail in one hand and the body in the other, firmly twist the tail away from the body, breaking the lobster in two. With kitchen shears, cut the bottom side of the tail's shell down the middle, and pull out the meat. Disjoint the claws from the body. With a mallet, crack them open and remove the meat.

{continued}

5. Fill each crêpe with ¼ cup of the prepared salad. Roll up tightly and serve each guest 2 crêpes topped with a dollop of Avocado Mousse (page 296).

OTHER WAYS TO DO IT
The lobster salad also makes a tasty sandwich filling or stuffing for tomatoes or melon. For an elegant hors d'oeuvre, place a spoonful of the salad on an endive spear and top it with a dollop of our Avocado Mousse.

DEVEINING SHRIMP
Generally shrimp should be peeled and deveined before they are cooked. However, when served cold, you can cook the shrimp in their shells, which will leave them plump and moist. When they have cooled, the method for deveining the shrimp is the same as if they were raw. Pull the shell away from the shrimp. Place the shelled shrimp flat on a work surface and make a shallow cut down the center of its curved back with a sharp paring knife. This cut exposes the thin black intestinal tract. Pull it out with your fingers or scrape it away with your knife and discard.

Chili- and Corn-crusted Calamari with Tangy Citrus Aïoli {Serves 4}

When traveling, we collect not only souvenirs but also ideas and inspiration. This calamari is an adaptation of some we had in a funky Jamaican restaurant in the Haight-Asbury section of San Francisco. Our version is encrusted with spicy cornmeal and accompanied by a creamy citrus dip. Squid requires careful cooking to prevent it from becoming too rubbery; it's best if fried until just cooked through.

TANGY CITRUS AÏOLI

Finely minced zest and juice of 1 lemon

¼ cups fresh orange juice

½ jalapeño pepper, seeded and minced

1 tablespoon minced garlic

1 cup Homemade Mayonnaise (page 287)

¼ teaspoon *nam pla* (Thai fish sauce, available in Asian markets and specialty food stores; see note, page 95)

Finely minced zest of 1 lime

Finely minced zest of 1 orange

½ cup yellow cornmeal

¼ cup chili powder

2 tablespoons all-purpose flour

Peanut oil

1 pound squid, cleaned, the mantles cut into ¼-inch rings and the tentacles into bite-size pieces (see note below)

1. Prepare the Tangy Citrus Aïoli: Combine the lemon juice, orange juice, jalapeño, and garlic in a small, nonreactive saucepan set over high heat. Bring to a boil and cook until the juice is very syrupy and reduced to about 3 tablespoons, about 10 minutes. Spoon the citrus reduction into a small bowl and let cool to room temperature.

2. Stir in the mayonnaise, *nam pla*, and all of the minced citrus zest. Mix well; the aïoli should be tart and tangy. If it tastes too sweet, add a squeeze of juice from the zested lime. If you want more spiciness, add the remaining half jalapeño. This can be made ahead and kept refrigerated for up to 2 days. Serve chilled.

3. Prepare the calamari: Sift together the cornmeal, chili powder, and flour in a small bowl. Heat 2 inches of peanut oil to 350°F in a deep-fryer or heavy-bottomed saucepan.

4. Toss the calamari in the cornmeal mixture and remove with tongs or a slotted spoon. When the oil is hot, carefully add half of the coated squid and fry until golden brown, about 1 minute. Remove with tongs or a slotted spoon, and drain on paper towels. Repeat with the remaining squid.

5. To serve, divide the squid among 4 plates and serve with the Tangy Citrus Aïoli and if you like, a leafy green salad dressed with Lemon–Olive Oil Vinaigrette (see page 90).

CLEANING SQUID

Fresh squid is usually available already cleaned (rinse it again at home), however it's less expensive if you clean it yourself. Here's how: Separate the head and the body by pulling them gently apart with your hands. Cut the tentacles from the head below the eyes and reserve. Discard the rest of the head. Remove the transparent plasticlike "pen" from the squid body. Rinse the inside of the body thoroughly with cold water to remove any remaining viscera. Scrape the purple skin off the squid's body with a knife or your fingers—it is edible but most people don't find it attractive. Slice the squid bodies into rings or prepare as directed.

Warm Shellfish and Asian Vegetables with Spicy Ginger-Lime Dressing {Serving 4}

Madame Dai, the proprietress of La Bibliothèque, our sister restaurant in Ho Chi Minh City, Vietnam, served the visiting White Dog Cafe contingency an exotic dish of warmed shellfish and crunchy vegetables. We loved it so much that we now feature our own version at the White Dog Cafe.

½ cup **Spicy Ginger-Lime Dressing**
  (page 288)

8 **littleneck clams, scrubbed**

8 **mussels, scrubbed and debearded**

1 **cup water**

2 **tablespoons olive oil**

8 **bay scallops**

8 **large shrimp, peeled and deveined**

½ **pound squid (see note, opposite page),**
  cleaned and cut into ½-inch-thin rings,
  leaving the tentacles whole

2 **cups thinly sliced savoy cabbage**

1 **cup carrot curls (use a vegetable peeler)**

1 **cup daikon curls (use a vegetable peeler)**

1 **red bell pepper, diced**

1 **cup cherry tomatoes, halved**

3 **scallions, thinly sliced**

4 **cups mizuma, watercress, or other**
  peppery salad green

4 **tablespoons toasted cashews**

1. Make the Spicy Ginger-Lime Dressing.

2. In a nonreactive sauté pan set over high heat, combine the clams, mussels and water. Bring to a boil, and then cover and steam until the shellfish open, 5 to 7 minutes. Pour off the liquid and reserve the shellfish (discard any clams or mussels that don't open).

3. Heat the oil until it ripples in a sauté pan set over high heat. Add the scallops, shrimp, and squid and stir-fry until just cooked through, 3 to 5 minutes.

4. Remove the pan from the heat. Add the reserved clams and mussels and all of the vegetables to the stir-fried seafood. Pour on the Spicy Ginger-Lime Dressing and toss quickly to coat evenly. Divide among 4 plates and top each with 1 tablespoon of the toasted cashews. Serve at once.

OTHER WAYS TO DO IT
Change the vegetables to suit your mood and the season.

ABOUT *NUOC CHAM*
Pronounced noo-AHK CHAHM, this is an important condiment on the Vietnamese table—used for dipping spring rolls, sprinkling over stir-fries and salads, and adding flavor to rice. It usually consists of fish sauce, lime juice, sugar, and chiles; however all cooks have their own version. We call ours Spicy Ginger-Lime Dressing and use it for dressing noodles, rice, raw or steamed vegetables, and as a marinade for grilled fish, meat, or chicken.

Lemon- and Pepper-grilled Calamari with Roasted Pepper–Balsamic Dressing {Serves 4}

Assertive fresh Italian parsley leaves lay the foundation for this salad of smoky grilled squid and a robust dressing made from roasted sweet bell peppers. Buy squid that has already been cleaned if you can find it (although it isn't difficult to clean; see note page 52). The calamari can also be cooked in a very hot cast-iron stovetop grill or skillet.

ROASTED PEPPER–BALSAMIC DRESSING

2 garlic cloves, peeled

1 roasted red bell pepper, peeled and seeded (see note, page 140)

1 roasted yellow bell pepper, peeled and seeded (see note, page 140)

1 teaspoon fresh thyme leaves

¼ cup plus 1 tablespoon balsamic vinegar

1 cup extra-virgin olive oil

¾ teaspoon salt

½ teaspoon freshly ground black pepper

MARINADE

½ lemon, seeded and finely chopped

1 tablespoon chopped fresh Italian parsley leaves

½ teaspoon hot red pepper flakes

½ teaspoon freshly ground black pepper

1 teaspoon *nam pla* (Thai fish sauce, available in Asian markets and specialty food stores; see note, page 95)

1 teaspoon minced garlic

2 tablespoons olive oil

12 ounces cleaned whole squid (see note, page 52)

1 bunch Italian parsley leaves

1. Prepare the Roasted Pepper–Balsamic Dressing: Combine the garlic, roasted bell peppers, thyme, and vinegar in a food processor or blender. Pulse to make a chunky purée, about 30 seconds.

2. With the motor running, slowly pour in the 1 cup of oil and process until just combined. Season with the salt and pepper. The dressing can be made up to 3 days in advance and kept refrigerated. Bring to room temperature before serving.

3. Preheat a gas grill or prepare a charcoal grill.

4. When the coals are just about ready, prepare the marinade: Whisk together the chopped lemon, parsley, pepper flakes, black pepper, *nam pla*, garlic, and the 2 tablespoons olive oil in a medium bowl. Add the squid and toss to coat with the marinade. Set aside for at least 5 minutes and no longer than 15 minutes.

5. Remove the squid from the marinade and grill quickly over high heat until the bodies puff up and the tentacles begin to curl, about 1 minute on each side. Set aside to cool to room temperature.

6. Slice the squid mantles into ¼ inch-rings and combine with the tentacles in a large bowl. Add the parsley leaves. To serve, place ¼ cup of the dressing in the center of each chilled plate. Top with some of the squid and parsley mixture. If you like, accompany this dish with Garlic Crostini (page 281) spread with Black Olive Tapenade (page 294).

OTHER WAYS TO DO IT

If you prefer, omit the parsley and serve the squid, whole, hot from the grill, drizzled with the dressing.

Marinated Goat Cheese with Fresh Tomatoes {Serves 4}

We know how lucky we are to have farm-fresh produce delivered right to our door year round, but we are especially grateful in mid-August, when succulent sun-ripened tomatoes abound. Our favorites are some recently rediscovered heirloom varieties that are sweet and juicy with that real tomato flavor we remember from summers long past. This simple salad of marinated cheese is best made when the tomatoes are ripened by the sun and bursting with juice. Be sure to marinate the cheese well ahead of time so it's ready to use when you want it.

½ cup extra-virgin olive oil

1 tablespoon chopped fresh Italian
    parsley leaves

1 tablespoon chopped fresh basil leaves

¼ teaspoon freshly ground black pepper

¼ teaspoon salt

Pinch of hot red pepper flakes

1 lemon, thinly sliced into rounds

8 ounces fresh (unaged) chèvre

4 ripe tomatoes, sliced

1. Whisk together the oil, parsley, basil, pepper, salt, and hot pepper flakes in a small bowl. Stir in the lemon rounds.

2. Divide the chèvre into 4 equal parts; shape each portion into a small disk. Arrange them in a single layer in a small bowl; pour on the lemon and oil marinade. Cover and set aside at room temperature for at least 6 hours, turning once. (If you're not going to use the cheese right away, it can be refrigerated for up to 1 week. Bring to room temperature before serving because the oil will solidify when chilled.)

3. To serve, arrange the tomatoes on 4 chilled salad plates. Top with a disk of the cheese and spoon some of the marinade over the top. Sprinkle with additional freshly ground black pepper to taste and serve.

OTHER WAYS TO DO IT
When tomatoes aren't in season, substitute leaves of crisp romaine, and rings of red and yellow bell peppers.

ABOUT GREYSTONE BRAND GOAT CHEESE
Our friend Douglass Newbold has a prize herd of Greystone Nubian goats from which she makes her famous Greystone Chèvratel. Fresh and mild, this goat cheese is so delicious and versatile that we use it in everything from appetizers to desserts. If you can't get this brand, use any soft, fresh (unaged) chèvre available.

Braised Fennel with Fresh Mozzarella and Sun-dried Tomato Vinaigrette {Serves 4}

Each winter this appetizer appears on the menu when we get a hankering for a salad of summer tomatoes and fresh mozzarella. The vinaigrette is a zesty purée of tangy sun-dried tomatoes spiked with sherry vinegar; its sharpness is mellowed by the sweet fennel and warm cheese. Be sure to prepare the Garlic Crostini (page 281) ahead of time—you can snack on them while the cheese melts.

16–20 Garlic Crostini (page 281)

SUN-DRIED TOMATO VINAIGRETTE
3 ounces sun-dried tomatoes

3 garlic cloves, chopped

1/2 small red onion, coarsely chopped

1 cup water

2 tablespoons sherry vinegar

1 tablespoon red wine vinegar

3 tablespoons tomato juice

1/2 teaspoon salt

Pinch of ground black pepper

1/4 cup olive oil

3/4 cup dry white wine

1/3 cup Pernod or Ricard

1/4 cup extra-virgin olive oil

1 tablespoon minced garlic

1 teaspoon sugar

1 teaspoon aniseed

1/2 teaspoon salt

1/2 teaspoon freshly ground black pepper

2 fennel bulbs, stalks removed, halved, cored, and thinly sliced

1/2 small red onion, thinly sliced

4 ounces fresh mozzarella, very thinly sliced

1. Prepare the Garlic Crostini.

2. Prepare the vinaigrette: Place the sun-dried tomatoes, garlic, and onion in a medium nonreactive saucepan and add the water. Bring to a boil over high heat. Reduce the heat to low and simmer for 15 minutes, until tomatoes and onions are soft. Remove from the heat and set aside to cool to room temperature.

3. Pour the cooled mixture into a food processor or blender. Add the sherry vinegar, red wine vinegar, tomato juice, salt, and pepper; purée until smooth, about 30 seconds. With the motor running, slowly pour in the oil and process to form a smooth emulsion. Serve at room temperature. Covered, this vinaigrette will keep in the refrigerator for 1 week.

4. Preheat the oven to 350°F.

5. Whisk together the wine, Pernod, oil, garlic, sugar, aniseed, salt, and pepper in a large bowl. Add the fennel and onion and toss to combine. Pour the mixture into a shallow nonreactive baking dish.

6. Cover with a lid or foil. Braise the fennel in the oven until tender but still firm to the bite, about 30 minutes.

7. Preheat the broiler. Uncover the baking dish and top the fennel with the slices of cheese. Broil until the cheese melts and bubbles, about 4 minutes.

8. To serve, spoon 1/4 cup of the Sun-Dried Tomato Vinaigrette onto the bottom of each of 4 salad plates. Divide the broiled fennel among the plates. Serve with the Garlic Crostini.

OTHER WAYS TO DO IT
To make a warm pasta salad, toss the fennel and vinaigrette with some just-cooked pasta shells or penne. Top with the cheese and then place under the broiler.

Broiled Black Mission Figs with Prosciutto, Fontina, and Sage Phyllo Flutes {Serves 4}

Even though we're located in Pennsylvania where fig trees can't survive year round, our farmer friend Paul Tsakos manages to supply us fresh figs each fall. His fig tree is planted in an old whiskey barrel that he wheels out of his barn each spring and wheels back inside before the first frost. Look for fresh figs in your grocery store from June through October.

FIGS

3 tablespoons balsamic vinegar

3 tablespoons extra-virgin olive oil

1 tablespoon chopped fresh rosemary leaves

Juice of $\frac{1}{2}$ lemon

Salt and freshly ground black pepper

8 fresh Black Mission figs (or other fresh figs), washed and dried

1 small red onion, sliced $\frac{1}{2}$-inch thick and separated into rings

PHYLLO FLUTES

1 cup grated Fontina cheese

$\frac{1}{4}$ cup finely diced prosciutto

2 tablespoons chopped fresh sage leaves

$\frac{1}{4}$ teaspoon freshly ground black pepper

1 package (1 pound) phyllo dough, thawed (see note, page 44)

Olive oil

Watercress or arugula, for garnish

1. Prepare the figs: In a medium bowl, whisk together the vinegar, oil, rosemary, and lemon juice. Season with salt and pepper to taste. Add the whole figs and the onion rings and gently toss in the marinade. Set aside to marinate for 30 minutes.

2. Preheat the oven to 400°F. Have ready a baking dish for the figs and onions and a baking sheet, preferably nonstick, for the flutes.

3. Prepare the flutes: Combine the Fontina, prosciutto, sage, and pepper in a small bowl and mix thoroughly.

4. Work with 1 sheet of phyllo at a time, and keep the remaining sheets covered with a damp towel to prevent them from drying out. Place 1 sheet of phyllo on a work surface with a long side toward you. Lightly brush the entire sheet with olive oil. Top with another sheet of phyllo. Cut the sheet lengthwise in half to make 2 rectangles. Spread one-fourth of the filling along the bottom edge of dough. Tightly roll up the dough into a flute or cylinder about 1 inch in diameter. Repeat this process to make a total of 4 flutes. Place the flutes a few inches apart on a nonstick baking sheet.

5. Pour the fig and onion mixture into a baking dish. Bake both the figs and flutes until the figs swell up and soften slightly and the flutes are golden brown, 8 to 10 minutes.

6. To serve, place a bouquet of watercress or arugula on each of 4 dinner plates. Using a pair of tongs or a slotted spoon, lean 2 figs against the greens. Angle the flute between the figs and greens. Spoon some of the cooking liquid around the figs and serve.

USING IMPORTED FONTINA

Fontina d'Aosta is from Italy's Piedmont region and is considered one of the world's greatest cheeses. It is buttery and mellow with a sweet, slightly smoky flavor and smooth semi-firm texture. It has a dark, golden-brown rind and smooth, pale, ivory interior that's dotted with very tiny holes. Make certain to purchase *true* Fontina d'Aosta with a brown rind, as the Fontinas in a bright red rind are nothing like the real thing.

Asian Barbecued Ribs with Gingered Snow Pea–Cabbage Slaw {Serves 4}

Once you start nibbling on these dainty ribs it's hard to stop; if plentiful, they'll end up being dinner. Part of their charm is eating them with the light and tangy Gingered Snow Pea–Cabbage Slaw. It cuts the richness of the meat, and its acidity contrasts nicely with the sweetness of the barbecue glaze.

5 cups Gingered Snow Pea–Cabbage Slaw (page 214)

2 pounds baby back ribs

Salt and freshly ground black pepper

2 tablespoons minced fresh ginger

1 tablespoon minced garlic

2 scallions, thinly sliced

1/2 cup hoisin sauce

1/4 cup oyster sauce

1/3 cup ketchup

1 tablespoon soy sauce

2 teaspoons hot chili paste (available in Asian markets and specialty food stores)

1/4 cup packed light brown sugar

1 teaspoon Asian sesame oil

1/4 cup rice wine vinegar

1. Prepare the Gingered Snow Pea-Cabbage Slaw.

2. Preheat the oven to 375°F. Fit a roasting pan with a flat rack.

3. Sprinkle both sides of the ribs with salt and pepper. Place on the rack in the pan. Bake for 45 minutes.

4. Meanwhile, combine the ginger, garlic, scallions, hoisin sauce, oyster sauce, ketchup, soy sauce, chili paste, brown sugar, sesame oil, and rice wine vinegar in a food processor. Process until smooth, about 30 seconds. Transfer the glaze to a bowl, or cover and refrigerate for up to 1 week.

5. Remove the ribs from the oven; leave the oven on. When they are cool enough to handle, slice the racks into individual ribs. Toss the ribs in the prepared glaze, coating well.

6. Place the ribs on a baking sheet and bake until the glaze caramelizes and the ribs are tender, 20 to 30 minutes more. Divide the ribs among 4 plates. Serve with the Gingered Snow Pea-Cabbage Slaw—and plenty of napkins.

USING BABY BACK RIBS

We like to use baby back ribs because they are small and dainty—about the size of your index finger—making them the perfect size for an appetizer. However this recipe will work well with any sort of ribs; simply adjust the cooking time accordingly. The barbecue glaze also is delicious on grilled chicken, pork, or even tuna.

Basil-dressed Melon and Prosciutto with Black Pepper–Orange Mascarpone {Serves 4}

We heighten the classic pairing of melon with prosciutto by adding a splash of sprightly basil mignonette (a vinaigrette minus the oil), luscious pepper-spiked cheese, and the surprise of a crisp curried cracker. The dramatic presentation and remarkable harmony of flavors in this dish linger long after it has been devoured.

BASIL MIGNONETTE

¼ cup minced shallots

¼ cup tightly packed minced basil leaves

1 cup Champagne vinegar

2 teaspoons sugar

1 teaspoon freshly ground black pepper

¼ teaspoon salt

BLACK PEPPER–ORANGE MASCARPONE

Grated zest of 1 orange

8 ounces (1 cup) mascarpone cheese

3 tablespoons fresh orange juice

¾ teaspoon freshly ground black pepper

¼ teaspoon salt

1 cantaloupe or other ripe melon, peeled, seeded, and cut into 8 wedges, for serving

8 thin slices of prosciutto, for serving

Poppy Seed Cracker Bread (page 241), for serving

1. Prepare the mignonette: Combine the shallots, basil, vinegar, sugar, pepper, and salt in a small bowl and mix well. Set aside briefly or cover and refrigerate overnight.

2. Prepare the mascarpone: Combine the orange zest, mascarpone, orange juice, pepper, and salt in a small bowl and mix well. Use immediately or cover and refrigerate for up to 5 days.

3. To serve, tightly wrap each wedge of melon with a slice of the prosciutto. Arrange 2 pieces of melon on each plate. Drizzle lightly with the basil mignonette and top with a dollop of the mascarpone. If desired, stand a large piece of Poppy Seed Cracker Bread in the mascarpone cheese for a dramatic crunch.

OTHER WAYS TO DO IT

Use the components of this dish for a dashing canapé: Break off 1½-inch pieces of the Poppy Seed Cracker Bread, spread them with the mascarpone, and top with small pieces of melon wrapped in prosciutto. Sprinkle lightly with the mignonette.

CHAPTER TWO

SOUPS, BISQUES
& CHOWDERS

SOUPS, BISQUES & CHOWDERS

Eating with the Enemy: A Vietnamese Tale 63

Sweet Potato and Lemon Grass Soup with Peanut "Pesto" 67

Ratatouille Bisque 68

Desert Garden Gazpacho with Margarita-Scallop Seviche 69

Chilled Cucumber Soup with Tomato-Tarragon Relish 70

Thai Three-Melon Soup 71

Artichoke Bisque 72

Curried Apple Bisque with Minted Yogurt 73

French Mushroom Soup 74

Garden Vegetable Minestrone 75

Lentil and Tomato Soup with Coriander and Cumin 76

Cuban Black Bean Soup 77

Chiapas Tortilla Soup 78

Asian Chicken Noodle Soup 79

Smoked Salmon and Corn Chowder 80

Creamy Mussel Chowder with Sorrel 81

Portuguese-style Mussel Stew 82

Beef Burgundy Stew 83

EATING WITH THE ENEMY: A VIETNAMESE TALE

OUR VAN OF AMERICAN TRAVELERS CAME TO A STOP AT THE LAKE OF THE SWORD, near the center of Hanoi, and I looked apprehensively out the window to see if anyone had noticed us. It was 1990, fifteen years after the end of the war, and the occasion of my first trip to Vietnam. On the drive from the airport we passed the Bach Mai Hospital, twice destroyed by U.S. bombers. I could still make out the pock marks on the landscape where American bombs had fallen. When I thought of Vietnam, it was only the war I pictured. And Hanoi, we had been taught, was the enemy capital. Now I wanted to understand it as a place and a people, to find a sister restaurant in this country where millions of Vietnamese had been killed or wounded in what they called the "American War." I had come to eat with the enemy, but what would they think of me—an American in Hanoi?

Stepping from the van, I heard explosions. "Tet," it was explained. The Tet Offensive flashed to mind, but it was not gunshot—rather the sound of firecrackers in celebration of the lunar New Year. I saw red splattered everywhere—not the red of war imprinted so vividly on my mind—but red balloons and flags, New Year's banners, and red berets worn by teenagers who gathered around us, their open faces smiling and full of curiosity. An older man walked slowly toward me, his beard like Ho Chi Minh's.

"American?" he asked. Now it had begun.

"Yes," I answered timidly.

"Good," he said, "may I have my picture taken with you? I like American."

He never mentioned the bombs of yesteryear.

Over tea and tangerines and a bowl of candied peanuts, coconut, and ginger, we were welcomed by a representative of the Vietnam-United States Society who spoke of the recent reforms allowing free enterprise after ten years of stagnation following the war.

"We are not communist or socialist," he explained. "We are a country trying to find its identity. We knew capitalism only during the oppression of colonialism, but on the other hand, we do not want dependency on the state. By opening the economy," he explained, "we have released the creative energy of our people."

White Dog Cafe patron, Howard Bilofsky, learns irrigation techniques in a Vietnamese rice patty during a sister restaurant visit

When I returned the following year with Kevin and a tour group of White Dog Cafe patrons, I could feel the entrepreneurial vitality in the air as new businesses sprang up everywhere. The first floors of the houses along the streets had turned into stores and cafes with lights strung along the sidewalks where it had been dark before. Unwanted elements were coming with it, just as the old guard had feared—materialism, classism, pollution, prostitution, AIDS, alcoholism, and crime. The old Hanoi, with its dignified, quiet streets and demure women in traditional dress, was disappearing. Just a year ago, the six-lane-wide boulevards had been filled only with thousands of bicycles, silently spinning by, miraculously weaving in and out of crowded intersections with no need for stop signs or lights. Then, there had been a seamless silent rhythm of motion as though a giant basket were being woven by a communality of diligence and grace. Now, the quietly streaming streets had been invaded by a chaos of roaring motorcycles and honking, smoking cars. At an intersection a rickshaw had been hit and now lay on its back motionless, like a helpless brown beetle, legs in the air. The car drivers didn't know how to weave and didn't care.

But change wasn't happening fast enough for a group of college students I later met on the beach in NaTrang who practiced their English with me while we sipped lemonade made from fresh-squeezed sugar cane and lemons. They expressed their impatience with the "old men in Hanoi" and wanted to see more rapid political reform. The government didn't allow them to listen to American music because they feared it taught bad values. When the police, who spoke no English, questioned the group of college students, they told the police it was Russian and they never knew the difference!

During a meal of fish soup with dill, squid, and leeks; deviled eggs with ground chicken, snails with ginger, sweet-and-sour pork, pot roast with potatoes, and candied fruit and nuts, we heard the views of an elder statesman, Madame Nguyeun Thi Binh, who, as foreign minister for the Vietcong, had negotiated with Kissinger at the Paris peace talks.

Vietnam was not a perfect democracy, she admitted, but progress was being made. As Minister of Education after the war, she had successfully addressed Vietnam's major concern. During French rule, there had been a ninety-five percent illiteracy rate. Now, fifteen years since independence, the statistics had been reversed. Current attention was on building the economy, hampered by the ongoing U.S. embargo (eventually lifted by President Clinton in 1994). A veteran in our group learned that the Vietnamese saw the American G.I.s as fellow victims of the war. Here in Vietnam he found the understanding and forgiveness that he had longed for but could not find at home.

Traveling down the coast, in every city we walked through open-air markets overflowing with fresh vegetables, fruits, fish, seafood, ducks, chickens, and freshly butchered meats. Kevin and I had never seen such an abundance of exotic foods—coriander, lemon grass, hot peppers and chiles, ginger, basil, garlic, scallions, shallots, so many different types of rice and noodles and foods that were totally new to us.

There was one food I did not want to try, of course. I had heard that dog was a delicacy in Vietnam. While swimming at China Beach, I saw a man walking toward the water holding a dog. I watched in horror thinking that he was going to drown it for a feast, until I realized that he was lovingly giving his pet a bath. *Maybe the name White Dog Cafe wouldn't be misinterpreted after all!* I thought

In Ho Chi Minh City the traditions of the north gave way to a more international flavor. Our sister restaurant, Madame Dai's La Biblioteque, is a blend of Vietnamese and French. A lawyer educated in Paris, Madame Dai had been a member of the South Vietnamese senate while discretely supporting the Vietcong, and after the war had turned the office in her house into a restaurant where her law books lined the dining room walls. Travelers from all corners of the world seemed to pass through her doors to share a glass of Johnnie Walker Black, kept on a shelf amidst a collection of antique pottery, and dine on spring rolls, stewed duck, and crème caramel.

For hundreds of years, the Vietnamese had fought invaders from

Madame Dai in her restaurant, La Bibliotéque, in Ho Chi Minh City, Vietnam

China, France, and the United States, and they had ingeniously adopted attributes of each culture into their own. Chinese noodles and French baguettes were a part of every meal. And from America? The sweet potato, for one. Our trip leader, Don Luce, famous

Judy, Kevin, and the Cafe's head bus boy, Scott Lee Lawrence, during a visit to a sister restaurant in Vietnam, 1995

in Vietnam for freeing political prisoners from South Vietnam's "Tiger Cages" during the war, had first come as an agriculture specialist in the 1950s to cultivate the sweet potato. Kevin's recipe for sweet potato soup, which blends the American sweet potato with the exotic flavors of Vietnam, is a tribute to Don, who has dedicated much of his life to bringing our countries together in friendship.

At the end of my last trip, sitting on the porch of the former South Vietnamese presidential palace, I tried to imagine the scene when North Vietnamese tanks crashed through the front gates to receive the surrender of the South and unite the country, as the last Americans were lifted from the embassy roof. It was hard to picture that now, gazing across the immaculate lawn and flower garden where all traces of war had vanished.

I thought of the Vietnamese people we had met and how much we shared in our desire for justice and freedom, and our hopes and fears for our children's futures, not to mention our mutual love of good food! The war was over, but the lesson of this great tragedy will not be forgotten. We had eaten with the enemy and found them to be our friends.

—JW

Sweet Potato and Lemon Grass Soup with Peanut "Pesto" {Serves 6 to 8}

This ever-popular soup originated at our sister restaurant, La Bibliothéque in Ho Chi Minh City, Vietnam, where they serve it chilled as a prelude to fiery curries and satés. We serve it iced in the warmer months, but it is equally delicious served hot when the monsoons blow through. It's quite easy to prepare ahead of time, and will stay perfectly tasty for up to two days in the refrigerator. The fragrant "pesto" garnish should be assembled no more than two hours before serving to preserve their crunch, color, and exotic perfume.

SOUP

2 pounds sweet potatoes, peeled and diced

3 stalks lemon grass, outer layers removed, bulbs split open

2 tablespoons olive oil

1 cup minced white onion

2 tablespoons minced garlic

1 jalapeño pepper, seeded and minced

1 piece (2 inches) fresh ginger, peeled and minced

1 can (14 ounces) coconut milk (preferably Chaokoh brand)

Juice of 1 lime

2 teaspoons salt

$1/4$ teaspoon cayenne pepper (optional)

PEANUT "PESTO"

$1/2$ cup unsalted peanuts, toasted (see note, page 144) and cooled

2 tablespoons chopped fresh basil leaves

2 tablespoons chopped fresh mint leaves

1 tablespoon chopped fresh cilantro leaves and stems

1. Place the sweet potatoes and lemon grass stalks in a large saucepan and cover with water. Bring to a boil over high heat. Reduce the heat to medium and simmer until the potatoes are fully cooked, about 20 minutes. Remove the lemon grass stalks. Drain the sweet potatoes, reserving the liquid and the potatoes separately.

2. While the potatoes are cooking, heat the oil in a small sauté pan set over medium heat until it ripples. Add the onion and cook until soft, about 5 minutes. Add the garlic and cook for 2 minutes. Add the jalapeño and minced ginger and sauté for 3 minutes more.

3. Combine the cooked sweet potatoes, cooked onion mixture, coconut milk, and 3 cups of the sweet potato cooking liquid in a food processor or blender. Process until smooth, about 30 seconds.

4. Pour the soup into a nonreactive saucepan set over medium heat and bring to a simmer. Stir in the lime juice, salt, and cayenne pepper, if desired. If the soup is too thick, add some more of the sweet potato cooking liquid, and adjust the seasonings to your taste. Serve the soup immediately while hot, or let cool to room temperature, and then refrigerate until well chilled, at least 1 hour.

5. Prepare the Peanut "Pesto": place the toasted peanuts on a cutting board or work surface and set a clean, heavy saucepan on top. Press down on the pan to break the peanuts into small, irregular pieces. Combine the crushed peanuts, basil, mint, and cilantro in a small bowl; toss well.

6. To serve, divide the soup among 6 to 8 bowls or soup plates. Sprinkle each serving with about 1 tablespoon of the Peanut "Pesto."

Ratatouille Bisque {Serves 8}

An uncomplicated soup, Ratatouille Bisque is indisputably healthy and delicious. We discovered it one particularly chilly autumn night when we found ourselves "souped out"—our customers had eaten up all of the soup in the house. We had just made a batch of ratatouille, so we took it, puréed it, then added some tomato juice to thin it, and some sherry vinegar to make it sparkle. Yum! An instant success.

1 head of roasted garlic (see note, page 38)

3 red bell peppers, diced

3 yellow bell peppers, diced

1 large yellow onion, diced

2 fennel bulbs, stalks removed, cored, and cut into large dice (see note, page 93)

½ cup olive oil

12 large, ripe plum tomatoes, halved

2 eggplants, halved lengthwise

3 cups tomato juice

3 cups water

1 teaspoon sugar

1 teaspoon salt

1 teaspoon freshly ground black pepper

2 tablespoons plus 1 teaspoon sherry vinegar (or balsamic vinegar or red wine vinegar)

Freshly grated Parmesan cheese, for serving

Polenta Croutons (page 283), for serving

Winter Herb Pesto (page 292), for serving

1. Prepare the roasted garlic.

2. Preheat the oven to 450°F.

3. In a bowl, toss the bell peppers, onion, and fennel with ¼ cup of the olive oil. Spread in a single layer on a baking sheet. Roast until lightly charred, about 45 minutes.

4. Toss the tomatoes with 2 tablespoons of the oil. Spread in a single layer on a nonstick baking sheet. Add to the hot oven and roast, stirring occasionally, until lightly charred, about 30 minutes.

5. Rub the eggplant halves with the remaining 2 tablespoons oil. Place them, cut sides down, on a baking sheet. Roast until soft, about 20 minutes.

6. When the vegetables are done, remove and let cool to room temperature. Remove the eggplant pulp by scraping it out of the skin with a large spoon. Reserve the pulp and discard the skin. Squeeze the roasted cloves of garlic from their skin.

7. Purée all of the roasted vegetables in batches in a food processor or blender. In a large nonreactive saucepan, combine the puréed vegetables with the tomato juice and water; bring to a simmer over medium heat. Stir in the sugar, salt, pepper, and vinegar. Thin with additional tomato juice and water, if desired; adjust the seasoning. Serve immediately, or let cool to room temperature, cover, and refrigerate for up to 3 days.

8. To serve, divide the soup among 6 warm bowls. If desired, serve with grated Parmesan, Polenta Croutons, and a dollop of Winter Herb Pesto.

OTHER WAYS TO DO IT
Grill the vegetables rather than roast them, and serve with Garlic Crostini (page 281) topped with chèvre.

Desert Garden Gazpacho with Margarita-Scallop Seviche {Serves 8}

If you're hot and tired there are few things more energizing than a bowl of icy gazpacho. We top ours with a refreshing seviche of scallops marinated in golden tequila and zesty citrus juices. Seviche is a Latin American dish that uses lime juice instead of heat to "cook" raw seafood. The acid in the citrus juices slowly changes the proteins in the scallops rendering them "cooked" after a few hours. The amount of tequila used in the marinade is just for flavor; if you prefer not to use it, it can be omitted.

MARGARITA-SCALLOP SEVICHE

Juice and grated zest of 2 limes

Juice and grated zest of 1 orange

3 tablespoons gold tequila

$^1/_2$ jalapeño pepper, seeded and minced

1 tablespoon chopped fresh cilantro leaves
and stems

2 scallions, thinly sliced

$^1/_2$ teaspoon salt

6 ounces sea scallops, cut into $^1/_4$-inch coins

DESERT GARDEN GAZPACHO

1 green bell pepper, diced

1 cup fresh corn kernels

1 cucumber, peeled, seeded, and diced

1 cup diced, peeled jicama (available
in most supermarkets)

$^1/_2$ small red onion, diced

2 pounds ripe tomatoes, seeded and diced
(about 4 cups)

1 teaspoon minced garlic

2 jalapeño peppers, seeded and minced

4 cups tomato juice

Juice of $1^1/_2$ limes

$^3/_4$ cup fresh orange juice

2 tablespoons chopped fresh cilantro leaves
and stems (see note, page 158)

$1^1/_2$ teaspoons salt

1. Prepare the seviche: Combine the lime juice and zest, orange juice and zest, tequila, jalapeño, cilantro, scallions, salt, and scallops in a small bowl. Cover and refrigerate for at least 4 hours and no longer than 6 hours. Serve well chilled.

2. Prepare the gazpacho: Combine the bell pepper, corn, cucumber, jicama, onion, tomatoes, garlic, and jalapeños in a large, nonreactive bowl. Stir in the tomato juice, lime juice, orange juice, cilantro, and salt. Cover and refrigerate until well chilled, at least 2 hours.

3. To serve, divide the soup among 8 well-chilled bowls. Top each with a spoonful of the Margarita-Scallop Seviche. This soup is best if eaten within 2 days.

OTHER WAYS TO DO IT

If you're in a hurry, the soup can be made by puréeing all of the vegetables in a food processor or blender, however the texture is much nicer if you take the time to cut them by hand.

Chilled Cucumber Soup with Tomato-Tarragon Relish {Serves 6}

Pastel green and garden-fresh, this soup typifies the kind of food we like to make in the summer. It can be prepared in a few minutes (without turning on the stove), and is invigoratingly icy—perfect for a refreshing lunch on a blazing hot summer day.

SOUP

4 large cucumbers (about 3 pounds), peeled, seeded, and cut into large chunks

1½ cups buttermilk

½ cup plain yogurt

2 whole scallions, thinly sliced

1½ teaspoons salt

¼ teaspoon freshly ground black pepper

TOMATO-TARRAGON RELISH

¾ cup diced, seeded, ripe tomato

2 tablespoons chopped fresh tarragon leaves

2 tablespoons extra-virgin olive oil

Pinch of salt

1. Prepare the soup: Place the cucumbers in a food processor or blender and process until liquefied, about 1 minute. Remove the purée to a bowl and whisk in the buttermilk, yogurt, scallions, salt, and pepper. Cover and refrigerate until well chilled, at least 1 hour. (The soup may be made 1 day in advance and will keep refrigerated for up to 3 days; however, the relish should be made just before serving.)

2. Meanwhile, prepare the relish: Combine the tomatoes, tarragon, oil, and salt in a small bowl and toss to combine.

3. To serve, divide the soup among 6 chilled bowls or plates. Top each serving with a spoonful of the relish.

Thai Three-Melon Soup {Serves 6}

Wandering outside the walls of the Imperial Palace in Bangkok, Thailand, Judy and I happened upon vendors offering a revitalizing melon drink to the overheated tourists. We loved it, and adapted it into a beautiful, coral-colored soup that we serve icy-cold topped with chilled poached shrimp and a splash of Thai fish sauce.

1 honeydew melon, peeled, seeded, and cut into large chunks

1 cantaloupe, peeled, seeded, and cut into large chunks

2 pounds watermelon (about 1/4 small), peeled, seeded, and diced

3 tablespoons chopped pickled ginger (see note below)

2 tablespoons fresh lime juice

18 chilled, poached, peeled, and deveined large shrimp

2 tablespoons chopped fresh cilantro leaves and stems, for garnish

2 tablespoons chopped fresh chives, for garnish

2 tablespoons *nam pla* (Thai fish sauce, available in Asian markets and specialty food stores), for serving

1. Combine the melons and pickled ginger in a food processor or blender and process until liquefied, about 1 minute (depending on the size of your food processor you may need to purée the melon in batches).

2. Pour the purée into a nonreactive bowl and stir in the lime juice. Cover and refrigerate until well chilled, at least 1 hour.

3. To serve, divide the soup among 6 icy-cold bowls or plates. Top each serving with 3 shrimp, a sprinkle of the herbs, and a splash of *nam pla.*

OTHER WAYS TO DO IT

This soup makes an exotic dessert if topped with a scoop of your favorite homemade or store-bought Orange sorbet instead of the shrimp and herbs. Or freeze it in a large shallow pan and scrape the frozen soup into bowls for a refreshing granita.

BUYING PICKLED GINGER

Pickled ginger is a widely used Asian condiment that is readily available in Asian markets and some specialty food stores. Many of our recipes call for pickled ginger juice, meaning the liquid that the ginger is packed in. It adds sparkle, life, and a jolt of flavor to soups, sauces, dressings, vinaigrettes, and relishes.

Artichoke Bisque {Serves 4}

Rich and velvet-textured, this bisque captures the essence of artichokes. Once the artichokes are cleaned, the preparation is effortless. The soup works equally well as an elegant beginning to a formal meal, or as a simple supper, served with antipasto and crusty bread.

4 tablespoons unsalted butter

2 leeks, trimmed and split lengthwise, washed well, green and white parts thinly sliced

1 tablespoon minced garlic

4 artichokes, leaves and chokes removed, bases and stems peeled and cut into $^1/_2$-inch pieces (see note below)

$^1/_2$ cup dry white wine or dry vermouth

1 large Idaho potato, peeled and cut into $^1/_2$-inch dice (about 2 cups)

4 cups Chicken Stock (page 277)

Salt and freshly ground black or white pepper

1. Melt the butter in a nonreactive saucepan over medium heat. Add the leeks and cook until limp and slightly translucent, about 5 minutes. Add the garlic and cook for 2 minutes.

2. Add the artichokes and wine. Reduce the heat to low, cover, and simmer for 10 minutes.

3. Stir in the potato and chicken stock and bring to a boil over medium heat. Reduce the heat, cover, and simmer until the potatoes are tender and begin to lose their shape, about 15 minutes.

4. Remove the solids with a slotted spoon and place them in a food processor, blender, or food mill. Process until smooth. Return the purée to the liquid and stir to combine. Season with salt and pepper to taste.

5. Keep the bisque warm until ready to serve, or let cool to room temperature and then refrigerate. When reheating you might need to add a few tablespoons of water, chicken stock, heavy cream, or milk to the bisque to thin it to a smooth, pourable consistency.

6. To serve, divide the soup among 4 warmed bowls or plates. If you like, sprinkle with Gremolata (page 285) or serve with a slice of a Burgundy-Rosemary Butter (see page 164).

CLEANING ARTICHOKES

Grasp the artichoke with the stem end pointing away from you (watch out for the spiny tips on the leaves). Starting with the leaves closest to the base, bend them back until they snap and twist them off. Continue removing all of the outer leaves until you reach the lighter colored yellow under leaves. Place the artichoke on a cutting board. With a sharp knife, slice the leaves off of the base and discard. With a sharp paring knife peel away the tough outer layer from the base and stem. Remove the stem from the base. Remove the fibrous choke from the base with a teaspoon or melon baller and discard. Keep the cleaned artichoke base and stem in water acidulated with a few drops of lemon juice to prevent discoloration.

Curried Apple Bisque with Minted Yogurt {Serves 6}

In the fall when the first cider is pressed, we use it as a "stock" for this savory-sweet bisque. The soup is very low in fat, but full of flavors that even kids like. Our homemade curry powder gives it a little heat that we like to temper with a splash of cool Minted Yogurt. Curry powders are as infinite in their variety as the people who make them. Ours is based loosely on curries from the Madras region of India.

MINTED YOGURT

1 cup low-fat plain yogurt

2 teaspoons minced fresh mint leaves

1/4 teaspoon salt (optional)

BISQUE

2 tablespoons olive oil

1 large yellow onion, diced (about 2 cups)

2 tablespoons minced fresh ginger

1 tablespoon minced garlic

1 tablespoon plus 1 teaspoon White Dog Cafe Curry Powder (page 284) or good-quality Madras curry powder

5 Granny Smith apples, peeled, cored, and diced (about 6 cups)

3 cups apple cider

2 cups water

1 teaspoon salt

1. Prepare the Minted Yogurt: Combine the yogurt, mint leaves and salt. Cover and store in the refrigerator until ready to use, or for up to 1 week.

2. Prepare the bisque: Heat the oil in a large sauce-pan set over medium heat. Add the onion and cook until translucent, about 5 minutes. Add the ginger and garlic and cook until soft, 2 to 3 minutes. (Do not let the garlic brown or it will give the bisque a bitter flavor.) Stir in the curry powder and cook, tossing and scraping the bottom of the pan so the mixture doesn't scorch for about 1 minute. Add the apples, cider, water, and salt and bring to a boil. Reduce the heat to low and simmer until the apples are completely soft, about 30 minutes.

3. Purée the bisque in batches in a food processor, blender, or food mill. Return to the saucepan and season with additional salt to taste. Serve warm, or let cool to room temperature, cover, and refrigerate for up to 3 days (or freeze for up to 3 months).

4. To serve, divide the bisque among 6 warmed bowls or plates. Top each portion with a generous dollop of the Minted Yogurt.

OTHER WAYS TO DO IT

We use Granny Smith apples in this recipe because they are available year-round. But you can substitute any ripe cooking apple, such as Rome, Cortland, Winesap, or Yellow Delicious in this recipe with excellent results. When you use red apples, leave the skins on. They give the bisque a lovely copper color.

TOASTING SPICES

We like to grind spices and then toast them to bring out all of their wonderful flavors. To toast spices, heat a sauté pan over medium high heat until a drop of water placed on it sizzles. Add the whole or ground spices to the pan and toast, stirring constantly, for about 30 seconds. Let cool to room temperature and use immediately.

French Mushroom Soup {Serves 6}

This puréed mushroom soup gets its creamy texture from Boursin, a buttery, triple-creme cheese from Normandy that's flavored with garlic and herbs. Calvados, an apple brandy also made in Normandy, enhances the cheese and balances its richness.

4 tablespoons unsalted butter

2 leeks, trimmed and split lengthwise, washed well, and thinly sliced

1 teaspoon minced garlic

2 pounds white mushrooms, sliced

2½ teaspoons salt

1 Idaho potato, peeled and diced

2 celery ribs, diced

4 cups Chicken Stock (page 277)

1 package (5.2 ounces) Boursin cheese

3 tablespoons Calvados

1½ teaspoons fresh lemon juice

1 tablespoon chopped fresh chervil leaves

½ teaspoon freshly ground black pepper

1. Melt the butter in a large, nonreactive saucepan set over medium heat. Add the leeks and cook until soft, about 3 minutes. Add the garlic and cook for 2 minutes. Add the mushrooms and ½ teaspoon of the salt and cook until the mushrooms begin to soften, about 5 minutes. Add the potato, celery, and chicken stock and bring to a boil. Reduce the heat to low, cover, and simmer until the potatoes are soft, about 30 minutes.

2. Purée the soup in batches in a food processor or blender. Return the puréed soup to the saucepan and crumble in the cheese. Whisk until thoroughly melted. Stir in the Calvados, lemon juice, chervil, pepper, and the remaining 2 teaspoons salt.

3. Serve immediately, or let cool to room temperature, cover, and refrigerate for up to 2 days.

Garden Vegetable Minestrone {Serves 6 to 8}

In Italian, minestrone means "big soup"—an apt description since this soup uses just about every vegetable in your garden. Use the vegetables suggested below as a guide and feel free to substitute whatever is coming up in your own backyard or farmers' market.

BEANS

1 cup dried white beans, such as great Northern or cannellini

4 garlic cloves, peeled

¹/₂ small yellow onion, peeled

2 bay leaves

SOUP

¹/₄ cup extra-virgin olive oil

1 large yellow onion, minced

3 tablespoons minced garlic

2 tablespoons tomato paste

1 small zucchini, diced

1 small yellow squash, diced

1 carrot, peeled and diced

1 small fennel bulb, stalks removed, cored, and diced

1 celery rib, diced

1 red bell pepper, diced

1 plum tomato, diced

1 cup dry white wine

2 cups (about 14 ounces) chopped canned tomatoes

2 cups water

2 teaspoons salt

¹/₂ teaspoon freshly ground black pepper

Pinch of hot red pepper flakes

1 tablespoon chopped fresh thyme leaves

¹/₂ cup fresh basil leaves

Freshly grated Parmesan cheese, for serving

1. Prepare the beans: Combine the beans, garlic cloves, peeled onion half, and 1 bay leaf in a large saucepan. Add water to cover by 4 inches. Bring to a boil over high heat. Reduce the heat to low and simmer until the beans are completely cooked through, about 1 hour. If necessary, add water to the beans while they are cooking to keep them submerged and to create a bean broth that will add body and liquid to the soup. Drain the beans, reserving the cooking liquid separately. Discard the garlic, onion, and bay leaf. Set the beans aside.

2. Prepare the soup: Heat the olive oil in a large, nonreactive stockpot set over medium-high heat until it ripples. Add the minced onion and sauté until translucent, about 5 minutes. Add the minced garlic and sauté for 2 minutes. Stir in the tomato paste and cook for 2 minutes more. Add the zucchini, yellow squash, carrot, fennel, celery, bell pepper, tomato, and the remaining bay leaf. Sauté until the vegetables begin to soften, about 4 minutes.

3. Add the wine, chopped tomatoes, reserved beans, and 3 cups of the bean broth. Stir in the water, salt, black pepper, pepper flakes, thyme, and basil. Bring the soup to a gentle boil. Reduce the heat to low and simmer for 20 minutes. Serve immediately, or let cool to room temperature, cover, and refrigerate for up to 3 days.

4. To serve, divide the soup among 6 to 8 warmed bowls or soup plates. Top with lots of the grated cheese. This soup is also delicious with a swirl of Basil Pesto (page 292) or Winter Herb Pesto (page 292).

Lentil and Tomato Soup with Coriander and Cumin {Serves 6}

In this hearty vegetarian soup, tender spinach leaves meet tomatoes and lentils in a garlicky, Indian-spiced broth. We like using tiny, dark-green lentilles du Puy (French lentils) because they retain their shape during cooking and have a pleasing texture. However, regular brown lentils can be substituted without affecting the flavor.

1 pound (2 cups) French or regular lentils, picked over and rinsed

1/4 cup extra-virgin olive oil

2 cups diced yellow onions

1/4 cup minced garlic

1 tablespoon ground coriander

1 tablespoon ground cumin

2 teaspoons mustard seeds

1 tablespoon fennel seeds

3/4 teaspoon cayenne pepper

1 can (14 ounces) plum tomatoes, undrained

3 cups tightly packed fresh spinach leaves, coarsely chopped

1 teaspoon salt

1 teaspoon freshly ground black pepper

1/4 cup chopped fresh cilantro leaves and stems, for serving

1. Place the lentils in a saucepan and add water to cover by 4 inches. Bring to a boil over high heat. Reduce the heat to low and simmer until the lentils are just tender, 20 to 30 minutes. Drain the lentils, reserving the cooking liquid separately.

2. In a nonreactive stockpot set over medium heat, heat the oil until it ripples. Add the onions and sauté until translucent, about 5 minutes. Add the garlic and sauté for 5 minutes. Add the coriander, cumin, mustard seeds, fennel seeds, and cayenne and cook for 1 minute. Stir in the tomatoes and their juice; break the tomatoes into large chunks with the back of a wooden spoon. Reduce the heat to low and simmer for 5 minutes.

3. Stir in the cooked lentils and 3 cups of the lentil cooking liquid. Bring to a simmer over medium heat. Stir in the spinach and cook until completely wilted. If the soup is too thick, add more of the lentil cooking liquid or water. Add the salt and pepper.

4. To serve, divide the soup among 6 warmed bowls. Top with the chopped cilantro. If you like, top with chunks of feta cheese in addition to the cilantro.

OTHER WAYS TO DO IT
This soup is also great when topped with a dollop of plain yogurt.

USING CANNED TOMATOES
For about ten months out of the year, canned tomatoes are superior to the Styrofoam-textured fresh ones offered in most grocery stores. We use them all winter, so they've found their way into many of our soup recipes. When looking for canned tomatoes, make sure that there is nothing added to them. The ingredient list should read simply: "Tomatoes."

Cuban Black Bean Soup {Serves 6 to 8}

Judy and I savored this thick, hearty soup in the sumptuous dining room of the Hotel Nacional in Havana, Cuba. It was my first experience with the Cuban version of black bean soup and I was pleasantly surprised by its creamy texture studded with whole black beans, its smoky aroma, and its warm spices. This soup was completely different from the smooth purées I was accustomed to eating in the States.

¼ cup olive oil

1 large white onion, minced

¼ cup minced garlic

1 green bell pepper, finely diced

2 celery ribs, finely diced

2 tablespoons dried oregano

1 tablespoon ground cumin

½ teaspoon coriander seeds, crushed

½ teaspoon ground allspice

2 cups (1 pound) dried black beans, picked over for stones and rinsed well

2 bay leaves

1 smoked ham hock (optional)

8 cups water

½ cup chopped fresh cilantro leaves and stems (see note, page 158)

2 tablespoons fresh lime juice

Salt and freshly ground black pepper

1. In a large pot set over medium heat, heat the oil until it ripples. Add the onion and cook until soft, about 5 minutes. Add the garlic, bell pepper, and celery and cook until soft, about 5 minutes. Stir in the oregano, cumin, coriander seeds, and allspice, and cook for 1 minute more.

2. Add the beans, bay leaves, ham hock, and water. Bring to a boil over high heat. Reduce the heat to medium, cover, and simmer until the beans are very tender, about 1 hour. If necessary, add a little water during the cooking to keep the beans from scorching.

3. Remove and discard the bay leaves. Reserve the ham hock. Ladle 1 cup of beans into a small bowl and mash them with the back of a fork. Return the mashed beans to the pot along with the cilantro, lime juice, and salt and pepper to taste. Remove the meat from the ham hock and finely dice. Add back to the soup. Keep the soup warm until ready to serve, or let cool to room temperature, cover, and refrigerate for up to 3 days. When reheating, you may need to add a little water to return the soup to its desired creamy consistency.

4. To serve, divide the soup among 6 to 8 warmed bowls. If you like, top with any of the following garnishes—chopped hard-cooked egg, diced avocado, chunky tomato salsa, chopped pineapple, sour cream, grated cheese, chopped scallions—or any combination of these.

OTHER WAYS TO DO IT

Dish up the beans over fluffy white rice for a main course of *Moros y Cristianos* (literally, Moors and Christians), a Cuban staple. For a traditional Southwestern-style black bean soup, prepare a recipe of Black Bean Refritos (page 212) and thin them to a soup-like consistency with tomato juice and water. Add a splash of lime juice, a sprinkling of chopped cilantro, some extra seasoning, and presto!

Chiapas Tortilla Soup {Serves 6 to 8}

High in the mountains of Mexico, in the charming colonial town of San Cristobal, Judy and I shared this soup of chicken, tortillas, and chiles with Lagondon Indians from the surrounding villages. The mountain twilight was cool, and we had little language in common, but the heat of this spicy soup helped to kindle new friendships as it warmed our bodies and spirits.

1 pound chicken thighs

1 small yellow onion, chopped

4 garlic cloves, peeled

2 jalapeño peppers, 1 halved and seeded, 1 seeded and minced

1 bunch fresh cilantro, stems reserved, leaves chopped (see note, page 158)

1 celery rib, chopped

1 carrot, peeled and chopped

6 cups water

2 tablespoons olive oil

1 large yellow onion, minced (about 2 cups)

3 tablespoons minced garlic

6 corn tortillas, torn into 1-inch pieces

1 tablespoon New Mexican chili powder (see note, page 130) or regular chili powder

2 tablespoons ground cumin

1 tablespoon dried Mexican oregano (see note below)

2$\frac{1}{2}$ cups seeded and chopped fresh or canned tomatoes

Juice of 1 lime

2 teaspoons salt

1. Combine the chicken thighs, chopped onion, garlic cloves, halved jalapeño, whole cilantro stems, celery, carrot, and water in a medium saucepan. Bring to a boil over high heat. Reduce the heat to low and simmer gently for 1 hour. Strain the stock, reserving the cooking liquid and the chicken thighs separately; discard the other solids. When the chicken thighs are cool enough to handle, remove the meat. Dice and reserve it.

2. Heat the olive oil in a large nonreactive saucepan set over medium heat until it ripples. Add the minced onion and cook until translucent, about 5 minutes. Add the minced garlic and minced jalapeño and cook for 3 minutes. Add the tortillas, chili powder, cumin, and oregano, and cook for 1 minute. Stir in the chopped tomatoes and 3$\frac{1}{2}$ cups of the reserved chicken broth. Reduce the heat to low and simmer until the tortillas have dissolved and the soup has thickened, about 30 minutes.

3. Add the diced chicken. If the soup looks too thick, add some of the reserved broth.

4. To serve, stir in the lime juice and salt. Ladle into 6 to 8 warmed bowls and top with the reserved chopped cilantro. Garnish this soup with fried tortilla crisps (see page 226) if you like.

USING MEXICAN OREGANO

Mexican oregano is more strongly flavored and pungent than its Mediterranean counterpart. You can find it in its dried form in Latin, Hispanic, and some gourmet supermarkets. We like its robust flavor and use it anytime we need dried oregano. As with any dried herb, buy it in small quantities and use it within a few months for maximum freshness and flavor.

Asian Chicken Noodle Soup {Serves 4 to 6}

This is a warming, cold-curing soup that we're sure will become part of your winter repertoire. It is fragrant with lemon grass, which has been used for centuries as a medicinal cure for colds and flu, stomach pains, and even backaches. We can't guarantee a quick recovery, but we promise this delicious soup will at least make you feel better while its going down!

1 pound chicken thighs

1 piece (4 inches) fresh ginger, cut in $\frac{1}{4}$-inch coins

4 garlic cloves, peeled

3 stalks lemon grass, outer layers removed, bulbs smashed with the bottom of a saucepan

1 bunch fresh cilantro, stems reserved, leaves chopped

6 cups water

1 teaspoon red Thai curry paste

1 can (14 ounces) coconut milk (preferably Chaokoh brand)

1 red bell pepper, diced

1 yellow bell pepper, diced

4 ounces shiitake mushrooms, stems removed and discarded, caps thinly sliced (about 1$\frac{1}{2}$ cups)

1 tablespoon fresh lime juice

2 tablespoons *nam pla* (Thai fish sauce, available in Asian markets and specialty food stores; see note, page 95)

$\frac{1}{2}$ teaspoon sugar

$\frac{1}{4}$ teaspoon freshly ground black pepper

12 ounces somen noodles (available in Asian markets and specialty food stores), cooked (see note below)

1. Combine the chicken thighs, ginger, garlic, lemon grass, cilantro stems, and water in a large saucepan. Bring to a boil over high heat. Reduce the heat to low and simmer for 1 hour.

2. Strain the stock into a large saucepan, reserving the chicken thighs separately; discard the other solids. When the chicken thighs are cool enough to handle, remove the meat. Dice and reserve it.

3. Bring the stock to a simmer over medium heat. Stir in the curry paste, coconut milk, bell peppers, mushrooms, and the reserved diced chicken. Simmer over medium heat until the vegetables are tender, about 10 minutes. Stir in the lime juice, *nam pla*, sugar, and pepper.

4. To serve, place a portion of the cooked somen in each bowl; ladle in about 1 cup of the soup. Sprinkle with the chopped cilantro.

OTHER WAYS TO DO IT

If you can't find somen noodles, substitute cooked angel hair pasta.

COOKING SOMEN NOODLES

The trick to cooking somen noodles is to avoid overcooking them. Each package of somen has 5 or 6 individually wrapped bundles of noodles in it. Unwrap the bundles before you begin. Bring a large pot of salted water to a rolling boil. Add the noodles all at once and cook until just tender, 2 to 3 minutes. Drain in a colander and rinse with cold running water until cool. Drain well. Toss with a little vegetable oil to keep the noodles from sticking together. Use immediately, or cover and refrigerate for up to 3 days.

Smoked Salmon and Corn Chowder {Serves 6}

In this recipe, creamy corn chowder is galvanized by the addition of smoked salmon, crunchy fennel, and fresh dill. This soup is best made with fresh corn kernels, but frozen corn will work in a pinch.

2 tablespoons unsalted butter

¼ cup diced smoked bacon (about 2 strips)

1 large yellow onion, minced

½ fennel bulb, stalks removed, cored, and minced

1 carrot, peeled and finely diced

1 celery rib, finely diced

1 red bell pepper, finely diced

¼ cup plus 2 tablespoons all-purpose flour

5 cups whole milk

3 cups sweet corn kernels (preferably fresh)

1 cup diced smoked salmon (about 6 ounces)

About 1 tablespoon salt

¼ teaspoon Tabasco sauce

½ teaspoon freshly ground black pepper

2 teaspoons fresh lemon juice

2 tablespoons chopped fresh dill

1. Melt the butter in a large, nonreactive saucepan set over medium heat. Add the bacon and cook until it renders its fat and starts to crisp, about 5 minutes. Add the onion and cook until soft, about 5 minutes. Add the fennel, carrot, celery, and bell pepper and cook for 5 minutes more.

2. Sprinkle the flour over the vegetables and stir well for 1 minute. Pour in the milk and whisk to combine. Bring to a simmer over medium heat, stirring constantly to avoid scorching. Reduce the heat to low and simmer for 20 minutes.

3. Stir in the corn kernels and smoked salmon and bring to a simmer over low heat. Season with the salt, Tabasco, pepper, lemon juice, and dill.

4. Serve immediately in warmed bowls, or let cool to room temperature, cover, and refrigerate for up to 2 days. Reheat slowly, and add more milk if the soup is too thick.

Creamy Mussel Chowder with Sorrel {Serves 6}

The lemony tartness of sorrel is a perfect complement to the rich cream and briny mussels in this chowder. If you wish, leave the mussels whole instead of chopping them, and if you prefer their flavor, clams work equally well. Substitute spinach leaves and add an extra tablespoon of fresh lemon juice if sorrel is unavailable.

2 cups dry white wine

1 bay leaf

1 teaspoon dried thyme

8 black peppercorns

2 pounds mussels, scrubbed and debearded

4 tablespoons unsalted butter

2 tablespoons olive oil

2 Idaho potatoes, peeled and diced
  (about 2 cups)

1 fennel bulb, stalks removed, cored,
  and diced

2 leeks, trimmed and split lengthwise,
  washed well, the white and light green
  parts thinly sliced

1 tablespoon minced garlic

¼ cup all-purpose flour

4 cups whole milk

½ cup tightly packed chopped sorrel leaves,
  stems removed (see note below)

½ teaspoon freshly ground black pepper

2 teaspoons *nam pla* (Thai fish sauce,
  available in Asian markets and specialty
  food stores; see note, page 95)

1 teaspoon salt

1 tablespoon fresh lemon juice

Pinch of cayenne pepper

1. Combine the wine, bay leaf, thyme, and peppercorns in a large, nonreactive saucepan set over high heat. Bring to a boil. Add the mussels, cover, and steam until the mussels open, 4 to 6 minutes. Let cool to room temperature. Discard any mussels that don't open. Remove the mussels from the shells; chop and reserve. Strain the cooking liquid through a double thickness of dampened cheesecloth or a fine sieve and reserve.

2. Melt the butter with the oil in a large, nonreactive saucepan set over medium heat. Add the potatoes and cook, stirring occasionally, for 5 minutes. Add the fennel, leeks, and garlic and cook, stirring occasionally, for 5 minutes. Stir in the flour and cook, stirring constantly, for 5 minutes.

3. Slowly whisk in the reserved cooking liquid and milk. Bring to a gentle boil. Reduce the heat to low and simmer for 15 minutes.

4. Stir in the reserved chopped mussels, sorrel leaves, pepper, *nam pla*, salt, lemon juice, and cayenne. Serve immediately, or let cool to room temperature, cover, and refrigerate for up to 2 days. Reheat gently before serving.

BUYING FRESH SORREL

Sorrel is an herb with soft, bright green leaves that resemble spinach. Its flavor is acidic with an almost lemony tang. Look for it at your farmers' market or grocery store mainly in the spring and summer. Choose leaves with delicate stems and no yellowing. The flavor is delicious in creamy soups like this one and makes an interesting addition to green salads.

Portuguese-style Mussel Stew {Serves 6}

We love hearty soups that double as one-dish meals. Dramatic in both presentation and taste, this adaptation of a Portuguese classic is one of our favorites. Much of its flavor comes from chorizo, a spicy pork sausage used in Spanish and Mexican cuisines. Chorizo is readily available in most larger supermarkets and specialty meat stores. As with all hearty, peasant-style cooking, the ingredients in this soup can vary with your larder and preferences.

¼ cup olive oil

2½ cups diced yellow onions

¼ cup minced garlic

5 ounces chorizo sausage, sliced

½ cup sliced pepperoni

2 teaspoons sweet paprika

¼ teaspoon hot red pepper flakes

2 bay leaves

½ cup dry white wine

1 can (28 ounces) plum tomatoes, undrained

4 cups Chicken Stock (page 277)

1 can (14 ounces) chickpeas (garbanzo beans), rinsed and drained

4 cups tightly packed whole green kale leaves

1½ pounds mussels, scrubbed and debearded (see note below)

1 teaspoon fresh lemon juice

½ teaspoon salt

2 tablespoons chopped fresh cilantro leaves and stems

2 tablespoons chopped fresh Italian parsley

1. In a large, nonreactive stockpot set over medium heat, heat the olive oil until it ripples. Add the onions and cook until soft, about 5 minutes. Add the garlic and cook for 2 minutes. Add the chorizo and pepperoni and cook for 5 minutes. Stir in the paprika, pepper flakes, and bay leaves, and cook for 1 minute. Pour in the wine and simmer until it is reduced by half, about 2 minutes. Add the tomatoes and their juice, breaking up the tomatoes with the back of a spoon. Stir in the chicken stock. Reduce the heat to low and simmer for 20 minutes.

2. Add the chickpeas and kale, cover, and simmer for 10 minutes.

3. Add the mussels, cover, and simmer until they open, 4 to 6 minutes. Discard any mussels that don't open. Stir in the lemon juice, salt, cilantro, and parsley. Serve immediately in large bowls.

OTHER WAYS TO DO IT
If you wish, prepare the stew through Step 2. Let the soup cool to room temperature, cover, and refrigerate overnight. To finish the dish, bring the stew to a simmer over medium heat. Add the mussels and complete Step 3.

BUYING AND CLEANING MUSSELS
Make sure their shells are tightly closed or will close if tapped lightly with your finger. To clean, scrub them well under cold running water with a stiff-bristled brush to remove all sand and grit. Discard any mussels that won't close or feel unusually heavy (they're probably filled with sand or mud). To debeard them, grasp the bit of stringy fibers that protrudes from the shell with your fingers and pull it off. Cover cleaned mussels with a damp cloth and store for up to two days in the refrigerator.

Beef Burgundy Stew {Serves 6}

Being a former Girl Scout, Judy enjoys cooking over open flames. She is a master of fireplace cookery and has been known to invite friends to her home for a fire-cooked supper. No one ever turns down an invitation when she is preparing this woodsy stew and hearth-baked bread, and no one has a better time than Judy enjoying friendship around the fire. She starts this hearty stew in an old Dutch oven on her range, and then slow-cooks it over the embers in her fireplace.

1 cup all-purpose flour

2½ teaspoons salt

1 teaspoon freshly ground black pepper

1 teaspoon dried thyme

2 pounds beef chuck, cut into 1- to 2-inch cubes

¼ cup olive oil

1 large yellow onion, diced (about 2 cups)

1 tablespoon minced garlic

1 can (14 ounces) Italian plum tomatoes, undrained

1 cup dry red wine

2 bay leaves

3 cups water

1 thyme sprig plus 1 teaspoon chopped fresh thyme leaves

1 cup diced carrot

2 celery ribs, diced

8 ounces button mushrooms, quartered (about 2 cups)

2 Idaho potatoes, peeled and cut into 1-inch cubes

1 teaspoon chopped fresh sage leaves

1. Combine the flour, 1 teaspoon of the salt, ½ teaspoon of the pepper, and the dried thyme in a bowl. Toss the meat in the mixture, coating well; shake off any excess.

2. Heat the oil in a nonreactive Dutch oven or large saucepan set over high heat until it ripples. Add the floured meat in small batches, and cook until browned on all sides. Remove the meat from the pan. Reduce the heat to medium. Add the onion, and cook until translucent, 6 to 8 minutes. Add the garlic and cook for 2 minutes. Add the tomatoes and their liquid, the wine, bay leaves, thyme sprig, browned meat, and water. Bring to a boil. Reduce the heat to low, cover, and simmer for 1 hour.

3. Add the carrot, celery, mushrooms, and potatoes. Cover and simmer until the vegetables are tender, about 30 minutes. Season with the chopped thyme and sage leaves, the remaining 1½ teaspoons salt and ½ teaspoon pepper. Serve immediately, or let cool to room temperature, cover, and refrigerate for up to 3 days. Reheat gently before serving.

CHAPTER THREE

SALADS, SANDWICHES
& LIGHT MEALS

SALADS, SANDWICHES & LIGHT MEALS

Eating Well, While Doing Good: A Farming Tale 87

Mixed Salad of Many Lettuces with Lemon–Olive Oil Vinaigrette 90

Romaine Salad with Egg-free Caesar Dressing 91

Warm Mushroom Spinach Salad 92

Spinach and Fennel Salad with Curried Pears and Gorgonzola 93

Country Bread and Roasted Vegetable Salad 94

Cool Island Cucumber Salad 95

Curried Chopped Vegetable Salad with Pesto Pita Wedges 96

Vietnamese Chicken Salad 97

Roasted Chicken and Mushroom Salad Balsamico 98

Waldorf-style Chicken Salad 99

Watermelon and Shrimp Salad with Jalapeño-Lime Dressing 100

Contessa Lisa's Tuscan Grain Salad 101

Cobb Salad Sandwich with Blue Cheese Mayonnaise 102

Italian Sausage Grinder 103

White Dog Cafe's Philly Cheese Steak 104

Tuna Sandwich à la Niçoise 105

Toasted Brioche with Ham and Brie 106

Southwestern Turkey Burger 107

Moroccan-spiced Lamb Burger with Pepper Relish 108

Salmon Burgers 109

Mexican Tortilla Roll Ups 110

Farm Stand Focaccia 111

Toasted Focaccia with Roasted Tomatoes, Olives, and Feta 112

EATING WELL, WHILE DOING GOOD: A FARMING TALE

EVERY HARVEST SEASON, WE INVITE THE LOCAL FARMERS WHO SUPPLY OUR PRO-duce to a dinner in their honor when our customers can meet the people who grow their food. The Farmers' Sunday Supper features ingredients from each of the farms, accompanied by a tasting of all-natural beers from local micro-breweries. During the dinner we learn about the farms and recognize the importance of organic agriculture to our good health and the crucial role played by farmers as stewards of the land.

Always dressed in his characteristic blue denim overalls, farmer Glenn Brendle brings us fresh fruits and vegetables from his Green Meadow Farm in Lancaster County. I picture him walking in our back kitchen door with a big smile, carrying a flat of the best-looking black raspberries you'll ever see. In addition to his own produce, Glenn organizes a distribution system for a collective of Amish farmers, each specializing in a different crop. Before his weekly trip into Philadelphia, Glenn picks up the produce from the other small farms in the surrounding Pennsylvania countryside. We've also arranged for Glenn to bring us free-range chicken and eggs and humanely raised pork and beef.

Finding poultry and meat raised free of the cruel and unsanitary conditions of factory farms is increasingly difficult, as corporate agribusiness controls a growing portion of our farmland and food supply. Family farmers who respect the land and the lives of farm animals are being lost at an astonishing rate, replaced by managers guided solely by profit, who feel no sense of connection to the animals or the land. Visiting Green Meadow for our annual staff picnic is like returning to a bygone era. I love to swing from a rope out over the water and drop into Farmer Glenn's swimming hole, enjoying what farm kids have done for generations and hoping that generations more will have the same opportunity.

From her herd of prize-winning Nubians at Greystone Farm, Douglass Newbold brings us the

Douglass Newbold of Greystone Farm, Chester County, PA, introducing her goats to White Dog Cafe Mentoring Program students

Farmer Mark Dornstreich of Branchcreek Farm, Bucks County, PA, showing herbs to a group of White Dog Cafe staff members

wonderful goat cheese that she calls Greystone Chevratel. Depending on the time of year, we feature the cheese in many different dishes. "Dougie" began raising goats in her backyard in Philadelphia, but as nervous neighbors watched her herd expand, she eventually found greener pastures in Chester County, where Greystone Farm is now home for ten Nubians and a menagerie of dogs, cats, chickens, peacocks, and a donkey. Dougie tends to her floppy-eared goats with personalized, loving care. The Nubians are milked twice a day, and the milk is then carefully pasteurized, cultured, hand-ladled, drained, and packaged before she drives into town in a car filled with at least two of her five dogs to deliver the fresh cheese to the Cafe. Dougie loves her animals so much that she would rather be milking her goats than vacationing on the Riviera, much to her non-farming, travel-loving husband's chagrin. I swear that the individualized love and attention that each goat at Greystone receives from Dougie makes that cheese the creamiest, most delicious you will ever taste.

Kimberton Hills Farm, a 400-acre, bio-dynamic farm in Chester County, supplies some of our humanely raised lamb and is part of the Camphill Village system inspired by German philosopher Rudolph Steiner. Coincidentally, Steiner was a leader of the Theosophical Society, the organization co-founded by Madame Blavatsky whose experience with a white dog gave the Cafe its name. Steiner later developed his own world view called "Anthroposophy" and influenced many fields with his ideas from bio-dynamic farming to Waldorf schools. Tom Griffith is the farm manager of the Village, a volunteer life-sharing community that includes adults who have disabilities. Much of the food for the community is grown on the farm, and other means for self-sufficient living are undertaken, such as spinning wool, sewing clothes, baking bread, and making ceramics. A few products of the farm are sold, including the lamb Tom delivers to the Cafe, which we often feature at the Farmers' Sunday Supper.

Back in the early days when the White Dog Cafe was her only Philadelphia account, Carol Stoudt delivered kegs of beer from her Lancaster County brewery in the back of her station wagon. The first new brewery in Pennsylvania since Prohibition, Stoudt's Brewery, now more than ten years old, has received national acclaim, winning several gold and silver medals at the All-American Beer Festival. One of the few female brewmasters in the country, Carol uses only natural ingredients and no preservatives. Her beers are some of the best you'll ever taste including the White Dog's Leg Lifter Lager, our own label, which pictures a fire hydrant with a white dog in characteristic pose!

Broccoli, beets, kale, cauliflower, peppers, beans, squash, eggplant, and tomatoes are just some of the beautiful organic vegetables that farmer Mark Dornstreich delivers twice a week from his 21-acre farm in Bucks County. During the winter months, greenhouses provide a year-round supply of fresh salad greens and herbs, so that our Salad of Many Lettuces from Branchcreek Farm is a favorite on our menu every day of the year. As anthropology students, Mark and his wife Judy were inspired by the peasant farmers they met in developing countries. Through their travels they realized how important it is to all life on Earth that farmers worldwide make a sustainable living through farming methods that do not use pesticides and chemical fertilizers, which destroy our topsoil and poison our food supply. Committed to that philosophy, they moved to Branchcreek Farm in 1978 and made farming their way of life. After years of struggling to learn growing techniques and find a market for their hard-earned products, Mark and Judy have built a successful business based on supplying restaurants with organic produce. A direct relationship with the land and with the customers who use the food they grow is important to them. "I know that Kevin truly appreciates the quality and taste of the produce we grow for him," Judy once told me, "so I gladly search through the basil patch to pick the most glorious leaves just for him because I know he'll be tickled." The amount of personal attention given the fresh herbs is remarkable, first by the farmers in growing, harvesting, and delivering the herbs to the Cafe and then by our kitchen staff as they painstakingly pluck the tiny leaves from their stems and incorporate them into many dishes on our menu.

The importance of the food we serve at the White Dog Cafe is not just in the final product and the fresh ingredients we use, but in the relationships we have with both our customers and our suppliers, and the way of life it supports from farm to table, which allows us to live our values through the work we do every day. At the Farmers' Sunday Supper we give thanks for that.   **—JW**

Mixed Salad of Many Lettuces with Lemon–Olive Oil Vinaigrette {Serves 6}

This is our house salad composed of hand-picked, young, organic leaves—straight from our local farmers. The vinaigrette is light and fresh yet bold. In addition to green salads, it marries well with pasta, grain salads, and seafood.

LEMON–OLIVE OIL VINAIGRETTE

1 clove garlic, peeled

1/2 lemon (pulp and rind), seeded and finely minced

1/4 cup chopped red onion

1 1/2 teaspoons Dijon mustard

1/2 cup fresh lemon juice

1/2 cup red wine vinegar

1/2 teaspoon sugar

1/2 teaspoon salt

1/2 teaspoon freshly ground black pepper

2 cups olive oil

LETTUCE

8 oz. (1/2 pound) mixed young lettuces and greens (such as arugula, spinach, green and red romaine, oak leaf, curley endive, red swiss chard, beet greens, lolla rossa, mache, radicchio, escarole, and mustard), gently washed and dried (see note, opposite page)

Edible flowers, as garnish (optional)

1. Prepare the vinaigrette: Combine the garlic, lemon, onion, mustard, lemon juice, vinegar, sugar, salt, and pepper in a food processor or blender. Process until smooth, about 30 seconds.

2. With the motor running, add the olive oil in a slow steady stream and process for 30 seconds more to form an emulsion. Use immediately or refrigerate in an airtight container for up to 2 weeks.

3. Prepare the lettuce: Gently toss the greens with the vinaigrette. Garnish with edible flowers, if desired. Serve immediately.

Romaine Salad with Egg-free Caesar Dressing {Serves 6}

Our Egg-free Caesar dressing may be healthier than its eggy counterpart but it's just as rich, creamy, and delicious. Food processors and blenders have made the egg unnecessary in Caesar dressing. Once, the egg functioned as an emulsifying agent that bound the ingredients together, but now, machines can whip the dressing so quickly, all that is needed to bind it is a little mustard, anchovies, and cheese.

2 cups Garlic Croutons (page 282)

EGG-FREE CAESAR DRESSING

1 can (2 ounces) oil-packed anchovy fillets, drained

1 tablespoon minced garlic

2 tablespoons freshly grated Parmesan cheese

1½ teaspoons red wine vinegar

1½ teaspoons Worcestershire sauce

1½ teaspoons Dijon mustard

1 tablespoon fresh lemon juice

½ teaspoon freshly ground black pepper

1 cup olive oil

½ cup water

SALAD

2 heads well-washed romaine lettuce, leaves torn into bite-size pieces (see note below)

1 small head radicchio, thinly sliced

2 tablespoons freshly grated Parmesan cheese

1. Prepare the Garlic Croutons.

2. Prepare the dressing: Combine the anchovies and their oil, the garlic, and Parmesan in a food processor or blender; process for 15 seconds. Add the vinegar, Worcestershire, mustard, lemon juice, and pepper; process for an additional 15 seconds. Scrape down the sides and process for 5 seconds. With the machine running, add the oil and water in a slow, steady stream. (The dressing can be made ahead and will keep refrigerated for up to 2 weeks.)

3. Prepare the salad: Combine the romaine and radicchio in a large bowl. Add 1 cup of the dressing and toss well to coat all the leaves. Divide the dressed greens among 6 plates. Sprinkle them evenly with cheese and the Garlic Croutons. Serve the salads immediately.

OTHER WAYS TO DO IT

This salad makes the perfect base for endless variations: You could top it with grilled salmon, shrimp, chicken, vegetables, steak, squid, or lamb. Just make sure whatever you combine with it is strong-flavored enough to stand up to the robust dressing. You can also use it to dress a cold pasta or rice salad.

CLEANING LETTUCE

The key to making a great salad is treating your greens with care. To wash salad greens, fill your sink with very cold water. Hold the head of lettuce by the stem end and dip the whole into the water and then remove it. Keep dipping the lettuce into the water until all of the sand and grit is gone. Avoid soaking the lettuce as it will absorb the water and lose its crunch. Dry the greens well; any water left on the greens will dilute the dressing and prevent it from clinging to the leaves. We recommend investing in a salad spinner—available in kitchenware stores—they do a terrific job of drying the lettuce without bruising it. Use your washed and dried greens as soon as possible, or cover them with damp paper towels and plastic wrap and store them in the refrigerator.

Warm Mushroom Spinach Salad {Serves 4}

This is our favorite spinach salad—a hearty salad of spinach leaves tossed with a mustard-thyme dressing and topped with red onion, sautéed mushrooms, and pancetta. Crumble some rich blue cheese on top and it easily becomes a meal.

DRESSING

2 teaspoons Dijon mustard

1 tablespoon red wine vinegar

¼ teaspoon sugar

½ cup olive oil

1 teaspoon chopped fresh thyme leaves

Salt and freshly ground black pepper

SALAD

¼ cup finely diced pancetta (see note below), or 4 slices smoked bacon, cut into ¼-inch strips

3 cups sliced white mushrooms

½ teaspoon salt

¼ cup dry white wine

1 tablespoon chopped fresh parsley

¼ teaspoon freshly ground black pepper

8 cups tightly packed washed and stemmed spinach leaves

1 small red onion, sliced into thin rings

1. Prepare the dressing: Combine the mustard, vinegar, and sugar in a small bowl. Drop by drop, whisk in the oil to form a thick emulsion. Whisk in the thyme and season with salt and pepper to taste. Reserve.

2. Prepare the salad: Heat the pancetta in a nonreactive sauté pan set over medium heat until it renders its fat and is brown and crisp, about 6 to 8 minutes. Remove the pancetta from the fat with a slotted spoon; drain on paper towels.

3. Add the mushrooms and salt to the pancetta drippings and sauté until dry, about 10 minutes. Stir in the wine, parsley, and pepper, and cook until the liquid evaporates, about 2 minutes. Keep warm.

4. Toss the spinach leaves with the dressing in a large bowl. Divide the dressed greens among 4 chilled plates. Top each salad with one-fourth of the red onion rings, crisped pancetta, and the warm mushrooms.

OTHER WAYS TO DO IT

This salad is delicious topped with crumbled Maytag blue cheese or Gorgonzola.

SUBSTITUTING PANCETTA FOR BACON

Pancetta is a cured Italian meat made from the same cut of pork as American bacon. However, instead of being smoked like the bacon, it's cured with salt and spices and wrapped into a large sausage-like roll. Use it in any recipe that calls for bacon and you'll be amazed at its superior flavor. Pancetta is available in most delis and gourmet markets.

Spinach and Fennel Salad with Curried Pears and Gorgonzola {Serves 4}

This composed salad takes advantage of ingredients found at the peak of ripeness and availability during the colder months. Young tender fennel, warm spiced pears, juicy navel oranges, and ever-green spinach are combined with tangy Gorgonzola and toasted hazelnuts for a festive luncheon main course.

PEARS

¼ cup fresh orange juice

1 tablespoon White Dog Cafe curry powder (page 284) or good-quality Madras curry powder

½ teaspoon ground ginger

1 tablespoon plus 1 teaspoon packed light brown sugar

¼ teaspoon salt

¼ teaspoon freshly ground black pepper

¼ cup olive oil

2 ripe pears, halved and cored

¾ cup Orange-Rosemary Vinaigrette (see page 39)

SALAD

6 cups tightly packed, washed and stemmed spinach leaves

1 small fennel bulb, stalks removed, cored, and thinly sliced

1 small red onion, sliced into thin rings

¼ cup hazelnuts, skinned and toasted (see note, page 144)

4 ounces Gorgonzola cheese, crumbled

1. Prepare the pears: Whisk together the orange juice, curry powder, ginger, brown sugar, salt, and pepper in a small bowl. Slowly whisk in the olive oil. Add the pears and toss to coat with the marinade. Let marinate at room temperature for at least 2 hours, or cover and refrigerate for up to 2 days.

2. About 30 minutes before you plan to bake the pears, preheat the oven to 400°F.

3. Place the pears, cut sides down, in a baking dish; pour the remaining marinade over them. Bake until tender, about 20 minutes.

4. Prepare the Orange-Rosemary Vinaigrette.

5. Prepare the salad: Toss together the spinach, fennel, onion, and vinaigrette in a large bowl. Divide the salad among 4 chilled plates. Top each salad with a warm pear half, one-fourth each of the toasted hazelnuts and the crumbled Gorgonzola.

ABOUT FENNEL

Fennel is a vegetable with long celery-like stalks that stem from a broad bulbous base. The stalks sport feathery fronds that resemble dill and can be used in much the same way. The stalks themselves are great in soups and braised dishes, while the bulb can be eaten raw in salads, or sautéed, roasted, or braised. Raw fennel is crunchy, slightly sweet, and has just a hint of licorice; however, when cooked, the licorice flavor becomes less noticeable. To prepare fennel, cut off the stalks, remove the core from the bottom of the bulb and then slice according to the recipe's instructions. Fennel is becoming more widely available these days; look for it in your supermarket from fall through early spring, its peak season being around late fall and winter. Select bulbs that are large and have no signs of splitting or browning, and store in a plastic bag in the refrigerator for up to 5 days.

Country Bread and Roasted Vegetable Salad {Serves 4}

The next time you see a nice crusty day-old loaf at your bakery, pick it up and try this hearty, healthful panzanella, or bread salad. The better the bread you use, the better your salad will be—we make it with leftover country-style sourdough. We think the salad is best when eaten just after it is mixed together. However to work ahead, you can prepare the vegetables and bread one day in advance and then combine them just before serving.

4 cups cubed (1 inch) country-style bread

1 red bell pepper, diced

1 yellow bell pepper, diced

1 red onion, diced

2 plum tomatoes, each cut into 8 wedges

1 small eggplant, diced

2 teaspoons dried basil

1 teaspoon dried oregano

1 teaspoon dried thyme

1/2 cup extra-virgin olive oil

2 tablespoons balsamic vinegar

1 tablespoon fresh lemon juice

3/4 teaspoon salt

1/2 teaspoon freshly ground black pepper

Crumbled goat cheese, Gorgonzola, or Parmesan shavings, for serving

1. Preheat the oven to 475°F.

2. Spread the bread cubes on a baking sheet. Toast in the oven, stirring occasionally, until crisp, about 5 minutes. Reserve.

3. Meanwhile, combine the bell peppers, onion, tomatoes, eggplant, basil, oregano, thyme, and 1/4 cup of the olive oil in a large bowl. Toss well to coat the vegetables lightly with the herbs and oil. Spread the vegetables in a single layer on 2 baking sheets. Roast until cooked through and just starting to brown, 10 to 15 minutes. Let cool to room temperature.

4. Combine the toasted bread cubes and roasted vegetables in a large mixing bowl. Add the remaining 1/4 cup olive oil, the vinegar, lemon juice, salt, and pepper; toss to mix well. Serve immediately on chilled plates and top with crumbled goat cheese, Gorgonzola, or shavings of Parmesan.

Cool Island Cucumber Salad {Serves 4}

It seems that wherever we travel, cucumbers have gotten there first—we've eaten various cucumber salads from Northern Europe to Southeast Asia. This is a cool, sweet-sour, Asian-style salad with the lip-tingling fire of hot chiles. If chile paste is unavailable, substitute jalapeño peppers; for a milder version, you can leave out the chiles altogether.

2 whole cucumbers

1 small red onion, thinly sliced

1/2 pint cherry tomatoes, halved

1/4 cup chopped cilantro

1/4 cup fresh lime juice

1/4 cup rice wine vinegar

1 teaspoon chile paste (available in Asian markets and specialty food stores)

1 teaspoon *nam pla* (Thai fish sauce, available in Asian markets and specialty food stores; see note below)

1 tablespoon sugar

1. Peel 4 lengthwise strips off each cucumber at 1/2-inch intervals using a vegetable peeler, leaving them striped. Slice the cucumbers in half lengthwise and scoop out the seeds. Cut the halves on the bias in 1/4-inch slices.

2. Combine the sliced cucumber, onion, cherry tomatoes, and cilantro in a large bowl. Whisk together the lime juice, vinegar, chile paste, fish sauce, and sugar in a separate bowl. Pour the dressing over the vegetables and toss well to combine. Serve immediately. This salad is best if eaten just after it is made.

ABOUT *NAM PLA*

***Nam pla*, or fish sauce, is a key seasoning ingredient in Southeast Asian food. It is a pungent sauce that is used much like soy sauce to add saltiness to food. When first encountered, you will find its scent odious, but magically, fish sauce tastes nothing like it smells. When combined with other foods its strange aroma vanishes and you will find that it enhances other ingredients and lends balance to any dish it touches. Because it is high in protein and B vitamins, fish sauce is also of dietary value. We use it in almost every Asian-style dish we make and in nontraditional ways, as well. We use it in place of salt in most dishes that contain fish or shellfish, like these Salmon Burgers. You will see that even though they aren't Asian inspired, they are greatly enhanced by the flavorful fish sauce. There are many different brands of fish sauce, some more strongly flavored than others; we recommend Tipiros brand because it is mild and fresh-tasting.**

Curried Chopped Vegetable Salad with Pesto Pita Wedges {Serves 4}

Easy to prepare and so good for you, this crunchy, healthful mix of chopped garden vegetables in a spicy dressing is a star on our lunch menu. Served atop the warm pesto sandwich, it is a full and satisfying meal. Feel free to experiment with the vegetables you include in the salad; whatever is in season will be delicious.

SALAD

1 carrot, finely diced

1 red bell pepper, finely diced

1 green bell pepper, finely diced

1 scallion, thinly sliced

1 cucumber, peeled, seeded, and finely diced

1 celery rib, finely diced

CURRY VINAIGRETTE

3 tablespoons cider vinegar

1 teaspoon Dijon mustard

1 teaspoon fresh lemon juice

1 tablespoon minced red onion

1/4 teaspoon minced garlic

1 teaspoon White Dog Cafe Curry Powder (page 284) or good-quality commercial Madras curry powder

1/2 teaspoon sugar

1/4 cup olive oil

Salt and freshly ground black pepper

PITA WEDGES

8 ounces unaged domestic chèvre

4 whole wheat pita rounds

1/4 cup Basil Pesto (page 292)

1. Preheat the oven to 400°F.

2. Combine the carrot, bell peppers, scallion, cucumber, and celery in a mixing bowl.

3. Prepare the vinaigrette: In a separate bowl, whisk together the vinegar, mustard, lemon juice, red onion, garlic, curry powder, and sugar. Slowly whisk in the oil to form an emulsion. Season with salt and pepper to taste. Pour the vinaigrette over the vegetables and toss well.

4. Divide the chèvre between 2 of the pitas, spreading the cheese over the surface of 1 side of each. Spread the remaining 2 pita breads with the basil pesto, covering the surfaces completely. Sandwich each cheese pita with a pesto-coated pita. Place sandwiches on a baking sheet. Bake until golden, about 12 minutes.

5. To serve, cut each pita sandwich into 4 wedges. Serve each person 2 wedges atop 1/2 cup of the chopped dressed vegetables.

OTHER WAYS TO DO IT

The chopped vegetables and vinaigrette also make a great salad mixed with cooked cold white rice or cottage cheese.

Vietnamese Chicken Salad {Serves 6 to 8}

This salad has been on our Bar and Grill menu since our first trip to Vietnam. While there, we became addicted to the spicy condiment nuoc cham, a blend of fish sauce, hot chiles, ginger, lime juice, garlic, and sugar. Meat is not the main ingredient in most everyday Vietnamese dishes; it's considered more of a garnish or condiment. The bulk of the dish is usually rice, noodles, vegetables, or fruit. That healthful Vietnamese way of eating is reflected in this recipe.

1 cup Spicy Asian Marinade (page 289)

4 boneless, skinless chicken breast halves

12 ounces somen noodles (available in Asian markets), cooked (see note, page 79)

$^1/_2$ cup Spicy Ginger–Lime Dressing (page 288)

1 carrot, grated

1 red bell pepper, thinly sliced

1 yellow bell pepper, thinly sliced

2 scallions, thinly sliced

1 cucumber, halved, seeded, and thinly sliced on the diagonal

$^1/_2$ cup sliced radishes

$^1/_2$ cup peanuts, toasted (page 144), crushed

1. Combine the Spicy Asian Marinade and the chicken breasts in a shallow dish. Cover and marinate in the refrigerator for at least 2 hours and up to 2 days.

2. Remove the chicken from the marinade and grill over charcoal or on a stovetop grill until cooked through, about 6 minutes on each side. (The chicken can also be roasted in the oven at 400°F for 10 to 15 minutes or until cooked through.) Reserve.

3. Toss together the cooked noodles, Spicy Ginger–Lime Dressing, carrot, bell peppers, scallions, cucumber, and radishes in a large mixing bowl.

4. Thinly slice the cooked chicken breasts (the chicken can be served warm or chilled, whichever you prefer).

5. Divide the salad and chicken among 6 chilled plates. Top each salad with a sprinkling of the toasted peanuts. If you like, garnish with a sprig of Thai basil (it has deep green leaves and purplish stems and buds, and tastes like a blend of basil and anise), which is available at Asian markets.

OTHER WAYS TO DO IT

You can substitute flank steak or pork tenderloin for the chicken.

Roasted Chicken and Mushroom Salad Balsamico {Serves 4}

People love to eat chicken salad for lunch, so we have developed many different varieties to keep them happy. This salad is one of our favorites; it is good hot or cold, and it is rare if a whole batch is ever eaten just by the customers—usually before we can put it away several cooks have made off with a plateful.

1½ tablespoons chopped fresh rosemary
  leaves

1½ tablespoons minced garlic

½ teaspoon freshly ground black pepper

Pinch of hot red pepper flakes

½ cup balsamic vinegar

¼ cup olive oil

3 tablespoons soy sauce

4 boneless, skinless chicken breast halves

12 ounces white mushrooms,
  stems removed

1 yellow bell pepper, diced

1 red bell pepper, diced

1 red onion, diced

Shaved Parmesan or crumbled Gorgonzola,
  for serving

1. Combine the rosemary, garlic, black pepper, pepper flakes, vinegar, olive oil, and soy sauce in a bowl and whisk well.

2. Place the chicken breasts, mushrooms, bell peppers, and onion in a shallow dish; add the marinade and toss to coat well. Cover and refrigerate for at least 2 hours or overnight.

3. Preheat the oven to 425°F.

4. Remove the chicken breasts from the marinade and place on a baking sheet. Pour the vegetables and marinade into a baking dish. Roast the vegetables until tender, about 20 minutes. Meanwhile, roast the chicken breasts until cooked through, about 12 minutes.

5. Let the vegetables and chicken cool to room temperature. Cut the chicken into 1-inch pieces. Combine the chicken with the vegetables and their cooking liquid. Serve at room temperature, or cover and refrigerate for up to 3 days.

6. If desired, serve over romaine leaves, spinach, or arugula and top with shaved Parmesan or crumbled Gorgonzola

OTHER WAYS TO DO IT
Cooked bow-tie or fusilli pasta can be incorporated to make a more substantial meal.

Waldorf-style Chicken Salad {Serves 4}

The classic Waldorf salad contained apples, celery, mayonnaise, and walnuts. Using these ingredients as a springboard, we developed this luscious salad that adds chicken, grapes, scallions, cider, and Gorgonzola to the traditional ingredients.

2 cups apple cider

1 fresh rosemary sprig plus 1 tablespoon chopped fresh rosemary leaves

1 bay leaf

5 black peppercorns

2 tablespoons cider vinegar

4 boneless skinless chicken breast halves

1 tablespoon minced shallot

1/2 cup Homemade Mayonnaise (page 287) or store-bought

1/2 cup sour cream

1 teaspoon salt

1/2 teaspoon freshly ground black pepper

1 celery rib, cut on the diagonal into 1/4-inch slices

2 crisp red eating apples (such as Jonathan or Red Delicious), cored and diced

1 cup seedless red grapes, stems removed

2 scallions, thinly sliced

1/2 cup walnut pieces, toasted (see note, page 144)

4 ounces Gorgonzola, crumbled

4 cups mixed salad greens

1. Combine the cider, rosemary sprig, bay leaf, peppercorns, and 1 tablespoon of the cider vinegar in a large nonreactive sauté pan. Bring to a simmer over medium heat. Add the chicken breasts in a single layer; they will be about two-thirds submerged in cider mixture. Reduce the heat to low, cover, and simmer very gently until the chicken is cooked through, 12 to 15 minutes. Check often to make sure the liquid doesn't boil (the chicken will be tough if it boils); it should just lightly simmer.

2. Remove the cooked chicken to a plate to cool. Increase the heat to high and boil the poaching liquid, uncovered, until it reduces to a thick syrupy consistency, about 10 minutes. Set aside to cool to room temperature.

3. Whisk together the cooled poaching liquid, the remaining 1 tablespoon cider vinegar, and the chopped rosemary. Mix in the shallot, mayonnaise, sour cream, salt, and pepper; reserve the dressing.

4. Cut the cooled chicken into pieces about the same size as a grape. Combine the chicken, celery, apples, grapes, scallions, walnuts, Gorgonzola, and the reserved dressing in a large bowl. Toss to mix well. Serve over mixed greens.

OTHER WAYS TO DO IT
In the spring we often omit the cheese and substitute fresh tarragon for the rosemary, tarragon vinegar for the cider vinegar, Granny Smith apples for the red apples, and toasted almonds for the walnuts.

POACHING PROTEIN
This method of cooking is used for naturally tender cuts of meat and fish. The food to be cooked is placed in barely simmering liquid often it's lightly covered with a piece of parchment or foil, and then cooked gently in the liquid. When poaching, it's important not to let the liquid boil. If it does, the meat will be tough and rubbery. Because a lot of flavor is transferred to the poaching liquid, it's generally reduced and used as a sauce, as demonstrated with the cider in this recipe.

Watermelon and Shrimp Salad with Jalapeño-Lime Dressing {Serves 4}

This is a light and spicy salad that makes a terrific first course for a summer lunch or a refreshing addition to a Fourth of July feast. Unless you've put Tabasco on your watermelon wedges, you probably won't believe how incredible watermelon and hot chiles are together—this salad is proof positive.

1 cup Avocado Mousse (page 296)

JALAPEÑO-LIME DRESSING
Juice and minced zest of 3 limes

1 tablespoon cider vinegar

2 tablespoons honey

¼ cup olive oil

1 jalapeño pepper, sliced into thin rings

1 teaspoon salt or *nam pla* (Thai fish sauce, available in Asian markets and specialty food stores; see note, page 95)

1 tablespoon chopped fresh cilantro leaves and stems

1 tablespoon chopped fresh mint leaves

SALAD
8 ounces cooked shrimp, peeled, deveined, and chilled

4 cups seeded watermelon cubes

1 small red onion, sliced into thin rings

1 head romaine lettuce

1. Prepare the Avocado Mousse.

2. Prepare the dressing: Whisk together the lime juice and zest, the cider vinegar, and honey in a small bowl. Slowly whisk in the olive oil. Stir in the jalapeño, salt (or *nam pla*), cilantro, and mint. Reserve.

3. Prepare the salad: In a large bowl, combine the shrimp, watermelon, and red onion rings. Add the dressing and toss to combine well. Arrange a few leaves of romaine on 4 chilled plates. Spoon the salad onto the lettuce and top with a dollop of the Avocado Mousse.

Contessa Lisa's Tuscan Grain Salad {Serves 6}

The historic Villa Capezzana is perched among vineyards and olive groves on a hillside near Florence, Italy. I attended a meeting of culinary professionals there to learn about the traditional culinary techniques of the Tuscan people and to sample their artisanal foodstuffs. My most memorable meal included this refreshing salad of ancient grain prepared by our hostess Contessa Lisa, who graciously shared her recipe with me.

1$\frac{1}{2}$ cups spelt (see note below)

6 cups water

1 cucumber, peeled, seeded, and finely diced (about 1 cup)

1 cup seeded diced tomato

2 scallions, thinly sliced

$\frac{1}{2}$ whole lemon, finely diced

1 teaspoon minced garlic

$\frac{1}{4}$ cup chopped fresh basil leaves

1 cup extra-virgin olive oil

1 teaspoon salt

1 teaspoon freshly ground black pepper

1. Place the spelt in a large saucepan and cover with the water. Bring to a boil. Reduce the heat to medium-low and simmer until tender, about 1$\frac{1}{2}$ hours (you may need to add additional water). Drain the spelt and let cool to room temperature.

2. In a large bowl, combine the cooled spelt, cucumber, tomato, scallions, lemon, garlic, basil, olive oil, salt and pepper; toss well. Serve at room temperature, or cover and refrigerate for up to 3 days. Bring to room temperature before serving. We like to serve this salad on a bed of baby arugula with thin slices of prosciutto and herb-cured olives.

OTHER WAYS TO DO IT
If you can't find spelt, substitute cooked barley instead.

ABOUT SPELT
Although you may never have heard of it, spelt (a cereal grain) has been cultivated and enjoyed by humans for 9,000 years. In Italy, it's known as *farro* and is ground into flour used to make pasta and pizzas. The cooked whole grain has a mellow, nutty flavor and resembles barley in appearance. Spelt is higher in protein than wheat and can be digested by people with wheat allergies. Look for it in health food stores and gourmet supermarkets.

Cobb Salad Sandwich with Blue Cheese Mayonnaise {Serves 4}

This sandwich has most of the fixins' of its popular namesake and truly is a meal in itself!

BLUE CHEESE MAYONNAISE

4 ounces blue cheese, crumbled and at room temperature

³/₄ cup Homemade Mayonnaise (page 287) or store-bought

1 tablespoon Dijon mustard

2 scallions, thinly sliced

¹/₂ teaspoon freshly ground black pepper

SANDWICHES

8 slices (each ¹/₂ inch thick) sourdough bread

4 skinless, boneless smoked chicken breasts halves, thinly sliced (see note below)

8 slices ripe tomato

8 slices bacon, cooked until crisp

1 ripe avocado, peeled and thinly sliced

4 large romaine lettuce leaves, washed

1. Make the Blue Cheese Mayonnaise: combine all of the ingredients in a small bowl and mix well. Use at once or cover and refrigerate for up to 3 days.

2. Spread 4 slices of the bread with a thick coating of the mayo. Top each with one-quarter of the sliced chicken, 2 slices of the tomato, 2 slices of the bacon, one-quarter of the sliced avocado, and a leaf of romaine. Top each with another piece of bread. Cut the sandwiches in half and serve. We like to serve our Spicy Sweet Potato Chips (page 195) on the side.

SMOKING CHICKEN

Smoking chicken at home is not a difficult task, although we do suggest that you do it in a kitchen with good ventilation. We recommend purchasing a stovetop smoker and following the manufacturer's instructions. However if you're feeling adventurous, you can also put some water-soaked hardwood chips (apple, cherry, hickory, or oak) or herb branches in the bottom of a roasting pan. Place a rack on top of the chips (the rack should be at least 2 inches above the chips) and place the roasting pan on a burner set over medium heat until the chips begin to smoke. Place the chicken on the rack and cover with a tight-fitting lid (very important). Smoke for 6 to 8 minutes, depending on the size of the breast. Before removing the lid, take the roasting pan outside or to a well-ventilated area; then, remove the chicken and finish cooking it in the oven.

Italian Sausage Grinder {Serves 4}

Philadelphia is hoagie heaven. The city is awash in hoagie shops, delis, and carts on the street that make some of the best hoagies, cheese steaks, and grinders you're likely to find anywhere. Although the term "grinder" may mean something different elsewhere, in Philadelphia it is a hoagie made with beef, pork, meatballs, or sausages that is heated in the oven. Our Italian Sausage Grinder is made with hot and sweet sausages from the Italian Market in South Philly. Top it with cheese and bake or broil until the cheese melts and, YO! Enjoy!

8 ounces sweet Italian sausage links

8 ounces hot Italian sausage links

2 tablespoons olive oil

1 large yellow onion, thinly sliced
   (about 2 cups)

1 tablespoon minced garlic

$\frac{1}{2}$ teaspoon hot red pepper flakes

1 red bell pepper, thinly sliced

1 yellow bell pepper, thinly sliced

$\frac{1}{2}$ cup water

3 plum tomatoes, cut into wedges

2 tablespoons red wine vinegar

$\frac{1}{2}$ teaspoon salt

4 Italian-style hoagie rolls, or 2 long
   soft-crusted baguettes

4 ounces smoked mozzarella cheese,
   thinly sliced

1. Preheat the oven to 400°F.

2. Place the sausage links in a large, nonreactive sauté pan and add $\frac{1}{2}$ inch of water. Bring to a simmer over low heat; cover and steam until cooked through, 8 to 10 minutes. Slice the links on the bias into 1-inch pieces. Reserve.

3. Pour out the water and wipe out the pan. Heat the oil in the same sauté pan set over medium heat. Add the onion and cook until soft, about 5 minutes. Add the garlic and cook for 2 minutes. Add the hot pepper flakes and bell peppers and cook for 5 minutes. Pour in the water and cook for 5 minutes more. Stir in the tomatoes and cook until soft, about 5 minutes. Add the sliced sausages, vinegar, and salt, and cook until the sausages are heated through, about 2 minutes.

4. Halve the rolls lengthwise. Fill with the sausage mixture; top each sandwich with one-fourth of the sliced cheese. Place them on a baking sheet and bake until the cheese melts, 4 or 5 minutes.

5. Serve hot from the oven with our Spicy Fried Potatoes (page 194) or Spicy Potato Chips (page 195).

VISITING THE ITALIAN MARKET

For food lovers visiting Philadelphia, your first stop (after the White Dog Cafe) should be the Italian Market, located in South Philadelphia on Ninth Street between Christian and Federal. A stroll down the blocks of the outdoor Italian market is a skip through time, back to an era when giant indoor supermarkets and shrink-wrapped vegetables were not the norm. The Italian Market is a marvel—you can barter with vendors who sell gorgeous produce at bargain prices, drool over sausage and pepperoni hanging in cheese shops, examine olive oils in myriad shades of green, and purchase everything from furred game suspended in a butcher shop window to fish flopping about on ice, and from shining copper cookware to the famed Italian water ice.

White Dog Cafe's Philly Cheese Steak {Serves 4}

A Philadelphia tradition, the cheese steak is now known the world over. According to local legend, the cheese steak was invented by Pat and Harry Olivieri, two brothers who had a hot dog stand during the Depression. They grew tired of eating hot dogs day in and day out; so, one afternoon they went to the butcher to see if he had any scraps. He gave them some beef, which they cooked up on their hot-dog griddle along with the onions from the condiment tray. A cab driver happened to pull up just as they were about to eat their new sandwich and asked if he could buy it from them. He loved it, and the rest is history. Provolone cheese was added in 1950, and today has been replaced by Cheez Whiz. Our cheese steak doesn't follow traditional guidelines, but we'd match it against a South Philly steak any day.

2 tablespoons olive oil

2 large yellow onions, thinly sliced (about 4 cups)

2 large portobello mushroom caps, thinly sliced (about 3 cups)

1½ teaspoons salt

1 pound trimmed flank steak, sliced as thinly as possible (preferably on a slicer)

½ teaspoon freshly ground black pepper

1½ cups grated Pepper-Jack cheese

2 soft-crusted long baguettes, or 4 Italian-style hoagie rolls

1. Preheat the oven to 400°F.

2. Heat the oil in a large nonreactive sauté pan set over medium-high heat until it ripples. Add the onions and cook until soft, about 5 minutes. Add the mushrooms and 1 teaspoon of the salt and sauté until tender, about 5 minutes. Add the flank steak, the remaining ½ teaspoon salt, and the pepper and sauté until the meat is cooked through about 5 minutes more.

3. Remove the pan from the heat. Sprinkle the cheese over the top, cover the pan, and set aside until the cheese melts, about 5 minutes.

4. Meanwhile, slice the baguettes lengthwise. Place, cut sides up, on a baking sheet, and toast in the oven until crisp, 4 to 5 minutes.

5. Fill the baguettes with the meat and cheese. Cut each into 2 portions. Serve immediately—with or without ketchup.

Tuna Sandwich à la Niçoise {Serves 4}

Consider doubling this recipe because you won't be able to stop yourself from eating most of the zesty, fresh salad before you can split the baguette. A la Niçoise refers to the use of tuna, tomatoes, black olives, capers, and garlic, ingredients that characterize the cuisine of this seaside city. Traditionally this salad is prepared with canned tuna, which is okay, but try it once with fresh tuna and you'll throw your can opener away!

---

1 cup **Creamy Basil Sauce (page 293)**

8 ounces **fresh yellowfin tuna fillet**

2 teaspoons **chopped garlic**

1/2 teaspoon **dried tarragon**

1/2 teaspoon **dried basil**

1 teaspoon **fresh lemon juice**

4 tablespoons **extra-virgin olive oil**

1/4 cup **drained capers, rinsed and minced**

2 **plum tomatoes, seeded and diced**

1/2 **small red onion, minced**

1/2 **small fennel bulb, stalks removed, cored, and minced (see note, page 93)**

1/2 cup **pitted, rinsed, and roughly chopped Niçoise olives**

1/4 **whole lemon, seeded and finely minced**

1 tablespoon **red wine vinegar**

1/2 teaspoon **freshly ground black pepper**

1 long **baguette (or your favorite bread)**

1. Prepare the Creamy Basil Sauce. Reserve.

2. Preheat the oven to 400°F.

3. Cut the tuna into 1-inch chunks. Place in large mixing bowl. Add the garlic, tarragon, basil, lemon juice, and 2 tablespoons of the olive oil; toss to coat each chunk evenly. Spread the fish on a greased baking sheet. Bake the fish to the desired doneness, 5 to 7 minutes for medium-rare. Set aside to cool to room temperature.

4. Combine the capers, tomatoes, onion, fennel, olives, and lemon in a large mixing bowl. Crumble in the tuna chunks and toss. Add the vinegar, pepper, and the remaining 2 tablespoons olive oil; toss to combine well. (The salad can be made up to 2 days in advance and kept refrigerated.)

5. Split the baguette lengthwise and spread the inside with the Creamy Basil Sauce. Fill the baguette with the tuna salad; cut into 4 portions.

6. Serve with a green salad dressed with Lemon–Olive Oil Vinaigrette (see page 90) or Egg-free Caesar Dressing (see page 91).

OTHER WAYS TO DO IT

Instead of filling a baguette, try hollowing out a tomato or sweet bell pepper and stuffing it with the salad. An anchovy or olive on top makes a nice garnish.

Toasted Brioche with Ham and Brie {Serves 4}

This sandwich echoes the famed Croque Monsieur, traditionally a ham and cheese sandwich dipped in beaten egg and browned in butter. Rather than dipping the sandwich in egg, we use our Brioche, a bread rich with butter and eggs, and we add a little of our Gingered Pear Chutney for some extra tang. We serve it for lunch and to late-night customers at our Bar and Grill with a mug of hot mulled cider.

8 slices (each ½ inch thick) Brioche (page 238) or store-bought

4 tablespoons whole-grain mustard

8 ounces thinly sliced ham, such as Black Forest, Smithfield, or county-cured Virginia ham

½ cup Gingered Pear Chutney (page 296) or store-bought chutney, such as Major Grey's

8 ounces Brie cheese, sliced

1 tablespoon unsalted butter

1. Spread each of 4 slices of the brioche with 1 tablespoon of the mustard. Top with one quarter of the ham, 2 tablespoons of the chutney, and one-quarter of the Brie. Top each sandwich with another piece of bread.

2. Heat the butter on a large griddle set over medium-low heat. Add the sandwiches and cook until the bread is golden brown and the cheese melts, about 4 minutes on each side. Cut the sandwiches in half and serve warm. If you like, serve this sandwich aside peppery watercress dressed with walnut oil and fresh lemon.

Southwestern Turkey Burger {Serves 4}

Each summer we reach the point that we just can't face another hamburger off the grill. Let these spicy turkey burgers inspire you to spark up your grill again and re-experience the delight of summer's first grilled burger.

1½ pounds ground turkey

1½ teaspoons minced garlic

1 teaspoon New Mexican chili powder
(see note, page 130)

1 teaspoon dried Mexican oregano
(see note, page 78)

½ teaspoon ground cumin

1 teaspoon Dijon mustard

1 chipotle chile pepper in adobo sauce
(available in Latin markets and
many supermarkets; see note below)

1½ teaspoons Worcestershire sauce

1 teaspoon salt

¼ teaspoon cayenne pepper

4 burger-size squares of corn bread, split

1 cup Avocado Mousse (page 296),
for serving

1. Prepare a charcoal grill.

2. Combine the turkey, garlic, chili powder, oregano, cumin, mustard, three-fourths of the chipotle chile, the Worcestershire, salt, and cayenne in a large mixing bowl; mix well. Shape the seasoned meat into 4 patties.

3. Grill the burgers until cooked through, about 6 minutes on each side. (The burgers can also be cooked with a little oil in a skillet set over medium heat for about 4 minutes on each side.) Place each burger in a corn bread "bun," and top with the Avocado Mousse and, if desired, some of our Firehouse Dalmatian Bean Salad (page 205).

FLAVORING WITH CHIPOTLE PEPPERS

Chipotle peppers are jalapeño peppers that have been dried and then smoked. They are smoky, slightly sweet, and very hot. We use them to add depth of flavor and heat to spicy dishes like black beans and enchiladas. They come dried or in small cans packed in adobo, a spicy tomato-based sauce. Look for chipotles in Latin markets and some gourmet supermarkets.

Moroccan-spiced Lamb Burger with Pepper Relish {Serves 4}

Ground lamb is available at most supermarkets; so the next time you're there, reach for it instead of ground beef and make these spicy lamb burgers. They are exotically seasoned with flavors of the Middle East—ordinary burgers just don't compare.

2 cups Pepper Relish (page 297)

1 pound ground lamb

2 tablespoons chopped fresh cilantro
  leaves and stems (see note, page 158)

2 tablespoons chopped fresh mint leaves

2 tablespoons chopped fresh oregano leaves

1 tablespoon chopped garlic

2 teaspoons sherry vinegar

1 teaspoon molasses

1½ teaspoons ground cumin

¼ teaspoon ground allspice

½ teaspoon hot red pepper flakes

1 teaspoon salt

½ teaspoon freshly ground black pepper

4 grilled pita breads

4 ounces feta cheese

1. Prepare the Pepper Relish.

2. Prepare a charcoal grill

3. Combine the lamb, cilantro, mint, oregano, garlic, vinegar, molasses, cumin, allspice, pepper flakes, salt, and pepper in a large mixing bowl; mix well. Shape the mixture into 4 patties.

4. Grill the burgers over the hot coals for about 6 minutes on each side or to the desired doneness (or heat a few drops of oil in a sauté pan over medium-high heat and cook until done). Place each burger on a grilled pita bread. Crumble 1 ounce of feta cheese over each and top with the Pepper Relish. If you like, serve alongside Cucumber Raita (page 298), Tomato Mint Chutney (see page 148), and Hummus (page 294).

INVESTING IN SHERRY VINEGAR

Sherry vinegar is a key ingredient in many dishes at the White Dog Cafe, and we recommend investing in it for your pantry. Sherry vinegar combines well with nut oils, mustards, grains, fruits, and vegetables.

Salmon Burgers {Serves 4}

Years ago we developed this burger to make use of the pieces of salmon that were too small to serve. Nowadays, we have to use whole fish to keep up with the demand for this plump, moist sandwich.

1½ pounds fresh salmon fillet,
   finely chopped

3 scallions, thinly sliced

1 tablespoon chopped fresh basil leaves

1 tablespoon *nam pla* (Thai fish sauce,
   available in Asian markets and specialty
   food stores; see note, page 95)

¼ teaspoon Tabasco sauce

2 tablespoons olive oil

4 tablespoons Tartar Sauce (page 290),
   for serving

1. Preheat the oven to 400°F.

2. Combine the salmon, scallions, basil, *nam pla*, and Tabasco in a large bowl; mix well. Shape the mixture into 4 patties.

3. Heat the oil in a large ovenproof skillet set over medium-high heat. Add the salmon patties and cook until golden on one side, 3 to 4 minutes. Carefully turn the patties over.

4. Place the skillet in the oven. Bake until just cooked through, about 5 minutes. If you like, serve on potato-dill bread with the Tartar Sauce, lettuce, and tomato with a simple cucumber and red onion salad dressed with our Lemon–Olive Oil Vinaigrette (page 90).

BUYING FRESH FISH

Always purchase fresh fish as close to the time you are going to prepare it as possible. When purchasing a whole fish, use your nose to determine freshness: Smell it first and select one with a fresh sealike aroma. Other indications of a fresh fish are firm and resilient flesh (no imprint should remain in the skin when pressed lightly with your finger), eyes clear and full, and gills red to maroon with no traces of gray or brown. Once you have purchased the fish, get it home as quickly as possible. Tightly wrap with plastic and place on a bed of ice.

Mexican Tortilla Roll Ups {Serves 4}

We serve these rolled sandwiches, which call for our Vegetable Seviche and our Mexican Hummus, to picnicking Roller Bladers Over 40. Although the idea to serve them at this particular party came to us because we liked the pun on the word "roll," they turned out to be a perfect picnic sandwich that keeps well without refrigeration for several hours.

MEXICAN HUMMUS

2 cups cooked chickpeas

2 tablespoons extra-virgin olive oil

2 garlic cloves, peeled

Juice of 1 lime

1 teaspoon ground cumin

1^1/$_2$ teaspoons New Mexican chili powder
  (see note, page 130)

^{1}/$_2$ teaspoon cayenne pepper

^{1}/$_2$ teaspoon salt

^{1}/$_4$ cup water

VEGETABLE SEVICHE

Juice and grated or minced zest of 1 lemon

Juice and grated or minced zest of 1 orange

Juice and grated or minced zest of 2 limes

1 jalapeño pepper, seeded and minced

2 tablespoons olive oil

2 teaspoons sugar

1 teaspoon salt

1 tablespoon chopped fresh cilantro leaves
  and stems (see note, page 158)

2 cucumbers, peeled, seeded, and
  finely diced

2 plum tomatoes, seeded and finely diced

1 carrot, peeled and grated

3 scallions, thinly sliced

1 red bell pepper, finely diced

8 large flour tortillas

2 ripe avocados, peeled and thinly sliced

2 cups shredded lettuce

1. Prepare the Mexican Hummus: Combine all of the ingredients in a food processor or blender and process until smooth, about 1 minute. To store, cover and refrigerate for up to 3 days.

2. Prepare the Vegetable Seviche: In a small bowl, whisk together the citrus juices and zests with the jalapeño, olive oil, sugar, salt, and cilantro.

3. Combine the cucumber, tomato, carrot, scallions, and bell pepper in a large bowl. Add the citrus mixture and toss to combine. Let stand at room temperature for 2 hours before serving. Or, cover and refrigerate for up to 2 days.

4. Spread each tortilla with ^{1}/$_4$ cup of the hummus. Top with ^{1}/$_2$ cup of the seviche, one-quarter of the avocado, and ^{1}/$_4$ cup of the shredded lettuce.

5. Carefully roll the filled tortillas into tight cylinders and serve at room temperature.

OTHER WAYS TO DO IT

You can add some sliced grilled chicken or steak to the roll ups if desired. To take on a picnic, wrap the roll ups tightly in plastic wrap, waxed paper, or foil.

Farm Stand Focaccia {Serves 8}

You won't believe your eyes when you pull this giant focaccia from the oven. Studded with farm-fresh vegetables and golden brown, it is glorious to behold. We make them for feeding crowds and they travel well; so gather a bunch of friends and at least a few bottles of wine and head for your favorite picnic spot.

2 pounds Parmesan Focaccia dough (page 239), omitting the Parmesan cheese and black pepper

1 small zucchini, cut into $\frac{1}{4}$-inch rounds

10 cherry tomatoes, halved

1 small red onion, sliced into rings

1 yellow bell pepper, cut into $\frac{1}{4}$-inch strips

1 tablespoon minced garlic

$\frac{1}{2}$ teaspoon hot red pepper flakes

1 teaspoon salt

$\frac{1}{2}$ cup extra-virgin olive oil

$\frac{1}{2}$ cup whole fresh basil leaves

6 ounces fresh mozzarella cheese, cut into $\frac{1}{2}$-inch cubes (about 1 cup)

1. Prepare the Parmesan Focaccia dough recipe through Step 4.

2. About 30 minutes before baking, preheat the oven to 400°F.

3. Combine the zucchini, tomatoes, onion, bell pepper, garlic, pepper flakes, salt, and olive oil in a large mixing bowl. Toss well to coat the vegetables with the oil. Pour the excess oil from the vegetables evenly over the top of the dough. Arrange the basil leaves over the surface of the dough; top with the oiled vegetables, pressing them lightly into the dough. Scatter the cubed cheese over the vegetables.

4. Bake the focaccia until the top is browned and the vegetables are tender, 25 to 30 minutes. Cut into wedges or slices and serve at once.

OTHER WAYS TO DO IT

For a knock-out sandwich, try slicing the baked focaccia in half and spread it with Lemon-Pepper Aïoli (page 291). Top with tomato slices, arugula leaves, and sliced prosciutto if desired.

ABOUT FOCACCIA

Focaccia is the forerunner to pizza as we know it. Originally baked on a stone beneath a fire's dying embers, the word focaccia comes from the Latin *panus focus*, which loosely translates as "bread from the fireplace floor." Today, it's a large flat Italian bread that's drizzled with olive oil, sprinkled with salt, and sometimes studded with savory morsels before being baked. Focaccia can be eaten straight from the oven or sliced in half and made into sandwiches. However, there are so many good things on top of this particular loaf that it's almost an open-faced sandwich already.

Toasted Focaccia with Roasted Tomatoes, Olives, and Feta {Serves 4}

One late summer day the pastry chefs made us so much beautiful focaccia we found we had more than was needed for dinner. At the same time a farmer brought in a surplus of perfect juicy plum tomatoes. We devised this warm salad/sandwich to make use of them both. It's the most boldly flavored and hearty open-faced sandwich that we offer at the White Dog Cafe. The ingredients are straightforward, yet work magically together. You can generally find good plum tomatoes in your market, but if not, save this for another time. Don't be put off by the whole garlic cloves, for they soften while cooking and become sweet and mellow. If feta is not to your liking, try fresh mozzarella or a dollop of creamy ricotta.

1 round of Parmesan Focaccia (page 239), prebaked and cooled

8 large plum tomatoes, cored and cut into 1-inch chunks

1 head of garlic, cloves separated and peeled

1 cup olive oil

1/2 teaspoon hot red pepper flakes

4 ounces feta cheese, crumbled

1/4 cup loosely packed fresh oregano leaves

1. Prepare the Parmesan Focaccia. Reserve.

2. Preheat the oven to 400°F.

3. Toss together the tomatoes, garlic, oil, and pepper flakes in a nonreactive roasting pan; cover with foil. Roast in the oven until the garlic is soft and the tomatoes are just starting to brown, about 30 minutes. (This mixture can be prepared a day in advance and kept refrigerated. Warm to room temperature when needed.)

4. While the vegetables roast, cut the prebaked focaccia into 4 equal pieces; split each piece horizontally in half as if for a sandwich. Arrange the bread, cut sides up, on a baking sheet and warm the bread in the oven until just toasted, about 5 minutes.

5. To serve, place a focaccia bottom on each of 4 plates. Spoon the warm tomato mixture over each portion. Crumble one-fourth of the feta over the tomatoes, and add oregano leaves; add the focaccia tops. If desired, serve with a simple salad of arugula dressed with Lemon—Olive Oil Vinaigrette (page 90).

OTHER WAYS TO DO IT

The tomato topping is wonderful over a bowl of just-cooked pasta.

BUYING IMPORTED OLIVES

There's nothing like a good-quality, imported cured olive to make a dish special. You'll find these at gourmet grocery stores, better delis, and health food stores. The curing process lightens the olive's natural bitterness and intensifies its flavor. Brine-cured olives are soaked in fresh water for eight days, and then soaked in saltwater for a month before being put up in barrels or bottles. Dry-cured olives are cured with salt. This method produces a shriveled olive that's flavorful but bitter; they are generally rubbed with olive oil and packed with fresh or dried herbs. The two most readily available types of imported olives are the Greek kalamata, a brine-cured, purplish-black olive with an almond shape, and the French Niçoise, a tiny brownish-black brine-cured olive.

MAIN COURSES

MAIN COURSES

Cuisine Perestroika: A Soviet Tale 117

Poultry & Game

Chicken Braised with Tomatoes, Black Olives, and Pepperoni 120

Sweet & Spicy Barbecued Chicken 121

Sautéed Chicken and Mushrooms in Marsala-Sage Sauce 122

Smoked Chicken in Rosemary Cream with Bow-Tie Pasta 123

Mediterranean Fried Chicken with Artichoke Salad 124

Spicy Chèvre-stuffed Chicken Breast with Roasted Corn Salsa 125

Spinach- and Ricotta-stuffed Chicken Breasts with Sun-dried Tomato–Olive Butter 126

Roast Cornish Hens with White Truffle Jus 128

Chili-rubbed Duck Breasts with Sun-dried Cherry Glaze 130

Roasted Duck with Native Grain, Brandied Fruits, and Pistachio Stuffing 131

Braised Rabbit with Tomatoes, Pancetta, and Green Peppercorns 132

Meats

Chilled Roast Beef Tenderloin with Horseradish Crème Fraîche 133

Grilled Beef Tenderloin with Balsamic-Pancetta Glaze 134

Betty's Beef Kabobs 135

Rosemary-Mustard London Broil with Wild Mushroom Glaze 136

Seared Peppered Sirloin with Red Wine–Chèvre Glaze 138

Nicaraguan Braised Beef Shins 139

White Dog Cafe Layered Meat Loaf 140

Veal Chops Roasted with Mushroom and Pine Nuts 142

MAIN COURSES

Sesame-roasted Pork Tenderloin with Ginger Glaze 143

Center-cut Pork Chops with Gorgonzola-Walnut Stuffing and Ruby Port Glaze 144

Pork Tenderloin with Caramelized Shallots and Apples 146

Sautéed Pork Medallions with Basil and Balsamic Vinegar 147

Derby Day Leg of Lamb with Tomato-Mint Chutney 148

Rosemary-roasted Leg of Lamb 149

Jamaican Curried Lamb Stew 150

Tarragon-braised Lamb Shanks 151

Seafood

Mediterranean Shellfish Stew with Green Goddess Sauce 152

Soft-Shell Crabs with Thai Curried Vegetables 153

Corn-crusted Crab and Shrimp Cakes with Summer Herbs Sauce 154

Seared Sea Scallops with Curried Apple "Sauce" and Crispy Fried Leeks 155

Trout Tropicale 156

Caribbean Grilled Mahi Mahi with Tropical Fruit Salsa 157

Roasted Trout with Potato-Shrimp Stuffing and Lemon-Thyme Sauce 158

Cuban-style Braised Tuna 160

Seared Tuna with Anise and Black Currant Balsamico 161

Crispy Red Snapper with Shiitake Mushroom Glaze 162

Leek- and Caraway-braised Swordfish with Lemon-Pepper Aïoli 163

Pan-roasted Salmon with Burgundy-Rosemary Butter 164

Rosemary and Lime-roasted Sea Bass with Mediterranean Salsa 165

(continued)

MAIN COURSES

Vegetarian

Wild Mushroom—Barley Risotto 166

Broccoli Risotto 167

Tomato and Sweet Corn Risotto 168

Fettuccine with White Beans, Sun-dried Tomatoes, and Rosemary 169

Savory Tart of Chanterelles, Swiss Chard, and Emmentaler 170

Curried Butternut Squash Ravioli with Winter Herb Pesto 172

Roasted Eggplant Marinara 174

Penne with Asparagus 175

Chiapas Pie 176

Mushroom-Corn Rellenos with Mole 178

Curry-roasted Vegetables with Indian Cheese Dumplings 179

Balsamic-roasted Portobello Mushrooms 180

Tangy Summer Vegetable Tian 181

CUISINE PERESTROIKA: A SOVIET TALE

WHEN SOVIET PRESIDENT MIKHAIL GORBACHEV INITIATED PERESTROIKA AND announced that restaurants would be the first privately owned businesses in the Soviet Union, I just had to go.

Through our international sister-restaurant program, I was eager to help fellow entre-preneurs in the fledgling free-enterprise movement and soon found myself experiencing a remarkable time in world history. The perfect opportunity for finding a Soviet sister restaurant came in 1988, when I joined the first culinary tour of the USSR organized by fellow Philadelphian Krista Bard. Before that trip I was largely unaware of the many different republics that made up the Soviet Union. All I had really understood was that back in the 1950s, when we crawled under our school desks during air raid practices, it was the Soviets we were hiding from. There was so much to learn about the people we had aimed our nuclear missiles toward since as far back as I could remember.

After much traveling and eating, I choose Stiklai, "The Glass-blower," as our new sister restaurant. It was the second privately owned business in the Soviet Union and the first in the republic of Lithuania. I was fascinated by the fortitude and ingenuity of the three proprietors in running a private business within an economic system in which everything else was owned by government. Romas, who previously worked in a state restaurant where he was voted "best bartender in the Soviet Union," went into partnership with two of his customers, Anna, an economist, and her husband

Kevin (ctr) in the kitchen of Stiklai, our Lithuanian sister restaurant, 1990

Shasha, a concert violinist. They remodeled a former glassblower's studio into a charm-ing restaurant in the old section of Vilnius, the capital city of Lithuania.

At first no one would take the chance of quitting their state jobs to work for them. From cooking to serving to washing the pots, they had done it all by themselves. Now thriv-ing with plenty of customers and staff, it was still very difficult for them to be the vanguard of a new way of doing business in a system where bribery, pilferage, and secrecy were learned from childhood as necessities for economic survival.

My invitation to visit us in America provided the state's prerequisite for receiving permission to leave the country, a long-awaited opportunity. The following year, with four of their staff, our Soviet friends came to Philadelphia and prepared a dinner at the White Dog Cafe with great success, returning home with many new ideas for their business. A year later, returning to the Soviet Union to complete our culinary exchange, I found that the rapid changes brought on by Gorbachev's reforms meant that we no longer had a Soviet sister restaurant—we had a Lithuanian one!

In July, 1990, Kevin and I, along with James Barrett, our pastry chef, visited our sister restaurant, Stiklai, to prepare an American dinner. Unable to reach our destination by air because of the Soviet blockade of Lithuania, we landed at the airport in Latvia, the republic just to the north. There we were warmly reunited with Romas, Anna, and Shasha. The six of us piled into a van, along with a driver, a translator, and a good supply of Lithuanian sparkling wine for the drive south across the border. To discourage the growing independence movement, the Soviets had blockaded the rebellious republic. Along with a visiting soccer team, we were the first foreigners to enter the republic since the roadblocks were lifted. As we drove through the capital city, we could sense the excitement, and it was proudly pointed out to us as we passed the town square that the Lithuanian flag now flew in place of the Soviet one, and that Lithuanian TV, seized from Soviet control, would be filming our dinner. We were surprised to find a photograph of our arrival on the front page of the paper the next morning, and realized that our presence here, as citizens of the free world, meant more than we had ever imagined.

Our hosts were eager to show us how they had put to good use what they had learned from their trip to America. Under the highly conformist Soviet system creativity was not encouraged. A chef was expected to prepare a dish just as it had been done by other chefs for generations before him. The great challenge was in finding the ingredients to replicate a classic dish in a country with many shortages. While working with Kevin in Philadelphia, the Stiklai staff had experienced an entirely different approach to cooking. Rather than starting with a standard recipe, Kevin looked first at what fresh ingredients were available that day and then created a dish around them. Our culinary exchange had brought them a new way of thinking that depended as much on innovation as traditional skill. At our first meal at Stiklai we were served a salad that seemed unremarkable to us at first glance, until the translator explained that in the Soviet Union, salads were shredded like coleslaw. This one featured whole leaves, a revolutionary concept here. Next our hosts proudly served a new entrée they had just created and named "Chicken Judy." Cuisine Perestroika had arrived!

Judy with White Dog Cafe Pastry Chef James Barrett, presenting a Statue of Liberty to two of the owners of Stiklai

Our American dinner at Stiklai was a major event in Vilnius. What did we want to say to them about our country through the food we served? Kevin created a menu that demonstrated American innovation and how we integrate the traditions of many cultures. From tacos with salsa to spring rolls to fried chicken and greens, we would celebrate America's diversity. For dessert, of course, there had to be apple pie. After overcoming the difficulties of cooking on strange stoves with a crew who spoke a different language the dinner was ready. Our hosts had attended to every detail in the dining room, from dusting the crystal chandeliers to arranging fresh flowers on white linen-covered tables. Once the guests were seated, I was introduced by Romas, who spoke of his trip to America. I explained how our sister restaurant program, "Table for Six Billion, Please!" envisioned a world of peace and abundance in which everyone had a place at the table. As each course was served, Kevin described the significance of the dish for the guests and TV audience. The governor of Lithuania had planned to attend the dinner but had been called to a meeting with President Gorbachev. Suddenly, the cameraman who'd filmed their meeting in Moscow arrived at Stiklai and brought us the news: He had heard Gorbachev promise that he would not prevent Lithuania from seceding. The road to independence was clear!

Boisterous toasts "To a free Lithuania!" were made all around. "And three cheers for Cuisine Perestroika!"

—JW

Chicken Braised with Tomatoes, Black Olives, and Pepperoni {Serves 4}

It's amazing how much intensity and depth of flavor can be brought together in just one dish. This dinner will delight you; it dirties only one pot, it doesn't need a lot of attention, and the results are incredibly rewarding— tender moist chicken in a stirring sauce of ripe tomatoes, spicy pepperoni, briny black olives, and fresh oregano.

½ cup all-purpose flour

1 tablespoon dried thyme

1 chicken (about 4 pounds), cut into serving pieces

Salt and freshly ground black pepper

¼ cup olive oil

1½ cups minced yellow onions

¼ cup minced garlic

2 tablespoons tomato paste (see note below)

1 cup (about 4 ounces) thinly sliced pepperoni

2 pounds fresh plum tomatoes, cut into ½ inch rounds (about 4 cups)

2 cups dry red wine

1 large pinch of hot red pepper flakes

2 sprigs fresh thyme

¾ cup brined kalamata olives, rinsed, pitted, and sliced

2 tablespoons chopped fresh oregano leaves

2 teaspoons fresh lemon juice

Pinch of sugar, optional

1. Combine the flour and dried thyme in a bowl. Rinse the chicken pieces and pat them dry. Sprinkle lightly with salt and pepper; dust with the flour mixture.

2. In a large, nonreactive Dutch oven set over high heat, heat the olive oil until it ripples. Working in batches, add the chicken pieces and cook until browned on all sides, about 15 minutes. Remove the chicken and reserve.

3. Reduce the heat to medium-high, add the onions and garlic and cook until the onions are translucent, about 5 minutes. Add the tomato paste and cook for 1 minute. Add the pepperoni and cook for 1 minute. Add the tomatoes and cook until they begin to soften, about 5 minutes.

4. Add the wine, hot pepper flakes, and thyme sprigs, and reduce the sauce to a simmer. Add the browned chicken pieces and bring back to a simmer. Reduce the heat to low, cover, and simmer very gently until the chicken is fork-tender and falling off the bone, about 45 minutes.

5. Transfer the chicken to a plate and keep warm. Simmer the sauce until it thickens slightly. Stir in the olives, chopped oregano, lemon juice, and a pinch of salt. Check for seasoning; if it tastes too acidic, add the pinch of sugar. Divide the chicken among 4 warm plates and top with the sauce. Serve with Fennel Roasted Potatoes (page 000) and sautéed spinach (page 000).

OTHER WAYS TO DO IT

It is also good served over a plate of steaming linguine with freshly grated Parmesan cheese.

COOKING TOMATO PASTE

When adding tomato paste to a recipe, its flavor is always enhanced and sweetened if you cook it for a little while in some oil, as we do in this recipe.

Sweet & Spicy Barbecued Chicken {Serves 4 to 6}

There are scores of recipes for barbecue sauce—each one different, but essentially the same. The basic formula incorporates three taste sensations: sweet, tart, and spicy. In our version, honey and orange supply the sweet, mustard and vinegar add the tang, and smoky chipotle peppers lend the fire. These ingredients not only fulfill the basic requirements for great barbecue, they also combine so well you'll hear involuntary lip smacking around the table.

8 tablespoons (1 stick) unsalted butter

2 cups minced yellow onions

2 tablespoons minced garlic

2 teaspoons minced chipotle pepper in adobo (see note, page 107)

1 cup ketchup

1 cup fresh orange juice

¼ cup plus 2 tablespoons honey

2 teaspoons Dijon mustard

2 tablespoons cider vinegar

2 teaspoons Worcestershire sauce

2 teaspoons dried thyme

½ teaspoon ground allspice

½ teaspoon salt

2 whole chickens, cut into serving pieces

1. In a nonreactive saucepan set over medium heat, melt the butter. Add the onions and cook for 1 minute. Add the garlic and cook for 4 minutes. Stir in the chipotle, ketchup, orange juice, honey, mustard, vinegar, Worcestershire, thyme, allspice, and salt. Simmer until thick, about 10 minutes. Let cool to room temperature.

2. Place the chicken pieces in a shallow dish. Pour half of the barbecue sauce on top; cover and reserve the remaining sauce. Turn to coat the pieces thoroughly. Cover and refrigerate for at least 2 hours or up to overnight.

3. Prepare a charcoal grill.

4. Lightly oil the grill rack. Grill the chicken over hot coals, turning occasionally and basting with the marinade, until cooked through, about 15 minutes.

5. Meanwhile, warm the reserved barbecue sauce in a pan. Serve on the side with the hot grilled chicken. This is good with Barley and Sweet Corn Tabbouleh (page 209) or grilled corn with our Cumin Butter (page 286). Also, use this sauce to barbecue ribs, pork chops, lamb, or duck.

AVOIDING FROZEN CHICKEN
Although it may be economical to stock up on chicken on sale and freeze it for later use, the quality of your prepared dish will suffer. Freezing changes the cell structure of the meat, which causes the bird to lose fluid that is rich in proteins and vitamins during the thawing stage, resulting in dry, tough meat.

Sautéed Chicken and Mushrooms in Marsala-Sage Sauce {Serves 4}

This combination of smoky Marsala and woodsy mushrooms is splendid. Here we combine the two with fresh sage to make a quick pan sauce for tender chicken medallions. Although the dish can be made with whole chicken breasts, the medallions give more surface area to drench with the luscious sauce.

4 boneless, skinless chicken breast halves

Salt and freshly ground black pepper

All-purpose flour, for dredging

2 tablespoons olive oil

2 tablespoons unsalted butter

¼ cup minced shallots

1 teaspoon minced garlic

2 cups sliced cremini or button mushrooms (about 5 ounces)

¼ cup dry Marsala

1 cup Chicken Stock (page 277)

2 tablespoons chopped fresh sage

1 teaspoon soy sauce

1. Place each chicken breast half between 2 sheets of plastic wrap and pound with a meat pounder until ¼ inch thick. Cut each pounded breast into 3 or 4 pieces to form medallions. Sprinkle each medallion lightly with salt and pepper and dip both sides in the flour, to coat.

2. In large, nonreactive sauté pan set over medium-high heat, heat the olive oil until it ripples. Sauté the chicken medallions until lightly browned and cooked through, about 1 minute on each side. Remove the cooked medallions to a plate and tent with foil to keep warm.

3. Add the butter to the pan and melt over medium heat. Add the shallots and cook for 1 minute. Add the garlic and cook for 3 minutes more. Add the mushrooms and ¼ teaspoon salt; cook until the mushrooms soften, about 4 minutes. Add the Marsala and boil until reduced by half. Add the chicken stock and boil until reduced to a consistency that will coat the back of a spoon, about 5 minutes. Remove from the heat and stir in the sage and soy sauce.

4. Divide the chicken medallions among 4 warmed plates and top with the sauce. We recommend serving this dish with Broccoli Risotto (page 167) and Green Beans with Onions (page 203).

Smoked Chicken in Rosemary Cream with Bow-Tie Pasta {Serves 4 to 6}

When this many toothsome ingredients are combined, the meal is guaranteed to be a smash hit. If you're not a rosemary fan, try flavoring the cream with basil, thyme, or oregano instead. The rosemary cream and the caramelized onions can be prepared 1 day in advance. This makes the final assembly quite simple

¼ cup unsalted butter

4 cups thinly sliced white onions

ROSEMARY CREAM

2 cups heavy cream

½ small yellow onion, peeled

3 sprigs (6 inches) fresh rosemary

1 bay leaf

5 black peppercorns

2 whole garlic cloves, peeled

1 pound dried bow-tie pasta

1 tablespoon olive oil

2 tablespoons minced garlic

3 cups coarsely chopped broccoli rabe (see note below)

1 tablespoon chopped fresh rosemary

4 skinless, boneless smoked chicken breast halves, cut into bite-sized chunks

1 cup sun-dried tomatoes, rehydrated and thinly sliced (see note, page 127)

½ cup freshly grated Parmesan cheese

¼ cup coarsely chopped walnuts, toasted (see note, page 144)

1 teaspoon salt

1 teaspoon freshly ground black pepper

1. Caramelize the white onions: Heat the butter in a large sauté pan set over medium heat. Add the white onions and cook until golden brown and caramelized, stirring occasionally for 30 minutes. Reserve.

2. Meanwhile, prepare the Rosemary Cream: combine the cream, yellow onion, rosemary sprigs, bay leaf, peppercorns, and garlic cloves in another saucepan set over medium heat. Bring to a simmer, reduce the heat to low and simmer gently for 30 minutes. Strain the cream and discard the solids. Keep warm until ready to serve. Otherwise, cool to room temperature, cover, and refrigerate overnight.

3. When ready to serve, bring a large pot of salted water to a boil over high heat. Cook the pasta until just firm to the bite, about 10 minutes. Drain and reserve.

4. In a large, nonreactive saucepan or sauté pan set over medium heat, heat the olive oil until it ripples. Add the minced garlic and cook for 2 minutes. Add the broccoli rabe and cook, stirring constantly, for 3 minutes more. Add the reserved rosemary cream, cooked pasta, chopped rosemary, chicken, onions, sun-dried tomatoes, cheese, walnuts, salt, and pepper. Toss to combine, and cook, stirring, until just heated through, 4 to 5 minutes. Serve immediately on warmed large plates.

COOKING WITH BROCCOLI RABE

Broccoli rabe (pronounced *rob*) has long and slender stalks with broccoli-like leaves and buds at the top. Oddly enough it tastes nothing like broccoli; its flavor is assertively bitter and will surprise you if you've never tried it before. It's easy to develop a taste for it since it adds a sharp note of contrast to any dish. Cut broccoli rabe into 2-inch pieces and use it the same way you'd use any braising green.

Mediterranean Fried Chicken with Artichoke Salad {Serves 4}

We coat tender chicken breasts with Parmesan cheese and bread crumbs before cooking them up golden brown in a splash of light olive oil. The results are crisp and tasty—you won't even miss the skin! Served with a salad of artichoke hearts, tomatoes, olives, and fresh basil, this dish is Mediterranean in flavor, style, and healthful attitude.

ARTICHOKE SALAD

1 cup (about 2 jars) store-bought marinated artichoke hearts, drained

3 plum tomatoes, cut into thin rounds

$\frac{1}{2}$ cup sliced and pitted kalamata olives

$\frac{1}{4}$ cup tightly packed basil leaves, thinly sliced

1 teaspoon minced garlic

$\frac{1}{4}$ cup extra-virgin olive oil

Juice of $\frac{1}{2}$ lemon

$\frac{1}{2}$ teaspoon red wine vinegar

$\frac{1}{2}$ teaspoon freshly ground black pepper

CHICKEN

1 cup fine, dry bread crumbs

1 cup freshly grated Parmesan cheese or Pecorino Romano

$\frac{1}{2}$ teaspoon salt

$\frac{1}{2}$ teaspoon freshly ground black pepper

2 eggs

4 boneless, skinless chicken breast halves

Olive oil, for frying

1. Prepare the salad: Combine the artichoke hearts, tomatoes, olives, basil, garlic, olive oil, lemon juice, vinegar, and pepper in a nonreactive bowl and toss to combine. Cover and refrigerate for 1 hour to allow the flavors to blend. Bring to room temperature before serving.

2. Prepare the chicken: Combine the bread crumbs, cheese, salt, and pepper in a mixing bowl. Whisk the eggs in a separate bowl. Dip each chicken breast half in the eggs and then in the bread crumb mixture.

3. In a large skillet set over medium heat, heat $\frac{1}{4}$ inch of olive oil until it ripples. Add the chicken breasts and sauté until golden brown and cooked through, about 6 minutes on each side. Drain on paper towels. Serve hot, topped with the artichoke salad and alongside Zucchini with White Beans and Mint (page 205), if desired.

Spicy Chèvre-stuffed Chicken Breasts with Roasted Corn Salsa {Serves 4}

The sun-drenched colors and flavors of the Southwest are displayed in this simple, tasty stuffed chicken breast that we serve with our Roasted Corn Salsa. This dish is also good accompanied by Maple-mashed Sweet Potatoes (page 197) and Sugar Snap Peas Sautéed with Scallions (page 201).

ROASTED CORN SALSA

1½ cups (about 2 ears) fresh corn kernels

1 red bell pepper, finely diced

1 green bell pepper, finely diced

1 jalapeño pepper, seeded and minced

½ cup minced red onion

4 tablespoons olive oil

1 garlic clove, minced

Juice and minced zest of 2 limes

Juice of 1 orange

2 tablespoons chopped fresh cilantro leaves and stems

¼ teaspoon salt

STUFFING

4 tablespoons olive oil

⅓ cup minced yellow onion

1 tablespoon minced garlic

2 teaspoons New Mexican chili powder (see note, page 130)

1 teaspoon ground cumin

1 tablespoon fresh orange juice

6 ounces (about ¾ cup) unaged chèvre, crumbled

1 scallion, thinly sliced

1 tablespoon chopped fresh cilantro leaves and stems (see note, page 158)

4 boneless, skinless chicken breast halves

Salt and freshly ground black pepper

1. Prepare the salsa: Preheat the broiler. Combine the corn, bell peppers, jalapeño, onion, and 2 tablespoons of the olive oil in a large bowl; mix well. Spread the oiled vegetables in a single layer on a baking sheet. Broil, stirring occasionally, until the vegetables start to brown, about 10 minutes. Remove the roasted vegetables to a mixing bowl.

2. Stir in the remaining 2 tablespoons oil, the garlic, lime juice and zest, orange juice, cilantro, and salt. Mix well to combine. Reserve, or cover and refrigerate for up to 1 day.

3. In a large nonreactive sauté pan set over medium heat, heat 2 tablespoons of the olive oil until it ripples. Add the onion and cook for 1 minute. Add the garlic and cook for 4 minutes more. Add the chili powder and cumin and cook for 1 minute. Transfer the mixture to a mixing bowl.

4. Pour the orange juice into the sauté pan and swirl to loosen any spices that adhere to the pan. Pour the mixture onto the spiced onions. Add the chèvre, scallion, cilantro, and ½ teaspoon salt; stir well to combine thoroughly. (The stuffing can be made up to 4 days ahead to this point and kept refrigerated.)

5. Preheat the oven to 400°F.

6. With a sharp paring knife, cut a pocket 2 inches long and about 1½ inches wide in the thickest part of each chicken breast. Using a small spoon or your fingers, stuff each chicken breast with one-quarter of the chèvre stuffing. Season both sides of the breasts with salt and pepper.

7. In a large ovenproof skillet set over high heat, heat the remaining 2 tablespoons oil until it ripples. Add the stuffed breasts and cook on the stovetop until they begin to brown on one side, about 2 minutes. Carefully turn the breasts over with a spatula. Place the skillet in the oven and bake until cooked through, about 8 minutes. Serve hot, topped with the warm Roasted Corn Salsa.

Spinach- and Ricotta-stuffed Chicken Breasts with Sun-dried Tomato–Olive Butter {Serves 6}

It isn't far-fetched to say that stuffing chicken breasts can be a form of creative expression. Just open your refrigerator, take a long, thoughtful look inside, and then make the stuffing by combining a few ingredients you're in the mood for. Presto! A quick and stylish dinner expressive of your whim. In this recipe, our spinach and ricotta stuffing is bound with an egg to keep it from loosening up while cooking. To make the chicken breasts extra-flavorful and moist, we top them with a zesty compound butter flecked with sun-dried tomatoes, kalamata olives, and minced lemon.

8 ounces (1 cup) Sun-dried Tomato–Olive Butter (page 287)

3 tablespoons olive oil

2 slices bacon, minced

1/3 cup minced white onion

2 teaspoons minced garlic

2 cups tightly packed, washed, and stemmed spinach leaves, finely chopped

1 tablespoon water

3/4 cup ricotta cheese

3 tablespoons freshly grated Parmesan cheese

1 large egg, beaten

1 teaspoon fresh lemon juice

1/4 teaspoon salt

Pinch of freshly ground black pepper

Pinch of freshly grated (or ground) nutmeg

6 boneless, skinless chicken breast halves

1. Make the Sun-dried Tomato–Olive Butter.

2. Heat 1 tablespoon of the olive oil in a large, nonreactive sauté pan set over medium heat, until it ripples. Add the bacon and cook until it renders its fat and browns, 6 to 7 minutes. Remove the bacon from the pan with a slotted spoon and reserve.

3. Add the onion cook for 1 minute. Add the garlic and cook for 4 minutes more. Add the spinach and water and cook until the spinach wilts and softens and the water evaporates, 3 to 4 minutes. Remove from the heat. When the spinach is cool enough to handle, squeeze out all of the moisture with your hands.

4. Combine the reserved bacon, chopped spinach mixture, ricotta, Parmesan, egg, lemon juice, salt, pepper, and nutmeg in a bowl; mix well.

5. Preheat the oven to 400°F.

6. With a sharp paring knife, cut a pocket 2 inches long and about 1½ inches wide in the thickest part of each breast half. Using a small spoon or your fingers, stuff 2 to 3 tablespoons of the filling into each breast. Season both sides of the breasts with salt and pepper.

USING COMPOUND BUTTERS
Compound butters are a wonderful way to add flavor to grilled or seared meats and fish, vegetables, and pasta. They're easy to make; just soften some butter and add a few flavorful ingredients—chopped herbs, anchovies, capers, or anything that strikes your fancy. Then roll it up in a log and refrigerate until firm. Slice off a few medallions to top your dinner, or freeze for up to 2 months.

(continued)

7. In a large ovenproof skillet set over high heat, heat the remaining 2 tablespoons oil until it ripples. Add the chicken breasts and cook on one side until they begin to brown, about 2 minutes. Carefully turn the breasts over with a spatula. Place the pan in the oven and bake until cooked through, about 8 minutes.

8. Top each chicken breast half with a few medallions of the Sun-dried Tomato–Olive Butter. Serve with Chèvre-Rosemary-Garlic Mashed Potatoes (page 192), Sautéed Green Beans with Onions (page 203), and Balsamic-Braised Kale (page 203).

REHYDRATING SUN-DRIED TOMATOES

Unless they are packed in oil, sun-dried tomatoes need to be rehydrated. Otherwise, they're difficult to cut and tough to eat. We like to save the liquid to add flavor to soups, stocks, sauces and vinaigrettes. Place the sun-dried tomatoes in a nonreactive saucepan; add cold water just to cover. Bring to a boil over medium-high heat. Remove from the heat and set aside to steep for 10 minutes. Strain the tomatoes, reserving the liquid separately. Let cool to room temperature and use tomatoes immediately or cover and refrigerate for up to 1 week. Refrigerate the sun-dried tomato liquid for up to 1 week.

Roast Cornish Hens with White Truffle Jus {Serves 4}

Tiny Cornish hens make an exquisite special-occasion dish that's perfect for entertaining. In this preparation we scent the birds with thyme and enrich the sauce of the pan drippings with the intoxicating oil of white truffles. You'll think it's heaven-sent.

---

4 Cornish game hens

Salt and freshly ground black pepper

1 large carrot, diced

1 celery rib, diced

1 leek, trimmed and split lengthwise, washed well, the white part cut into 1-inch pieces

5 tablespoons unsalted butter, melted

1 teaspoon dried thyme

1 cup dry white wine

4 tablespoons cold unsalted butter, cubed

1 tablespoon white truffle oil

1. Preheat the oven to 450°F.

2. Rinse the hens inside and out and pat dry. Reserve the giblets. Cut the tip joint off each wing and reserve. Salt and pepper the birds inside and out.

3. Truss the birds: Cut a $^1\!/_2$ inch slit on the right side of the bird in the fleshy flap of skin located just above the tail. Cross the left leg over the right and carefully insert it through the incision so that each hen's legs are tightly crossed. If the skin tears and does not hold, tie the legs together with kitchen string. Tuck the wings behind the back of the bird.

4. In a roasting pan, make a nest of the carrot, celery, leek, wing tips, and giblets. Arrange the birds on top. Combine the melted butter and thyme in a small bowl. With a pastry brush, baste the birds with the mixture.

5. Place the birds in the oven and roast for 15 minutes.

6. Reduce the oven temperature to 350°F. Roast the birds for 30 minutes more.

7. Pour the wine over the birds and roast until the juices run clear when the thickest part of the thigh is pierced with a fork, about 15 minutes more. If the birds are not a beautiful golden brown color when finished, place under the broiler for a minute to crisp and brown the skin.

BUYING WHITE TRUFFLE OIL

White truffle oil is a wonderful way to experience white truffles without having to mortgage your house. It is becoming increasingly available these days in specialty food stores, although you should select a bottle with care as some brands can be disappointing. Look for oils that contain white truffle extract or white truffle essence; those that contain white truffle aroma have chemically reproduced the smell of the truffle without using any of the truffle itself. Then, ask the merchant if you can smell the oil before you buy it. If it smells like plain olive oil, you don't want it; but if you smell an intoxicating woodsy, garlicky aroma, then you've found what you're looking for.

{continued}

8. Remove the birds from the pan. Strain the liquid into a small saucepan, discarding the vegetables and giblets. Ladle off the fat and discard. Place the saucepan over high heat and boil to reduce the liquid to $\frac{1}{3}$ cup. Remove the pan from the heat and whisk in the cold, cubed butter and white truffle oil. Season to taste with salt and freshly ground black pepper.

9. Serve each hen topped with the White Truffle Jus. We like to serve the hens perched on a nest of Sautéed Greens (Swiss chard) and Garlic (page 202) or on a mound of Lavender-Honey Roasted Butternut Squash (page 198).

Chili-rubbed Duck Breasts with Sun-dried Cherry Glaze {Serves 4}

Inspired by a trip to Santa Fe, New Mexico, where native grains thrive, fruits and vegetables are dried in the sun, and game is abundant, this is the most talked-about duck dish we've ever done. Game meats have an affinity for sweet-tart sauces, particularly this one—its rich caramel color and plump sun-dried cherries enhance and tame even the wildest beast.

SUN-DRIED CHERRY GLAZE

1/3 cup (about 2 ounces) sun-dried cherries

1/3 cup ruby port

1/4 cup sherry vinegar

1 tablespoon packed light brown sugar

1 tablespoon minced shallots

5 black peppercorns

1 bay leaf

1 cup Veal Demi-Glace (page 279)

1/2 teaspoon salt

1/4 teaspoon freshly ground black pepper

MARINADE

3 tablespoons New Mexican chili powder
  (see note below)

1 1/2 tablespoons honey

1 1/2 tablespoons cider vinegar

1 teaspoon soy sauce

4 skinless, boneless duck breast halves

2 tablespoons olive oil, if cooking
  in a grill pan

1. Make the Sun-dried Cherry Glaze: Combine the cherries, port, vinegar, sugar, shallots, peppercorns, and bay leaf in a small, non-reactive saucepan and bring to a boil over medium heat. Reduce the heat to low and simmer until the liquid evaporates, about 5 minutes.

2. Stir in the Veal Demi-Glace and simmer for 2 minutes. Stir in the salt and pepper; taste for seasoning. Remove the bay leaf. Serve hot, or let cool to room temperature, cover, and refrigerate for up to 1 week. Spoon off any congealed fat that rises to the top and reheat before serving.

3. Prepare the duck breasts: Combine the chili powder, honey, vinegar, and soy sauce in a small bowl and mix well. Place the duck breasts in a shallow dish and rub them with the marinade. Cover and refrigerate for at least 2 hours or up to overnight.

4. Prepare a charcoal grill, or pour the oil onto a stovetop grill pan and set over high heat until smoking.

5. Grill the duck breasts to the desired doneness, about 5 minutes on each side for medium-rare. If you like your duck cooked a little more, finish the breasts in a 400°F oven for a few minutes.

6. Serve the duck at once, topped with the warm Sun-dried Cherry Glaze. We like to serve this dish with Native Grains Pilaf (page 208) and Sugar Snap Peas Sautéed with Scallions (page 201).

OTHER WAYS TO DO IT

Try grilling the duck breasts over a mesquite or charcoal fire. If you can't find duck breasts, try roasted or smoked turkey, game hens, venison, goose, or pork instead.

ABOUT NEW MEXICAN CHILI POWDER

Most chili powders found in the supermarket contain dried chiles as well as salt, garlic, oregano, cumin, coriander, and cloves. The chili powder called for in this recipe is simply dried ground New Mexican chiles. New Mexican chili powder can be found in many spice stores and specialty markets; if you can't find it, regular chili powder will do.

Roasted Duck with Native Grains, Brandied Fruits, and Pistachio Stuffing {Serves 8}

Although we'd love to, it isn't practical to serve whole stuffed birds like turkey or duck or goose at the restaurant. They're really best suited for family-style meals. Thankfully, we do get to prepare these succulent roast ducklings stuffed with jewel-toned dried fruits, pistachio nuts, and native grains each year for the holiday staff party. The crisp skin of duck is a decadent indulgence, and this bird makes a festive meal for large holiday gatherings.

$\frac{1}{3}$ cup dried black currants

$\frac{1}{3}$ cup sun-dried cherries

$\frac{1}{3}$ cup quartered dried apricots

$\frac{3}{4}$ cup brandy

2 tablespoons unsalted butter

1 cup minced yellow onion

$\frac{1}{2}$ cup minced celery

$1\frac{1}{2}$ cups cooked wild rice, at room temperature (see note, page 215)

$1\frac{1}{2}$ cups cooked hominy, at room temperature (see note, page 215)

1 pound unsalted pistachio nuts, shelled, toasted (see note, page 144), and coarsely chopped (about 1 cup)

2 teaspoons chopped fresh thyme leaves

1 teaspoon salt

$\frac{1}{4}$ teaspoon freshly ground black pepper

2 ducklings (each about 4 pounds), washed and patted dry

1. In a small bowl, combine the currants, cherries, apricots, and brandy. Set aside to plump for 1 hour.

2. Melt the butter in a large sauté pan set over medium-high heat. Add the onion and cook until translucent, about 5 minutes. Add the celery and cook for 2 minutes. Remove from the heat.

3. Combine the cooked onion and celery, plumped fruits, wild rice, hominy, and pistachios in a large bowl. Add the thyme, salt, and pepper; mix well to combine. (The stuffing can be made up to 2 days in advance; let cool to room temperature, refrigerate, and bring back to room temperature before stuffing the ducks.)

4. Preheat the oven to 400°F.

5. Prick the skin of the ducks all over with the tip of a knife or fork, being careful not to pierce the meat. Season the ducks inside and out with additional salt and pepper. Divide the stuffing in half and loosely stuff each duck cavity. (If you have any extra stuffing, place it in a buttered ovenproof dish and bake until golden on top.) Tightly truss the legs with kitchen string.

6. Place the ducks, breast sides down, on a rack set in a roasting pan; add $\frac{1}{2}$ inch of water to the pan. Roast for 30 minutes.

7. Turn the ducks breast sides up and roast until the thigh juices run clear when pierced with a fork, about 45 minutes more.

8. Remove the stuffing from the ducks. Carve the birds and serve each portion with some of the stuffing.

9. If desired, serve with Winter Herb Pesto (page 292), Caraway-Roasted Vegetables (page 199), and a simple watercress salad.

Braised Rabbit with Tomatoes, Pancetta, and Green Peppercorns {Serves 4}

This is a wintry, soul-warming dish that's so delicious it quells hesitation in those with more affection than appetite for our furred friends. The rabbit slowly simmers in a rich tomato sauce studded with piquant green peppercorns and pancetta until it falls from the bones to melt in your mouth.

$\frac{1}{2}$ cup all-purpose flour

3 tablespoons dried thyme

1 fresh or frozen rabbit (about 3$\frac{1}{2}$ pounds),
   cut into 6 or 7 pieces

1 teaspoon freshly ground black pepper

$\frac{1}{2}$ teaspoon salt

$\frac{1}{4}$ cup olive oil

$\frac{1}{2}$ cup finely diced pancetta (or bacon)

1$\frac{1}{2}$ cups minced yellow onions

1 carrot, finely diced

1 celery rib, finely diced

1 cup ruby port

3 cups Chicken Stock (page 277)

2$\frac{1}{2}$ cups chopped canned tomatoes

$\frac{1}{4}$ cup fresh thyme sprigs

2 tablespoons minced garlic

1 tablespoon drained brined
   green peppercorns

1 bay leaf

1. Preheat the oven to 350°F.

2. Combine the flour and 1 tablespoon of the dried thyme in a small bowl. Pat the rabbit pieces dry; season lightly with the pepper and salt. Dust each piece with the flour mixture until lightly coated.

3. In a large, nonreactive, ovenproof Dutch oven set over high heat, heat the oil until very hot. Add the rabbit pieces and cook until deep golden brown, about 4 minutes on each side. Remove the rabbit and reserve.

4. Pour off the excess oil from the pan. Add the pancetta and cook over medium heat until it is crisp and has rendered most of its fat, about 5 minutes. Add the onions, carrot, and celery; cook until the vegetables begin to soften, about 5 minutes. Add the port and simmer for 2 minutes.

5. Add the remaining 2 tablespoons dried thyme, the chicken stock, chopped tomatoes, fresh thyme, garlic, green peppercorns and bay leaf. Bring the sauce to a simmer. Add the rabbit pieces and bring to a simmer again.

6. Cover with a lid and braise in the oven until the rabbit is fork-tender and falling off the bone, about 1 hour. Remove the bay leaf.

7. Divide the rabbit among 4 warmed plates and top with the green peppercorn sauce. If desired, serve with Herbed Parmesan Polenta (page 210) and Sautéed Greens (Swiss chard) and Garlic (page 202).

OTHER WAYS TO DO IT
Try this with chicken or duck—they are wonderful slow-cooked.

CHOOSING PEPPERCORNS BY COLOR
The differences of hue and flavor among peppercorns have to do with different stages of ripeness. Green peppercorns are unripe berries that have been picked while still soft and then packed in brine. Black peppercorns have ripened longer on the vine. Once harvested, they're dried until the outer skin shrivels and turns black. White peppercorns (which we find less flavorful) are berries that have been fully ripened, skinned, and dried.

Chilled Roast Beef Tenderloin with Horseradish Crème Fraîche {Serves 6}

Each year on Bastille Day—July 14—we showcase this rare-roasted beef tenderloin topped with Horseradish Crème Fraîche as part of an elegant outdoor soirée celebrating French Independence. Ideal for summer entertaining, this dish can be roasted a day in advance and chilled. Simply slice the roast and arrange on a platter an hour before your guests arrive. Any leftovers makes knockout sandwiches! Anyone sensitive to hot food can adjust horseradish amounts, to taste.

BEEF

½ cup Dijon mustard

½ cup dry red wine

2 tablespoons fresh chopped rosemary leaves

1 tablespoon minced garlic

¼ cup minced shallots

½ teaspoon freshly ground black pepper

¼ cup olive oil

1 center-cut beef tenderloin (about 2 pounds)

HORSERADISH CRÈME FRAÎCHE

1 cup Crème Fraîche (page 288) or
  sour cream

2 teaspoons Worcestershire sauce

¼ cup grated fresh horseradish (see note
  below) or prepared horseradish to taste

¼ teaspoon Tabasco sauce, or to taste

¼ teaspoon freshly ground black pepper

¾ teaspoon salt

1. Marinate the beef: Combine the mustard, wine, rosemary, garlic, shallots, pepper, and olive oil in a small bowl; whisk together. Place the beef in a shallow baking dish and rub with the marinade to coat thoroughly. Cover and refrigerate for 2 hours or up to overnight.

2. Preheat the oven to 450°F.

3. Prepare the Horseradish Crème Fraîche : Whisk together the crème fraîche, Worcestershire, horseradish, Tabasco, pepper, and salt in a small bowl. Cover and chill. (The sauce can be made up to 3 days in advance.)

4. Place the beef on a rack set in a roasting pan. Roast in the middle of the oven until medium-rare, 35 to 40 minutes. An instant-read thermometer should read 135°F when inserted in the middle of the roast. Let cool to room temperature. Cover and refrigerate for at least 2 hours or until well chilled.

5. Thinly slice the beef across the grain; serve with the chilled Horseradish Crème Fraîche. We enjoy this dish with Dijon Potato Salad (page 195), chilled asparagus, and a country-style loaf of French bread.

OTHER WAYS TO DO IT

The beef can also be grilled over a charcoal fire and served hot.

MEATS

USING FRESH HORSERADISH

Freshly grated horseradish is a treat not to be missed. Look for its lengthy gnarled brown roots in your supermarket. It is available all year long, but you'll find it most often in the spring and fall. To use, peel off the tough outer skin with a vegetable peeler and then grate it on a box grater. Sprinkle the freshly grated horseradish over sliced meats, mashed potatoes, or green salads and incorporate it in sauces, vinaigrettes, and Bloody Marys.

Grilled Beef Tenderloin with Balsamic-Pancetta Glaze {Serves 4}

We serve this elegant dish on New Year's Eve. Its festive colors and assertive flavors can dazzle even the most holiday-party-weary diner.

BALSAMIC-PANCETTA GLAZE

2 tablespoons olive oil

2 tablespoons finely diced pancetta or bacon

2 tablespoons finely diced carrot

2 tablespoons finely diced celery

2 tablespoons finely diced red bell pepper

2 tablespoons minced shallot

1 tablespoon all-purpose flour

¼ cup balsamic vinegar

1½ cups Veal Demi-Glace (page 279)

¼ teaspoon salt

BEEF

4 beef tenderloin steaks (about 6 ounces each)

Salt

Freshly ground black pepper

1. Prepare a charcoal grill or preheat the broiler.

2. Heat the oil in a nonreactive saucepan. Add the pancetta and cook over medium heat until the fat renders and the meat is crisp and brown, 5 to 7 minutes. Add the carrot, celery, bell pepper, and shallot and sauté until crisp-tender, about 2 minutes. Sprinkle the flour over the vegetables and cook, stirring constantly, for 1 minute. Stir in the balsamic vinegar and cook for 1 minute. Stir in the Veal Demi-Glace and simmer for 5 minutes. Add ¼ teaspoon salt and taste for seasoning. Serve the glaze hot, or let it cool to room temperature, cover, and refrigerate for up to 1 week. Spoon off any congealed fat that rises to the top and reheat before serving.

3. Season the steaks on both sides with salt and pepper. Grill over a solid bed of glowing charcoal for 5 to 6 minutes on each side, or to the desired doneness. If broiling the steaks, broil for about 6 to 8 minutes on each side.

4. Serve the steaks hot, topped with the glaze. We like to serve the steak atop a Roasted Red Pepper and Potato Cake (page 191) and a bed of wilted spinach.

MAKING YOUR OWN VEAL DEMI-GLACE

Many of the sauces we serve with meat are based on Veal Demi-Glace (page 279), which is made by reducing veal stock to a thick sauce-like consistency. There is no way around the fact that making demi-glace takes time (it's more precious than gold in our kitchen). The stock has to simmer for many hours and then reduce for many hours more. It does freeze well however, so if you have a day to spend around the house, you can make enough demi-glace to last you many months and to make fabulous "restaurant-style" sauces.

Betty's Beef Kabobs {Serves 4}

When Judy first started the White Dog Cafe, she wanted to serve the foods she relished as a child. Her mother Betty Wicks, a great cook and a renowned hostess, gave her this old family recipe for beef kabobs when the only kitchen at the Cafe was a charcoal grill in the backyard. Customers loved it then and they still ask for it today. Betty's Kabobs remain a summer barbecue classic.

MARINADE

1 cup vegetable oil

$^3/_4$ cup soy sauce

$^1/_2$ cup fresh lemon juice

$^1/_2$ cup Dijon mustard

1 tablespoon freshly ground black pepper

2 garlic cloves, minced

$1^1/_2$ pounds beef sirloin, trimmed of excess fat and cut into 1-inch cubes

16 mushroom caps

1 small red bell pepper, cut into $1^1/_2$-inch squares

1 small yellow bell pepper, cut into $1^1/_2$-inch squares

1 small white onion, cut into $1^1/_2$-inch pieces

8 cherry tomatoes

8 long metal skewers, or 8 wooden skewers soaked in water for at least 1 hour

1. Prepare the marinade: Whisk together the oil, soy sauce, lemon juice, mustard, black pepper, and garlic in a large bowl.

2. Add the cubed meat and mushroom caps to the bowl and toss to coat with the marinade. Cover and refrigerate for 4 to 6 hours.

3. Prepare a charcoal grill or preheat the broiler.

4. Evenly divide the marinated meat, mushrooms, and all of the remaining vegetables among the 8 skewers. Transfer the marinade to a saucepan and bring to a boil for 1 minute. Reserve the marinade.

5. Grill the kabobs over a solid bed of glowing coals, turning frequently and basting with the reserved marinade, for 5 to 8 minutes for medium-rare. To broil the kabobs, set them a few inches from the broiler and turn frequently for 8 to 10 minutes. Serve hot, with Lemon-Garlic Rice (page 210) and, if desired, grilled corn with our Cumin Butter (page 286).

OTHER WAYS TO DO IT

Try substituting chicken, turkey, swordfish, or shrimp for the beef. Adjust cooking times as necessary.

Rosemary-Mustard London Broil with Wild Mushroom Glaze {Serves 6}

We've heard that Americans are moving away from red meat, but this dish remains the single most-ordered item on our menu. Our customers find it irresistible. Maybe it's the rich marinade, which is terrific on any red meat as well as chicken, or perhaps it's the wonderfully rich, woodsy glaze made flavorful with wild mushrooms and a dash of Worcestershire. It could be simply that Americans love beef.

MARINADE

1/4 cup Dijon mustard

2 shallots, chopped

1/2 jalapeño pepper, seeded

2 tablespoons chopped fresh
  rosemary leaves

2 tablespoons soy sauce

1 teaspoon freshly ground black pepper

3/4 cup olive oil

3 pounds flank steak, trimmed of all fat

WILD MUSHROOM GLAZE

2 tablespoons unsalted butter

2 tablespoons minced shallot

2 cups sliced wild mushrooms (about 5
  ounces), such as shiitake, chanterelle,
  or oyster

3/4 cup dry red wine

5 black peppercorns

1 allspice berry

1 bay leaf

1 1/2 cups Veal Demi-Glace (page 279)

1 tablespoon Worcestershire sauce

1/4 teaspoon salt

1/2 teaspoon freshly ground black pepper

1. Prepare the marinade: Combine the mustard, shallots, jalapeño, rosemary, soy sauce, and pepper in a food processor. Blend to a smooth paste, about 1 minute. With the motor running, slowly pour in the oil to form a thick emulsion. (This marinade can be made ahead and kept refrigerated for up to 1 week.)

2. Marinate the meat: Rub the meat with the marinade and place in a shallow baking dish. Cover with plastic and refrigerate for at least 8 hours and up to 2 days. The texture of flank steak benefits from long marinating.

3. Prepare the glaze: Melt the butter in a small, nonreactive saucepan set over medium-high heat. Add the shallot and sauté until translucent, about 3 minutes. Add the mushrooms and sauté until they release their juices and cook dry, about 10 minutes.

4. Stir in the wine, peppercorns, allspice, and bay leaf. Reduce the heat to medium and simmer until almost all of the liquid evaporates, about 5 minutes.

5. Stir in the Veal Demi-Glace and Worcestershire and simmer for 2 minutes. Remove and discard whole spices and bay leaf. Season with the salt and pepper. Serve immediately or let cool to room temperature, cover, and refrigerate for up to 1 week. (Reheat before serving.)

6. When ready to serve, preheat the broiler and a broiler pan.

IDENTIFYING TRUE FLANK STEAK

The term London broil refers to flank steak, but because of its popularity (and the fact that each animal has only two flanks) butchers have creatively named some other less desirable cuts of meat London broil as well. Ask your butcher to make sure that what you're buying is flank steak so you won't be disappointed.

{continued}

7. Broil the steak until medium-rare, about 5 minutes on each side. Let rest for 5 minutes.

8. Slice the steak as thinly as possible against the grain. Serve warm, with the Wild Mushroom Glaze. We like to serve this dish with sides of White Cheddar and Red-Skinned Potato Gratin (page 189) and Green Beans with Onions (page 203).

OTHER WAYS TO DO IT
If there are no wild mushrooms available, substitute domestic mushrooms. If you like, grill the flank steak rather than broil it.

Seared Peppered Sirloin with Red Wine–Chèvre Glaze {Serves 4}

Since we're not known as a steak house, it is always surprising when guests tell us this is the best steak in town, and we gladly accept their accolades. The glaze is what transforms this steak into something unforgettable; it's savory with lots of freshly cracked black pepper, tangy chèvre, and red wine.

RED WINE–CHÈVRE GLAZE

2 tablespoons minced shallot

5 black peppercorns

1 bay leaf

1 allspice berry

1 cup dry red wine

1½ cups Veal Demi-Glace (page 279)

3 tablespoons crumbled unaged chèvre

1½ teaspoons freshly ground black pepper

¼ teaspoon salt

STEAKS

4 sirloin steaks (each about 8 ounces) trimmed of all excess fat

Salt and freshly ground black pepper

1 tablespoon olive oil

1. Make the glaze: In a small, nonreactive saucepan, combine the shallot, peppercorns, bay leaf, allspice, and red wine and bring to a boil over medium heat. Reduce the heat and simmer until most of the liquid evaporates, about 5 minutes.

2. Stir in the demi-glace and simmer for 5 minutes. Add the chèvre and whisk over low heat until incorporated and smooth. Strain through a fine sieve and stir in the pepper and salt. Keep warm or let cool to room temperature, cover, and refrigerate for up to 1 week. Reheat before serving.

3. Cook the steaks: Season the steaks on both sides with a little salt and lots of freshly ground black pepper. Heat the oil until very hot in a large cast-iron skillet set over high heat. Add the steaks and sear for 3 minutes on each side or to the desired doneness.

4. Serve the steaks topped with the glaze. We like to serve them with our Chèvre-Rosemary-Garlic Mashed Potatoes (page 192) and Sautéed Greens with Garlic (page 170).

SEARING MEAT

Searing food in a home kitchen is always a bit more of a challenge than it is in a restaurant where a powerful ventilation system hangs above the stove to clear the air. To sear this steak properly, you must have a very hot pan with very hot (almost smoking) oil in it. When you add the steaks they will smoke and splatter, and if you're in a small apartment, might even set off your smoke alarm! We suggest opening the windows and turning on the vent if you have one or temporarily covering the smoke alarm with a cloth if you don't. The result is definitely worth a few smoky minutes; a succulent juicy steak with a crisp browned exterior.

Nicaraguan Braised Beef Shins {Serves 4 to 6}

We adopted this intensely flavored, slow-simmering, one-pot meal from the kitchen of our Nicaraguan sister restaurant, Selva Negra. There they serve a wide array of long-simmered stews that make use of inexpensive, less-tender cuts of meat. In this recipe, beef shins are rendered sublime by lengthy braising with beer, red beans, and smoky chipotle peppers.

2 teaspoons ground cumin

1½ teaspoons New Mexican chili powder
  (see note, page 130)

¼ teaspoon freshly ground black pepper

1¼ teaspoons salt

4 pounds beef shins, cut 1½ inches thick

½ cup yellow cornmeal

¼ cup olive oil

1 cup finely diced white onion

1 tablespoon minced garlic

2 teaspoons minced canned chipotle pepper
  in adobo (see note, page 107)

1 tablespoon tomato paste

1 cup diced red tomatoes

1 cup diced green tomatoes

1 cup diced green bell pepper

12 ounces (1½ cups) beer

1 cup water

1 teaspoon dried Mexican oregano
  (see note, page 78)

1 bay leaf

1 cup dried pinto or kidney beans,
  picked over for stones and rinsed well

Juice of ½ lime

1. Combine the cumin, chili powder, black pepper, and ¼ teaspoon of the salt in a small bowl; mix well. Rub the spice mixture over the beef shins and place them in a baking dish. Let rest at room temperature for 30 minutes.

2. Put the cornmeal in a shallow dish. Coat each of the beef shins evenly on all sides.

3. Heat the oil in a large, deep, preferably cast-iron Dutch oven or nonreactive casserole set over medium-high heat. Add the beef shins and brown for about 2 minutes on each side. Remove the browned meat and reserve. Add the onion and garlic and cook for 2 minutes. Add the chipotle pepper, tomato paste, and any spices left from the rub for the beef; cook for 1 minute. Add the red tomatoes, green tomatoes, and bell pepper and cook for 1 minute. Add the beer, water, oregano, bay leaf, beans, and the browned beef. Bring to a gentle simmer.

4. Cover and reduce the heat to low so that the liquid just simmers. Simmer gently until the beans are soft and the meat is fork-tender, about 2 hours. At the end of the cooking period there should not be much liquid left in the pan and the beans should form a thick sauce. If there is excess liquid, remove the meat and boil the mixture uncovered for a few minutes to reduce it. If there is too little liquid, add some water to loosen the sauce. Stir in the lime juice and the remaining 1 teaspoon salt.

5. Divide the beef among 4 warm plates; top with the sauce. If you like, serve with warm Corn, Cheddar, and Sun-dried Tomato Muffins (page 237).

OTHER WAYS TO DO IT

If green tomatoes are unavailable, substitute tomatillos or regular tomatoes. Feel free to cut down on the amount of chipotle peppers used if you want to tame the heat of this dish. Substitute Chicken Stock (page 277) for the beer if you want to avoid alcohol.

White Dog Cafe Layered Meat Loaf {Serves 6}

We keep our lunch menu at the White Dog Cafe on the lighter side, as many people don't like to eat a heavy meal in the middle of the day. However, some of our customers make a long commute from the suburbs to their jobs in the city, and without time for breakfast, they arrive at our doorstep starving. We've added some hearty lunches to accommodate their appetites and this meat loaf is always a sellout. It's great for dinner, too, or for a late-night meat loaf sandwich!

2 tablespoons olive oil

3 teaspoons minced garlic

2 cups sliced white mushrooms

Salt and freshly ground black pepper

2 tablespoons dry Marsala or dry white wine

4 cups tightly packed fresh spinach leaves, stemmed and well washed

1½ pounds lean ground veal

¼ cup minced yellow onion

¼ cup dry red wine

2 eggs, lightly beaten

½ cup fine, dry bread crumbs

2 tablespoons chopped fresh sage leaves

2 tablespoons chopped fresh parsley leaves

12 thin slices prosciutto

2 red bell peppers, roasted (see note below), peeled, seeded, and cut into thin strips

1. Preheat the oven to 350°F.

2. Heat 1 tablespoon of the olive oil in a nonreactive sauté pan set over medium heat. Add 1 teaspoon of the garlic and cook for 1 minute. Add the mushrooms, ¼ teaspoon salt, and ¼ teaspoon pepper and cook until the liquid from the mushrooms evaporates, about 10 minutes. Add the Marsala and cook until it evaporates, about 2 minutes. Reserve.

3. Heat the remaining 1 tablespoon olive oil in another nonreactive sauté pan set over medium heat. Add 1 teaspoon of the remaining garlic and cook for 1 minute. Add the spinach and cook until the spinach wilts, about 2 minutes. Remove to a colander and let cool to room temperature. Squeeze the excess moisture from the spinach.

4. Combine the veal, onion, red wine, eggs, bread crumbs, sage, parsley, ½ teaspoon salt, and the remaining 1 teaspoon garlic in a large bowl; mix well.

5. Line the inside of an 8 x 4-inch loaf pan with 11 slices of the prosciutto, allowing 2 inches of the ham to overhang on all sides.

6. Press one-quarter of the meat mixture into the bottom of the pan. With your fingers, make a shallow trench about 2 inches

ROASTING PEPPERS

Place the pepper in the flames of a gas burner set on high. Use tongs or a fork to rotate the pepper occasionally until all sides are evenly charred. The skin will turn entirely black in 15 minutes. Alternately, lightly oil the pepper and place on a baking sheet under a broiler. Roast, turning occasionally, until all sides are evenly charred. (The broiling method takes about 20 minutes.) Transfer the roasted pepper to a bowl and tightly cover with plastic wrap. Let sit for 10 minutes or until cool enough to handle. Scrape off all of the charred skin. Resist the temptation to rinse the pepper under running water to remove the skin; this rinses away much of its flavor. Remove the seeds and chop the pepper according to the recipe instructions.

{continued}

wide down the center of the pan. Press the spinach into the trench. Top the layer with one-third of the remaining meat. Make a trench in the middle of the meat and fill it with the mushrooms. Top with half of the remaining meat. Make another trench and fill it with the roasted peppers. Top with the remaining meat. Fold the prosciutto over the top of the meat loaf; arrange the remaining slice over the top to encase it entirely. Cover tightly with foil. Bake the meat loaf for 55 minutes.

7. Remove the foil. Bake uncovered for 10 minutes more.

8. Let rest for 5 minutes. Unmold the loaf onto a serving platter and cut into 1-inch-thick slices. We serve this dish with Rustic Tomato and Basil Sauce (page 290), Chèvre-Rosemary-Garlic Mashed Potatoes (page 192), and Green Beans with Onions (page 203).

Veal Chops Roasted with Mushrooms and Pine Nuts {Serves 4}

Organic, humanely raised veal is becoming more widely available, largely a result of consumer concern about modern farming methods. Your butcher can show you the difference between milk-fed veal, which is pale and lack-luster in flavor, and mother nursed, free-range grass-fed veal, which is rosy-pink and vastly more flavorful. This is a simple dish to prepare that yields a lush sauce—garlicky and lemony-tart.

$1/2$ whole lemon, seeded and finely minced

1 tablespoon minced garlic

1 teaspoon salt

$1/4$ teaspoon freshly ground black pepper

1 bay leaf, crumbled

1 cup dry white wine

$1/4$ cup plus 2 tablespoons extra-virgin olive oil

4 veal rib chops (about 8 ounces each)

20 domestic mushrooms, stems removed

$2^1/2$ tablespoons pine nuts

2 tablespoons minced fresh chives

1. Preheat the oven to 400°F.

2. Combine the lemon, garlic, salt, pepper, bay leaf, wine, and $1/4$ cup olive oil in a large bowl. Add the veal chops and turn to coat thoroughly with the marinade. Cover and set aside at room temperature for 30 minutes.

3. Transfer the chops to a plate. Add the mushroom caps to the marinade and toss gently.

4. Heat the remaining 2 tablespoons olive oil in a nonreactive large ovenproof skillet set over high heat. Add the chops and sear until browned, about 2 minutes on each side. Add the mushroom and marinade mixture to the skillet: sprinkle the pine nuts over the top. Roast in the upper third of the oven until just cooked through, usually about 10 minutes (depending upon the size of the chops). The meat should look slightly pink inside and appear juicy throughout.

5. Divide the veal chops and mushrooms among 4 warm plates. Add the chives to the sauce in the pan and bring to a simmer over medium heat. Spoon the sauce over the chops. Serve with buttered angel hair pasta and broccoli sautéed with sweet and hot peppers.

Sesame-roasted Pork Tenderloin with Ginger Glaze {Serves 6}

The menu at the Cafe changes every day so we can use fresh seasonal ingredients and keep the cooks and the customers intrigued with what we're serving. However some items are so popular that when we try to discontinue them and make something new, customer outrage forces them back on the menu. This Asian-inspired pork tenderloin with its rich ginger glaze is one of those dishes: a White Dog Cafe classic.

---

3 pork tenderloins (about 12 ounces each), trimmed of excess fat

1 cup Spicy Asian Marinade (page 289)

1 cup dry sherry

¼ whole lemon

2 tablespoons coarsely chopped fresh ginger

1 shallot, minced

5 black peppercorns

1 allspice berry

1 bay leaf

1½ cups Veal Demi-Glace (page 279)

1 tablespoon minced fresh ginger

¼ teaspoon salt

1. Place the pork tenderloins in a shallow dish and cover with the marinade. Cover and refrigerate for at least 4 hours and up to 12 hours.

2. In a nonreactive saucepan, combine the sherry, lemon, coarsely chopped ginger, shallot, peppercorns, allspice, and bay leaf. Bring to a boil over low heat. Simmer until most of the liquid evaporates, about 10 minutes.

3. Add the Veal Demi-Glace and simmer for 2 minutes. Strain the glaze through a fine sieve into another nonreactive saucepan; discard the solids.

4. Stir the minced ginger and salt into the strained glaze. Keep warm or let cool to room temperature, cover, and refrigerate for up to 1 week. (Spoon off any congealed fat that rises to the surface and reheat before serving.)

5. Preheat the oven to 400°F.

6. Place the marinated tenderloins a few inches apart on a roasting pan. Roast in the center of the oven until a meat thermometer inserted in the thickest part of the meat reads 160°F, 12 to 15 minutes. Let the meat rest for 5 minutes.

7. Slice the pork into ¼-inch medallions. Fan the slices out on 6 warmed plates and top with the reserved Ginger Glaze. If you like, serve with Spicy Sweet Potato Chips (page 195) and Steamed Sesame Snow Peas (page 202) and garnish the plate with white and black sesame seeds, if desired.

OTHER WAYS TO DO IT
The pork is also terrific grilled. Try serving it with Stir-Fried Wild Rice (page 204) and Sesame-roasted Asparagus (page 204).

Center-cut Pork Chops with Gorgonzola-Walnut Stuffing and Ruby Port Glaze {Serves 6}

Succulent and juicy, these chops incorporate one of our favorite ingredient combinations: port, Gorgonzola, and walnuts. They are even more delicious when we know that the pork that we use comes from a farm where pigs are humanely raised and slaughtered.

RUBY PORT GLAZE

2 tablespoons unsalted butter

1 shallot, minced

1 small carrot, finely diced

1/2 celery rib, finely diced

1 bay leaf

5 black peppercorns

1 fresh thyme sprig

1/3 cup red wine vinegar

1 cup ruby port

1 1/2 cups Veal Demi-Glace (page 000)

1/2 teaspoon salt

1/4 teaspoon freshly ground black pepper

STUFFING AND CHOPS

4 cups cubed (1/2 inch) hearty wheat bread (use walnut bread, if available)

1/3 cup chopped toasted walnuts (see note below)

3/4 cup (about 3 ounces) crumbled Gorgonzola cheese

2 scallions, thinly sliced

1 teaspoon chopped fresh thyme leaves

2 tablespoons dry sherry

1. Prepare the Ruby Port Glaze: Melt the butter in a nonreactive small saucepan set over medium heat. Add the shallot, carrot, and celery and cook over low heat until the shallot is translucent, about 5 minutes. Add the bay leaf, peppercorns, thyme, and vinegar and boil over moderate heat until all of the vinegar evaporates, about 1 minute. Pour in the port and simmer until it reduces to about 3 tablespoons and becomes syruplike, about 10 minutes. Add the demi-glace and simmer for 2 minutes.

2. Strain the glaze through a fine sieve; discard the solids. Stir in the salt and pepper. Serve hot or let cool to room temperature, cover, and refrigerate for up to 1 week. Reheat before serving.

3. Prepare the stuffing and chops: Preheat the oven to 350°F.

4. Combine the bread, nuts, cheese, scallions, thyme, sherry, and 1/2 teaspoon pepper in a mixing bowl. Pour the melted butter over the stuffing and mix well.

5. Carefully stuff each chop pocket with 3/4 cup of the stuffing. Pack the stuffing in tightly so it won't come loose during cooking. Season both sides of each chop with salt and pepper.

6. Heat the oil in a large skillet set over high heat. Add the pork chops and sear until golden brown, about 2 minutes on each side.

TOASTING NUTS AND SEEDS

Toasting nuts and seeds brings out their best flavor. This method works for all types, but you'll need to vary the cooking time according to what you're toasting. Use your nose and eyes for close surveillance; nuts and seeds change from toasted to burned in moments. Preheat the oven to 375°F. Spread the nuts or seeds in a single even layer on a baking sheet. Toast in the oven for about 5 minutes. Shake the pan once or twice during their toasting to move the nuts and seeds around and turn them. Watch very carefully lest they burn. Let cool to room temperature and use immediately. Alternately, set a large skillet over high heat for a few minutes. Add the nuts or seeds; shake and stir constantly until they are golden brown.

{continued}

Freshly ground black pepper

8 tablespoons (1 stick) unsalted
  butter, melted

6 center-cut pork chops (each about
  8 ounces), with pockets cut for stuffing
  (see note below)

Salt

2 tablespoons olive oil

Remove the chops to a roasting or jelly-roll pan. Roast in the oven until the meat is cooked and the stuffing is heated through, about 12 minutes.

7. Serve hot, topped with the Ruby Port Glaze. If desired, serve this dish with Cider-braised Cabbage (page 200) and Honey-glazed Turnips (page 198).

OTHER WAYS TO DO IT
A different but equally wonderful sauce for these chops is Red Grape Compote (see page 48).

BUTCHERING CHOPS FOR STUFFING
Ask your butcher to cut pockets in the chops so they can be stuffed, or you can cut the pockets yourself: With a sharp paring knife, make a 1½-inch incision along the side of the chop opposite the bone and carefully run the blade back and forth to cut a deep, large pocket.

Pork Tenderloin with Caramelized Shallots and Apples {Serves 4}

Too elegant to be called a skillet dinner, but just as easy, this unfussy dish of roasted pork tenderloin combines the autumnal flavors of apples and shallots caramelized in cider with the forest scents of juniper and bay.

4 tablespoons unsalted butter

½ cup thinly sliced shallots

5 juniper berries, crushed

2 bay leaves

2 teaspoons chopped fresh thyme leaves

1 cup apple cider

½ cup heavy cream

2 tablespoons olive oil

2 pork tenderloins (about 12 ounces each), trimmed of all excess fat, halved crosswise

Salt and freshly ground black pepper

1 large apple, peeled, cored, and cubed (¾ inch)

1. Preheat the oven to 400°F.

2. Melt the butter in a sauté pan set over medium heat. Add the shallots, juniper berries, bay leaves, and thyme and cook until the shallots brown, about 5 minutes. Increase the heat to high, add the cider, and boil until syrupy and reduced by about half, 6 to 8 minutes. Stir in the cream and reduce, stirring constantly, until thickened to a saucelike consistency, about 3 minutes. Keep the sauce warm.

3. In a large, cast-iron skillet set over medium heat, heat the olive oil until it ripples. Meanwhile, lightly season the pork with salt and pepper. Sear the tenderloins in the oil for 3 minutes, turning to brown all the sides. Scatter the apple around the pork.

4. Place the skillet in the oven and roast until the pork is just cooked through, 8 to 10 minutes.

5. Remove the pork to a cutting board and let rest for 5 minutes Add the cooked apples and any accumulated cooking juices to the sauce; season to taste with salt and pepper and remove the bay leaves.

6. Thinly slice the pork against the grain, and top with the sauce. If desired, serve with Savoy Cabbage with Pancetta and Oyster Mushrooms (page 200) and wild rice.

OTHER WAYS TO DO IT
Try this dish with crispy potato pancakes or buttered egg noodles.

Sautéed Pork Medallions with Basil and Balsamic Vinegar {Serves 4}

Balsamic vinegar combines beautifully with the flavors of Asia. The sauce for these sautéed pork medallions marries balsamic and rice wine vinegars, ginger, garlic, and fish sauce to demonstrate this kinship perfectly. It's smooth, mellow, and delightful.

½ cup balsamic vinegar

1 tablespoon rice wine vinegar

2 teaspoons cornstarch

1 tablespoon minced fresh ginger

1 tablespoon minced garlic

2 teaspoons *nam pla* (Thai fish sauce, available in Asian markets and specialty food stores; see note, page 95)

3 tablespoons packed light brown sugar

½ cup cold water

2 tablespoons vegetable oil

2 pork tenderloins (each about 12 ounces), cut into 16 medallions, each slice pounded until about ¼ inch thick

Salt and freshly ground black pepper

¼ cup chopped fresh basil leaves

4 scallions, thinly sliced

1. Preheat the oven to 350°F.

2. In a bowl, whisk together the balsamic vinegar, rice wine vinegar, cornstarch, ginger, garlic, *nam pla*, brown sugar, and cold water. Mix well and reserve.

3. In a nonreactive large sauté pan set over high heat, heat the oil until it ripples. Meanwhile, lightly season both sides of the pork medallions with salt and pepper. Working in batches, cook the pork until golden, about 1 minute on each side. Transfer the pork medallions to a jelly-roll pan.

4. Place the pork in the oven and roast until just cooked through, 4 to 5 minutes.

5. Meanwhile, add the reserved vinegar mixture to the sauté pan and bring to a simmer over medium heat. Simmer for 1 minute. Stir in the basil and scallions. Remove the pork from the oven and pour any accumulated juices into the sauce. Bring to a simmer and remove from the heat.

6. Pour the warm sauce over the pork medallions. Serve with Sesame-roasted Asparagus (page 204) and Stir-Fried Wild Rice (page 204).

OTHER WAYS TO DO IT

Try serving the pork medallions with steamed white rice and Sesame-Steamed Snow Peas (page 202).

Derby Day Leg of Lamb with Tomato-Mint Chutney {Serves 8}

This dish incorporates the ingredients of that famous drink traditionally served at the Kentucky Derby, the Mint Julep. Leg of lamb makes great picnic fare since it can be made a day in advance, chilled, and then sliced and served cold. Paired with Tomato-Mint Chutney, some crusty bread, and a pitcher of White Dog Cafe Mint Juleps (page 232), you'll have a sensational picnic for the Derby or in your own backyard.

TOMATO-MINT CHUTNEY

2 tablespoons extra-virgin olive oil

2 cups minced white onions

4 cups diced fresh tomatoes
  (about 2 pounds)

2 tablespoons sugar

$1/4$ cup red wine vinegar

$1 1/4$ teaspoons salt

$1/2$ teaspoon freshly ground black pepper

1 tablespoon bourbon

$1/2$ cup tightly packed fresh mint leaves,
  finely chopped

LAMB

$1/4$ cup minced shallots

1 tablespoon minced garlic

$1/4$ cup stone-ground mustard

2 tablespoons honey

$1/4$ cup bourbon

$1/2$ cup chopped fresh mint leaves

1 teaspoon salt

1 teaspoon freshly ground black pepper

1 boned and tied leg of lamb (about 6 pounds)

1. Prepare the Tomato-Mint Chutney: In a nonreactive saucepan over medium-high heat, heat the olive oil until it ripples. Add the onions, tomatoes, sugar, vinegar, salt, and pepper and stir to combine. Bring to a boil. Reduce the heat to low and simmer until the tomatoes soften and reach a thick, saucelike consistency, 30 to 45 minutes. Remove from the heat and let cool to room temperature.

2. Stir in the bourbon and the mint. Taste for seasoning and serve immediately. The chutney can be refrigerated for up to 5 days.

3. Whisk together the shallots, garlic, mustard, honey, bourbon, mint, salt, and pepper in a small bowl. Rub the marinade over the leg of lamb. Cover and refrigerate for at least 2 hours or overnight.

4. Preheat the oven to 500°F.

5. Place the leg of lamb on a rack set in a roasting pan. Roast for 10 minutes.

6. Reduce the oven temperature to 375°F. Roast until an instant-read thermometer inserted in the center of the leg reads 140°F, 45 to 60 minutes more. Allow the roast to rest for 10 minutes. Remove the strings before slicing across the grain.

7. Serve warm or chilled topped with the Tomato-Mint Chutney, and, if desired, alongside Dijon Potato Salad (page 195) and chilled asparagus.

BUYING A LEG OF LAMB

Leg of lamb is available in most supermarkets. Ask your butcher to remove the bone and tie the lamb into a roast for you. Although purchasing a whole leg of lamb is expensive, it will feed eight to ten people. It is more economical than its hefty price tag might suggest.

Rosemary-roasted Leg of Lamb {Serves 8}

Lamb and rosemary make a combination we never tire of. This unstudied preparation doesn't embellish the leg of lamb with many ingredients—just rosemary, garlic, lemon, and olive oil. The flavor of the lamb is enhanced by the marinade and proves that a few well-chosen fresh ingredients can produce fantastic food—simplicity can be stunning.

1 tablespoon salt

1 teaspoon freshly ground black pepper

2 tablespoons chopped fresh rosemary leaves

Juice of 1 lemon

¼ cup olive oil

¼ cup minced garlic

1 boned and tied leg of lamb (about 6 pounds)

1. Whisk together the salt, pepper, rosemary, lemon juice, olive oil, and garlic in a large bowl. Add the leg of lamb to the marinade and turn to coat evenly. Cover and refrigerate for at least 2 hours or overnight.

2. Preheat the oven to 500°F.

3. Place the lamb on a rack set in a roasting pan. Roast on the middle rack of the oven for 10 minutes.

4. Reduce the oven temperature to 375°F. Roast until an instant-read thermometer inserted in the center of the roast reads 140°F, 45 to 60 minutes more. Let the roast rest for 10 minutes. Remove the strings before carving across the grain.

5. Slice the meat thinly against the grain. Serve with Chévre-Rosemary-Garlic Mashed Potatoes (page 192) and Roasted Vegetables Balsamico (page 201), or with Black Olive Tapenade (page 294), Zucchini with White Beans and Mint (page 205), and Sautéed Greens and Garlic (page 202).

ROASTING FATTY MEATS
When roasting meat at high temperatures or with a high fat content—like duck, goose, or ribs—roast the meat on a rack set in a roasting pan that has about ½ inch of water in the bottom. This way, the fat that drips onto the bottom of the pan won't smoke.

Jamaican Curried Lamb Stew {Serves 6}

In the dog days of summer when Philadelphia is blanketed in heat and humidity, we stir up some breeze with Rum and Reggae, an annual Caribbean street party. It features a live reggae band and lots of exotic rum drinks that excite us to dance in the street (tropical attire suggested). For dinner we serve this fiery Jamaican lamb stew topped with freshly grated coconut, fresh pineapple chunks, and mango chutney to help cool us down. As a special treat, serve along with White Dog Cafe Rum Punch (page 233).

2 pounds lamb shoulder, trimmed of all excess fat and cut into 1½-inch cubes

1 tablespoon White Dog Cafe Curry Powder (page 284) or Madras curry powder

½ teaspoon ground allspice

2 teaspoons salt

¼ teaspoon freshly ground black pepper

Juice and grated zest of 1 lime

¼ cup olive oil

2 cups finely diced white onions

2 tablespoons minced garlic

1 tablespoon minced fresh ginger

1 tablespoon chopped fresh thyme leaves

1 Scotch bonnet pepper (or other fiery chile), seeded and minced (see note, page 36)

1 (14-ounce) can unsweetened coconut milk (available in Asian markets and specialty stores)

1 bay leaf

1¾ cups water

2 large carrots, cut into 1-inch lengths (about 2 cups)

2 large Idaho potatoes, cut into 1-inch cubes

¼ cup dark rum

1 tablespoon cornstarch

1 tablespoon distilled white vinegar

1. Combine the cubed lamb, curry powder, allspice, 1 teaspoon of the salt, the pepper, and the lime juice in a large bowl. Toss to coat the meat with the spices. Marinate at room temperature for 30 minutes.

2. Heat the oil in a large Dutch oven set over high heat. Add the seasoned meat and brown evenly, turning occasionally, 6 to 8 minutes. Add the onions, garlic, ginger, thyme, and chile pepper, and cook for 2 minutes. Stir in the coconut milk, bay leaf, and water. Bring to a simmer. Reduce the heat to low, cover, and simmer for 30 minutes.

3. Add the carrots and potatoes. Cover and continue to simmer gently for 1 hour.

4. Whisk together the rum and cornstarch in a small bowl. Add the mixture to the stew and bring to a simmer. Stir in the vinegar, lime zest, and the remaining 1 teaspoon salt. Remove and discard the bay leaf. Serve hot over steamed white rice with Crispy Plantain Fritters (page 213), or let cool to room temperature, cover, and refrigerate for up to 3 days. Reheat before serving. If desired, serve with White Dog Cafe Rum Punch.

Tarragon-braised Lamb Shanks {Serves 4}

There are few things to eat that are as satisfying as long-cooked lamb shanks. They are easy enough to get into the oven and once there, simmer slowly for several hours, filling the kitchen with whiffs of ambrosia. We braise these shanks in a mixture of tarragon vinegar, white wine, and chicken stock that melds into a delicate, velvety sauce spiked with Dijon mustard and fresh herbs. During winter's last stand, this meal is a gentle push toward spring.

¼ cup olive oil

4 lamb shanks

Salt and freshly ground black pepper

All-purpose flour, for dredging

1½ cups finely diced white onions

1 tablespoon minced garlic

2 carrots, peeled and finely diced

2 celery ribs, finely diced

¼ cup tarragon vinegar

1 cup dry white wine

3 cups Chicken Stock (page 277)

2 bay leaves

2 teaspoons Dijon mustard

2 tablespoons chopped fresh sage leaves

2 tablespoons chopped fresh tarragon leaves

1. Preheat the oven to 350°F.

2. In a nonreactive Dutch oven set over medium-high heat, heat the oil until it ripples. Meanwhile, season the shanks liberally with salt and pepper and dust them with the flour. Add the shanks to the pan and sear, turning frequently, until browned on all sides, about 10 minutes.

3. Remove the shanks from the pan and reserve. Add the onions, garlic, carrots, and celery to the pan and cook for 2 minutes. Stir in the vinegar and wine and cook until the liquid reduces by half, about 3 minutes. Add the chicken stock, bay leaves, and browned shanks to the pan; bring to a simmer. Cover the pot and braise in the oven until the shank meat is fork-tender and falling off the bone, about 2 hours.

4. Transfer the shanks to a plate and tent with foil to keep warm. Place the Dutch oven on the stovetop and boil the liquid over high heat until it reduces by half and is thick and saucelike, about 5 minutes. Remove from the heat and stir in the mustard, sage, tarragon, and ¼ teaspoon salt. Remove the bay leaves.

5. Place 1 shank on each plate and top with about ½ cup of the sauce. For a simple side dish, serve with parsleyed new potatoes and steamed asparagus.

OTHER WAYS TO DO IT

These shanks are also delicious with buttered egg noodles and sautéed spinach.

SLOW-COOKING SHANK MEATS

Beef shins and other shank meats are quite tough (and also inexpensive) because they contain lots of connective tissue. However slow, moist cooking softens and dissolves the connective tissue and tenderizes the meat. Plus, the cooking liquid makes a tasty sauce.

Mediterranean Shellfish Stew with Green Goddess Sauce {Serves 4 to 6}

The essence of this lusty stew, similar to the bouillabaisse of Marseille, comes from saffron, the dried stigma of the delicate purple crocus. It takes 70,000 blossoms to yield only one pound of saffron, which accounts for its high price; however there's no substitute for the color and distinctive flavor it imparts. Always use saffron in thread form.

_{1/3} cup Green Goddess Sauce (page 293)

2 tablespoons extra-virgin olive oil

1/2 cup minced white onion

2 tablespoons minced garlic

1 small fennel bulb, stalks removed, cored, and diced

1 green bell pepper, diced

1 teaspoon saffron threads

5 black peppercorns

1 bay leaf

1 cup dry white wine

3 cups chopped canned tomatoes

5 cups Fish Stock (page 279)

1/2 orange

1/3 cup chopped Italian parsley leaves

1/8 teaspoon hot red pepper flakes

1 tablespoon *nam pla* (Thai fish sauce, available in Asian markets and specialty food stores; see note, page 95)

8 ounces littleneck clams, scrubbed

8 ounces sea scallops, side muscles removed if necessary

8 ounces mussels, scrubbed and debearded (see note, page 82)

8 ounces shrimp, peeled and deveined

8 ounces cleaned squid (see note, page 52), mantles cut into 1/4-inch rings, tentacles into bite-size pieces

2 cups kale leaves (or other leafy greens such as Swiss chard, spinach, or escarole)

2 cups cooked pasta shells

1. Prepare the Green Goddess Sauce. Reserve.

2. Heat the oil in a large, nonreactive saucepan set over medium-high heat. Add the onion and sauté until translucent, about 5 minutes. Add the garlic and cook for 1 minute. Add the fennel and bell pepper and sauté for 3 minutes. Add the saffron, peppercorns, bay leaf, and wine. Bring to a boil. Reduce heat and simmer until the liquid reduces to 1/2 cup, about 5 minutes.

3. Add the tomatoes, fish stock, orange, parsley, pepper flakes, and *nam pla*. Simmer over low heat for 10 minutes.

4. Add the clams and scallops to the stew, cover, and simmer for 5 minutes. Add the mussels, shrimp, squid, and kale; cover and simmer for 5 minutes. Add the cooked pasta shells and heat through, about 1 minute.

5. Ladle the stew into large warm bowls. Top each with the Green Goddess Sauce and serve with lots of crusty bread to mop up the delicious broth.

OTHER WAYS TO DO IT

Feel free to change the seafood used in this dish according to your taste and what is fresh and available. Occasionally we use medallions of a firm-fleshed fish such as bluefish, monkfish, swordfish, or tuna instead of just shellfish.

BUYING LIVE CLAMS

Choose clams with a sweet aroma and tightly closed shells. Scrub well under cold running water with a stiff-bristled brush. Discard any that won't close when you tap them with your finger or any that feel heavy (they may contain sand or mud). Keep live clams covered with a damp towel in the refrigerator for no longer than 2 days.

FISH & SEAFOOD

Soft-shell Crabs with Thai Curried Vegetables {Serves 4}

Succulent soft-shell crabs are available from April through September. They are actually blue crabs that have just molted their hard outer shells. Within a few days they develop a rigid new shell; but for the short time in limbo, their soft exterior is deliciously edible. Make sure the crabs you purchase are alive. It takes some pluck to clean them but the rewards are great—particularly when paired with this spicy vegetable curry.

THAI CURRY SAUCE

1 lemon grass stalk, minced

Minced zest of 1 lime

1/4 cup tightly packed fresh mint leaves

1/4 cup tightly packed fresh basil leaves

1/4 cup tightly packed fresh cilantro leaves

2 teaspoons red Thai curry paste (available in Asian markets and specialty food stores)

1 teaspoon *nam pla* (Thai fish sauce, available in Asian markets and specialty food stores; see note, page 95)

1 tablespoon minced fresh ginger

1 teaspoon minced garlic

1 can (14 ounces) unsweetened coconut milk (available in Asian markets and most grocery stores)

VEGETABLES AND CRABS

4 tablespoons vegetable oil

1 carrot, peeled and cut into 1/2-inch coins

1 red bell pepper, diced

1 yellow bell pepper, diced

1/2 bunch scallions, thinly sliced

4 cups thinly sliced bok choy, Asian cabbage, or spinach leaves

8 soft-shell crabs, cleaned (see note below)

Salt and freshly ground black pepper

1. Prepare the sauce: Combine the lemon grass, lime zest, mint, basil, cilantro, curry paste, *nam pla*, ginger, garlic, and coconut milk in a food processor or blender; purée until smooth, about 1 minute. Reserve. (The sauce can be made 1 day in advance and kept refrigerated.)

2. In a large, nonreactive sauté pan set over high heat, heat 2 tablespoons of the oil until it ripples. Add the carrot, bell peppers, scallions, and bok choy; stir-fry until just cooked through, about 4 minutes. Add the reserved sauce and bring to a simmer. Remove from the heat and keep warm.

3. In a large sauté pan set over medium-high heat, heat 1 tablespoon of the oil until very hot. Lightly season both sides of the crabs with salt and black pepper. Add 4 crabs (or as many as will fit without crowding), top sides down, and cook until the skin blisters and they are cooked through, about 3 minutes on each side. (Be careful while cooking the crabs because they have a high water content and can splatter hot oil.) Remove the cooked crabs to a plate and keep warm. Add the remaining 1 tablespoon oil to the pan and cook the remaining crabs.

4. To serve, divide the vegetables and sauce among 4 warmed plates. Top each serving with 2 crispy crabs and if you like, serve with mounds of steamed jasmine rice, although any white rice is fine.

OTHER WAYS TO DO IT

Substitute shrimp, scallops, or chicken if soft-shell crabs aren't available. For a lighter version, leave out the meat altogether and add more vegetables.

CLEANING SOFT-SHELL CRABS

Place a crab, right side up, on a work surface. Lift the pointed top shell on each side and scrape away and discard the gills found underneath. With a sharp knife or kitchen shears, cut the face off just behind the eyes and discard. Turn the crab over and pull back the tail flap. Grasp the tail flap and pull while gently twisting to remove the intestinal tract; discard.

Corn-crusted Crab and Shrimp Cakes with Summer Herbs Sauce {Serves 4}

We make these crab cakes only in the summertime when the New Jersey corn is at its best and the blue crabs from Maryland are sweet, plump, and plentiful. Served with our creamy Summer Herbs Sauce, these corn-crisped cakes are the tasty quintessence of summer.

SUMMER HERBS SAUCE

1 cup Homemade Mayonnaise (page 287) or store-bought

½ cup sour cream

2 tablespoons chopped fresh cilantro leaves and stems

2 tablespoons chopped fresh basil leaves

2 tablespoons chopped fresh tarragon leaves

2 tablespoons chopped fresh dill

2 tablespoons minced fresh chives

Minced zest of 1 lemon

1 tablespoon fresh lemon juice

½ teaspoon salt

¼ teaspoon freshly ground black pepper

CRAB AND SHRIMP CAKES

8 ounces jumbo lump crabmeat, picked over

8 ounces shrimp, peeled, deveined, and roughly chopped

1 red bell pepper, finely diced

3 scallions, thinly sliced

1 celery rib, finely diced

1 cup fresh corn kernels

½ cup Homemade Mayonnaise (page 287) or store-bought

¾ cup dry bread crumbs

1 egg, beaten

1 teaspoon salt

½ teaspoons Tabasco sauce

1 cup cornmeal

¼ cup olive oil

1. Prepare the Summer Herbs Sauce: Combine all of the ingredients in a small bowl and whisk together. Cover and refrigerate for 1 hour before serving. The sauce will keep in the refrigerator for up to 3 days.

2. Combine the crabmeat, shrimp, bell pepper, scallions, celery, corn, mayonnaise, bread crumbs, egg, salt, and Tabasco in a large bowl; mix well.

3. Place the cornmeal in a shallow dish. Shape the crab and shrimp mixture into 8 equal cakes. Dredge each cake in the cornmeal to coat both sides well.

4. In a large skillet set over medium-low heat, heat the oil until it ripples. Carefully add 4 of the crab cakes and cook until golden brown and cooked through, about 4 minutes on each side. Cook the remaining cakes, adding more oil, if necessary. Serve warm, with the Summer Herbs Sauce and our crunchy, Tangy Six-Vegetable Slaw (page 214).

OTHER WAYS TO DO IT

These cakes are also delicious with Curried Chopped Vegetable Salad (see page 96) and Creamy Basil Sauce (page 293).

Seared Sea Scallops with Curried Apple "Sauce" and Crispy Fried Leeks {Serves 4}

This recipe perfectly exemplifies how new food combinations and dishes are inspired. We were testing the Curried Apple Bisque recipe for this cookbook and had a batch of it that we liked. We didn't want to discard it, but because it makes only about 4 bowls, there was no way to serve it as soup at the restaurant. We decided to use the soup as a "sauce" for the scallops and paired them with the grain salad we had just developed. We thought the mingling of flavors and textures was phenomenal, and our guests agreed.

CRISPY FRIED LEEKS

2 cups julienned leeks, (white and green parts about ¹/₁₆ inch thick and 3 inches long), washed and dried thoroughly

Vegetable or peanut oil for frying

Salt

4 cups Native Grains Pilaf (page 208)

1 cup Curried Apple Bisque (page 73)

SEA SCALLOPS

1½ pounds (about 24) sea scallops, side muscles removed, if necessary

Salt and freshly ground black pepper

2 tablespoons olive oil

1. Prepare the leeks: In a deep fryer or small saucepan, heat 2 inches of oil to 350°F, or until a small cube of bread dropped in the oil browns in about 2 minutes. Fry the leeks in two batches until lightly golden, about 4 minutes.

2. Remove with a slotted spoon and drain on paper towels. Sprinkle with salt and serve immediately, or reserve for up to 8 hours.

3. Prepare the Native Grains Pilaf and the Curried Apple Bisque. Keep warm.

4. Pat the scallops dry; season with salt and pepper to taste. Heat 1 tablespoon of the olive oil until it ripples in a large heavy skillet set over high heat. Add half of the scallops to the pan and sear for 1 to 2 minutes on each side. Don't disturb them as they're searing or they won't develop a crisp, browned exterior. Also, be careful not to overcook the scallops; their centers should remain translucent. Remove the scallops and keep them warm. Repeat with the remaining 1 tablespoon oil and scallops.

5. Serve the scallops atop a bed of the warm Native Grains Pilaf. Drizzle some Curried Apple Bisque around the plate and top with a bouquet of the Crispy Fried Leeks.

Trout Tropicale {Serves 4}

Coated in toasted Brazil nuts and served with a citrus and rum sauce, this trout recipe is light, fresh, and exotic—not quickly forgotten. We remember this truth every time we try to take it off of the menu—our guests ask for it again and again. If you don't like to look your dinner in the eye, you can use trout fillets instead of the whole fish for a less dramatic presentation.

CORNMEAL-NUT-COATING

6 ounces (about 1½ cups) unsalted brazil nuts, toasted (see note, page 144)

1 cup cornmeal

Salt and freshly ground black pepper

TROUT

4 small whole trout (8 ounces each), scaled and cleaned, with head and tail intact

¼ cup vegetable oil

SAUCE

1 cup fresh grapefruit juice

2 tablespoons dark rum

4 tablespoons unsalted butter, cut into 1-inch cubes

¼ cup chopped fresh cilantro leaves (see note, page 158)

1. Preheat the oven to 400°F.

2. Prepare the coating: Combine half of the nuts, the cornmeal, 1 teaspoon salt, and ½ teaspoon pepper in a food processor. Process until the nuts are finely ground, about 30 seconds. Remove to a shallow bowl or baking dish. Coarsely chop the remaining nuts by hand; reserve.

3. Prepare the trout: Sprinkle the cavity of each trout with salt and pepper. Dredge the skin of each trout in the cornmeal and nut mixture, coating both sides well.

4. In a large, nonreactive sauté pan set over medium heat, heat the oil until it ripples. Add 2 of the trout and cook until golden brown on one side, 2 to 3 minutes. Carefully turn the trout over and cook for 1 minute. Remove the trout to a baking sheet and reserve. Repeat with the remaining 2 trout. Place the trout in the oven and bake until the flesh is opaque and flaky, about 5 minutes.

5. Meanwhile, prepare the sauce: Pour off any oil from the sauté pan and wipe out the pan with a paper towel. Set the pan over high heat and add the grapefruit juice, rum, the reserved coarsely chopped nuts, and ½ teaspoon freshly ground black pepper. Boil until reduced by half, about 3 minutes. Whisk in the butter and cilantro; season with salt to taste. Remove the sauce from the heat and spoon some over each trout.

6. Serve with Crispy Plantain Fritters (page 213), Lemon-Garlic Rice (page 210), and snow peas sautéed with grapefruit and lump crabmeat.

OTHER WAYS TO DO IT

Fillets of red snapper, sea bass, or halibut are great prepared this way, as are soft-shell crabs.

Caribbean Grilled Mahi Mahi with Tropical Fruit Salsa {Serves 4}

This platter of island delights conjures up tropical breezes, sandy beaches, and the rhythm of steel drums.

MARINADE

1 tablespoon ground allspice

1 tablespoon dried thyme

1½ teaspoons cayenne pepper

1½ teaspoons freshly ground black pepper

2 tablespoons garlic powder

1 tablespoon sugar

½ cup distilled white vinegar

¼ cup soy sauce

¼ cup fresh lime juice

1 Scotch bonnet pepper (see note, page 36) or 2 jalapeño peppers, seeded and minced

¼ cup dark rum

1 cup minced white onion

1 cup olive oil

4 mahi mahi fillets (each about 6 ounces)

TROPICAL FRUIT SALSA

2 cups diced (¼ inch) mixed tropical fruits, such as mango, papaya, pineapple, or melon

½ cup sliced scallions

½ cup diced red bell pepper

½ cup diced yellow bell pepper

1 jalapeño pepper, seeded and minced

3 tablespoons chopped fresh mint leaves

3 tablespoons chopped fresh basil leaves

3 tablespoons chopped fresh cilantro leaves

1 teaspoon minced garlic

2 teaspoons minced fresh ginger

¼ cup fresh lime juice

¼ cup ginger ale

¼ cup unsweetened pineapple juice

2 teaspoons pickled ginger juice (see note, page 71)

1 tablespoon *nam pla* (Thai fish sauce, available in Asian markets and specialty food stores)

1 tablespoon olive oil

1. Prepare the marinade: Combine the allspice, thyme, cayenne, black pepper, garlic powder, and sugar in a large mixing bowl. Add the vinegar, soy sauce, lime juice, chile pepper, rum, and onion and stir to combine. Slowly whisk in the olive oil. The marinade can be made up to 1 week in advance and kept refrigerated.

2. Arrange the fish fillets in a shallow dish. Pour on the marinade, cover, and refrigerate for 1 to 2 hours.

3. Make the Tropical Fruit Salsa: Combine all of the ingredients and toss to mix well. Serve immediately at room temperature or cover and refrigerate for up to 2 days.

4. Prepare a charcoal grill or preheat the oven to 400°F.

5. Grill the marinated fish over the hot coals until cooked through, about 5 minutes on each side. If cooking in the oven, place the fillets on an oiled baking sheet and roast until the flesh is opaque and flaky, 10 to 12 minutes.

6. Serve with the Tropical Fruit Salsa, and perhaps our crunchy Cool Island Cucumber Salad (see page 95), Crispy Plantain Fritters (page 213), and Black Beans and Rice (page 211).

OTHER WAYS TO DO IT

The marinade can also be used for pork, chicken, shrimp, or other firm-fleshed fish as our twist on classic Jamaican "jerk."

Roasted Trout with Potato-Shrimp Stuffing and Lemon-Thyme Sauce {Serves 6}

When we receive our just-caught farm-raised rainbow trout from our friend Farmer Glenn, we smoke them, grill them, sauté them, and in this preparation (our favorite), we fill them with a creamy potato-shrimp stuffing and roast them in the oven.

LEMON-THYME SAUCE

1 cup dry white wine

2 teaspoons dried thyme

2 allspice berries

5 black peppercorns

2 shallots, minced

1 bay leaf

1 cup Chicken Stock (page 277)

³/₄ pound (3 sticks) unsalted butter, cut into 1-inch cubes

1 tablespoon dry sherry

1¹/₂ teaspoons *nam pla* (Thai fish sauce, available in Asian markets and specialty food stores; see note, page 95)

2 teaspoons chopped fresh thyme leaves

1¹/₂ teaspoons fresh lemon juice

POTATO-SHRIMP STUFFING

2 Idaho potatoes, peeled and finely diced

Salt

5 black peppercorns

1 bay leaf

8 ounces shrimp, peeled and deveined

1 egg

¹/₄ cup Homemade Mayonnaise (page 287) or store-bought

¹/₄ cup sour cream

1. Prepare the Lemon-Thyme Sauce: Combine the wine, dried thyme, allspice, peppercorns, shallots, and bay leaf in a small, nonreactive saucepan set over medium heat. Simmer until all of the liquid evaporates, about 10 minutes. Add the Chicken Stock and simmer until it's reduced by half, about 5 minutes.

2. Strain the reduction through a fine sieve into another non-reactive pan; discard the solids. Set over very low heat and add the butter 1 cube at a time, whisking constantly until melted and incorporated. Stir in the sherry, *nam pla*, thyme leaves, and lemon juice. Serve immediately, or keep warm for up to 2 hours.

3. Preheat the oven to 400°F.

4. Make the stuffing: Combine the potatoes, 1 teaspoon salt, peppercorns, and bay leaf in a saucepan and add cold water to cover by 2 inches. Bring to a boil over medium heat. Reduce the heat and simmer until just cooked through, about 10 minutes.

5. Drain the potatoes; discard the peppercorns and bay leaf. Spread out on a baking sheet, and roast in the oven for 1 minute to remove any excess moisture. Let cool to room temperature. Leave the oven on.

6. In a food processor, purée half of the shrimp to a smooth paste, about 30 seconds. Coarsely chop the remaining shrimp with a knife. Combine the puréed and chopped shrimp; reserve.

USING FRESH CILANTRO

The roots and stems of the cilantro plant hold much of its refreshing flavor. Whenever we use cilantro, we chop the leaves and the stems together. In this recipe, we separate them and imbue the chicken stock with the essence of the stems only. If the cilantro you purchase has the roots attached, wash them well and add them to the stock, too.

(continued)

2 teaspoons *nam pla* (Thai fish sauce, available in Asian markets and specialty food stores)

¹/₂ teaspoon Tabasco sauce

1 tablespoon Pernod or Ricard

2 teaspoons Worcestershire sauce

1 red bell pepper, finely diced

1 yellow bell pepper, finely diced

3 scallions, thinly sliced

¹/₂ celery rib, finely diced

2 tablespoons chopped fresh basil leaves

2 tablespoons chopped fresh cilantro leaves (see note, opposite page)

2 tablespoons chopped fresh dill

TROUT

6 small whole trout (about 8 to 10 ounces each), scaled and cleaned, heads and tails intact

Freshly ground black pepper

7. Whisk together the egg, mayonnaise, sour cream, *nam pla*, Tabasco, Pernod, and Worcestershire in a large bowl. Add the cooled potatoes, shrimp, bell peppers, scallions, celery, and herbs; mix well.

8. Lightly sprinkle each trout inside and out with salt and black pepper. Fill the cavity of each fish with about 1 cup of the stuffing. Close the trout and place them on a baking sheet. Roast until the stuffing is completely cooked through and the fish is flaky, about 20 minutes. Serve immediately with the warm Lemon-Thyme Sauce and, if you like, steamed asparagus, broccoli, or green beans, and roasted cherry tomatoes.

Cuban-style Braised Tuna {Serves 4}

Cuban cuisine is inherited from many cultures including Ciboney Indian, African, Chinese, and Spanish. The most evident flavors are from Spain, which can be found in everything from saffron-infused rice dishes and flan to chorizo and olives and their oil. In this piquant sauce, almonds, capers, and olives speak of the early Spaniards who brought the flavors of the Mediterranean to the islands of the Caribbean.

¼ cup extra-virgin olive oil

1½ cups thinly sliced white onions

2 tablespoons minced garlic

4 cups roughly chopped fresh
  plum tomatoes

¼ cup drained capers, rinsed and
  squeezed dry (see note below)

⅔ cup sliced pimiento-stuffed green olives

Pinch of hot red pepper flakes

1½ cups dry white wine

4 yellowfin tuna steaks (about
  6 ounces each)

¼ cup chopped fresh cilantro leaves

¼ cup slivered almonds, toasted
  (see note, page 144)

1. Heat the oil in a large, nonreactive sauté pan or skillet over medium-high heat. Add the onions and cook until soft, about 4 minutes. Add the garlic and cook for 1 minute. Add the tomatoes and sauté until they begin to soften, about 3 minutes. Add the capers, olives, pepper flakes, and wine; bring to a simmer.

2. Add the tuna steaks to the sauce. Reduce the heat to low, cover, and simmer until the tuna is completely cooked through, 10 to 15 minutes, depending upon the thickness of the steaks.

3. Remove the tuna and keep warm. If the sauce looks too loose, increase the heat and simmer until it reduces to the desired consistency. Stir in the cilantro. Top the fish with the warm sauce; sprinkle with the toasted almonds. Serve with Lemon-Garlic Rice (page 210) or Spicy Fried Potatoes (page 195) topped with Saffron Aïoli (see page 194).

ABOUT CAPERS
Capers are the flowering bud of a shrub found along the Mediterranean and in Asia. They are dried in the sun and then packed in brine or coarse sea salt, which gives them their distinctive piquant flavor. Before using capers, rinse them well under cool running water, and then squeeze them dry in your hand or a towel to remove excess salt.

Seared Tuna with Anise and Black Currant Balsamico {Serves 4}

Made from concentrated white Trebbiano grape juice and aged in wooden barrels, balsamic vinegar has a natural sweetness and velvety texture that has been revered for centuries. Its full-bodied, complex flavor is so rich and meaty that sometimes we use it as a substitute for veal demi-glace. In this recipe, we treat tuna as a red meat and top it with a mouthwatering sauce of caramelized shallots, currants, and balsamic vinegar.

¼ cup dried black currants

½ cup good-quality balsamic vinegar

4 yellowfin tuna steaks (about 6 ounces each)

Salt and freshly ground black pepper

Aniseeds (or anise seeds), for coating

3 tablespoons olive oil

2 large shallots, thinly sliced (about ¼ cup)

4 garlic cloves, thinly sliced

1 tablespoon fresh thyme leaves

2 bunches arugula, washed and dried

¼ cup walnuts, toasted (see note, page 144) and coarsely chopped

1. Combine the currants and vinegar in a small bowl and set aside to soak for 1 hour.

2. Sprinkle both sides of each tuna steak with salt, pepper, and a heavy coating of aniseeds.

3. In a large, nonreactive skillet set over high heat, heat 1 tablespoon of the oil until it ripples. Add the tuna steaks and sear for about 3 minutes on each side, or cook to the desired doneness. Remove the fish to a plate and keep warm.

4. Turn the heat to medium-high and add the remaining 2 tablespoons oil to the pan. Add the shallots and sauté until browned and crisp, 3 to 5 minutes. Add the garlic and cook until golden, about 2 minutes. Add the thyme leaves and the currants and balsamic vinegar mixture. Bring to a boil and simmer for 1 minute.

5. Arrange the arugula over 4 warmed plates. Place 1 tuna steak on each plate; top the fish with the balsamic sauce and sprinkle with the toasted walnuts. If you like, serve with crispy Polenta Croutons (page 283) but omit the aniseeds in the croutons because they're already on the fish.

OTHER WAYS TO DO IT

If arugula is unavailable, use spinach leaves. Rosemary-Roasted Potatoes (page 192) are also a great accompaniment to this dish.

USING ARUGULA

Arugula is a flavorful leafy green that is most widely used in Italian food. Its leaves resemble radish leaves and its taste is bitter and peppery. Arugula is generally eaten raw, although like spinach, it can be braised, steamed, or sautéed. Arugula is sold in bunches with the roots attached at better supermarkets and health food stores. To use, remove the roots and wash it well as it's usually quite sandy.

Crispy Red Snapper with Shiitake Mushroom Glaze {Serves 4}

This colorful dish is as attractive as it is tasty. If you haven't made many Chinese-inspired dishes before, combine these ingredients and, amazingly, you'll instantly be transported to your favorite Chinese restaurant. It's well worth a trip to your Asian market to pick up the necessary ingredients (some supermarkets carry them, too).

4 tablespoons peanut oil

2 tablespoons minced fresh ginger

2 tablespoons minced garlic

3 scallions, thinly sliced

$\frac{1}{2}$ teaspoon hot chile paste (preferably Sambal Oelek brand, available in Asian markets and specialty food stores)

1 red bell pepper, finely diced

2 cups sliced, stemmed shiitake mushrooms

1 cup plus 2 tablespoons cold water

$\frac{1}{4}$ cup oyster sauce (available in Asian markets and many supermarkets)

1 tablespoon hoisin sauce (available in Asian markets and many supermarkets)

2 tablespoons ketchup

1 tablespoon packed light brown sugar

1 teaspoon soy sauce

1 tablespoon rice wine vinegar

1 tablespoon cornstarch

$1\frac{1}{2}$ pounds red snapper fillets, skin side scored, cut into 4 equal portions

Salt and freshly ground black pepper

1. Heat 2 tablespoons of the oil in a nonreactive saucepan set over medium heat. Add the ginger, garlic, and scallions and cook until soft, about 5 minutes. Stir in the chile paste and cook for 1 minute. Add the bell pepper and mushrooms and cook until the mushrooms soften, about 5 minutes.

2. Stir in 1 cup of the water. Stir in the oyster sauce, hoisin sauce, ketchup, brown sugar, soy sauce, and rice wine vinegar; bring to a gentle simmer. Meanwhile, in a small bowl, whisk together the cornstarch and the remaining 2 tablespoons cold water. Whisk the cornstarch mixture into the simmering sauce and bring to a boil. Reduce the heat to low and simmer for 5 minutes, or until clear and thickened. Remove from the heat and keep warm.

3. In a large sauté pan set over high heat, heat the remaining 2 tablespoons oil until it ripples. Sprinkle both sides of the fish with salt and pepper. Sear the fish, skin side down, until golden brown, about 5 minutes. Carefully turn the fillets over and cook through, 3 to 6 minutes, depending upon the thickness of the fillet.

4. Place the fish on 4 warmed dinner plates; top with the shiitake glaze. Serve with Sesame-roasted Asparagus (page 204) and Stir-fried Wild Rice (page 204).

OTHER WAYS TO DO IT

The sauce is great over any tuna, salmon, halibut, grilled chicken, pork, or beef. If you want a spicier sauce, add more chile paste.

SCORING FISH SKIN

When preparing this dish it's important to score the skin side of the fish so that it will retain its shape and cook evenly. If you don't, the skin shrinks as it cooks and curls the flesh up along with it. To score the fish, take a sharp knife or single-edged razor blade and make several shallow diagonal cuts, just slicing through the skin of the fish.

Leek- and Caraway-braised Swordfish with Lemon-Pepper Aïoli {Serves 4}

This is an adaptation of a luncheon entrée that we enthusiastically consumed at Chez Panisse in Berkeley, California. The simplicity and freshness of this dish demonstrate Chef Alice Water's cooking philosophy: Use seasonal organic ingredients and allow their integrity to shine though. In the fall, when cauliflower is at its peak, this popular dish hits the menu.

½ cup **Lemon-Pepper Aïoli (page 291)**

4 swordfish steaks (about 6 ounces each)

Salt and freshly ground black pepper

Caraway seeds, for coating

2 tablespoons olive oil

1 large leek, trimmed and split lengthwise, washed well, the white and light green parts sliced

1 cup Fish Stock (page 279)

1 small cauliflower, trimmed and cut into florets, the florets blanched and cooled

1 large carrot, peeled into curls

1 small bunch (about 1 pound) Swiss chard, cut into 2-inch pieces

1 tablespoon *nam pla* (Thai fish sauce, available in Asian markets and specialty food stores; see note, page 95)

1. Prepare the Lemon-Pepper Aïoli.

2. Sprinkle both sides of the swordfish steaks with salt, pepper, and a heavy coating of caraway seeds. In a large, nonreactive skillet set over high heat, heat the oil until it ripples. Add the swordfish and sear until the bottom starts to brown, about 3 minutes. Turn the fish over and add the leek. Cook until the leek begins to soften, about 3 minutes.

3. Pour in the fish stock. Add the cauliflower, carrot curls, Swiss chard, and *nam pla*. Cover and braise until the vegetables are tender, 3 to 4 minutes.

4. Divide the vegetables and broth among 4 shallow bowls. Serve the swordfish steaks on the vegetables and top each with 2 tablespoons of the Lemon-Pepper Aïoli.

OTHER WAYS TO DO IT
Tuna steaks are delicious prepared this way as well.

FINDING READY-MADE FISH STOCK
Fish stock is easy and economical to make at home; however, if you're pressed for time, look for it in your local seafood shop. Many better fishmongers make stock daily and sell it by the quart.

Pan-roasted Salmon with Burgundy-Rosemary Butter {Serves 4}

In this unique preparation, oyster mushrooms sear themselves to the salmon forming a crisp and beautiful crust. The Burgundy-Rosemary Butter merges seamlessly with the salmon, woodsy mushrooms, and earthy lentils.

BURGUNDY-ROSEMARY BUTTER

1 cup Burgundy or other dry red wine

¼ cup minced shallots

½ teaspoon salt

½ teaspoon freshly ground black pepper

⅛ teaspoon ground allspice

½ pound (2 sticks) unsalted butter, at room temperature

16 oyster mushrooms, stems removed

4 salmon fillets (about 6 ounces each)

1. Prepare the Burgundy-Rosemary Butter: Combine the wine and shallots in a small, nonreactive saucepan set over high heat. Boil to reduce the mixture until the wine is almost evaporated, about 10 minutes.

2. Combine the wine and shallot reduction, salt, pepper, allspice, and butter in a small bowl. Mix well with a fork or wooden spoon until evenly combined.

3. Shape the butter into a log 2 inches in diameter and roll up in waxed paper or plastic wrap. Refrigerate until firm for up to 1 week, or freeze for up to 2 months. Slice for serving.

4. Preheat the oven to 475°F. Oil a baking sheet.

5. Arrange 4 mushrooms, cap sides down, in a row on the baking sheet. Make sure their edges touch slightly. Season a salmon fillet with salt and pepper; set it, rounded side down, on the mushrooms. Repeat with the remaining mushrooms and salmon. Roast on the bottom rack of the oven for 8 to 10 minutes, or 6 to 8 minutes if you like your fish less well done.

6. After roasting, the mushrooms should adhere to the bottom of the fish; carefully slide a metal spatula under them and remove the fish from the baking sheet.

7. Serve the fillets, mushroom sides up. Top with a few slices of the Burgundy-Rosemary Butter. We like to serve this dish on a bed of Warm French Lentils (page 206) alongside Savoy Cabbage with Pancetta, but omitting the Oyster Mushrooms (see page 200).

OTHER WAYS TO DO IT

If you can't find oyster mushrooms, shiitake mushrooms with the stems removed make a good substitute.

Rosemary- and Lime-roasted Sea Bass with Mediterranean Salsa {Serves 6}

This is a showstopping preparation of sea bass served head to tail. We roast it on a bed of dried rosemary branches, which sends a heavenly aroma wafting through the kitchen and imparts a delicate smoky flavor to the fish. If you don't have any rosemary branches, a roasting rack will work. Also, you may need a piece of foil that extends beyond your roasting pan that you'll place under the head and tail of the fish to collect any juices that might drip from them.

MEDITERRANEAN SALSA

1 cup diced seeded tomato

1 cup finely diced fennel

1 red bell pepper, finely diced

$\frac{1}{2}$ cup finely diced red onion

$\frac{1}{2}$ cup sliced kalamata olives

$\frac{1}{4}$ cup drained capers, rinsed and squeezed dry

1 teaspoon minced garlic

$\frac{1}{2}$ lemon (pulp and rind), seeded and chopped

2 tablespoons chopped fresh parsley leaves

$\frac{1}{4}$ cup chopped fresh basil leaves

3 tablespoons red wine vinegar

Juice and minced zest of 1 orange

$\frac{1}{4}$ cup plus 2 tablespoons extra-virgin olive oil

$\frac{1}{4}$ teaspoon salt

$\frac{1}{2}$ teaspoon freshly ground black pepper

SEA BASS

1 whole sea bass (about 5 pounds), scaled and cleaned with head and tail intact

Salt and freshly ground black pepper

$\frac{1}{2}$ red onion, sliced into thin rings

1 lime, cut into thin rounds

3 sprigs (6 inches long) fresh rosemary

2 garlic cloves, thinly sliced

Dried rosemary branches for roasting (optional)

2 tablespoons olive oil

1. Prepare the Mediterranean Salsa: Combine all of the ingredients in a large bowl and toss to mix well. Let sit at room temperature for 30 minutes to allow the flavors to blend before serving or cover and refrigerate for up to 2 days.

2. Preheat the oven to 400°F.

3. Rinse the fish well under cold running water (to make sure the cavity is clean of any entrails) and pat it dry. With a sharp knife, make 4 deep diagonal incisions down to the bone on each side of the fish. Sprinkle the cavity with salt and pepper. Lay the onion rings, lime rounds, and rosemary sprigs in the cavity; close the fish. Insert the garlic slivers into the incisions.

4. Tie the fish together in 3 or 4 places with butcher's twine to close the cavity. Place the fish on a bed of rosemary branches (or a rack) set in a large roasting pan. Rub the fish with the olive oil; sprinkle with salt and pepper.

5. Roast the fish until completely cooked through, about 40 minutes. (A good rule of thumb is to cook the fish for 10 minutes for each inch of thickness.)

6. Transfer the fish to a large platter and remove the twine; top with the Mediterranean Salsa. You can also serve this fish on a bed of spinach or arugula leaves with a side of warm orzo tossed with a little chopped fresh parsley and olive oil.

OTHER WAYS TO DO IT

If a whole fish is unavailable or you look at a whole fish with trepidation, marinate fillets of fish in the rosemary, lime, garlic, black pepper, salt, and olive oil. Roast them in the oven or grill them over a charcoal fire.

Wild Mushroom–Barley Risotto {Serves 4 to 6}

Risotto is a classic Italian specialty—onions and Arborio rice are sautéed in butter or olive oil and the rice is stirred constantly as hot broth is gradually added to the pot. The friction from stirring softens the outer hull of the rice grains, creating an inimitable creaminess. In this dish we substitute barley for the rice, so technically it's not a risotto, but the results are surprisingly similar. The stirred barley retains its nubby texture while exuding a luxurious creaminess, its nutty flavor perfectly complementing the woodsy porcini.

½ ounce dried porcini or other dried wild mushroom

6 cups water

2 tablespoons extra-virgin olive oil

⅓ cup minced shallots

1 tablespoon minced garlic

3 cups chopped portobello or button mushrooms

2 cups raw barley

½ cup dry Marsala

1 cup freshly grated Parmesan cheese

1 teaspoon salt

½ teaspoon freshly ground black pepper

1 tablespoon fresh thyme leaves

1. Combine the dried mushrooms and the water in a saucepan; bring to a boil over high heat. Remove from the heat and set aside to steep for 15 minutes. Strain the mushrooms and reserve the liquid separately. Coarsely chop the mushrooms and reserve.

2. In a nonreactive saucepan set over medium heat, heat the olive oil until it ripples. Add the shallots and cook until translucent, about 4 minutes. Add the garlic and cook for 1 minute. Turn the heat to high and add the chopped fresh mushrooms. Cook until they release their juices and cook dry, 5 to 6 minutes.

3. Add the barley and stir for 1 minute. Pour in the Marsala, and enough of the reserved mushroom broth to just cover the barley. Add the reserved dried mushrooms and bring to a gentle simmer and stir. As the barley absorbs the liquid, add more mushroom broth, a ladleful at a time, stirring before and after each addition. After about 20 minutes the barley should be tender. If it is still chewy, add a little more broth and continue to stir until tender.

4. Stir in the Parmesan, salt, pepper, and thyme. Taste for seasoning. Serve immediately alone or as an accompaniment to roasted chicken.

VEGETARIAN

Broccoli Risotto {Serves 4 to 8}

An all-American twist on an Italian classic, this dish blends broccoli and cheese in a luxurious risotto. Try it topped with sliced Balsamic-roasted Portobello Mushrooms (page 180).

6 cups water

1 head of broccoli, stems and florets cut into 2-inch pieces

2 tablespoons olive oil

1 cup minced white onion

2 cups Arborio rice

1 cup dry white wine

1 teaspoon salt

1/2 teaspoon freshly ground black pepper

1 (5.2-ounce) package Boursin cheese with garlic and herbs

1/2 cup freshly grated Parmesan cheese

1. Bring the water to a rolling boil. Add the broccoli and cook until tender, 3 to 5 minutes. Drain the broccoli, reserving the cooking liquid; immediately plunge the broccoli in ice water. When cool, drain the broccoli, finely chop, and reserve.

2. In a nonreactive saucepan set over medium heat, heat the olive oil until it ripples. Add the onion and cook until translucent, about 5 minutes. Add the rice, toss to coat with the oil, and cook, stirring until it has a nutty aroma, about 1 to 2 minutes. Continue stirring and add the wine. When the wine is absorbed, add enough of the broccoli broth to just cover the rice. Bring to a gentle simmer and stir. As the rice absorbs the liquid, add more broth, a ladleful at a time, stirring before and after each addition (you will not use all of the broccoli broth). After about 20 minutes the rice should be tender but still firm in the center.

3. Stir in the chopped broccoli, salt, and pepper; cook, stirring constantly, for 3 to 5 minutes more. Add more broth if the rice isn't quite cooked or becomes sticky. Stir in the Boursin and Parmesan just before serving. The risotto should be pourable but not runny; the grains of rice and liquid should not be separate. Taste for seasoning. Serve hot.

CREATING YOUR OWN VEGETARIAN ROUNDUP

In putting together the recipes for this chapter we wrestled with the problem of how to present our most popular vegetarian meal, the Vegetarian Roundup—a dazzling array of the best vegetables, grains, and legumes prepared in our kitchen on any given day. We think (and our customers seem to agree) that serving lots of small dishes is an exciting way to eat a vegetarian meal, as it offers more diversity of flavor, temperature, and texture than, for instance, a piece of eggplant Parmesan. In addition, some of our best-loved vegetable dishes are too marvelous to be relegated only to the side and eclipsed by a piece of meat; they demand to be the focus of a meal. As you plan a vegetarian meal, consider choosing several different vegetable dishes to create your own Roundup: some dips and spreads, a roasted vegetable dish, some quick-cooked green vegetables, and some grains and legumes.

Tomato and Sweet Corn Risotto {Serves 4}

This is one of our favorite summer risottos. The opposing tang of the tomatoes and the sweetness of the corn is bridged by a large handful of chopped fresh basil. Served with a green salad, some crusty bread, and a crisp white wine, it is a heavenly meal. For the broth we use a quick and easy corn stock, made by simmering corn cobs and aromatics—to reinforce the sweet corn flavor.

CORN STOCK

4 ears of sweet corn

3 garlic cloves, peeled

1 small onion, peeled

6 basil stems

5 black peppercorns

1 bay leaf

1 teaspoon salt

10 cups water

2 cups coarsely chopped fresh or canned tomatoes

RISOTTO

2 tablespoon extra-virgin olive oil

1 cup diced leeks (white part only)

1 teaspoon minced garlic

1½ cups Arborio rice

½ cup dry white wine

1 cup finely diced fresh ripe tomato

½ cup chopped fresh basil leaves

¾ cup freshly grated Parmesan cheese

½ teaspoon salt

½ teaspoon freshly ground black pepper

1. Make the stock: With a sharp knife, remove the corn kernels from the ears of corn and reserve for the risotto. Place the corn cobs, garlic, onion, basil stems, peppercorns, bay leaf, salt, and water in a large stockpot set over high heat. Bring to a boil. Reduce the heat and simmer for 1 hour. Strain the stock into a clean saucepan; discard the solids.

2. Combine 1 cup of the corn stock with the coarsely chopped tomatoes in a blender or food processor and purée until smooth. Add the purée to the remaining corn stock and set over low heat.

3. Make the risotto: In a large, nonreactive saucepan set over medium heat, heat the olive oil until it ripples. Add the leeks and cook until translucent, about 2 minutes. Add the garlic and cook for 1 minute. Add the rice, toss to coat with the oil, and cook until it exudes a nutty aroma, 1 to 2 minutes. Continue stirring and add the wine. When the wine is absorbed, add enough of the corn-tomato stock to just cover the rice. Bring to a gentle simmer and stir. As the rice absorbs the liquid, add more stock, a ladleful at a time, stirring before and after each addition (you might not use all of the stock). After about 20 minutes the rice should be tender but still firm in the center.

4. Stir in the reserved corn kernels and diced tomato. Taste the rice for doneness. If it is still starchy in the center, add a little more broth and continue to stir until the broth is absorbed. The rice should be tender yet firm, loose but not runny. Stir in the basil, Parmesan, salt, and pepper. Adjust seasoning to taste. Serve immediately.

Fettuccine with White Beans, Sun-dried Tomatoes, and Rosemary {Serves 4}

A comforting winter meal of pasta, white beans, and sun-dried tomatoes, this dish demonstrates the economy of a restaurant kitchen. It incorporates cooking liquid from the beans and the soaking liquid saved from rehydrating the sun-dried tomatoes into a lush sauce—not a drop of flavor goes to waste. We always save sun-dried tomato jus (natural juices) as its subtle richness adds flavor and complexity to soups, sauces, and vinaigrettes. It will keep indefinitely in the refrigerator.

5 to 6 fresh rosemary sprigs, leaves minced and stems reserved

$3/4$ cup dried Great Northern beans

1 bay leaf

5 black peppercorns

3 garlic cloves, peeled

9 cups water

$1/2$ cup tightly packed sun-dried tomatoes

$1/4$ cup extra-virgin olive oil

1 cup thinly sliced red onion

$1/4$ cup minced garlic

Pinch of hot red pepper flakes

Juice of $1/2$ lemon

$3/4$ teaspoon salt

$1/4$ teaspoon freshly ground black pepper

1 pound Food Processor Pasta Dough (page 281), cut into fettuccine or 1 pound store-bought

4 ounces unaged chèvre, crumbled and at room temperature,

4 ounces ($1^1/3$ cups) Pecorino Romano, grated

1. Combine the rosemary stems, beans, bay leaf, peppercorns, garlic, and 8 cups of the water in a large saucepan. Bring to a boil over medium-high heat. Reduce the heat and cook until the beans are tender, about 1 hour. Drain the beans and reserve the broth. Remove and discard the rosemary stems, bay leaf, peppercorns, and garlic cloves.

2. Meanwhile, combine the sun-dried tomatoes and the remaining 1 cup of water in a small, nonreactive saucepan. Bring to a boil. Remove from the heat and let stand for 15 minutes. Drain the tomatoes and reserve the liquid. Thinly slice the tomatoes.

3. Heat the olive oil in a large, nonreactive skillet over medium-high heat. Add the onion and cook until translucent, about 5 minutes. Add the garlic, minced rosemary leaves, and red pepper flakes; cook for 2 minutes. Add the beans, sun-dried tomatoes, $1^1/2$ cups of the reserved bean cooking liquid, and $1/2$ cup of the sun-dried tomato soaking liquid. Stir in the lemon juice, salt, and pepper. Taste for seasoning. Remove from the heat and keep warm.

4. Cook the fettuccine in a large pot of salted boiling water until just al dente, about 4 minutes for fresh. Drain and toss with the bean sauce.

5. Divide the pasta and beans among 4 plates. Top each serving with one-fourth of the chèvre and one-fourth of the Pecorino Romano. Start with Garden Vegetable Minestrone (page 74) or our Warm Mushroom–Spinach Salad (page 92) for a healthy yet hearty meal.

FLAVORING DRIED BEANS

When cooking dried beans, we add ingredients to the cooking water to give it flavor, and make the beans more flavorful. Depending upon what the beans are being used for, we might add an onion, garlic cloves, bay leaves, peppercorns, cinnamon sticks, allspice berries, or herb stems.

Savory Tart of Chanterelles, Swiss Chard, and Emmentaler {Serves 4}

Savory tarts are a showcase for each season's bounty and cook's ingenuity. The dough is basic, but the filling can be flexible: asparagus and Brie in the spring, tomatoes and pesto in the summer, pears and Gorgonzola for fall. We serve this rich, earthy tart of wild mushrooms, Swiss cheese, and Swiss chard to warm us in the depths of winter. Don't worry if you can't find chanterelles; any wild or domestic mushroom will suffice, and spinach is a good substitute for the Swiss chard.

2 tablespoons unsalted butter

1½ cups thinly sliced yellow onions

8 ounces chanterelle mushrooms, torn into bite-size pieces

2 teaspoons chopped fresh thyme leaves

2 teaspoons chopped fresh sage leaves

½ cup dry white wine

½ teaspoon salt

⅛ teaspoon freshly ground nutmeg

¼ teaspoon freshly ground black pepper

2 tablespoons extra-virgin olive oil

4 cups tightly packed Swiss chard leaves and stems, cut into 1-inch pieces

2 to 4 tablespoons cold water

1 pound, 12 ounces Basic Pie Dough (page 280)

1 tablespoon fine dry bread crumbs

6 ounces Emmentaler or other Swiss cheese, grated (about ¾ cup)

1 egg yolk

1. Melt the butter in a large, nonreactive sauté pan set over medium heat. Add the onions and cook until translucent, about 5 minutes. Add the chanterelles, thyme, and sage and sauté until the chanterelles release their liquid, about 5 minutes. Increase the heat to high, add the wine, and cook until all of the liquid evaporates, 5 to 6 minutes. Season with ¼ teaspoon salt, the nutmeg, and the pepper. Set aside to cool to room temperature.

2. In a large sauté pan set over high heat, heat the olive oil until it ripples. Add the chard and sauté until the leaves begin to wilt. Sprinkle on 2 to 3 tablespoons water and continue to sauté until the leaves are wilted and the stems are tender, about 5 minutes. Set aside to cool to room temperature.

3. Preheat the oven to 425°F.

4. On a floured work surface, roll out the pie dough to a 15-inch round about ⅛ inch thick. Carefully transfer the dough to a baking sheet, letting the dough hang over the edges.

5. Sprinkle the bread crumbs in a 10-inch circle in the center of the dough. They will absorb any excess liquid in the filling so the pastry remains crisp. Spread half of the cooled mushroom filling on top of the bread crumbs; sprinkle with one-third of the grated cheese.

6. Squeeze out all excess moisture from the chard with your hands. Season with the remaining ¼ teaspoon salt. Spread the

COOKING WITH SWISS CHARD

Swiss chard is a marvelous, delicious, and gorgeous vegetable. Tasting vaguely of spinach and bok choy, it's also endlessly versatile (you can sauté it with garlic and olive oil, wrap its giant leaves around savory stuffing, bake it into a creamy gratin, and stir it into soups). Look for large, pale green- or deep crimson-veined leaves.

{continued}

chard in an even layer on top of the cheese. Top this with half of the remaining cheese, the remaining mushroom filling, and the rest of the cheese.

7. Whisk together the egg yolk and the remaining 1 tablespoon water. Brush the exposed dough with some of the egg wash. Fold the edges of the dough up over the filling, leaving about 5 inches of the filling exposed. Brush the top of the dough with the remaining egg wash.

8. Bake the tart for 10 minutes.

9. Reduce the oven temperature to 350°F. Bake for 50 minutes more, or until the crust is golden and the cheese has melted. Remove and allow to cool slightly on a rack. Cut into wedges and serve with a salad of peppery watercress and bright red cherry tomatoes

Curried Butternut Squash Ravioli with Winter Herb Pesto {Serves 4 to 5}

Warm Indian spices and sweet winter squash merge in these healthful, handsome ravioli. We serve them in the fall and early winter when butternut squash are bountiful and arrive from the farms every day. The curry powder in the pasta dough adds flavor and brilliant color to the dish; topped with the emerald-hued Winter Herb Pesto, they are striking and delicious.

1 large butternut squash

4 tablespoons unsalted butter, melted

1 teaspoon minced garlic

1 tablespoon Garam Masala (page 285) or store-bought

2 cups all-purpose flour

2 eggs, lightly beaten

1 tablespoon White Dog Cafe Curry Powder (page 284) or good-quality Madras curry powder

1 tablespoon water

1 scallion, thinly sliced

2 tablespoons chopped fresh cilantro leaves

1/2 teaspoon salt, or to taste

1 cup Winter Herb Pesto (page 292)

1. Preheat the oven to 350°F.

2. Peel, halve, and seed the squash. Cut the flesh into 1-inch cubes (there will be about 6 cups). Combine the squash, melted butter, garlic, and garam masala in a small roasting pan and toss well. Cover with foil and bake until the squash is tender, about 30 minutes. Let cool to room temperature.

3. Meanwhile, combine the flour, eggs, and curry powder in a food processor. Process, adding the water, drop by drop, until the dough resembles coarse meal. Press the dough into a ball. If it won't come together, return it to the food processor, add a few drops more water and process for a few seconds; the dough should be firm and elastic. Wrap the dough in plastic. Let rest at room temperature for 45 minutes, or refrigerate for up to 1 week.

4. When the squash has cooled, purée it in a food processor, blender, or food mill until smooth. Remove to a bowl. Stir in the scallion, cilantro, and salt. Use immediately, or let cool to room temperature, cover, and refrigerate for up to 3 days.

5. Prepare the Winter Herb Pesto.

6. Assemble the ravioli: Cut the pasta dough into 2 equal pieces. Either by hand or with a pasta maker, roll out each piece of dough into a very thin sheet, 1/16-inch-thick. Trim the sheets so that they are the same length. Lay out 1 of the sheets on a work surface. Using a pastry brush or spray bottle, lightly moisten the pasta with water. Spacing them about 2 inches apart, spoon 1-tablespoon mounds of the squash filling onto the moistened pasta

ABOUT GARAM MASALA
Garam masala is a warm blend of up to 12 different ground spices from northern India somewhat akin to curry. We recommend making it in small batches to retain freshness.

{continued}

sheet in 2 rows running the length of the sheet. Drape the second sheet of dough over the mounds of filling. Firmly press around the mounds, taking care to press out any air that may be trapped inside. With a fluted pastry cutter or a sharp knife, cut the ravioli into 2-inch squares. Firmly press around the edges to seal well.

7. Bring a large pot of salted water to a rolling boil. Cook the ravioli until they float to the surface and the dough is just tender to the bite, 5 to 7 minutes. Drain the ravioli and divide them among 4 warmed plates. Top with the Winter Herb Pesto and serve at once.

OTHER WAYS TO DO IT

The ravioli can be fried instead of boiled. Heat a few inches of peanut oil in a saucepan to 350°F. Cook a few ravioli at a time, turning occasionally until they are puffed and golden brown, 3 to 4 minutes. Transfer with a slotted spoon to a baking sheet lined with paper towels. Keep warm in the oven while frying the remaining ravioli. If desired, serve with Cucumber Raita (page 298) and Gingered Pear Chutney (page 296).

Roasted Eggplant Marinara {Serves 6 to 8}

This is a chunky garden-style marinara substantial enough to rival any meat sauce! We serve it over a tangle of fresh linguine and arugula leaves, crowned with some chèvre or shaved Pecorino Romano cheese. It also is fabulous with grilled fish or chicken, a bowl of creamy polenta, or a simple piece of crusty bread.

¼ cup plus 3 tablespoons extra-virgin olive oil

2 cups minced white onions

¼ cup plus 2 tablespoons minced garlic

1 small fennel bulb, cored and diced

4 cups chopped canned tomatoes with their liquid

2 cups Vegetable Stock (page 277) or water

2 bay leaves

Pinch of hot red pepper flakes

Freshly ground black pepper

Salt

1 small eggplant (about 1 pound), cut into 1-inch dice

8 ounces white mushrooms, halved

1 red bell pepper, roasted (see note, page 140), cut into ½-inch dice

1 green bell pepper, roasted (see note, page 140), cut into ½-inch dice

1 yellow bell pepper, roasted, (see note, page 140), cut into ½-inch dice

½ cup chopped fresh basil leaves

½ cup chopped fresh parsley leaves

1. Preheat the oven to 425°F.

2. In a large, nonreactive saucepan set over medium heat, heat the ¼ cup of the olive oil until it ripples. Add the onions and cook until translucent, about 5 minutes. Add ¼ cup of the garlic and cook for 2 minutes. Add the fennel and cook for 3 minutes. Add the tomatoes, vegetable stock, bay leaves, pepper flakes, a pinch of freshly ground black pepper, and 1 teaspoon of salt. Simmer over low heat for 45 minutes.

3. Meanwhile, combine the eggplant and mushrooms in a large bowl and toss with the remaining 3 tablespoons oil, 2 tablespoons of the remaining garlic, a pinch of salt and the red pepper flakes. Spread in an even layer on a baking sheet. Roast in the oven until cooked through and starting to brown, 15 to 20 minutes. Reserve.

4. After the tomato sauce has simmered 45 minutes and has reached a thick, saucelike consistency, add the cooked eggplant, mushrooms, and roasted peppers. Stir well and bring to a simmer. Remove from the heat and stir in the basil and parsley. Taste for seasoning. Serve immediately or let cool to room temperature, cover, and refrigerate for up to 2 days. Reheat before serving.

OTHER WAYS TO DO IT

For a more robust sauce, try grilling the eggplant and mushrooms. Cut the eggplant into long slices and grill until cooked through, a few minutes on each side. Use portobello mushrooms instead of white mushrooms (so they won't slip through the grill) and grill until cooked through, a few minutes on each side. Cut the eggplant and mushrooms into 1-inch cubes and add to the sauce.

PRESERVING FRESH HERB FLAVOR

Notice that we add the chopped fresh herbs to this dish at the end, just before serving it. Fresh herbs lose their flavor and fragrance if they are cooked for too long, so adding them at the last minute gives maximum flavor.

Penne with Asparagus {Serves 4}

This dish is a quick springtime sauté of tender asparagus, leeks, mushrooms, peas, and fresh herbs tossed with penne. We cook the penne in the water used to blanch the asparagus, which gives it added flavor and saves room on the stovetop. Assemble all of the ingredients before you start cooking this dish, as you would for a stir-fry— once started it's finished in minutes.

12 ounces asparagus, trimmed of tough ends, cut diagonally into 1$\frac{1}{2}$-inch lengths

1 pound dried penne

3 tablespoons extra-virgin olive oil

1$\frac{1}{2}$ cups washed, thinly sliced leeks (white part only) or scallions

2 tablespoons minced garlic

8 ounces white or cremini mushrooms, sliced (about 3 cups)

$\frac{1}{4}$ cup dry vermouth

2 cups Vegetable Stock (page 277)

1 cup fresh or frozen peas

3 tablespoons chopped fresh mint leaves

3 tablespoons chopped fresh dill

Salt and freshly ground black pepper

$\frac{1}{2}$ cup fine dry bread crumbs

$\frac{1}{2}$ cup freshly grated Parmesan cheese

1. In a large pot of salted boiling water, blanch the asparagus until tender yet firm, 1 to 2 minutes, depending upon its size. Remove the asparagus with a slotted spoon or small strainer and plunge in ice water until chilled. Drain and reserve.

2. Bring the asparagus blanching water back to a rolling boil. Add the pasta and cook until al dente. Drain well and toss with 1 tablespoon of the olive oil.

3. While the pasta cooks, heat the remaining 2 tablespoons olive oil in a large sauté pan set over medium-high heat until it ripples. Add the leeks and cook until translucent, about 3 minutes. Add the garlic and cook, without browning, for 1 minute. Add the mushrooms and sauté until they release their moisture and cook dry, about 5 minutes. Pour in the vermouth and cook until it evaporates. Add the vegetable stock and bring to a simmer. Add the reserved asparagus, peas, mint, and dill. Simmer until heated through, 1 to 2 minutes. Season with salt and pepper to taste.

4. Divide the cooked pasta among 4 warmed bowls. Top each with the vegetables and stock. Sprinkle the bread crumbs and Parmesan on top of each portion. Serve immediately.

OTHER WAYS TO DO IT
Shrimp or scallops can be added while sautéing the mushrooms, if desired, but for me, omit the cheese.

Chiapas Pie {Serves 4 to 6}

La Casa del Pan, our vibrant sister restaurant in Chiapas, Mexico, features a unique and wholly vegetarian menu. It was there, in their rustic kitchen, engulfed by the scents of blazing dried chiles, fragrant herbs, exotic vegetables, and fresh tortillas, that we grasped the subtleties of both vegetarian cuisine and the regional foods of Mexico. This dish is a tribute to La Casa del Pan; it captures the magic of that kitchen in layer upon layer of roasted vegetables, succulent cheese, spicy tomato sauce, fresh herbs, and corn tortillas. The vegetables in this dish can be varied according to what's available; the pie can be assembled a day in advance and baked just before serving.

SAUCE

2 tablespoons olive oil

1 cup diced white onion

2 tablespoons minced garlic

1 jalapeño pepper, seeded and minced

2 teaspoons New Mexican chili powder (see note, page 130)

1 teaspoon ground cumin

2 cups chopped fresh tomatoes

¼ cup coarsely chopped fresh cilantro leaves (see note, page 158)

1 cup water

FILLING

1 large sweet potato, peeled and cut into ¼-inch dice (about 2 cups)

1 small yellow squash, halved lengthwise, cut into ½-inch slices

1 small zucchini, halved lengthwise and cut into ½-inch slices

Kernels cut from 2 ears of corn, or 1 cup thawed frozen corn kernels

1 cup diced yellow onion

1 tablespoon minced garlic

Juice of 1 orange

1 teaspoon dried Mexican oregano (see note, page 78)

1. Preheat the oven to 400°F.

2. Make the sauce: In a large nonreactive saucepan set over medium heat, heat the olive oil until it ripples. Add the white onion and cook until translucent, about 4 minutes. Add the garlic and jalapeño and cook for 2 minutes. Add the chili powder and cumin and cook for 1 minute. Add the tomatoes, cilantro, and water; simmer the sauce for 20 minutes, uncovered.

3. Meanwhile, make the filling: Combine the sweet potato, squash, zucchini, corn, yellow onion, garlic, orange juice, oregano, chili powder, cumin, 1 teaspoon salt, pepper, and olive oil in a large bowl. Toss well to coat the vegetables evenly with the oil and spices. Spread the vegetables in a single layer on a large baking sheet. Roast, stirring occasionally, until the vegetables are cooked through, 15 to 20 minutes.

4. Remove filling to a bowl and toss with the black beans. Taste for seasoning.

5. Combine the yogurt, sour cream, cilantro, scallions, and a pinch of salt in a small bowl and mix well.

6. Scrape the tomato sauce mixture into a food processor or blender. Add ½ teaspoon salt and the lime juice. Process the mixture to a purée.

BUYING AND USING ANAHEIM CHILES

Anaheim chiles are quite common and are available in most grocery stores. They are medium green (sometimes red) and look like a long narrow green bell pepper. They are very mild, with only a hint of spiciness and are available fresh, or roasted, peeled, and canned. For this recipe the roasted, peeled, canned variety work well; however, you can easily roast and peel fresh chiles yourself.

(continued)

1 tablespoon New Mexican chili powder

1 teaspoon ground cumin

Salt

1 teaspoon freshly ground black pepper

2 tablespoons olive oil

1 cup cooked black beans

3/4 cup plain yogurt

3/4 cup sour cream

2 tablespoons chopped fresh cilantro leaves and stems

1/2 cup thinly sliced scallions

10 (6-inch) corn tortillas

Juice of 1 lime

4 Anaheim chiles, roasted (see note, opposite page), peeled, and seeded

1 cup (4 ounces) grated Monterey Jack cheese

7. Assemble the pie: Reduce the oven temperature to 350°F. Oil a 10-inch pie pan. One at a time, dip 5 of the tortillas into the tomato sauce to coat generously. Place the coated tortillas in the pie tin overlapping them slightly to cover the bottom and side of the pan. Spread half of the roasted vegetable-bean mixture over the tortillas. Top with a few tablespoons of the tomato sauce. Arrange the roasted chiles in a single layer over the vegetables; spoon half of the sour cream-yogurt mixture on top. Dip 3 more tortillas in the tomato sauce and layer them over the sour cream. Top with the remaining roasted vegetables, the remaining sour cream mixture, and 1/2 cup of the jack cheese. Stack the remaining 2 tortillas and cut them into 4 even strips. Dip the strips into the tomato sauce. Arrange the round-edged strips around the circumference; weave the straight strips into a lattice pattern in the center of the pie.

8. Bake the pie for 30 minutes.

9. Sprinkle with the remaining 1/2 cup cheese. Bake until the cheese is melted and bubbling, about 10 minutes more. Let set for 5 to 10 minutes and cut into wedges. If desired, start this meal with Chilled Desert Garden Gazpacho (page 69) or Watermelon and Shrimp Salad (page 100). Lemon-Garlic Rice (page 210) and Cool Island Cucumber Salad (page 95) are delicious accompaniments.

Mushroom-Corn Rellenos with Mole {Serves 4}

These stuffed chiles are characteristic of the cooking at La Casa del Pan and incorporate the many indigenous ingredients found at the local market. Mildly spicy and slightly sweet, this quick version of a classic mole adds richness to these atypical rellenos. Rather than being stuffed with heavy cheese and batter-fried, we fill our chiles with mushrooms, corn, and just a bit of fresh farmer's cheese before baking them.

MOLE

4 dried ancho chiles, seeded, stemmed, and torn into small pieces

1/4 cup raisins

2 cups water

2 large tomatoes, coarsely chopped

1 tablespoon tomato paste

4 large garlic cloves

1 medium white onion, chopped

1 tablespoon sesame seeds

3 tablespoons peanuts, toasted (see note, page 144)

1 teaspoon fresh thyme leaves

1 teaspoon dried Mexican oregano (see note page 78)

1/2 teaspoon ground cinnamon

1 tablespoon olive oil

1/2 teaspoon salt

3 tablespoons grated unsweetened chocolate (1/2 ounce)

FILLING

2 tablespoons olive oil

1 cup diced white onion

2 tablespoons minced garlic

1 pound cremini mushrooms, trimmed and sliced (about 6 cups)

1/2 teaspoon salt

Kernels cut from 4 ears of sweet corn, or 2 cups thawed frozen corn kernels

1/4 teaspoon freshly ground black pepper

1/4 cup (about 2 ounces) queso fresca or farmer's cheese

4 large or 8 small whole poblano chiles, roasted (see note, page 140), peeled, slit on one side, seeds removed)

1. Make the Mole: Place the ancho chili pieces and raisins in a small saucepan. Add the water and bring to a boil over high heat. Remove from the heat and let steep for 15 minutes. Strain the solids from the liquid, and reserve each separately.

2. Combine the rehydrated chiles and raisins, tomatoes, tomato paste, garlic, onion, sesame seeds, peanuts, thyme, oregano, and cinnamon in a food processor or blender. Process to a smooth paste.

3. In a large nonreactive sauté pan set over medium-high heat, heat the oil until it ripples. Add the puréed chile mixture and cook, stirring occasionally, for 5 minutes. Whisk in 1 1/2 cups of the reserved liquid from the chiles. Turn the heat to low and simmer for 10 minutes.

4. Remove the pan from the heat. Stir in the salt and grated chocolate. Taste for seasoning. Keep warm.

5. Preheat the oven to 375°F.

6. Make the filling: In a large sauté pan set over medium-high heat, heat the olive oil until it ripples. Add the onion and cook until translucent, 4 to 5 minutes. Add the garlic and cook for 1 minute. Add the mushrooms and the salt and cook until the mushrooms release their juices and cook dry, 5 to 6 minutes. Add the corn and cook for 1 minute. Remove from the heat. Stir in the pepper and cheese and mix well. Let cool to room temperature. (The filling can be made 1 day in advance, covered and refrigerated.)

7. Carefully stuff the whole, split roasted chiles with the filling. Close the chiles and place them, split-side down on an oiled baking sheet. Bake until heated through, about 20 minutes. Top each pepper with a spoonful of the mole sauce and, if desired, serve with Lemon-Garlic Rice (page 210) and our sweet-tart Vegetable Seviche (see page 110).

Curry-roasted Vegetables with Indian Cheese Dumplings {Serves 4; makes 8 dumplings}

Although curry powders abound on every supermarket shelf, you'll find that making your own is well worth the time and effort. The exquisite layers of flavor achieved with homemade curry powder dance circles around flat supermarket brands. We make this dish as part of a vegetarian feast served every fall to celebrate Mahatma Gandhi's birthday. The Indian cheese dumplings help to cool the fire of the curry; however, if you're pressed for time, a dollop of plain yogurt will do.

DUMPLINGS
1$\frac{1}{2}$ cups plain yogurt

$\frac{1}{4}$ cup chopped fresh cilantro leaves
   and stems

Salt and freshly ground black pepper

SAUCE AND VEGETABLES
$\frac{1}{4}$ cup extra-virgin olive oil

2 cups minced white onion

$\frac{1}{4}$ cup minced garlic

2 tablespoons minced fresh ginger

2 tablespoons White Dog Cafe Curry Powder
   (page 284)

1 teaspoon cumin seeds

1 teaspoon fennel seeds

1 teaspoon fenugreek seeds

2 cups canned tomatoes (see note, page 76),
   chopped and undrained

1 teaspoon salt

$\frac{1}{4}$ teaspoon hot red pepper flakes, or to taste

Pinch of freshly ground black pepper

1 pound red-skinned potatoes, cut into
   $\frac{1}{2}$-inch wedges

4 ounces green beans, trimmed

1 eggplant (about 1 pound), cut into
   $\frac{3}{4}$-inch dice

3 large carrots, peeled and cut into
   $\frac{1}{2}$-inch coins

4 celery ribs, cut diagonally into 2-inch pieces

1. Prepare the dumplings: Line a colander or strainer with a double layer of dampened cheesecloth or a coffee filter and set over a bowl. Place the yogurt in the strainer and refrigerate until the yogurt is drained of excess moisture and is firm and compact, about 6 hours.

2. Place the yogurt in a bowl; stir in the cilantro and salt and pepper to taste. Shape into 8 round dumplings. Cover and refrigerate until needed.

3. Prepare the sauce and vegetables: In a large, nonreactive sauté pan set over medium-high heat, heat the olive oil until it ripples. Add the onion and cook until translucent, about 5 minutes. Add the garlic and ginger and cook for 2 minutes. Add the curry powder, cumin seeds, fennel seeds, and fenugreek seeds; cook, stirring constantly, for 1 minute. Stir in the tomatoes, salt, pepper flakes, and black pepper; bring to a simmer. Remove from the heat and allow to cool slightly. (The sauce can be prepared ahead of time up to this point. Let cool to room temperature, cover, and refrigerate for up to 2 days.)

4. Preheat the oven to 400°F.

5. Spread the vegetables evenly over 2 large jelly-roll pans. Pour the curry sauce over the vegetables, and toss to coat them well with the sauce. Roast the vegetables, stirring once or twice, until cooked through and starting to brown, 20 to 30 minutes. Divide the vegetables among four dinner plates and top each serving with 1 dumpling.

Balsamic-roasted Portobello Mushrooms {Serves 4}

Marinated in balsamic vinegar and soy sauce, these fleshy mushrooms have a surprisingly meaty flavor. They are simple to prepare and are terrific grilled; if you offer them as a vegetarian alternative at your next barbecue, you'll find you have more hamburgers left than mushrooms. We serve them with creamy herb-flecked polenta to temper any sharpness from the vinegar, and with spinach sautéed with roasted garlic and pine nuts.

4 large portobello mushrooms, stems discarded, caps brushed free of dirt

$1/2$ cup balsamic vinegar

$1/2$ cup soy sauce

$1/2$ cup olive oil

1 teaspoon minced garlic

2 tablespoons chopped fresh rosemary leaves

$1/2$ small red onion, minced

1 teaspoon freshly ground black pepper

$1/2$ cup water

1. Place the mushrooms, stem sides up, in a shallow baking dish.

2. Whisk together the balsamic vinegar, soy sauce, olive oil, garlic, rosemary, onion, pepper, and water. Pour the liquid over the mushrooms, coating well. Cover and refrigerate for at least 4 hours or up to 2 days.

3. About 30 minutes ahead of time, preheat the oven to 450°F. Remove the baking dish from the refrigerator.

4. Roast the mushroom caps until soft and cooked through, 12 to 15 minutes.

5. Serve at once, with Herbed Parmesan Polenta (page 210) and Sautéed Greens and Garlic (page 202), sprinkled with pine nuts.

OTHER WAYS TO DO IT

The mushrooms are also fabulous when grilled, or try serving them in an open-faced focaccia sandwich that is spread with pesto and broiled under fresh mozzarella.

ABOUT PORTOBELLO MUSHROOMS

Did you know that "exotic" portobello mushrooms are just overgrown cremini mushrooms? Cremini mushrooms are a brownish and firmer cousin of the regular white or cultivated mushroom.

Tangy Summer Vegetable Tian {Serves 4 to 8}

This dish makes use of late summer's surplus of tomatoes, basil, and zucchini. It is best served at room temperature, making it a natural supper for sultry nights. We squeeze as many vegetables as possible into the tian, so it must be pressed when it comes out of the oven to make it more compact and easier to serve.

½ cup chopped fresh basil leaves

2 tablespoons chopped fresh oregano leaves

1 tablespoon chopped fresh thyme leaves

¼ cup plus 2 tablespoons extra-virgin olive oil

¼ cup plus 2 tablespoons red wine vinegar

1 large eggplant, sliced into ¼-inch rounds

½ cup freshly grated Parmesan cheese

2 tablespoons minced garlic

Salt and freshly ground black pepper

3 large tomatoes, cut into ¼-inch slices

1 large zucchini, cut diagonally into ¼-inch slices

2 portobello mushrooms, stems removed, cut into ¼-inch slices

1 medium red onion, thinly sliced and separated into rings

1 medium yellow summer squash, cut diagonally into ¼-inch slices

1. Preheat the oven to 400°F. Oil a 10 x 7-inch baking dish or pan.

2. Combine the basil, oregano, and thyme in a small bowl. In a separate bowl, whisk together the olive oil and vinegar.

3. Arrange a single layer of the eggplant slices in the bottom of the prepared baking dish. Sprinkle with a few tablespoons of the vinaigrette, some of the mixed herbs, a sprinkling of the cheese, a pinch of the minced garlic, a pinch of salt, and a grinding of black pepper. Top with a single layer of sliced tomatoes. Sprinkle the tomatoes with more of the vinaigrette, herbs, cheese, garlic, salt, and pepper. Repeat with the zucchini, mushrooms, onion, yellow squash, remaining eggplant, vinaigrette, herbs, cheese, garlic, salt, and pepper. When finished, the layered vegetables will probably be higher than the sides of the pan.

4. Oil a piece of aluminum foil and tightly cover the vegetables with it. Set on the middle rack of the oven with a baking sheet underneath to catch any juices. Bake for 1 hour and 15 minutes. Remove from the oven, uncover, and carefully pour all of the excess juices into a bowl. Reserve the liquid.

5. Place the tian on a baking sheet and re-cover it with the foil. Place another baking pan of the same size on top of it and weigh down with something heavy (ideally a brick, but a few cans of soup will work). When the weight is placed on, some juices may spill over the sides. Set aside at room temperature for 1 hour.

6. Remove the weights and foil. Pour off any liquid and combine with the reserved juices in a saucepan. Bring to a boil over high heat. Reduce the heat and cook until syrupy, about 5 minutes.

7. Cut the tian into wedges and serve at room temperature. Drizzle each piece with some of the reduced vegetable juices. If desired, serve with our White Bean–Feta Brandade (page 295) or Basil Pesto (page 292).

CHAPTER FIVE

VEGETABLES & SIDE DISHES

VEGETABLES & SIDE DISHES

The Organic Growers of Graterford: A Prison Tale 186

White Cheddar and Red-skinned Potato Gratin 189

Truffled Potato Croquettes with Chèvre 190

Roasted Red Pepper—Potato Cake 191

Chèvre-Rosemary-Garlic Mashed Potatoes 192

Rosemary-roasted Potatoes 192

Fennel-roasted Potatoes 193

Country-Style Potatoes 193

Spicy Fried Potatoes with Saffron Aïoli 194

Spicy Potato (or Sweet Potato) Chips 195

Dijon Potato Salad 195

Summer Garden Vegetable Potato Salad 196

Maple-mashed Sweet Potatoes 197

Lavender- and Honey-roasted Butternut Squash 198

Honey-glazed Turnips 198

Caraway-roasted Vegetables 199

Cider-braised Cabbage 200

Savoy Cabbage with Pancetta and Oyster Mushrooms 200

Roasted Vegetables Balsamico 201

Sugar Snap Peas Sautéed with Scallions 201

Sesame-steamed Snow Peas 202

Sautéed Greens and Garlic 202

Balsamic-braised Kale 203

Green Beans with Onions 203

VEGETABLES & SIDE DISHES

Sesame-roasted Asparagus 204

Stir-fried Wild Rice 204

Firehouse Dalmatian Bean Salad 205

Zucchini with White Beans and Mint 205

Warm French Lentils 206

Black Olive Couscous 207

Native Grains Pilaf 208

Barley and Sweet Corn Tabbouleh 209

Herbed Parmesan Polenta 210

Lemon-Garlic Rice 210

Black Beans and Rice 211

Black Bean Refritos 212

Crispy Plantain Fritters 213

Gingered Snow Pea–Cabbage Slaw 214

Tangy Six-Vegetable Slaw 214

THE ORGANIC GROWERS OF GRATERFORD: A PRISON TALE

AFTER TRAVELING ABOUT FORTY-FIVE MINUTES NORTH OF PHILADELPHIA, I turned the restaurant's van off a rural highway and through a gate with a sign reading "Graterford State Correctional Institution." I was trying out our concept of using food to increase understanding. Our "Eating with the Enemy" program had taken us to the Soviet Union, Vietnam, and Cuba, so why not some place closer to home? I drove over a creek and along the dusty road, past open farmland and woods. Although I understood where I was headed, I still gasped when I rounded a bend and saw the massive stone walls that suddenly loomed before me. There was something so frightening and primitive about this medieval-like scene, with the turreted guard towers at each end of the long imposing wall. My destination was a garden outside of the walls where a dozen inmates with good behavior were permitted to raise organic vegetables. I had come with a group of Cafe patrons to tour the garden and have dinner with the inmates—the Organic Growers of Graterford.

Aware that our criminal-justice system fails to rehabilitate offenders, often sending them back onto our streets angrier and more violent than when they entered the system, I appreciated the importance of the gardening program, run by volunteers who believed in the restorative power of working with plants and maintaining a healthful diet. I arrived at the outbuilding to unload the vegetarian buffet dinner of organic vegetable and grain dishes that Kevin had prepared for us just as the other cars, filled with patrons of the White Dog Cafe, pulled up. After sending out a newsletter announcing events, I'm always curious to see who responds. Today I was surprised to see three elderly ladies, perhaps in their eighties. I recognized them as regular patrons of the Cafe, who often dined together at our dinner-discussion series. I was a little concerned about them walking across the uneven, muddy ground

Graterford inmate-gardener proudly displays organically grown tomatoes

where we would view the gardens, but as I headed out with Omar, the inmate leader, and Violet, the volunteer coordinator, I looked over

The Organic Growers of Graterford tending their garden

my shoulder at a picture that will stay in my memory forever. The three little ladies were walking arm-in-arm with two huge, burly inmates. All five smiling faces were lit brightly by the late afternoon sun as it shown across the fields to the now distant stone fortress left behind. Big, heavy boots below gray uniforms and tiny black shoes below thin, hose-covered legs were making their way slowly but steadily across the bumpy ground of the open fields, toward a sign painted with colorful flowers, "Welcome to our garden. The Organic Growers of Graterford."

Our group of about thirty, including our dinner speaker who had written a book on the relationship between crime and diet, walked down rows of tomatoes, peppers, broccoli, corn, herbs, and flowers, chatting with inmates about their gardening techniques, plans for the next season, and courses they had taken in cooking and flower arranging, taught by volunteers who were among our guests. After we gathered at two long tables, cramped under the low ceiling of the windowless outbuilding, Omar said grace, and we enjoyed a delicious meal that included White Cheddar and Red-skinned Potato Gratin, and Honey Glazed Turnips. After dinner, the inmates took turns standing to tell us about their gardening experiences. Many were shy to speak and had to be coaxed by Omar and Violet. Their stories brought tears to many eyes and enthusiastic applause from the three ladies and other diners.

"Nobody ever cared about me, and so I never cared about nothing," the first began. "I was angry when I dug the dirt the first day, and I dug harder and harder. When I planted the seeds and the plants came up, I felt happy like I never did before. And I take good care of them. When I wake up in the morning and I see my garden, I get a peaceful feeling."

Another began, "I worry about my family and how they get by without me being there. When I came here, I was angry and frustrated that I couldn't do nothing for them. Now it's my plants that calm me down and keep me company."

An older inmate, a leader in the group, told this folk story: "Long ago in an ancient society in Persia, when a man committed a crime, he was imprisoned until he could successfully grow a plant. The type of plant differed with the severity of the crime, from a simple flower to a tall oak. It wasn't until the offender had nurtured the plant to maturity that he was set free to rejoin his community."

Finally, the youngest of the inmates spoke: "My mom, she loves to garden. I guess that's where I get it from. But I never paid her no mind before. I was too busy being in trouble. Now I wrote her that when I get out, I'm gonna help in her garden. She's so happy."

Often when I eat the fresh vegetable dishes we enjoyed at that dinner, I think of the Organic Growers of Graterford out under the sun, in the fresh air, with hands in the earth, nurturing their plants, and with them, their own humanity.　　　　　　　　　**—JW**

White Cheddar and Red-skinned Potato Gratin {Serves 6 to 8}

We serve this rich, bubbling, thyme-flecked gratin of white cheddar cheese and red-skinned potatoes with Rosemary-Mustard London Broil with Wild Mushroom Glaze (page 136) and Green Beans with Onions (page 203).

$1\frac{3}{4}$ **pounds red-skinned potatoes, scrubbed**

1 cup heavy cream

1 cup whole milk

2 cups shredded sharp white cheddar cheese

1 tablespoon dried thyme

$1\frac{1}{2}$ **teaspoons salt**

1 teaspoon freshly ground black pepper

1. Preheat the oven to 325°F. Butter an 11 x 7-inch casserole, gratin, or baking dish.

2. Slice the potatoes as thinly as possible. Drop the slices into cold water to keep them from discoloring.

3. Combine the cream, milk, cheese, thyme, salt, and pepper in a large mixing bowl. Drain the potatoes thoroughly. Add the potatoes to the cream mixture. Spoon the mixture into the prepared dish. Cover and bake for 1 hour. Remove cover and continue baking until cooked through, golden brown, and bubbling, about ½ hour.

Truffled Potato Croquettes with Chèvre {Serves 8}

This dish is potatoes at their height of elegance; here, the common Idaho is creamed with luxurious white truffle oil and wrapped around nuggets of lush chèvre. For an elegant brunch, offer these croquettes with softly scrambled eggs with chives, or serve them as a first course with sautéed spinach and radishes. They are, of course, a perfect addition to almost any vegetarian meal and will win raves no matter how you present them.

---

2 pounds Idaho potatoes, peeled and quartered

1 whole egg plus 3 egg yolks, whisked together

2 tablespoons white truffle oil (see note, page 128)

2 tablespoons unsalted butter

1 teaspoon salt

$\frac{1}{4}$ teaspoon freshly ground black pepper

4 ounces unaged chèvre, at room temperature

All-purpose flour, for dusting

Vegetable oil

1. Preheat the oven to 400°F.

2. Place the potatoes in a saucepan and add water to cover by 2 inches. Bring to a boil over high heat. Reduce the heat and simmer until just cooked through, about 15 minutes.

3. Drain the potatoes; arrange them in a single layer on a baking sheet. Roast in the oven for 2 minutes to dry off any excess moisture. Leave the oven on.

4. In a large bowl, mash the potatoes with a ricer, potato masher, or sturdy whisk. Stir in the beaten egg and yolks and mix well to combine. Stir in the white truffle oil, butter, salt, and pepper. Taste for seasoning.

5. Shape the chèvre into 8 small disks, each about 1$\frac{1}{2}$ inches in diameter and $\frac{1}{4}$ inch thick. When the potato mixture is cool enough to handle, divide it into 8 equal portions. Shape each portion around a piece of chèvre, forming a 3-inch patty with a piece of cheese in the center. (The croquettes can be made to this stage up to 2 days in advance and kept refrigerated.)

6. Dust each croquette with flour, to coat all sides. In a large sauté pan set over medium-high heat, heat $\frac{1}{8}$ inch of oil until it ripples. Working in batches, cook the croquettes until golden brown, about 3 minutes on each side. Remove the cooked croquettes to a baking sheet. Bake in the oven until the cheese melts and the croquettes are heated through, about 5 minutes. Serve hot.

Roasted Red Pepper–Potato Cake {Serves 4}

These cheesy, crimson-flecked potato cakes are studded with roasted red peppers and fresh thyme. They are great aside the Tangy Tian of Summer Vegetables (page 181) or as part of any vegetarian meal topped with Winter Herb Pesto (page 292). They can also dress up a meat-and-potato meal, like the Grilled Beef Tenderloin with Balsamic-Pancetta Glaze (page 134).

1 pound red-skinned potatoes, scrubbed

Salt

¼ cup plus 2 tablespoons olive oil

1 cup minced yellow onion

1 tablespoon chopped fresh thyme leaves

1 teaspoon minced garlic

2 red bell peppers, roasted (see note, page140), peeled, seeded, and finely diced

¾ cup freshly grated Parmesan

1 egg yolk, whisked

Freshly ground black pepper

All-purpose flour, for dusting

1. Combine the potatoes and a pinch of salt in a saucepan and add water to cover by 2 inches. Bring to a boil over high heat. Reduce the heat and simmer until the potatoes are easily pierced with a fork, about 20 minutes.

2. Meanwhile, heat the 2 tablespoons olive oil in a sauté pan set over medium-high heat. Add the onion and cook until translucent, about 5 minutes. Add the thyme and garlic and cook for 2 minutes. Reserve.

3. Drain the potatoes well. Return them to the saucepan and set over low heat. Toss the potatoes for a minute to evaporate any excess moisture.

4. Mash the hot, dried potatoes in a large bowl with a sturdy whisk or potato masher. Add the reserved onion and garlic mixture, the bell peppers, cheese, egg yolk, and pepper. Mix thoroughly with a spoon.

5. Shape the mixture into 4 large cakes, each about 5 inches in diameter. (The cakes can be made to this point up to 2 days in advance. Let cool to room temperature, cover, and refrigerate until needed.)

6. Lightly dust both sides of the cakes with flour. In a large sauté pan set over medium heat, heat the remaining ¼ cup oil until it ripples. Carefully add the potato cakes and cook until golden brown, about 4 minutes on each side. Serve hot.

Chèvre-Rosemary-Garlic Mashed Potatoes {Serves 8}

Sweet garlic, tangy chèvre, and fragrant rosemary conspire to make one of the best mashed potatoes we've ever tasted. Serve this rich mash with leg of lamb, grilled steak or chicken.

8 large russet potatoes, peeled and quartered

4 tablespoons unsalted butter

1/2 cup whole milk

4 ounces unaged chèvre

1 head of garlic, roasted (see note, page 38), the pulp squeezed from the cloves

1 tablespoon chopped fresh rosemary leaves

2 teaspoons salt

1 teaspoon freshly ground black pepper

1. Place the potatoes in a large saucepan and add water to cover by 2 inches. Bring to a boil over high heat. Reduce the heat and simmer until fork tender, 20 to 25 minutes.

2. While the potatoes are cooking, melt the butter in the milk in a small saucepan set over low heat.

3. Drain the potatoes in a colander. Return them to the saucepan and set over low heat. Toss for a minute to evaporate any excess moisture. Add the butter and milk mixture and mash the potatoes with a sturdy whisk. Crumble in the chèvre, roasted garlic, rosemary, salt, and pepper; mash to combine. Taste for seasoning. Serve immediately.

OTHER WAYS TO DO IT

To make sour cream and chive mashed potatoes, substitute 1 1/4 cups sour cream for the chèvre, reduce the milk in the recipe to 1/4 cup, and add 1/4 cup minced chives. Omit the rosemary.

Rosemary-roasted Potatoes {Serves 4 to 6}

Garlicky, rosemary-scented, and hot from the oven, these are beyond compare; we serve them with everything from sirloin to swordfish.

1 pound red-skinned potatoes, scrubbed and quartered

2 tablespoons olive oil

1 tablespoon chopped fresh rosemary leaves

1 tablespoon chopped garlic

1/2 teaspoon salt, or to taste

Pinch of hot red pepper flakes

1. Preheat the oven to 450°F.

2. Combine the potatoes, olive oil, rosemary, garlic, salt and pepper flakes in a mixing bowl. Toss to combine well.

3. Spread the potatoes in a single even layer on a baking sheet. Roast, stirring occasionally, until cooked through and lightly golden, 20 to 30 minutes. Serve immediately.

Fennel-roasted Potatoes {Serves 4 to 6}

A simple, fragrant accompaniment for roasted or grilled meats and fish or for part of a vegetarian meal with Sun-dried Tomato Vinaigrette (page 56).

4 large Idaho potatoes, cut lengthwise into thin wedges

¼ cup extra-virgin olive oil

2 tablespoons minced garlic

1 teaspoon salt

2 teaspoons fennel seed

Pinch of hot pepper flakes

Combine the potato wedges with with the other ingredients in a large bowl and toss well. Spread them on a baking sheet and roast in a 400°F oven for 25 minutes, turning occasionally with a spatula until golden brown and tender when pierced with a fork. Serve immediately.

Country-style Potatoes {Serves 4 to 6}

A hearty peasant dish of potatoes simmered with onions and garlic in an herbed tomato broth, this makes a warming supper alongside braised greens or as part of a vegetarian feast. It also pairs well with meat, game, or poultry.

⅓ cup extra-virgin olive oil

1 large yellow onion, cut into 1-inch cubes

4 garlic cloves, slivered

1 tablespoon tomato paste

4 plum tomatoes, cut into 1-inch-thick rounds

4 Idaho potatoes, peeled and cut into large cubes

1 tablespoon chopped fresh sage leaves

1 tablespoon chopped fresh rosemary leaves

1 tablespoon chopped fresh oregano leaves

Pinch of hot red pepper flakes

1 teaspoon salt

1 tablespoon fresh lemon juice

1. In a large nonreactive skillet or sauté pan set over medium-high heat, heat the oil until it ripples. Add the onion and cook until browned, about 8 minutes.

2. Add the garlic and cook for 1 minute. Stir in the tomato paste and cook for 1 minute. Add the tomatoes, potatoes, pepper flakes, and salt. Pour in enough water to cover all but the top ½ inch of the potatoes. Bring to a boil over high heat. Reduce the heat to a simmer, cover, and cook for 10 minutes.

3. Remove the cover, increase the heat to medium-high, and cook until the potatoes are tender and in a thick sauce, about 10 minutes more.

4. Stir in the lemon juice and chopped fresh herbs and taste for seasoning. Serve immediately, or let cool to room temperature, cover, and refrigerate for up to 2 days. Reheat before serving.

OTHER WAYS TO DO IT
For a richer, nonvegetarian version of this dish, omit the tomato paste and replace the water with a light veal or chicken stock.

Spicy Fried Potatoes with Saffron Aïoli {Serves 4}

We serve these crisp, golden, spiced potatoes topped with large dollops of our homemade Saffron Aïoli.

SAFFRON AÏOLI

1/2 cup dry white wine

1 teaspoon saffron threads

1 teaspoon minced garlic

2 cups Homemade Mayonnaise (see note, page 287) or store-bought

1/2 teaspoon *nam pla* (Thai fish sauce, available in Asian markets and specialty food stores; see note, page 95)

1/2 teaspoon freshly ground black pepper

SPICY SEASONING MIX

1 teaspoon salt

1/2 teaspoon chili powder

1/2 teaspoon cayenne pepper

1/2 teaspoon hot paprika

1/2 teaspoon dried oregano

1/2 teaspoon garlic powder

1/4 teaspoon ground cumin

Peanut oil, for frying

1 pound red-skinned potatoes, scrubbed and thoroughly dried

1. Prepare the Saffron Aïoli: Combine the wine, saffron and garlic in a small, nonreactive saucepan set over low heat. Simmer until almost all of the liquid evaporates, about 5 minutes. Remove from the heat. Transfer to a medium bowl, and let cool to room temperature.

2. Stir in the mayonnaise, *nam pla*, and pepper. Taste for seasoning. Use the aïoli immediately or refrigerate in an airtight container for up to 4 days.

3. Preheat the oven to 200°F.

4. Prepare the seasoning mix: Combine the salt, chili powder, cayenne, paprika, oregano, garlic powder, and cumin in a small bowl. Reserve.

5. Prepare the potatoes: In a deep fryer or heavy saucepan, heat 2 inches of peanut oil to 350°F, or until a cube of bread dropped in the oil turns golden brown within 1 to 2 minutes.

6. While the oil is heating, slice the potatoes as thinly as possible. When the oil has reached the correct temperature, fry half of the potatoes until golden and crisp, 5 to 7 minutes. Remove the potatoes from the oil with a slotted spoon to a paper-towel-lined baking sheet. Set in the preheated oven to keep warm while frying the remaining potatoes.

7. Sprinkle the potatoes with some of the reserved seasoning to taste. Serve immediately topped with the Saffron Aïoli. Any leftover seasoning can be stored in a jar and used later.

Spicy Potato (or Sweet Potato) Chips {Serves 4}

Homemade potato chips are simple to make and better than anything you'll find in a bag. Use a good-quality peeler to produce large, uniform chips that fry nicely. We've found that plastic Y-shaped peelers work best.

1 pound red-skinned potatoes or sweet potatoes, scrubbed and thoroughly dried

Peanut oil, for frying

Spicy Seasoning Mix (see opposite page) or salt and freshly ground black pepper

1. Peel the skin off the potatoes with a peeler and discard.

2. Peel the potatoes into long, even chips and place in cold water for 1 hour, changing the water twice. This keeps them from discoloring and removes some starch from the potato, which can cause them to stick together when fried.

3. Remove the potatoes from from the water and drain thoroughly in a colander. Then pat dry on a clean kitchen towel.

4. When the oil has reached 350°F, fry the chips in small batches until lightly golden brown, 4 to 5 minutes.

5. With a slotted spoon, remove the chips to a paper-towel-lined plate. Season with the Spicy Seasoning Mix. Serve immediately.

Dijon Potato Salad {Serves 6 to 8}

A picnic-perfect salad of red-skinned potatoes bathed in an herbed mustard vinaigrette, this dish is elegant enough to accompany a piece of grilled salmon or tuna, but isn't out of place with coleslaw and a burger.

2 pounds red-skinned potatoes, cut into ¼-inch slices

2 tablespoons Dijon mustard

2 tablespoons red wine vinegar

2 tablespoons chopped fresh dill

2 tablespoons chopped fresh tarragon leaves

1 teaspoon sugar

½ teaspoon freshly ground black pepper

½ teaspoon salt

¼ cup olive oil

1 celery rib, finely diced

2 scallions, thinly sliced

1. Place the potatoes in a saucepan and add water to cover by 2 inches. Bring to a gentle boil over high heat. Reduce the heat and simmer until just cooked through, about 10 minutes. Drain well and spread in a single layer on a baking sheet to cool.

2. Combine the mustard, vinegar, dill, tarragon, sugar, pepper, and salt in a small bowl. Slowly drizzle in the oil, whisking constantly to form an emulsion.

3. Combine the cooled potatoes, celery, and scallions in a large bowl. Toss with the dressing. Serve immediately, or cover and refrigerate for up to 3 days.

Summer Garden Vegetable Potato Salad {Serves 6 to 8}

Emerald green pesto and white balsamic vinegar dress this colorful salad of red-skinned potatoes and summer vegetables. White balsamic vinegar isn't aged in wooden barrels so it retains its light hue and delicate fruity flavor. Look for it in specialty food stores and better supermarkets. If you can't find it, substitute apple cider vinegar. This salad is best if served the day it is made.

1½ pounds red-skinned potatoes, cut into ½-inch wedges

1/4 pound trimmed green beans, halved

1 small zucchini cut into ¼-inch coins

1 red bell pepper, diced

1 yellow bell pepper, diced

8 cherry tomatoes, halved

2 scallions, thinly sliced

¾ cup Basil Pesto (page 292)

2 tablespoons white balsamic vinegar

Salt and freshly ground black pepper to taste

1. Place the potatoes with a pinch of salt in a large saucepan and add water to cover. Bring to a boil over high heat. Lower the heat and simmer until the potatoes are just cooked through, about 10 minutes. Drain the potatoes and spread them on a baking sheet. Sprinkle with vinegar. Cool to room temperature. Reserve.

2. Bring a small pot of salted water to a boil. Blanch the green beans in the boiling water for 1 minute. Remove and shock in ice water until chilled. Drain well and reserve. Blanch the zucchini and yellow squash in the boiling water for 30 seconds or until just cooked through. Remove and shock in ice water until chilled. Drain well. Reserve.

3. Combine the potatoes, green beans, zucchini, yellow squash, bell peppers, cherry tomatoes, scallions and basil pesto in a large bowl. Toss well. Season to taste with salt and freshly ground black pepper. Serve at room temperature, or cover and refrigerate until chilled.

Maple-mashed Sweet Potatoes {Serves 6 to 8}

Pure Vermont maple syrup adds another dimension to this creamy thyme-spiked mash of sweet potatoes. We serve it with all of our favorite pork dishes, Nicaraguan Braised Beef Shins (page 139) and Chili-rubbed Duck Breasts with Sun-dried Cherry Glaze (page 130).

8 sweet potatoes, peeled and halved

5 tablespoons unsalted butter

¼ cup pure maple syrup

2 tablespoons chopped fresh thyme leaves

1 teaspoon salt

½ teaspoon freshly ground black pepper

1. Place the potatoes in a large saucepan and add water to cover by 2 inches. Bring to a boil over high heat. Reduce the heat and simmer until the potatoes are easily pierced with a fork, about 20 minutes.

2. Meanwhile, melt the butter with the maple syrup in a small saucepan over low heat.

3. Drain the potatoes in a colander. Return them to the saucepan and set over low heat. Toss for 1 minute to evaporate any excess moisture. Add the butter and syrup to the potatoes and mash with a potato masher or a strong whisk. Stir in the thyme, salt, and pepper. Serve immediately.

OTHER WAYS TO DO IT

If you want to change their flavor altogether, omit the thyme and add 1 tablespoon of minced chipotle peppers (or more depending upon your taste for fire) to the mashed potatoes. The smoky fire of the chipotles mingles with the sweet syrup and potatoes in this highly spirited version of a classic home-style dish.

Lavender- and Honey-roasted Butternut Squash {Serves 4 to 6}

The current incarnation of this dish evolved over many months. Originally, we imported lavender honey from France to make lavender-honey ice cream, which we served with roasted fresh figs. When fig season was over, several jars of the perfumed honey remained. We tried glazing winter squash with it and fell in love with the combination. Today we use locally produced honey and dried lavender flowers in this singular roasted butternut squash. Look for dried lavender flowers in specialty food stores and spice shops; they are quite fragrant, so use them sparingly.

1 small butternut squash (1$\frac{1}{2}$ to 2 pounds)

4 tablespoons unsalted butter, cut into $\frac{1}{2}$-inch cubes

2 tablespoons honey

1 teaspoon dried lavender

1 teaspoon dried thyme

$\frac{1}{2}$ teaspoon salt

$\frac{1}{4}$ teaspoon fresh ground black pepper

1. Preheat the oven to 400°F.

2. Peel the squash, halve lengthwise and scoop out the seeds. Cut the flesh into $\frac{1}{2}$-inch cubes and spread in a single layer in a large roasting pan.

3. Dot the squash with the cubed butter and drizzle with the honey. Sprinkle with the lavender, thyme, salt, and pepper.

4. Cover with foil and roast, stirring occasionally, until tender, about 30 minutes. Serve immediately or let cool to room temperature, cover, and refrigerate for up to 2 days. Reheat before serving.

Honey-glazed Turnips {Serves 4}

In this beautiful preparation, we cook the turnips uncovered in water that is sweetened with honey and enriched with butter. As the water evaporates and the turnips cook, the honey and butter form a caramel that coats the vegetables, lending them golden color and deep, rich flavor. This method of cooking works well for carrots, rutabagas, and winter squash, too.

4 tablespoons unsalted butter

$\frac{1}{4}$ cup honey

1 cup hot water

4 small turnips, peeled and cut into $\frac{1}{2}$-inch cubes

Salt and freshly ground black pepper

1. Combine the butter, honey, and water in a large cast-iron skillet. Bring to a boil over high heat.

2. Add the turnips and the additional water, if necessary, to just cover the turnips with liquid. Cook over high heat until the liquid evaporates, about 10 minutes. Note, however, that as the water evaporates, the honey and butter begin to caramelize on the bottom of the pan. Toss the turnips constantly as the caramel forms, coating them evenly, until fork tender and golden brown. Serve immediately.

Caraway-roasted Vegetables {Serves 4 to 6}

A relic of ancient Greece, caraway seeds lend a distinctive bite to any dish they grace. In this vivid mélange of caramelized fall vegetables, rich autumnal flavors are livened by crunchy bright-green Brussels sprouts and fresh sage. This dish is especially good with roast beef, grilled fish, or as part of a Thanksgiving dinner.

1 large white onion, cut into 1-inch cubes

1 pound red-skinned potatoes, scrubbed and quartered

4 tablespoons olive oil

2 teaspoons minced garlic

2 teaspoons caraway seeds

1 teaspoon rubbed sage

2 large carrots, peeled and cut into 1-inch pieces

6 ounces button mushrooms, cleaned

8 ounces Brussels sprouts

2 tablespoons chopped fresh sage leaves

½ teaspoon salt

¼ teaspoon freshly ground black pepper

1. Preheat the oven to 450°F.

2. In a medium bowl, toss together the onion, potatoes, 2 tablespoons of the olive oil, 1 teaspoon each of the garlic and caraway seeds, and ½ teaspoon of the rubbed sage. Spread the vegetables in a single layer on a baking sheet. Roast, stirring occasionally, until golden brown and cooked through, about 25 minutes. Keep warm.

3. Meanwhile, using the same bowl, toss together the carrots, mushrooms, the remaining 2 tablespoons of the olive oil, the remaining 1 teaspoon each minced garlic and caraway seeds, and the remaining ½ teaspoon rubbed sage. Spread the vegetables in a single layer on a baking sheet. Roast, stirring occasionally, until slightly golden and just tender, about 15 minutes. Keep warm.

4. While the vegetables roast, bring 2 quarts of salted water to a boil. Trim the end off each Brussels sprout with a paring knife. Make two shallow incisions at the base of each, forming an X. Blanch the sprouts until just cooked through, about 4 minutes. To test the Brussels sprouts for doneness, remove 1 from the pot and cut it in half. If cooked through to the center, it's done. Drain and reserve.

5. Toss together the warm roasted vegetables and Brussels sprouts in a large bowl. Season with the chopped fresh sage, salt, and pepper. This dish tastes and looks its best when served immediately, while the Brussels sprouts are bright green. However, if necessary, let cool to room temperature, cover, and refrigerate for up to 2 days. Reheat in a warm oven before serving.

Cider-braised Cabbage {Serves 6 to 8}

We serve this cabbage with rich, meaty, wintry dishes; its sharp tang offers nice contrast.

---

1 tablespoon olive oil

1/3 cup finely diced hickory-smoked bacon

1 small white onion, minced

1 carrot, peeled and finely diced

1 small red or white cabbage, halved, cored, and thinly sliced

1 cup apple cider

3/4 cup apple cider vinegar

2 tablespoons sugar

1 bay leaf

5 black peppercorns

Salt and freshly ground black pepper

1. In a large nonreactive saucepan set over medium heat, heat the oil until it ripples. Add the bacon and cook until browned and crisp.

2. Add the onion and carrot and cook 3 to 4 minutes, until soft. Add the cabbage and toss to coat with the oil. Stir in the apple cider, cider vinegar, sugar, bay leaf, and peppercorns; cook until the cabbage begins to wilt, 2 or 3 minutes. Cover tightly and set over very low heat.

3. Braise slowly until the cabbage is very tender, 45 to 60 minutes. Remove from the heat and season to taste with salt and pepper. Remove the bay leaf. Serve immediately, or let cool to room temperature, cover, and refrigerate for up to 2 days. Reheat before serving.

Savoy Cabbage with Pancetta and Oyster Mushrooms {Serves 4}

Sweet cabbage, salty pancetta, and delicate oyster mushrooms merge in this quick sauté. We serve it at the White Dog Cafe with Warm French Lentils (page 206) and Pan-seared Salmon with Burgundy-Rosemary Butter (page 164).

---

1 ounce pancetta, cut into 1/4-inch dice (about 1/3 cup)

2 ounces oyster mushrooms (about 1 cup), tough stems removed, caps torn into bite-size pieces, or 1 cup sliced button mushrooms

4 cups (about 1 pound) thinly sliced savoy cabbage

1/4 cup water

Freshly ground black pepper

1. Slowly cook the pancetta in a sauté pan set over medium-low heat until all the fat is released and the pancetta is crispy, 5 to 7 minutes.

2. Turn the heat to medium-high, add the mushrooms, and cook until they begin to soften, about 3 minutes. Add the cabbage and 1/4 cup water. Cook, tossing, until the water evaporates and the cabbage is tender, about 5 minutes. Season with pepper to taste. Serve immediately.

Roasted Vegetables Balsamico {Serves 4}

Serve this flavorful dish alongside roast leg of lamb, chicken, or a meaty fish like tuna or swordfish. It also works well as part of a vegetarian dinner with Herbed Parmesan Polenta (page 210) and Sautéed Greens and Garlic (page 202).

1 small zucchini, cut into 1-inch dice

1 small yellow squash, cut into 1-inch dice

1 red bell pepper, cut into 1-inch dice

1 yellow bell pepper, cut into 1-inch dice

1 red onion, cut into 1-inch dice

4 tablespoons olive oil

3 tablespoons minced garlic

3 teaspoons dried thyme

3 teaspoons dried basil

1 small eggplant, cut into 1-inch dice

1 tablespoon plus 1 teaspoon
    balsamic vinegar

1 tablespoon soy sauce

¼ teaspoon freshly ground black pepper

1. Preheat the oven to 425°F.

2. Combine the zucchini, yellow squash, bell peppers, and onion in a large bowl; sprinkle with 2 tablespoons of the olive oil, 2 tablespoons of the minced garlic, 2 teaspoons of the thyme, and 2 teaspoons of the basil. Toss well to coat all of the vegetables with the oil and seasonings. Spread in an even layer on a baking pan and roast, stirring occasionally, until golden, about 20 minutes.

3. Meanwhile, using the same bowl, toss the eggplant with the remaining 2 tablespoons olive oil, the remaining 1 tablespoon garlic, and the remaining 1 teaspoon each thyme and basil. Spread in an even layer on a baking sheet and roast, stirring occasionally, until lightly golden, about 15 minutes.

4. Toss all of the cooked vegetables together in a large bowl. Sprinkle with the vinegar, soy sauce, and black pepper; toss to mix well. Serve hot or at room temperature. The vegetables will keep, refrigerated, for up to 2 days. Bring to room temperature before serving.

Sugar Snap Peas Sautéed with Scallions {Serves 6}

Nothing could be greener, fresher, or more sweet or brilliantly colored than quick-cooked scallions and peas. After more than a few minutes in the pan they begin to fade, so make haste to the table.

1 tablespoon butter

2 scallions, thinly sliced

1 pound sugar snap peas

Salt and black pepper

1. Heat the butter in a pan set over medium-high heat.

2. Add the scallions and toss for a few seconds. Add the peas and a few tablespoons of water.

3. Cook, stirring, until tender but still crisp, about 5 minutes. Season to taste and serve immediately.

Sesame-steamed Snow Peas {Serves 6}

Try these peas with any Asian-style meal. We serve them with Sesame-roasted Pork Tenderloin with Ginger Glaze (page 143) and Sweet Potato Chips (page 195) or aside Crispy Red Snapper with Shiitake Mushroom Glaze (page 162) or Sautéed Pork Medallions with Basil and Balsamico (page 147).

1 pound snow peas

2 tablespoons Asian sesame oil

Pinch of sesame seeds, toasted (see note, page 144)

Salt and freshly ground black pepper

1. Bring a few tablespoons of water to a boil in a large sauté pan set over high heat.

2. Add the peas and steam, uncovered, until just tender and the water is almost evaporated. Add the sesame oil and seeds, and season to taste. Serve immediately.

Sautéed Greens and Garlic {Serves 4}

I can't think of a meal that isn't enhanced by the addition of sautéed greens. I like the textural contrast and earthy undertones they introduce, not to mention the healthful vitamins and fiber.

3 tablespoons olive oil

6 cloves garlic, minced

1¼ pounds spinach, washed well, tough stems removed and discarded

or

1¼ pounds kale, washed well, tough stems removed and discarded, and cut into 2-inch strips (if leaves are large)

or

2 pounds Swiss chard, washed well, whole stalks cut into 2-inch strips

or

2 pounds broccoli rabe, washed well, and cut into 2-inch strips

or

2 pounds bok choy, washed well, leaves and tender part of the stems cut into 2-inch pieces, tough stems discarded

or

1¼ pounds arugula, washed well, tough stems removed and discarded

Salt and freshly ground black pepper

1. To cook any of the greens listed, heat the olive oil in a large nonreactive sauté pan set over medium-high heat.

2. Add the minced garlic and sauté for 1 minute.

3. Add the cleaned greens, a few tablespoons of water, and season to taste.

4. Cover and cook, stirring and turning, until the greens are tender and wilted. (For the spinach and arugula, cook for only a matter of seconds, until slightly wilted. For the kale and broccoli rabe, the cooking time can take up to 5 minutes.) Taste the greens for doneness and adjust the seasoning with salt, pepper, and a sprinkling of lemon juice or balsamic vinegar, if desired. Serve immediately.

NOTE: If you're going to cook the greens immediately after washing them, they do not need to be dried. The moisture clinging to the leaves will produce steam as they cook. If you aren't going to use them right away, dry the leaves in a clean towel or salad spinner.

Balsamic-braised Kale {Serves 4}

Kale is a leafy member of the cabbage family that flourishes in hues from purple to yellow to brilliant green—the most common American variety is dark green with frilly leaves, resembling giant parsley. Although it's commonly seen covering the ice on a salad bar buffet, kale has merit far beyond its decorative value. When braised, it becomes tender without losing its texture—perfect for soups, stews, as well as a lively side dish by itself.

8 cups tightly packed kale leaves, stemmed and cut into large pieces

2 tablespoons extra-virgin olive oil

1 tablespoon minced garlic

1 tablespoon balsamic vinegar

Salt and freshly ground black pepper

1. Set the kale in a colander and rinse well.

2. Heat the oil in a large sauté pan set over medium-high heat until it ripples. Add the garlic and cook for 2 minutes. Add the kale leaves. Turn the heat to medium and cover. Braise until tender, 10 to 15 minutes. The water on the kale leaves should provide enough liquid to braise them, however check the kale occasionally and add more water if necessary.

3. Remove the lid, raise the heat to high, and cook off any excess liquid. Remove from the heat. Pour on the vinegar and toss well. Season to taste. Serve immediately.

THE WAY WE DO IT
This method of cooking works well with other leafy greens as well. Try it with Swiss chard, spinach, escarole, or arugula.

Green Beans with Onions {Serves 6}

Crisp green beans and sweet onions are an all-time favorite pairing; we serve them alongside Rosemary-Mustard London Broil with Wild Mushroom Glaze (page 136) or with Sautéed Chicken and Mushrooms in Marsala-Sage Sauce (page 122), but they'll enhance any home-style meal.

2 tablespoons olive oil

1 cup white onion, thinly sliced

1 teaspoon minced garlic

1½ pounds trimmed green beans, blanched

salt and freshly ground black pepper

1. Heat the oil in a sauté pan set over medium heat until it ripples.

2. Add the onion and cook, stirring occasionally, until it caramelizes. Add the garlic and cook for 1 minute.

3. Add the beans and a few tablespoons of water and cook, stirring, until the water evaporates and the beans are crisp-tender. Season to taste and serve immediately.

Sesame-roasted Asparagus {Serves 4}

Sesame oil, the dark nutty elixir pressed from toasted sesame seeds, has a fantastically potent flavor and fragrance. It can easily overpower most foods, so we add it carefully. In this dish it is combined with a light sprinkling of sesame seeds, soy sauce, sherry, and hot pepper flakes to lace the asparagus with flavor without covering its wonderful character.

1 pound asparagus spears, trimmed

2 tablespoons dry sherry

2 tablespoons vegetable oil

1 tablespoon soy sauce

1 tablespoon sesame seeds

1 teaspoon Asian sesame oil

Pinch of red pepper flakes

1. Preheat the oven to 450°F.

2. Arrange the asparagus in a single layer in a large baking dish.

3. Whisk together the sherry, vegetable oil, soy sauce, sesame seeds, sesame oil, and pepper flakes in a small bowl. Drizzle over the asparagus and roll the spears to coat evenly.

4. Roast until tender, 6 to 8 minutes, depending on the thickness of the spears. Taste for seasoning. Serve immediately.

Stir-fried Wild Rice {Serves 4}

Sweet with grated carrot and fragrant with black pepper, this dish is easy to toss together and surprisingly filling. Nutty wild rice lends it a character and texture superior to its white rice counterparts. We serve it with wok-seared red snapper, or stir in a cracked egg and some diced cooked chicken or shrimp during the last minute of cooking to make it a meal.

1 cup uncooked wild rice, rinsed well

Salt

2 tablespoons vegetable oil

1 tablespoon minced garlic

1 tablespoon minced fresh ginger

4 scallions, thinly sliced

1 carrot, peeled and grated

1 celery rib, finely diced

2 tablespoons plus 1 teaspoon soy sauce

2 tablespoons chopped fresh cilantro, leaves and stems (see note, page 158)

¹/₄ teaspoon freshly ground black pepper

1. Combine the wild rice and a pinch of salt in a saucepan; add water to cover by 4 inches. Bring to a boil over high heat. Reduce the heat to medium and simmer, uncovered, until the rice grains split open and are tender, 45 to 60 minutes. (You may need to add more water to the rice as it cooks to keep it submerged.) Drain the rice in a colander.

2. In a large sauté pan set over high heat, heat the oil until it ripples. Add the garlic, ginger, and scallions and cook, without browning, for 2 to 3 minutes. Add the carrot and celery and cook until just tender, 2 to 3 minutes. Add the drained rice and toss until heated through. Add the soy sauce, cilantro, and pepper; mix well. Taste for seasoning. Serve immediately.

Firehouse Dalmatian Bean Salad {Serves 4}

Black and white beans flecked with bell and jalapeño peppers make a colorful, spicy salad. We serve it with our Southwestern Turkey Burger (page 107) or Cobb Salad Sandwich with Blue Cheese Mayonnaise (page 102).

¼ cup fresh orange juice

Grated zest and juice of 1 lime

1 jalapeño pepper, seeded and minced

1 tablespoon New Mexican chili powder (see note, page 130)

1 tablespoon ground cumin, toasted (see notes, page 73)

2 teaspoons minced garlic

2 teaspoons salt

½ cup olive oil

1 red bell pepper, finely diced

1 green bell pepper, finely diced

1 carrot, peeled and finely diced

¼ cup tightly packed fresh cilantro leaves and stems, chopped (see note, page 158)

2 cups cooked black beans

2 cups cooked white beans, such as Great Northern

1. Whisk together the orange juice, lime zest and juice, jalapeño, chili powder, cumin, garlic, and salt in a small bowl. Whisk in the oil in a slow steady stream. Reserve.

2. Toss together both of the bell peppers, the carrot, cilantro, cooked black and white beans, and the reserved vinaigrette in a large bowl. Taste and adjust the seasoning, if necessary. The salad is best if you let it sit at room temperature to allow the flavors to blend for a few hours before serving.

3. Cover and refrigerate for up to 3 days. Bring to room temperature before serving.

OTHER WAYS TO DO IT

This salad is delicious to eat by itself, however if you want to serve it the way we do at the White Dog Cafe, sprinkle black pepper over small rounds of fresh chèvre and bake in a 400°F oven until soft. Serve the warmed cheese over mounds of the bean salad and some mixed lettuce leaves.

Zucchini with White Beans and Mint {Serves 4}

White beans and zucchini are startlingly delicious paired with fresh mint. Use a fruity full-flavored olive oil for optimum results and shave some Parmesan on top just before serving.

2 tablespoons extra-virgin olive oil

½ teaspoon minced garlic

3 or 4 small zucchini, cut into long (¼ x ¼-inch) strips

1 cup cooked cannellini beans (see note, page 215)

½ tablespoons chopped fresh mint leaves

Salt and freshly ground black pepper

1. In a large sauté pan set over medium-high heat, heat the oil until it ripples. Add the garlic and cook for 2 minutes. Add the zucchini and a few drops of water. Cook, tossing gently, until just tender, about 4 minutes. Add the beans and heat through.

2. Remove the pan from the heat. Stir in the mint and salt and pepper to taste. Serve hot, or let cool to room temperature, cover, and refrigerate for up to 2 days. Reheat before serving.

Warm French Lentils {Serves 6}

We add an oignon piqué or "pricked onion" (a bay leaf attached to a peeled onion using a clove as a tack) to the pot with the lentils for this recipe. Adding a piqué, herb stems, or peppercorns to the pot helps flavor the water. And because lentils absorb the flavor as they cook, they become richer tasting.

1 small onion, peeled

1 bay leaf

1 whole clove

2 cups (1 pound) dried French lentils, picked over for stones and rinsed well

3 tablespoons sherry vinegar

2 teaspoons Dijon mustard

¼ cup vegetable oil

3 tablespoons walnut oil

1 teaspoon fresh thyme leaves

1 teaspoon salt

¾ teaspoon freshly ground black pepper

1 small carrot, peeled and finely diced

2 scallions, thinly sliced

¼ cup walnuts, toasted (see note, page 144) and minced

1. Prepare the onion piqué: Attach the bay leaf to the peeled onion using the clove as a tack.

2. Combine the lentils and the onion piqué in a saucepan; add enough water to cover by 4 inches. Bring to a boil over high heat. Reduce the heat to low and simmer until the lentils are just cooked through, about 20 minutes. Skim off any foam that rises to the surface.

3. Meanwhile, whisk together the sherry vinegar and mustard in a small bowl. Slowly whisk in the vegetable and walnut oils to form an emulsion. Stir in the thyme, salt, and pepper.

4. When the lentils are fully cooked, drain them and discard the onion piqué. Place them in a bowl and add the carrot, scallions, walnuts, and the dressing; toss to combine well. Taste for seasoning. Serve warm, or let cool to room temperature, cover, and refrigerate for up to 3 days. Reheat before serving.

Black Olive Couscous {Serves 4 to 6}

A staple food of North Africa, couscous, which is granular semolina or coarsely ground wheat, is as versatile as rice. Precooked dried semolina is available in most grocery stores and takes only minutes to prepare. In this recipe we toss it with garlic, olives, lemon, parsley, and cracked black pepper for a quick, flavorful side dish.

2 garlic cloves, smashed and peeled

2 tablespoons extra-virgin olive oil

$\frac{1}{2}$ teaspoon salt

2 cups water

2 cups precooked couscous

1 cup kalamata olives, pitted and cut into rings

$\frac{1}{2}$ whole lemon, seeded and finely minced

$\frac{1}{4}$ cup chopped fresh parsley leaves

$\frac{1}{2}$ teaspoon freshly ground black pepper

1. Combine the smashed garlic cloves and the olive oil in a small bowl; set at room temperature for 1 hour. Remove and discard the garlic; reserve the oil.

2. Meanwhile, combine the salt and water in a large saucepan; bring to a boil over high heat.

3. Pour the couscous in the saucepan of boiling water and turn off the heat. Cover and let stand for 5 minutes.

4. Place the cooked couscous in a large bowl and fluff the couscous with a fork. Add the reserved olive oil, the olives, lemon, parsley, and black pepper; toss to combine thoroughly. Taste for seasoning. Serve immediately, or let cool to room temperature, cover, and refrigerate for up to 3 days. The couscous can be served warm or chilled.

Native Grains Pilaf {Serves 8 to 10}

This warm salad of wild rice, barley, and hominy tossed with sunflower and pumpkin seeds combines perfectly with a piquant dressing that features apple cider, Dijon mustard, sherry vinegar, walnut oil, and fresh sage. We serve the pilaf alongside Chili-rubbed Duck Breasts with Sun-dried Cherry Glaze (page 130) or Veal Chops Roasted with Mushrooms and Pine Nuts (page 142).

1 tablespoon apple cider

1 1/2 teaspoon Dijon mustard

1 1/4 teaspoons sherry vinegar

1 teaspoon soy sauce

3/4 teaspoon maple syrup

1/4 cup vegetable oil

1 1/2 teaspoon walnut oil

1 1/2 teaspoons chopped fresh sage leaves

1/4 teaspoon freshly ground black pepper

2 cups cooked wild rice (see page 215)

2 cups cooked barley (see page 215)

2 cups cooked hominy (see page 215)

2 tablespoons water

1/4 cup sunflower seeds, toasted
   (see note, page 144)

1/4 cup pumpkin seeds, toasted (see note,
   page 144)

1. Whisk together the cider, mustard, vinegar, soy sauce, and maple syrup in a small bowl. Whisk in the vegetable and walnut oils in a slow, steady stream. Stir in the chopped sage and pepper. Set aside.

2. Combine the cooked grains and the water in a large saucepan. Warm over low heat, stirring constantly, until heated through. (Both the grains and dressing can be made a day in advance and refrigerated until needed. To finish the dish, simply complete the step below.)

3. Toss the warm grains with 1/2 cup of the dressing and mix well. Stir in the sunflower and pumpkin seeds. Serve immediately. Refrigerate any extra dressing in an airtight container for up to 2 weeks.

ABOUT HOMINY
Hominy is corn that's been dried and then soaked in an alkaline solution that removes its hull. Canned hominy, which is ready-to-eat, is available in many supermarkets. Dried hominy is available in natural food stores and has to be reconstituted before it's edible. (For cooking directions, see page 215.)

Barley and Sweet Corn Tabbouleh {Serves 6}

This is a lemon-flecked tabbouleh of barley, sweet corn, and tomatoes that embodies summer eating. It enhances any alfresco menu from casual hot dogs at the beach to an elegant city-rooftop soirée. There is delicious tension between the sweet summer corn and tart bits of lemon, creating a compelling salad that tastes slightly different with each bite. The tabbouleh is best if made a few hours before serving so that the barley has a chance to absorb some of the lemon and tomato juices.

1 cup uncooked barley

Salt

2 cups fresh corn kernels

2 cups diced fresh tomatoes
 (about 1 pound)

1 whole lemon, seeded and finely minced

Juice of 1 lemon

4 scallions, thinly sliced

3/4 cup extra-virgin olive oil

1/2 cup chopped fresh parsley leaves

1/4 cup chopped fresh mint leaves

1/4 cup chopped fresh cilantro leaves

1/2 teaspoon minced garlic

1/2 teaspoon freshly ground black pepper

1. Combine the barley and a pinch of salt in a saucepan and add water to cover by 2 inches. Bring to a boil over high heat. Reduce the heat to medium and simmer, uncovered, until tender, about 20 minutes. Drain the barley in a colander. Rinse well under cold running water until cool. Drain well.

2. Combine the cooled barley, corn, tomatoes, minced lemon, lemon juice, scallions, oil, parsley, mint, cilantro, garlic, black pepper, and 1 1/2 teaspoons salt in a large bowl. Toss to mix well. Taste for seasoning. Cover and let sit at room temperature for a few hours before serving, or cover and refrigerate for up to 2 days.

OTHER WAYS TO DO IT

For a light supper try the salad as a stuffing for fresh vine-ripened tomatoes or radicchio leaves, topped with Creamy Basil Sauce (page 293).

USING WHOLE LEMON RIND

You'll notice in this recipe and others throughout the book that we call for whole minced lemon—rind and all. Classically, anytime citrus rind is called for in a recipe, just the outer part is used, the white part, or pith, is considered too bitter. However, since your palate responds to four basic taste sensations—sweet, sour, salty, and bitter—adding tiny bits of minced lemon to a dish can stimulate the bitter receptive taste buds and add complexity and depth to what you taste.

Herbed Parmesan Polenta {Serves 4}

Hot creamy polenta is warming food for the soul. This version has Parmesan cheese and fresh herbs stirred in at the end (to go over the top, stir in some butter as well). It is the perfect mate for braises and stews, or a meal in itself served with Roasted Eggplant Marinara (page 174) and Sautéed Greens and Garlic (page 202).

1½ teaspoons salt

4 cups water

1¼ cups cornmeal

⅓ cup freshly grated Parmesan cheese

1 tablespoon chopped fresh rosemary or thyme leaves

Freshly ground black pepper

1. Combine the salt and water in a large saucepan set over medium heat. Bring to a gentle boil.

2. A small handful at a time, gradually sift the cornmeal into the simmering water; whisk constantly to avoid lumps. Continue to stir, slowly adding the cornmeal until all is incorporated. Reduce the heat to low and simmer gently, stirring often, until the polenta is smooth and creamy, 20 to 30 minutes.

3. Remove from the heat and stir in the cheese, rosemary, and pepper to taste. Serve immediately.

Lemon-Garlic Rice {Serves 4}

This flavorful rice is imbued with lemon and garlic, making it the perfect counterpoint for dishes seasoned with curry and chiles. Try making it with lime or orange juice instead of lemon, if desired. We serve it with Cuban-style Braised Tuna (page 160) or Jamaican Curried Lamb Stew (page 150).

2 tablespoons olive oil

½ cup minced white onion

2 tablespoons minced garlic

1 cup uncooked long-grain white rice

2 cups water

Salt

Juice of ½ lemon

Grated or minced zest of 1 whole lemon

Freshly ground black pepper

1. In a saucepan set over medium-high heat, heat the oil until it ripples. Add the onion and cook until soft, about 5 minutes. Add the garlic and cook for 1 minute. Add the rice and toss for a minute to coat with the oil.

2. Pour in the water, a pinch of salt, and the lemon juice. Bring to a boil. Cover and reduce the heat to low. Simmer until the rice is cooked and the liquid absorbed, 20 to 25 minutes. Remove from the heat.

3. Fluff the rice with a fork; toss with the lemon zest. Season to taste with salt and pepper. Serve immediately.

Black Beans and Rice {Serves 4 to 6}

We serve these cinnamon-scented black beans and rice alongside Caribbean Grilled Mahi Mahi with Tropical Fruit Salsa (page 157) and Cool Island Cucumber Salad (page 95).

2 cups (1 pound) dried black beans, picked over for stones and rinsed well

1 cinnamon stick

3 garlic cloves, peeled

1/2 medium white onion, peeled

1 bay leaf

3 tablespoons olive oil

1 cup minced white onion

2 tablespoons chili powder

4 cups cooked white rice

1 teaspoon ground cinnamon

1 1/2 teaspoons salt

1. Combine the beans, cinnamon stick, garlic, peeled onion, and bay leaf in a large saucepan and add water to cover by at least 2 inches. Bring to a boil over high heat. Reduce the heat and simmer, uncovered, until the beans are soft but still retain their shape, 1 to 1 1/2 hours. (Add water as needed to keep the beans submerged.) Skim off any foam that rises to the surface. Drain the beans; remove and discard the cinnamon, garlic, onion, and bay leaf. Reserve the cooked beans.

2. In a large sauté pan set over medium-high heat, heat the oil until it ripples. Add the minced onion and cook until translucent, about 5 minutes. Add the chili powder and toss for 1 minute, being careful not to burn it. Add the cooked rice and toss to coat with the chili powder. Add the reserved beans, the ground cinnamon, and the salt; cook until heated through. Serve hot, or let cool to room temperature, cover, and refrigerate for up to 2 days. Reheat before serving.

Black Bean Refritos {Makes 4 cups}

These spicy, smoky beans are perfect on nachos, over a bowl of Lemon-Garlic Rice (page 210), and, of course, on our Huevos Chihuahua (page 226).

2 cups (1 pound) dried black beans, picked over for stones and rinsed well

2 tablespoons olive oil

1 cup thinly sliced white onions

4 garlic cloves, minced

1 tablespoon New Mexican chili powder (see note, page 130)

2 teaspoons ground cumin

2 teaspoons dried oregano

1/2 teaspoon minced chipotle pepper (available in most supermarkets and specialty food stores; see note, page 107)

2 teaspoons salt

1. Place the beans in a large pot and add water to cover by at least 2 inches. Bring to a boil over high heat. Reduce the heat and simmer uncovered until the beans are very soft, about 1 hour. (Add water as needed to keep the beans submerged.) Skim off any foam that rises to the surface. When the beans are soft, pour off most of the cooking water leaving enough to just cover the beans.

2. In a sauté pan set over medium heat, heat the oil until it ripples. Add the onions and cook until soft and starting to brown, about 10 minutes. Add the garlic, chili powder, cumin, oregano, and chipotle pepper; cook until lightly toasted, about 1 minute.

3. Combine the beans and their liquid and the onion mixture in a food processor. Pulse a few times to form a chunky purée. Season with the salt. Serve immediately, or let cool to room temperature, cover, and refrigerate for up to 4 days. Reheat before serving.

Crispy Plantain Fritters {Serves 4}

Look for plantains that are soft with brownish black skins; they have the best flavor and texture.

2 ripe plantains

Peanut or vegetable oil

1. Peel the plantains and cut into 1½-inch circles.

2. Heat ½ inch of peanut oil to 350°F in a small saucepan. Carefully add half of the plantains, and cook, turning frequently, until all sides are golden brown, 4 to 5 minutes. Remove the browned plantains from the oil with a slotted spoon and drain on paper towels. Cool to room temperature

3. Stand a piece of cooled plantain on end. Place a flat metal spatula on top of the plantain. Slowly apply pressure, pushing down on the plantain until it is about ¼ inch thick. Flatten all of the remaining plantain pieces. The fritters can be prepared ahead through this step, and refrigerated for up to 24 hours. Complete step 4 just before serving.

4. Just before serving, reheat the oil to 350°F. Fry the flattened plantains in the oil until golden brown, about 30 seconds on each side. Remove from the oil with a slotted spoon and drain on paper towels for a minute. Serve hot.

PEELING PLANTAINS

Peeling a plantain is a bit different than peeling a banana. First, cut off about 1 inch from each end of the plantain. Then with a sharp paring knife, make 3-4 vertical cuts about one-half to three-fourths of an inch apart just through the skin to the flesh. Peel away the skin in strips one at a time. That's it.

Gingered Snow Pea–Cabbage Slaw {Makes 5 cups}

Tossed with Spicy Ginger-Lime Dressing, this tangy, light, and healthful salad is a far cry from traditional mayonnaise-based slaws. It can be made with virtually any thinly sliced crunchy vegetable that strikes your fancy.

2 cups thinly sliced white or napa cabbage

1 cup thinly sliced snow peas

1 red bell pepper, thinly sliced

1 carrot, peeled and grated

1 cup Spicy Ginger-Lime Dressing (page 288)

Toss all of the vegetables with the dressing. Allow to stand at room temperature for 30 minutes before serving. Or cover and refrigerate for up to 4 days.

Tangy Six-Vegetable Slaw {Makes about 2 quarts; serves 8}

A light and healthful medley of colorful vegetables in a tangy red wine vinegar dressing, this side dish is a casual yet dressy companion for seafood and barbecue.

³/₄ cup red wine vinegar

3 tablespoons sugar

1¹/₂ teaspoons salt

1¹/₂ teaspoons dry mustard powder

1 teaspoon aniseed

1 teaspoon celery seed

¹/₂ teaspoon cayenne pepper

¹/₄ cup plus 3 tablespoons olive oil

1 red bell pepper, thinly sliced

1 yellow bell pepper, thinly sliced

1 carrot, peeled and grated

2 cups (¹/₂ pound) thinly sliced red cabbage

2 cups (¹/₂ pound) thinly sliced white cabbage

4 scallions, thinly sliced

1. Combine the vinegar, sugar, salt, mustard powder, aniseed, celery seed, and cayenne pepper and in a bowl and whisk together. Slowly whisk in the olive oil. Reserve.

2. Combine the bell peppers, carrot, red cabbage, white cabbage and scallions in a large bowl and toss together to combine well. Pour the reserved dressing over the vegetables and toss well. Allow the slaw to sit at room temperature for 30 minutes before serving to allow the vegetables to absorb the flavors of the dressing.

3. Taste for seasoning and serve, or cover and refrigerate for up to 2 days.

Cooking Grains and Beans

Dried beans and grains appear in countless forms on every section of our restaurant menu: in drinks (beer), salads (Contessa Lisa's Tuscan Grain Salad), soups (Cuban Black Bean Soup), entrées (Fettuccine with White Beans, Sun-dried Tomatoes, and Rosemary), side dishes (Warm French Lentils), and desserts (James' Giant Oatmeal Cookies). Most are readily available in supermarkets; however, health food stores and some gourmet shops are your best source for organic grains and beans. We are fond of them because they're delicious, non-perishable, plus they're good for the body as well as the budget. Here are general cooking guidelines:

BARLEY
Rinse the barley well. Cook it uncovered over low heat in boiling water at a ratio of 3 cups liquid to 1 cup barley until tender, 35 to 40 minutes. When the barley is cooked but still slightly firm to the bite, drain in a colander and use immediately.

WILD RICE
Rinse the grains well under cold running water. Place 1 cup of rice, 3 cups of water, and a pinch of salt in a saucepan set over high heat. Bring to a boil. Reduce the heat to medium-low, cover, and simmer until tender and some, but not all, of the grains have begun to split open, 35 to 60 minutes. You might need to add more water during the cooking time. Drain off any liquid that remains in the pan.

HOMINY
Whole dried hominy is available at Hispanic markets and some gourmet supermarkets. Soak 1 cup of hominy in a generous amount of water overnight. Combine the drained hominy and 6 cups water in a large saucepan set over high heat. Bring to a boil. Reduce the heat to medium and simmer, uncovered, until pliable and tender, 2 to 3 hours. Check occasionally to make sure the hominy is submerged in plenty of water; add more, if necessary.

DRIED BEANS
Sift through the beans and remove any stones or impurities. Rinse the beans in cold water. Place the beans in a saucepan and add water to cover by at least 2 inches. Bring to a boil over high heat. Lower the heat and simmer, uncovered, until the beans are tender but still retain their shape, 45 minutes to $1\frac{1}{2}$ hours (depending upon the type of bean you are cooking). Drain the beans and use immediately, or spread out on a baking sheet and let cool to room temperature. Cover and refrigerate for up to 3 days. The increased popularity of beans makes soaking them before cooking unnecessary these days.

CHAPTER SIX

BRUNCHES & BAKED GOODS

BRUNCHES & BAKED GOODS

Using Food to Build Community: A Neighborhood Tale 219

Broiled Grapefruit with Star Anise Sugar 222

Roasted Red Pepper and Shrimp Grits 223

Provençal Egg Salad 224

Scrambled Eggs with Smoked Salmon, Cream Cheese, and Dill 224

Shepherd's Hash and Baked Eggs 225

Huevos Chihuahua 226

Six-Grain Pecan Pancakes with Apple Cider Syrup 227

Banana-Buttermilk Pancakes with Honey-Pecan Syrup 228

Corn and Blueberry Pancakes with Maple–Pine Nut Butter 229

Cranberry-Buckwheat Pancakes with Orange-Honey-Thyme Butter 230

Brioche French Toast with Apricot–Grand Marnier Sauce 231

White Dog Cafe Granola 232

White Dog Cafe Mint Julep 232

Bloodhounds 233

White Dog Cafe Rum Punch 233

Sour Cream Coffee Cake 234

Orange and Black Currant Scones 235

Blueberry Muffins 236

Banana-Nut Muffins 236

Corn, Cheddar, and Sun-dried Tomato Muffins 237

Brioche 238

Parmesan Focaccia 239

Rosemary-Parmesan Biscotti 240

Curried Poppy Seed Crackers 241

USING FOOD TO BUILD COMMUNITY: A NEIGHBORHOOD TALE

WITH A STREET MAP IN HAND AND A LIST OF ADDRESSES, I HEADED OFF IN search of Philadelphia's prize-winning inner-city gardens and wall murals. The neighborhoods I drove through were thought to be the city's most disadvantaged and crime-ridden, so I wasn't surprised by the graffiti-covered walls, boarded-up row houses, and littered streets. What was unexpected, and why I have returned year after year, is the courageous spirit of community survival and renewal that I found in the heart of Philadelphia's "Badlands." My discoveries have led to a series of annual neighborhood tours combined with meals and discussions at the White Dog Cafe, providing an opportunity for understanding and relationship-building across the economic and racial barriers that divide our community.

Community activist, Father Paul Washington, depicted in a mural (located in North Philadelphia) featured in the White Dog Cafe Community Garden and Wall Mural Tour

On my initial outing, finding the gardens was no easy task, and I became lost in the confusing maze of tiny one-way streets. At first, I was afraid to ask directions and felt out of place knowing that a white person driving in this neighborhood was a rare sight. The stern faces I observed didn't encourage me, but when I finally stopped to ask, I was delighted to find how helpful and friendly people were. I realized that the sternness I had perceived from a distance was probably no different from the look on my own face, before conversation brought on smiles. A half block from my destination, a one-way sign blocked my entry, so I parked and walked up the narrow street. The first three houses in the row were abandoned, and broken glass was scattered across the sidewalk where a window had fallen out. I could see nothing green on the block—only the brick faces and concrete stoops of the nineteenth-century row houses, set along crumbling sidewalks and a patched asphalt street marked with potholes. Ahead on the left was an opening where one house had been demolished, usually a place for a trash-heaped lot.

When I reached the opening, I stood in wonder at the site before me. Here was the most beautiful garden of artfully composed flower beds and lush green trees. A neat brick-lined pebble path bordered by pink and white impatiens wound from the gate past crab apple and juniper trees, under a rose-covered arbor, and around a circular bed of concentric rows of red, white, and blue flowers. In the corner, a stand of blossoming birds of paradise poked their orange-and-purple heads above the back of a garden bench. On the entire wall behind, from ground to roof, was painted a mural which transported me into a land of green forests and blue sky, far away from the harsh man-made world that loomed behind me.

This, I thought, *is something my customers have just got to see*, and the White Dog Community Garden and Wall Mural Tour was born.

A woman passing by noticed my interest and ran to get Daisy, the garden club president. Soon, across the street, a door opened in a tidy house with white curtains and flowering window boxes, and an older woman walked toward me, pulling from her apron pocket the key to the garden gate. We strolled along the path as she proudly pointed out the varieties of flowers and plants and told me of the garden's history. I noticed a memorial plaque on the bench, and Daisy explained that the garden had been built in memory of the fourteen-year-old son of one of the gardeners—the same woman who'd gone to get Daisy. Her young son had been stabbed to death.

Several years previously, Daisy recalled, a group of neighbors cleaned the trash from the lot and planned the colors and patterns of the flower beds and trees. Holding a broom and turning in a circle, Daisy had made the outline for the circular flower bed. Start-up supplies and technical assistance had been provided by Philadelphia Green, a project of the Pennsylvania Horticultural Society, which awarded the community garden prizes that Daisy's garden had won for the past several years. Funds for upkeep and replanting are raised each year by the neighbors who pay dues of one dollar a month and hold what

Jane Golden, director of the Phila. Mural Arts Program, shows a proposal for a mural depicting racial harmony

they call a "pantry party." Each family contributes ingredients for a meal. Bags of groceries, which might contain the makings for a chicken dinner or a bacon-and-eggs break-

Flossie Narducci (left) of Philadelphia Green with community gardeners and many White Dog Cafe patrons

fast, are put on tables along the sidewalk beside the garden to be raffled off along with a bake sale of homemade pies and cakes. It wasn't easy, she confessed, when vandals had torn out the rose bushes and broken down young trees, and it was discouraging to work hard cleaning the block, only to find it full of trash again the next day. Some disheartened homeowners had moved out of the neighborhood and had been replaced by renters who didn't care. Undaunted, Daisy teaches the new neighbors by her own example, sweeping the streets, picking up trash, and tending the garden with pride. "This garden is what keeps me going. I come out here with the flowers and trees and look up at the mural—it's my pathway into the wilderness."

The next month and for the following six years I've returned to Daisy's garden with a group of our customers as part of our annual brunch tour. Beginning on Saturday morning with orange-and-black currant scones and coffee at the Cafe and an introduction by Flossie Narducci of Philadelphia Green and Jane Golden, art director of the city's Mural Arts Program, our tour by motorized trolley may take us to a Korean vegetable garden in West Philadelphia or a flower garden in the barrio with a mural of Puerto Rican history. Gardening enthusiasts from the suburbs stroll along paths in North Philadelphia discussing growing techniques with urban gardeners, while art lovers from Center City chat with young neighborhood artists who helped paint the murals and are proud to point out that there is no graffiti on them.

At each stop the gardeners and mural artists hop aboard the trolley and as we head home to the Cafe we all chatter merrily, looking forward to the brunch that awaits us. Back at the Cafe we gather around antique oak tables in our large sunshine-filled back dining room where our Table Talk programs are held. While enjoying a brunch of Broiled Grapefruit and Roasted Red Pepper and Shrimp Grits we listen to community leaders share stories of how the paint brush and the garden hoe have helped build communities in Philadelphia.   **—JW**

Broiled Grapefruit with Star Anise Sugar {Serves 4}

Although grapefruit is perfect just halved and eaten, we like to offer our customers something they don't often eat at home, so we dress it up a little with a sprinkling of star anise sugar and a quick flash under the broiler. In Asian cuisine, the peppery licorice flavor of anise is often combined with citrus; we think it is remarkably delicious paired with grapefruit. Try it for a special-occasion brunch.

4 tablespoons sugar

1 star anise pod, crushed

2 grapefruits, halved

1. Preheat the broiler.

2. Combine 2 tablespoons of the sugar and the crushed star anise pod in a spice grinder or mortar and grind to powder. Stir in the remaining 2 tablespoons of sugar. (The star anise sugar will keep in an airtight container for 1 month.)

3. With a sharp paring knife, section the grapefruit halves by cutting along each side of the membranes that form the triangular wedges. Arrange the grapefruit halves on a baking sheet and sprinkle each with 1 tablespoon of the anise sugar. Broil until the sugar melts and bubbles, 2 to 3 minutes. Serve immediately.

OTHER WAYS TO DO IT
You can substitute vanilla for the star anise by scraping the seeds of a split vanilla bean into the sugar.

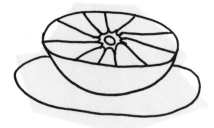

USING STAR ANISE
Star anise, a star-shaped, licorice-flavored seed pod from an evergreen tree of the magnolia family is an important ingredient in five-spice powder and is often used when braising and stewing meats in Chinese cuisine.

Roasted Red Pepper and Shrimp Grits {Serves 6}

In the White Dog kitchen, we have very few fixed rules about food, however one of them is to never combine fish and cheese. Of course, there are exceptions to every rule, and these rich creamy grits are a glorious one.

2 tablespoons unsalted butter

1 large yellow onion, minced (about 2 cups)

1 tablespoon minced garlic

1 cup quick-cooking grits

4 cups whole milk

1 cup water

2 teaspoons salt

$\frac{1}{2}$ teaspoon freshly ground black pepper

$\frac{1}{4}$ teaspoon Tabasco sauce

2 red bell peppers, roasted (see note, page 140), peeled, seeded, and puréed

8 ounces shrimp, peeled and deveined

8 ounces (2 cups) grated cheddar or Monterey Jack cheese

1. Melt the butter in a saucepan set over medium heat. Add the onion and sauté until soft, about 5 minutes. Add the garlic and cook for 2 minutes. Stir in the grits. Stir in 2 cups of the milk and simmer until the liquid is absorbed, about 5 minutes. Add the remaining 2 cups of milk and simmer, stirring occasionally, until it is absorbed, about 5 minutes. Add the water and simmer until the grits are soft and thick, 35 to 40 minutes.

2. Preheat the oven to 400°F.

3. Add the salt, pepper, Tabasco, and puréed bell peppers to the grits; mix well. Pour the mixture into a 10 x 6 x 1$\frac{3}{4}$-inch casserole. (The grits may be prepared to this point 1 day in advance. Let cool to room temperature, cover, and refrigerate overnight. Bring to room temperature before proceeding.)

4. Spread the shrimp evenly over the grits and top with the grated cheese. Bake on the top rack of the oven until the shrimp are cooked through and the cheese is melted, about 15 minutes.

IDENTIFYING TRUE GRITS

Grits is corn that has been through many changes. It starts out as dried yellow or white corn kernels. These kernels are soaked in an alkaline solution made from ashes of lime, which removes the hull and germ from the corn. The whole kernels can then be cooked in water to create hominy or finely ground to make grits.

Provençal Egg Salad {Serves 4 to 6}

This saucy egg salad is for neither the faint of heart nor the garlic-shy! Try it as an eye-opening bagel spread atop a salad of fresh spinach leaves, or topped with tomato between a few slices of hearty pumpernickel.

8 whole, unshelled eggs

Pinch of salt

2 tablespoons rinsed, chopped, and pitted Niçoise olives

1 small red onion, minced

3 tablespoons capers, rinsed and chopped (see note, page 160)

1 cup Basic Aïoli (page 291)

2 tablespoons chopped fresh basil leaves

½ teaspoon freshly ground black pepper

½ teaspoon fresh lemon juice

1. Hard-cook the eggs: Carefully place them into a pot with the salt, and add enough cold water to cover the eggs completely. Bring to a boil over high heat. Immediately remove the pot from the heat, cover with a tight-fitting lid, and let the eggs cool to room temperature in the cooking water. Peel the eggs under running water and use immediately, or store refrigerated in an airtight container for no more than 1 week.

2. Combine all of the ingredients in a large bowl and mix well. Cover and refrigerate until chilled. The egg salad will keep for 2 days in the refrigerator.

3. If desired, serve in a crusty baguette with roasted red peppers, arugula leaves, and a few anchovy fillets. For a perfect accompaniment, try our Spicy Fried Potatoes (page 194).

Scrambled Eggs with Smoked Salmon, Cream Cheese, and Dill {Serves 6}

The addition of cream cheese to scrambled eggs makes them silky and rich, and we can't resist adding smoked salmon and dill for an unforgettably decadent breakfast.

8 eggs

4 ounces (½ cup) cream cheese, cut into small chunks

4 ounces smoked salmon, cut thin slices into ¼-inch strips

1 tablespoon chopped fresh dill

½ teaspoon salt

¼ teaspoon freshly ground black pepper

1 tablespoon unsalted butter

1. Place the eggs in a large bowl, and whisk until frothy. Add cream cheese, smoked salmon, dill, salt, and pepper; whisk to combine.

2. Melt the butter in a skillet set over medium heat. Pour in the egg mixture and cook, constantly scraping and stirring the eggs from the pan's bottom and sides, until they achieve the desired doneness, about 8 minutes. (It's okay if the cream cheese doesn't melt entirely.)

3. Divide the eggs among 6 warmed plates and serve with toast.

OTHER WAYS TO DO IT

Try this scramble served on top of homemade potato pancakes.

Shepherd's Hash with Baked Eggs {Serves 6}

One year, when Valentine's Day fell on a Sunday, we dubbed this hash "Shattered Dreams and Broken Hearts Hash" and served more orders of it than had ever been sold in the history of the White Dog Cafe. We think it was a hit because it's the kind of comfort food that can mend a broken heart. Don't be daunted by preparing the lamb shanks because there's nothing to it; they just take some time to cook. If desired, you can prepare them a day ahead.

4 tablespoons olive oil

2 pounds lamb shanks

Salt and freshly ground black pepper

2 cups water

$\frac{1}{2}$ cup dry white wine

1 Idaho potato, peeled and cut in $\frac{1}{4}$-inch dice

1 white onion, finely diced

1 fennel bulb, stalks removed, cored, and finely diced

1 carrot, peeled and finely diced

$\frac{1}{2}$ cup fresh or thawed frozen peas

$\frac{1}{2}$ teaspoons minced garlic

2 teaspoons chopped fresh rosemary leaves

$\frac{1}{2}$ cup heavy cream

6 eggs

1. Preheat the oven to 325°F.

2. In a casserole or ovenproof Dutch oven set over high heat, heat 2 tablespoons of the olive oil until it ripples. Sprinkle the lamb shanks with salt and pepper; sear in the hot oil, turning frequently, until browned on all sides, 6 to 8 minutes.

3. Pour in the water and wine; cover tightly. Braise in the oven until the meat falls off the bone, about 3 hours.

4. Let the shanks cool to room temperature. Remove the meat from the bones and discard the bones and any excess fat. Coarsely chop the meat and reserve until needed, or refrigerate up to 2 days.

5. Preheat the oven to 400°F.

6. Heat the remaining 2 tablespoons olive oil in a large skillet set over medium heat. Add the potato, cover, and cook, stirring occasionally, for 10 minutes. Add the onion, fennel, carrot, peas, and garlic; cover and cook, stirring occasionally, for 15 minutes or until tender. Stir in the reserved lamb, rosemary, cream, 1 teaspoon salt, and $\frac{1}{2}$ teaspoon pepper. Bring to a simmer.

7. Spoon the hash into a 10 x 6 x 1$\frac{3}{4}$-inch casserole.

8. Make 6 evenly spaced indentations in the hash with the back of a kitchen ladle. Crack 1 egg into each indentation and sprinkle with salt and pepper. Bake until the eggs are set, yet jiggle a little when shaken, about 15 minutes. Serve immediately.

OTHER WAYS TO DO IT
Use chicken in place of the lamb, if desired.

Huevos Chihuahua {Serves 6}

We call our version of Huevos Rancheros "Huevos Chihuahua"—they're Mexican in style and as feisty as their namesake. If you don't want to make the fried corn tortilla crisps called for in this recipe, simply wrap everything up in a warm flour tortilla instead. Although we serve them for brunch, these eggs are great at any time of day.

GAZPACHO SAUCE

1 tablespoon olive oil

1/2 cup diced red onion

1/2 teaspoon minced garlic

1 teaspoon New Mexican chili powder
(see note, page 130)

1/2 teaspoon ground cumin

1/2 pound fresh plum tomatoes, diced,
or 2 cups chopped canned tomatoes

1/2 cup diced zucchini

1/2 yellow bell pepper, diced

1/2 green bell pepper, diced

1 teaspoon Tabasco sauce

1 1/2 teaspoons chopped fresh oregano leaves

1 1/2 teaspoons chopped fresh basil leaves

1 1/2 teaspoons chopped fresh cilantro leaves
and stems

1 1/2 teaspoons fresh lime juice

1 1/2 teaspoons fresh orange juice

1/2 teaspoon salt

6 corn tortillas

3 cups Black Bean Refritos (page 212)

6 eggs, fried

Salt and freshly ground black pepper

Grated Pepper-Jack cheese

Sour cream, guacamole, and sliced
scallions, for serving (optional)

1. Prepare the Gazpacho Sauce: Heat the olive oil in a large non-reactive sauté pan set over high heat. Add the onion and cook until soft, 3 to 5 minutes. Add the garlic and cook for 2 minutes. Stir in the chili powder and cumin and cook for 30 seconds. Add the tomatoes, zucchini, bell peppers, and Tabasco. Reduce the heat to low and simmer, stirring occasionally, until the vegetables are tender and the sauce thickens, 8 to 10 minutes.

2. Remove from the heat and stir in the oregano, basil, cilantro, lime juice, orange juice, and salt. Season with more Tabasco to taste. Keep warm, or let cool to room temperature, cover, and refrigerate for up to 3 days.

3. Prepare the corn tortilla crisps: Heat 1/4-inch of oil in a sauté pan set over high heat until it ripples. Carefully add 1 corn tortilla and cook for about 30 seconds on each side or until crisp. Drain on paper towels. Repeat with the remaining tortillas. Sprinkle with salt and pepper and reserve.

4. Prepare the Black Bean Refritos; keep warm. Fry the eggs; keep warm.

5. Arrange a tortilla on each plate. Top each tortilla with 1/2 cup of the warmed Black Bean Refritos, a fried egg, and a large spoonful of the Gazpacho Sauce. Season to taste and sprinkle with the cheese. If desired, top with sour cream, guacamole, and sliced scallions, like we do.

Six-Grain Pecan Pancakes with Apple Cider Syrup {Makes 12 to 16 pancakes}

These are not normal pancakes! They are so full of healthy grains that you're probably adding minutes to your life as you eat them. And they're scrumptious as well. Look for the grains in your health-food store, where you should be able to buy them in small amounts. If you have to buy 1-pound bags of each grain, mix them together and store in an airtight container for up to 2 months. You'll have them on hand for your next batch of pancakes.

APPLE CIDER SYRUP

3 cups apple cider

2 whole allspice berries

1 cinnamon stick

2 whole cloves

$^3/_4$ cup light corn syrup

$^1/_4$ cup packed light brown sugar

$^1/_8$ teaspoon salt

4 tablespoons unsalted butter

PANCAKES

$^1/_2$ cup cornmeal

$^1/_2$ cup rolled oats

$^1/_2$ cup whole wheat flour

$^1/_2$ cup rye flour

$^1/_2$ cup wheat bran

$^1/_2$ cup flax seeds

1 tablespoon baking powder

$1^1/_2$ teaspoons baking soda

$^3/_4$ teaspoon salt

3 eggs

3 cups buttermilk (see note, page 228)

$^3/_4$ cup honey

$^1/_4$ pound (1 stick) unsalted butter, melted and cooled

1 cup pecan pieces, toasted (see note, page 144)

1. Prepare the syrup: Combine the cider, allspice, cinnamon stick, and cloves in a small nonreactive saucepan set over medium heat. Simmer until the mixture reduces to 1 cup of liquid, about 20 minutes. Stir in the corn syrup, brown sugar, and salt and bring to a simmer. Whisk in the butter until it melts.

2. Strain to remove the solids. Keep warm, or cover and refrigerate for up to 2 weeks.

3. Prepare the pancakes: Combine the cornmeal, oats, whole wheat and rye flours, wheat bran, flax seeds, baking powder, baking soda, and salt in a large bowl. Mix well.

4. In a separate bowl, whisk together the eggs, buttermilk, honey, and melted butter.

5. Add the wet ingredients to the dry ingredients and mix until just combined. (If you overmix the batter, the cakes will be tough; a few lumps are okay.) Gently stir in the pecans.

6. Heat a griddle over medium-high heat until a drop of water sprinkled on it sizzles. Pour scant $^1/_2$ cupfuls of the batter onto the griddle and cook until the bubbles that form around the outside edge pop, 2 to 3 minutes. Flip the pancakes and cook the other sides until golden brown. Repeat with the remaining batter.

7. Serve with the warm Apple Cider Syrup.

OTHER WAYS TO DO IT

These pancakes are also great topped with warm applesauce or with apple or pear butter and maple syrup.

Banana-Buttermilk Pancakes with Honey-Pecan Syrup {Makes 12 to 16 pancakes}

The key to light fluffy pancakes lies in not overmixing the batter. If you blend the batter too much, the gluten in the flour begins to develop and makes the batter elastic. This is something desirable in a nice loaf of bread but not in a pancake—so when you're mixing it all up, use a light hand and know that a few lumps are fine.

HONEY-PECAN SYRUP

3/4 cup honey

3/4 cup light corn syrup

4 tablespoons unsalted butter

1 cup pecans, toasted (see note, page 144) and coarsely chopped

PANCAKES

2 cups all-purpose flour

2 tablespoons sugar

2 teaspoons baking powder

1/2 teaspoon baking soda

1/2 teaspoon salt

2 eggs

2 cups buttermilk (see note below)

1/2 cup whole milk

2 tablespoons unsalted butter, melted and cooled

3 very ripe bananas, peeled and mashed

1. Prepare the syrup: Bring the honey and corn syrup to a simmer in a small saucepan set over medium heat.

2. Whisk in the butter and pecans. Keep warm, or cover and refrigerate for up to 2 weeks.

3. Prepare the pancakes: Sift together the flour, sugar, baking powder, baking soda, and salt in a large bowl. In a separate bowl, whisk together the eggs, buttermilk, whole milk, and melted butter. Add the wet ingredients to the dry ingredients and mix just to combine. Fold in the mashed bananas.

4. Heat a griddle over medium-high heat until a drop of water sprinkled on it sizzles. Pour scant 1/2 cupfuls of the batter onto the griddle and cook until the bubbles that form around the outside edges pop, 2 to 3 minutes. Flip the pancakes and cook the other sides until golden brown. Repeat with the remaining batter.

5. Serve with the warm Honey-Pecan Syrup.

MAKING HOMEMADE BUTTERMILK

If you don't have buttermilk on hand or don't want to purchase a whole quart, try making your own. Simply follow the ratio of 1 tablespoon of white vinegar or fresh lemon juice to 1 cup of whole milk. Mix together and let stand at room temperature for 1/2 hour before proceeding with your recipe.

Corn and Blueberry Pancakes with Maple–Pine Nut Butter {Makes 12 to 16 pancakes}

We make these pancakes when the New Jersey corn is high and the blueberries are plump and juicy—from mid-July through August. You can make them with frozen corn kernels and frozen blueberries but some of the sweetness is lost, so you'll want to add a bit more sugar.

MAPLE–PINE NUT BUTTER

½ pound (2 sticks) unsalted butter, at room temperature

½ cup pure maple syrup

¼ cup plus 2 tablespoons pine nuts, toasted (see note, page 144) and coarsely chopped

PANCAKES

4 tablespoons unsalted butter

1 cup fresh or frozen sweet corn kernels (fresh is best)

¾ cup all-purpose flour

¼ cup cornmeal

3 tablespoons sugar

1½ teaspoons baking powder

¾ teaspoon baking soda

¼ teaspoon salt

¼ teaspoon ground allspice

1 egg

½ cup buttermilk (see note, opposite page)

½ cup whole milk

1 cup fresh blueberries

1. Prepare the nut butter: Place the butter in a food processor and process for 30 seconds to whip. With the motor running, slowly pour in the syrup and process for 15 seconds. Scrape down the sides. Process until smooth, about 10 seconds.

2. Transfer the butter to a small bowl and fold in the pine nuts. Serve immediately, or place the whipped butter on a piece of plastic wrap or parchment paper and roll it into a cylinder 2 inches in diameter. Refrigerate until firm and then slice into medallions before serving. The roll of butter can be frozen for up to 2 months.

3. Prepare the pancakes: Melt the 4 tablespoons butter in a sauté pan set over medium-high heat. Add the corn and sauté for 1 minute; reserve.

4. Sift the flour, cornmeal, sugar, baking powder, baking soda, salt, and allspice into a large bowl. In a separate bowl, whisk together the egg, buttermilk, whole milk, and sautéed corn.

5. Add the wet ingredients to the dry ingredients and mix until just combined (a few lumps are okay.) Fold in the blueberries.

6. Heat a griddle over medium-high heat until a drop of water sprinkled on it sizzles. Pour scant ½ cupfuls of the batter onto the griddle and cook until the bubbles that form around the outside edges pop, 2 to 3 minutes. Flip the pancakes and cook the other sides until golden brown. Repeat with the remaining batter.

7. Serve with a medallion of Maple–Pine Nut Butter.

Cranberry-Buckwheat Pancakes with Orange-Honey-Thyme Butter {Makes 12 large pancakes}

Of all of the pancakes we serve, these are our favorite. The buckwheat batter is substantial and wholesome, and when smothered in maple syrup, the tart cranberries are nuggets of pure joy. We serve them with Orange-Honey-Thyme Butter and lots of maple syrup.

ORANGE-HONEY-THYME BUTTER
Juice and grated zest of 2 oranges

1/2 pound (2 sticks) unsalted butter, at room temperature

1/2 cup honey

1 tablespoon minced fresh thyme leaves

Pinch of salt

PANCAKES
1 cup buckwheat flour

1 cup all-purpose flour

3 tablespoons sugar

1 tablespoon baking powder

1/2 teaspoon baking soda

2 eggs, separated

1 cup buttermilk

1 cup whole milk

3 tablespoons unsalted butter, melted and cooled

2 cups fresh (or thawed frozen) cranberries

Maple syrup, for serving

1. Prepare the thyme butter: Bring the orange juice to a simmer in a small nonreactive saucepan set over medium heat. Simmer until the juice reduces to 1 tablespoon and is a syrupy consistency, about 5 minutes. Let cool to room temperature.

2. Combine the orange syrup and butter in a food processor and process to combine, about 30 seconds. With the motor running, pour in the honey and process for 1 minute. Scrape down the sides, add the orange zest, thyme, and salt and process for 10 seconds.

3. Serve immediately, or place the whipped butter on a piece of plastic wrap or parchment paper and roll it into a cylinder 2 inches in diameter. Refrigerate until firm and then slice into medallions before serving. The roll of butter can be frozen for up to 2 months.

4. Prepare the pancakes: Combine the buckwheat flour, all-purpose flour, sugar, baking powder, and baking soda in a large bowl; mix well. In a separate bowl, whisk together the egg yolks, buttermilk, whole milk, and melted butter. Add the wet ingredients to the dry and mix until just combined. (There will be some lumps in the batter.)

5. Meanwhile, with an electric mixer, beat the egg whites to stiff peaks, about 2 minutes.

6. Fold the egg whites and cranberries into the pancake batter.

7. Heat a griddle over medium-high heat until a drop of water sprinkled on it sizzles. Pour scant 1/2 cupfuls of the batter onto the griddle and cook until the bubbles around the outside edges pop, 2 to 3 minutes. Flip the pancakes and cook the other sides until golden brown. Repeat with the remaining batter.

8. Serve warm with the Orange-Honey-Thyme Butter and syrup.

Brioche French Toast with Apricot–Grand Marnier Sauce {Serves 6}

Brioche, a luxurious French bread made with butter and eggs, is our first choice for French toast, because it is tender, rich, and able to soak up all of the wonderful custard. Top it with our Apricot-Grand Marnier Sauce and breakfast can't get more decadent.

APRICOT–GRAND MARNIER SAUCE

2 cups thinly sliced sun-dried apricots

3 cups fresh orange juice

1/2 vanilla bean, split

1/4 cup Grand Marnier

BRIOCHE FRENCH TOAST

2 whole eggs

6 egg yolks

2 cups heavy cream

2 cups half-and-half

1/2 cup sugar

1 teaspoon ground cinnamon

1/4 teaspoon ground nutmeg

1 teaspoon pure vanilla extract

1 (9 x 5-inch loaf) Brioche (page 238 or store-bought), cut into 12 slices (each about 3/4 inch thick)

3 tablespoons unsalted butter

1. Prepare the Apricot–Grand Marnier Sauce: Combine the apricots, orange juice, and vanilla bean in a small nonreactive saucepan. Simmer over medium-low heat until the apricots are quite soft and the liquid reduces to a thick syrup, about 1 hour.

2. Stir in the Grand Marnier and simmer for 5 minutes.

3. Remove and discard the vanilla bean. Keep warm, or let cool to room temperature and refrigerate for up to 1 week. (If refrigerated, reheat before serving.)

4. Prepare the French toast: Combine the whole eggs, egg yolks, cream, half-and-half, sugar, cinnamon, nutmeg, and vanilla in a large bowl; whisk to combine the custard well.

5. Place the slices of brioche in a shallow baking dish or on a jelly-roll pan and pour the custard over them. Set aside until most of the liquid has been absorbed by the bread, about 5 minutes.

6. In a large skillet set over medium heat, melt 1 tablespoon of the butter. Add as many of the bread slices as will fit in a single layer and cook until golden on the bottom, 2 to 3 minutes. Turn the slices over to brown the other sides. Repeat with the remaining butter and slices.

7. Serve immediately with the warm Apricot-Grand Marnier Sauce.

White Dog Cafe Granola {Makes 8 cups}

Granola is a brunch staple at our restaurant, although no two batches are ever exactly the same. This recipe allows for endless variations—try it with nuts, grains, dried fruits, even chocolate chips.

2 cups rolled oats

1 cup wheat germ or wheat bran

1 cup oat bran

1/2 cup shelled sunflower seeds

1/2 cup shelled pumpkin seeds

1/2 cup unsweetened shredded coconut

1/2 cup slivered almonds

1 cup peanut butter

1/2 cup honey

2 teaspoons ground cinnamon

1 cup mixed dried fruits such as black currants, cherries, golden raisins, and diced apricots

1. Preheat the oven to 300°F.

2. Combine the oats, wheat germ, oat bran, seeds, coconut, almonds, peanut butter, honey, and cinnamon in large bowl. With your hands, mix well to combine thoroughly and coat all of the ingredients with the peanut butter, honey, and cinnamon. Spread the granola in a single even layer over 2 baking sheets. Bake, stirring every 10 minutes, until deep golden brown, about 30 minutes.

3. Let the granola cool to room temperature. Toss in the dried fruits. Serve, or store for up to 2 weeks in an airtight container.

4. If desired, serve with plain yogurt and lots of sliced bananas, strawberries, melon, or whatever fruit is readily available. This granola is also delicious eaten as a breakfast cereal with warm or cold milk poured over it, or out of hand as a late-night snack.

OTHER WAYS TO DO IT

This granola recipe can vary according to your preferences. If you like, keep the peanut butter, honey, and cinnamon the same, and substitute like amounts of your favorite nuts, grains, and dried fruits for some or all the ones we use in this recipe.

White Dog Cafe Mint Julep {Serves 2}

This refreshing drink is also perfect with our Derby Day Leg of Lamb (page 148).

40 fresh mint leaves plus 2 sprigs, for garnish

2 teaspoons sugar

1/4 cup water

Crushed ice

4 ounces bourbon

Combine the mint leaves, sugar, and water in the bottom of a rocks glass. Crush together with the back of a wooden spoon until the sugar dissolves and the mint leaves are well broken up. Fill the glass with crushed ice. Pour the bourbon over the ice; stir well. Garnish with the mint sprig.

Bloodhounds {Serves 4}

Here's a Bloody Mary that's guaranteed to make you howl.

3 cups tomato juice

2 teaspoons prepared horseradish

1 tablespoon Worcestershire sauce

Juice of $\frac{1}{2}$ lemon

$\frac{1}{2}$ teaspoon celery seeds

$\frac{1}{2}$ teaspoon freshly ground black pepper

1 large dash of Tabasco sauce

Celery salt or coarse kosher salt

Ice

6 to 8 ounces vodka

Cucumber spears, carrot spears, celery ribs, whole scallions, lime wedges, and lemon wedges, for garnish

1. Combine the tomato juice, horseradish, Worcestershire, lemon juice, celery seeds, pepper, and Tabasco in a pitcher; stir.

2. Coat the bottom of a small plate with celery salt. Rub the rims of 4 glasses with a lime wedge, and dip the rims in the celery salt, coating well.

3. Fill the glasses with ice and divide the vodka among them. Pour in the tomato juice mixture and garnish each drink with the cucumber, carrot, celery, scallions, and lemon and lime wedges.

White Dog Cafe Rum Punch {Makes 2 quarts}

Whether it's for brunch or a dance party, this drink will have you doing the limbo in no time.

8 ounces dark rum

8 ounces light rum

2 cups fresh orange juice

2 cups pineapple juice

$\frac{1}{2}$ cup fresh lime juice

12 ounces ($1\frac{1}{2}$ cups) lemon-lime soda

$\frac{1}{4}$ cup grenadine

1 orange, sliced into thin rounds

1 lime, sliced into thin rounds

Combine all of the ingredients and mix well. Serve over lots of ice.

Sour Cream Coffee Cake {Serves 8}

Elizabeth Fitzgerald, our sous-chef, swears that her mother, Nancy, makes the best coffee cake she's ever tasted. Fortunately for us, Nancy gave us her recipe for the buttery, rich coffee cake she's been making for thirty years. It is very easy to assemble and one of the quickest-disappearing breakfast foods you'll ever make.

½ pound (2 sticks) unsalted butter, melted and cooled

2 cups granulated sugar

2 eggs, beaten

1 cup sour cream

1 teaspoon vanilla extract

1½ cups all-purpose flour

¼ cup wheat germ or wheat bran

1 teaspoon salt

1 teaspoon baking powder

1 cup chopped pecans

2 tablespoons packed dark brown sugar

2 teaspoons ground cinnamon

1. Preheat the oven to 350°F. Butter and flour a 10 x 6-inch baking dish or pan.

2. Combine the melted butter, granulated sugar, eggs, sour cream, and vanilla in a large bowl; mix well. Stir in the flour, wheat germ, salt, and baking powder, and mix until just combined. (Do not overmix the dough.)

3. In a separate bowl, combine the nuts, brown sugar, and cinnamon and toss to mix well.

4. Pour half of the batter into the prepared pan. Sprinkle on half of the nut mixture. Cover with the remaining batter, and sprinkle the remaining nut mixture over the top. Bake until golden on top and firm, 45 to 50 minutes.

5. Cool on a rack for 10 minutes. Serve warm.

Orange and Black Currant Scones {Makes 16}

These scones are a tradition at the White Dog Cafe, and as soon as you try them, we bet they'll become a tradi-tion at your house, too. We like them best with homemade raspberry jam and a pot of whipped cream.

4 cups all-purpose flour

3 tablespoons granulated sugar

2 teaspoons baking powder

2 teaspoons baking soda

$1/4$ teaspoon salt

$1/2$ pound (2 sticks) cold unsalted butter, diced

Grated zest of 2 oranges

2 eggs

1 cup plus 2 tablespoons buttermilk

$1^1/2$ cups dried black currants

Raw or granulated sugar

Raspberry jam, for serving (optional)

Whipped cream, for serving (optional)

1. Combine the flour, granulated sugar, baking powder, baking soda, and salt in a large bowl; mix well. With a pastry blender or your fingers, cut in the butter and orange zest until the mixture resembles fine granules.

2. Whisk together the eggs and buttermilk in a small bowl. Pour over the dry ingredients and sprinkle on the currants. Stir just until the ingredients come together and a soft dough forms. (Be careful not to overmix the dough or your scones will be tough.)

3. Divide the dough into 16 mounds and place them 1 inch apart on an ungreased baking sheet. Sprinkle the mounds with a little of the raw sugar, cover, and refrigerate for 15 minutes or up to overnight.

4. Meanwhile, preheat the oven to 375°F.

5. Bake the chilled scones until lightly browned on top, about 20 minutes. Cool on a rack. Serve at room temperature. The scones are best if eaten the day they are made.

Blueberry Muffins {Makes 12}

The White Dog Cafe's first incarnation was as a muffin shop, so we have a rich muffin history and repertoire. We wanted to share this recipe because it has more fresh blueberries than any other we've found. If you can't find fresh blueberries, use the fresh-frozen ones found in your grocer's freezer.

3½ cups cake flour (not self-rising)

1½ cups sugar

1½ tablespoons baking powder

¼ teaspoon salt

1 egg

¾ cup vegetable oil

1½ cups buttermilk

3 cups blueberries, preferably fresh

1. Preheat the oven to 400°F. Butter a 12-cup muffin tin.

2. Sift together the flour, sugar, baking powder, and salt into a large bowl. In a separate bowl, whisk together the egg, oil, and buttermilk. Add the wet ingredients to the dry ingredients and mix just until combined. (Be careful not to overmix or the muffins will be tough.) Fold in the blueberries.

3. Fill each muffin cup to the rim with batter. Bake on the center rack until firm to the touch and just starting to brown, 30 to 35 minutes. Cool for 2 to 3 minutes, then turn the muffins out onto a wire rack to cool. Serve warm or at room temperature.

Banana-Nut Muffins {Makes 12}

These are the richest, moistest, and most banana-filled muffins you'll ever try—each muffin contains half a banana! They are out of this world.

1½ cups cake flour (not self-rising)

1¼ teaspoons baking powder

1¼ teaspoons baking soda

¼ teaspoon salt

2 eggs

2½ cups mashed ripe bananas (about 6 large)

1½ cups packed dark brown sugar

⅓ cup vegetable oil

⅓ cup buttermilk

½ teaspoon vanilla extract

½ cup pecans or walnuts, toasted (see note, page 144) and chopped

1. Preheat the oven to 400°F. Butter a 12-cup muffin tin.

2. Combine the flour, baking powder, baking soda, and salt in a large mixing bowl; mix well. Mix together the eggs, bananas, sugar, oil, buttermilk, and vanilla in a separate bowl. Add the wet ingredients to the dry ingredients and mix just until combined. (Be careful not to overmix or the muffins will be tough.) Fold in the nuts.

3. Fill each muffin cup to the rim with batter. Bake until firm to the touch and golden on top, 25 to 30 minutes. Cool for 2 to 3 minutes and serve warm or at room temperature.

Corn, Cheddar, and Sun-dried Tomato Muffins {Makes 12}

This is our version of a gussied-up corn muffin. We serve them at brunch as a savory alternative to all of the sweets. They are also great spread with pesto or served alongside either the Chiapas Tortilla Soup (page 78) or Cuban Black Bean Soup (page 77).

½ cups cake flour (not self-rising)

1 cup yellow cornmeal

½ tablespoons baking powder

1½ tablespoons sugar

½ teaspoon salt

½ teaspoon freshly ground black pepper

6 ounces (1½ cups) grated sharp white cheddar cheese

¾ cup chopped rehydrated sun-dried tomatoes (see note, page 127)

½ cup thinly sliced scallions

1½ cups warmed whole milk

6 ounces (1½ sticks) unsalted butter, melted and cooled

⅓ cup vegetable oil

1 egg

1. Preheat the oven to 400°F. Butter a 12-cup muffin tin.

2. Combine the flour, cornmeal, baking powder, sugar, salt, and pepper in a large mixing bowl; mix well. Add the cheese, sun-dried tomatoes, and scallions and toss well.

3. Whisk together the warm milk, melted butter, oil, and egg in a separate bowl.

4. Add the wet ingredients to the dry and mix together just until a soft dough forms. (Be careful not to overmix the dough.) Fill the prepared muffin cups to the rim with batter. Bake until the tops start to brown slightly, 20 to 25 minutes.

5. Cool for 2 to 3 minutes, then turn out onto a wire rack to cool. Serve warm or at room temperature.

Brioche {Makes one 9 x 5-inch loaf}

Brioche is an elegant, airy, yeasty, and buttery rich egg bread. We use it for French toast, stuffings, toasted sandwiches, and as a snack, spread with butter and sprinkled with sugar and cinnamon. In this recipe, the dough must be refrigerated overnight, so be sure to start the bread the day before you need it.

3 tablespoons whole milk

1½ teaspoons active dried yeast

1 tablespoon plus 1½ teaspoons sugar

3 eggs

2 to 2½ cups all-purpose flour

½ teaspoon salt

13 tablespoons unsalted butter, cut into 1-inch cubes, at room temperature

1. Warm the milk to about 110°F (it should feel just warm to the touch). Pour the milk into the bowl of an electric mixer. Add the yeast and the 1½ teaspoons sugar and stir to combine. Let sit for 5 minutes to proof.

2. Add the eggs to the bowl. Mix with a dough hook if you have one, or standard beaters, on low speed for 1 minute. Sift together 2 cups of the flour, the salt, and the remaining 1 tablespoon sugar.

3. Add the dry ingredients to the egg mixture. Mix on low speed until the dough forms a ball that cleans the sides of the bowl, 4 to 6 minutes. Continuing on low speed, add the butter cubes, 1 at a time, waiting until each cube is fully incorporated before adding another. Mix for 2 minutes more; the dough will be loose, not stiff. Slowly add more flour, and beat until the dough cleans the side of the bowl again. Transfer the dough to a large, buttered bowl, cover with plastic wrap, and refrigerate overnight.

4. Remove the dough from the refrigerator. It will have risen slightly overnight. Punch down the dough and press it into a buttered 9 x 5-inch loaf pan. Cover with a towel and set the pan in a warm, draft-free spot to rise until it's 2½ times its original size, 2 to 3 hours.

5. About 30 minutes before baking, preheat the oven to 350°F.

6. Bake on the middle rack of the oven until cooked through and golden brown, 20 to 25 minutes. The loaf will pull away from the sides of the pan when it is done. Turn the loaf out of the pan and let cool to room temperature on a wire rack. Use immediately, or wrap tightly and refrigerate for a few days, or freeze for up to 2 weeks.

Parmesan Focaccia {Makes about 2 pounds; Serves 8}

The focaccia we make every day at the White Dog Cafe uses a sourdough starter that we have been cultivating for years, so it isn't a recipe that translates well. This a hassle-free recipe requires no starter and yields a golden, tender focaccia. We top it with grated Parmesan cheese, but fresh herbs, garlic, sea salt, sun-dried tomatoes, olives, or cherry tomatoes are all viable alternatives.

2 cups whole milk

1 envelope (2½ teaspoons) active dried yeast

6 cups all-purpose flour

½ cup wheat bran or wheat germ

1 tablespoon salt

2 teaspoons sugar

2 eggs

¼ cup extra-virgin olive oil

½ cup freshly grated Parmesan cheese

½ teaspoon freshly ground black pepper

1. Warm the milk in a small saucepan set over low heat to about 110°F (it should feel just warm to the touch). Stir in the yeast and set aside to proof for 10 minutes.

2. Combine the flour, wheat bran, salt, and sugar in the bowl of an electric mixer fitted with a dough hook if you have one, or standard beaters. Add the yeast mixture and the eggs. Mix on low speed to combine. Continue mixing until the dough comes together and pulls away from the sides of the bowl. Knead on low speed until the dough is smooth and elastic, 6 to 8 minutes. If working by hand, knead the dough on a floured surface until smooth and elastic, about 15 minutes.

3. Place the dough in a large, well-oiled bowl and cover with a dish towel or plastic wrap. Set the dough in a warm, draft-free spot to rise until doubled in bulk, 1 to 2 hours.

4. Generously oil a jelly-roll pan. Punch down the dough. Spread the dough into the prepared pan to a uniform 1-inch thickness. Cover with a dish towel. Set aside to rise in a warm draft-free spot until doubled in bulk, about 1 hour.

5. About 30 minutes before baking, preheat the oven to 400°F.

6. Make a dozen evenly spaced shallow indentations in the dough with the handle of a wooden spoon or your index finger. Drizzle the dough with the olive oil. Sprinkle on the Parmesan and pepper. Bake until golden brown, 20 to 25 minutes. Serve warm.

Rosemary-Parmesan Biscotti {Makes about 3 dozen}

Biscotti are twice-baked sweet Italian biscuits that are made by baking the dough into a loaf, slicing the loaf, and then baking the slices again. Our savory recipe produces an exceptionally crunchy cheese cracker studded with pine nuts and rosemary—they're one of our favorite snack foods. We serve them spread with Black Olive Tapenade (page 294) alongside Lemon- and Pepper-grilled Calamari with Roasted Pepper–Balsamic Dressing (page 54)—or anytime we need a cracker for dips or spreads.

$2^{1}/_{3}$ cups all-purpose flour

$1^{1}/_{2}$ teaspoons salt

$^{3}/_{4}$ teaspoon baking powder

$^{1}/_{2}$ cup freshly grated Parmesan

2 teaspoons freshly ground black pepper

2 tablespoons chopped fresh
    rosemary leaves

$1^{1}/_{2}$ teaspoons dried thyme

$^{1}/_{3}$ cup pine nuts, toasted (see note,
    page 144)

4 eggs

$^{1}/_{3}$ cup cold water

1. Preheat the oven to 350°F. Oil a baking sheet.

2. Combine the flour, salt, baking powder, Parmesan, pepper, rosemary, thyme, and pine nuts in a large bowl. In a separate bowl, whisk together 3 of the eggs with the cold water.

3. Make a well in the center of the dry ingredients and pour the whisked eggs into the well. Slowly stir the eggs into the flour until combined.

4. Flour your hands and a work surface. Knead the dough until smooth, about 3 minutes, adding additional flour, if necessary. Shape the dough into a $2^{1}/_{2}$ x 8-inch log. Set the log on the oiled baking sheet.

5. Whisk the remaining egg. Lightly brush over the top of the log to glaze it. Bake until golden brown, about 30 minutes. Lower the oven temperature to 325°F.

6. Let the loaf cool to room temperature on a wire rack. Use a serrated knife to slice the loaf on a diagonal into $^{1}/_{4}$-inch-thick slices. Arrange the slices, cut sides down, in a single layer on a baking sheet. Return to the oven and bake until lightly golden and crisp, about 15 minutes.

7. Cool the biscotti on a rack. Store in an airtight container for up to 2 weeks.

Curried Poppy Seed Crackers {Makes about 16 large crackers}

These crackers are easy to make and magnificent to behold; crisp, craggy pieces of bright yellow cracker dotted with black poppy seeds. The recipe makes a big batch of crackers, but they'll keep in an airtight container for several weeks. Recrisp in a warm oven, if necessary.

¼ cup plus 2 tablespoons lukewarm (110°F) water

1½ teaspoons active dried yeast

½ teaspoon sugar

1½ teaspoons White Dog Cafe Curry Powder (page 284) or other high-quality curry powder

½ teaspoon salt

1 egg, separated

1½ cups all-purpose flour, plus more as needed

1 tablespoon poppy seeds

1. Pour the lukewarm water into a large mixing bowl. Sprinkle the yeast on top of the water and stir until it dissolves. Stir in the sugar, curry powder, and salt. Whisk in the yolk. Add 1 cup of flour and mix with a wooden spoon until smooth. Gradually add ½ cup of the flour until the dough becomes too difficult to stir.

2. Turn out the dough onto a floured surface and knead in enough additional flour to form a cohesive dough. Continue kneading and adding small amounts of flour until the dough is firm, resilient, and no longer sticks to the work surface. Transfer to a greased bowl and cover with plastic wrap. Set aside in a draft-free place to rise until doubled in bulk, about 1 hour.

3. Preheat the oven to 425°F.

4. Invert a jelly-roll pan and generously oil what is now the top. When the dough has doubled in bulk, punch it down and divide it into 8 equal portions. Place 1 portion at a time on the oiled, upside-down baking sheet. Use a rolling pin to roll out the dough as thinly as possible. Wet your hands in cold water and use your fingertips to spread the dough out farther, until it's stretched to the point where it has holes and is almost translucent. Using a pastry brush, lightly coat the dough with cold water. Sprinkle some of the poppy seeds onto the moistened dough. Gently press the seeds into the dough with your fingertips. Repeat with the remaining pieces of dough.

5. Bake each batch on the inverted pan until crisp and golden, 5 to 7 minutes. Let cool on the pan. Break each batch in half or thirds. Store in an airtight container.

CHAPTER SEVEN

DESSERTS

DESSERTS

The Hip Hop: An Urban Youth Tale 245

Apple-Cranberry Deep-dish Streusel Pie 248

Harvest Fruit Crisp 249

Nana's Strawberry Pie 250

Double-crusted Peach-Blueberry Pie 251

Lavender Biscuits with Mixed Summer Berries 252

Pumpkin and Walnut Shortbread Tart with Cranberry Coulis 253

Lemon Curd and Almond Shortbread Tart 254

Havana Banana Cake with Pineapple-Rum Compote 255

Rose Geranium Pound Cake 256

White Chocolate—Raspberry Cheesecake 257

Creamy Chèvre Torte in Pine Nut Crust with Zinfandel-spiked Cherries 258

White Dog Cafe Milk Chocolate Cream Pie 260

Dense Bittersweet Chocolate Torte 262

Orange-Pistachio Biscotti 263

Cappuccino Crème Brûlée 264

Anne-Marie's Kitchen Cabinet Cookies 265

James's Giant Oatmeal Cookies 266

Homemade Caramel Sauce 267

Hot Fudge Sauce 267

THE HIP HOP: AN URBAN YOUTH TALE

SEAN WAS IN THE KITCHEN TAKING HIS POPPY SEED POUND CAKES OUT OF THE oven. In the dining room, Chris was setting places for ten people at each banquet table. Lakia stood on a chair looping yellow and red streamers as Tanya joined the other end to a cluster of balloons. These were tenth graders from the local public high school, and tonight was The Hip Hop at the White Dog Cafe, the culminating celebration of our restaurant's nine-month-long mentoring program with them. The idea had first come to me in 1991, as I watched the students while driving by the school one day. It had occurred to me then that this is where my own children would be if I hadn't sent them to private school. Like most urban high schools, with barred windows and graffiti-covered metal doors, the local school looked more like a prison than an educational institution. The students there were all African-American. These were the kids of my own neighborhood, yet all I knew about them were the generalizations I read in books and newspapers or watched in the movies or on TV. *Who are they?* I thought to myself. I needed to know.

Over the next few months, in talking with school administrators about starting an off-site mentorship program, I soon discovered the school had one of the lowest SAT scores in the city and one of the highest rates of poverty and violence. The students' lunch break was only twenty minutes long so they would have no time for fighting. The food offered in the school cafeteria was so unappealing that most kids ate candy bars and potato chips from the vending machines. I also learned that one of the students joining the program, David, had been suspended for having a knife, which he carried for protection from the larger boys. David, who'd never met his father and whose mother had problems, lived with his aunt. I realized then that this was going to be a whole new experience for all of us.

The next fall, our first group of students and ten White Dog Cafe staff mentors began a process of

White Dog Cafe staff and students of the Mentoring Program serving patrons at the Hip Hop

becoming in some small way, a part of each other's lives. How shy we all were, like foreigners to each other. The students kept their eyes down, never making contact, acting disinterested while watching everything. The boys, smileless and sullen, tried hard to maintain the cool, detached demeanor of the streets.

Starting out with showing where our food originates, we took them on a field trip to the family farms that supply the Cafe. After a long ride out into the country we clambered out of the school bus and into the open spaces of Bucks County, where we followed the farmer through the fields as he explained the process of organic farming. Hesitantly the students tried little bites of fresh herbs that we picked along the way—basil, lemon thyme, rosemary—flavors and smells they'd never experienced before. Next we all piled back into

A student of the White Dog Cafe Mentoring Program serving patrons during the Hip Hop

the bus and took off to the goat farm that produces fresh chèvre for the Cafe. There, we romped in the pasture with the goats and, in the barn, quietly held an egg up to our ears, listening to an unborn chick pecking at its shell.

The next week, after working his first shift in the Cafe, helping the maitre d' show customers to their seats, one student remarked of his surprise at how easy it was to be nice to people! Smiling came more easily to the students when we ventured out to basketball games, movies, and ice skating—or just enjoyed pizza and soda together.

Working in the Cafe's kitchen is always the favorite activity for the students, where the ever-patient pastry chef teaches some simple skills in making desserts. One student, Lakia, wrote in her school paper, "First I worked downstairs with the pastry chef and chopped some macadamia nuts to put on the apple pies. Then I cut the apples and next I rolled dough and put a plastic bag over so it could rise again. I worked with Kevin making desserts and I ate a piece of chocolate cake. I loved all of my jobs and being a chef is like being a painter. Maybe I could take a plate home for my grandma so she can taste the great food I've been talking about when I go home."

This year's Hip Hop was another great success. The students had sold tickets for the dinner and in came their customers—moms, dads, grandmothers, sisters and brothers, girlfriends and boyfriends, teachers, even the school janitor. Having read about The Hip Hop in our Cafe's newsletter, many of our regular cus-

Cafe staff with students from the Mentoring Program, 1997

tomers, some with children, helped fill the eighty seats.

Chosen by the students, the menu was simple, home-style foods including barbecue chicken and ribs, potato salad, and Sean's poppy seed pound cake (from a family recipe) for dessert—all served by the students. After dinner, each student took a turn at the microphone to make an announcement or say a thank you. Standing up in front of others is always the scariest part, but how pleased they were afterwards, and how proud everyone was of them for all they had accomplished.

Soon after, the music started as deejay "Baby D" got the crowd on its feet. Suddenly the dance floor was packed. Three of Tanya's sisters put the rest of us to shame with their coordinated dance steps. After a few exhausting dances, I stood to the side to catch my breath and watch the crowd. More familiar faces began appearing as graduates of our program from past years (some who had received college scholarships from the White Dog program) arrived for the party. In came David, wearing a suit and a big smile. He was back from his sophomore year at college and had brought his girlfriend to meet us. How very glad we all were to see him.

Who are they? I had once asked myself while driving past the school. I knew now. They are our children.

—JW

Apple-Cranberry Deep-dish Streusel Pie {Serves 8}

This amazing apple pie is a heaping mound of apples and cranberries baked in a flaky pie crust and topped with a buttery walnut streusel. It wins consistent raves and is as good for breakfast as it was for dessert the night before.

STREUSEL

¾ cup firmly packed light brown sugar

1 cup all-purpose flour

2 teaspoons ground cinnamon

1 teaspoon ground allspice

½ teaspoon salt

1 cup walnuts, roughly chopped

6 tablespoons cold unsalted butter, cut into small cubes

FILLING

1¼ cups granulated sugar

1 tablespoon ground cinnamon

⅓ cup cornstarch

9 Granny Smith apples, peeled, cored, and sliced (about 8 cups)

2 cups fresh or thawed frozen cranberries

¼ pound (1 stick) unsalted butter, sliced

1 prebaked single pie crust (made from Basic Pie Dough, page 280)

1. Preheat the oven to 350°F.

2. Make the streusel: Combine the brown sugar, flour, cinnamon, allspice, salt, walnuts, and butter in the bowl of an electric mixer fitted with the paddle attachment. Beat on low speed until the mixture has the texture of coarse meal, about 2 minutes. Reserve.

3. Make the filling: Combine the sugar, cinnamon, and cornstarch in a small bowl and mix well. Combine the apples, cranberries, and butter in a large mixing bowl. Add the sugar mixture and toss well to coat the fruits and butter evenly. Mound the filling in the prebaked pie crust. Carefully pat the streusel topping over the top. Place the pie on a baking sheet. Bake until the topping is evenly browned and crisp and the apples are cooked through and tender, 1 to 1¼ hours.

4. Let the pie cool slightly on a wire rack. Serve warm.

FREEZING FRESH CRANBERRIES

Fresh cranberries are fabulous but pretty scarce from January through September. If you want, stock up on fresh cranberries in the fall, and keep them in your freezer for up to a year.

Harvest Fruit Crisp {Serves 6}

Harvest fruits are all of the gorgeous fruits the farmers bring us during the late summer and early autumn—apples, pears, peaches, grapes, cranberries, gooseberries, plums—and any combination of them can be baked into a bubbling crisp that will make your mouth water. This dessert is terrific for crowds; we make it when we have eighty people coming for a Table Talk dinner and all must be served their dessert at the same time. It can be made in the morning and warmed just before serving. Top it with some vanilla ice cream or a dollop of whipped cream and a sprinkle of cinnamon.

TOPPING

1 cup firmly packed light brown sugar

1 cup all-purpose flour

1½ cups rolled oats

1 teaspoon ground cinnamon

½ teaspoon ground ginger

Pinch of salt

1 cup coarsely chopped pecans

¼ pound (1 stick) cold unsalted
    butter, cubed

FILLING

4 large, firm, tart apples, such as
    Granny Smith, McIntosh, or Ida Red,
    cored and sliced

3 ripe pears, such as Bartlett or Bosc,
    cored and sliced

1½ cups seedless red grapes,
    stems removed

1½ cups fresh or thawed frozen cranberries

1½ cups granulated sugar

3 tablespoons cornstarch

2 teaspoons ground cinnamon

1 teaspoon ground ginger

½ teaspoon ground cloves

1. Preheat the oven to 350°F. Butter an 8 x 8-inch baking dish.

2. Make the topping: Combine the brown sugar, flour, oats, cinnamon, ginger, salt, pecans, and butter in the bowl of an electric mixer fitted with the paddle attachment. Blend on low speed until the butter is incorporated and the topping is the consistency of coarse meal, about 2 minutes. Reserve.

3. Make the filling: Combine the apples, pears, grapes, and cranberries in a large mixing bowl. Combine the sugar, cornstarch, cinnamon, ginger, and cloves in a separate bowl and mix well. Add the sugar mixture to the fruits and toss to coat evenly.

4. Spread the fruit mixture into the prepared baking dish. Cover with the crumb topping. Place on a baking sheet. Bake until the juice is thick and the topping is browned, about 50 minutes. If the topping browns before the fruit is cooked, cover with foil, and bake until the fruit is tender. Serve warm, or let cool to room temperature, cover, and refrigerate for up to 2 days. Rewarm before serving.

Nana's Strawberry Pie {Serves 6 to 8}

In early summer when you find yourself with ripe, juicy strawberries still warm from the sun, the time is right to make Judy's grandmother's celebrated strawberry pie.

3 pints (6 cups) strawberries, rinsed, hulled, and stemmed

1 cup sugar

3 tablespoons cornstarch

2 tablespoons unsalted butter

Juice of 1/2 lemon

1 prebaked single pie crust (see Basic Pie Dough, page 280)

Whipped cream, for serving

1. Reserve 1 pint of the best-looking strawberries.

2. Place the remaining berries in a bowl and crush with a pastry blender, potato masher, or strong wire whip. Combine the crushed berries, sugar, cornstarch, butter, and lemon juice in a nonreactive saucepan set over medium heat. Bring to a simmer and cook until thick and uncloudy, 8 to 10 minutes. Let cool to room temperature.

3. Pour the filling into the prebaked pie shell. Arrange the reserved whole berries, stem side down, in concentric circles over the top of the filling. Chill for at least 2 hours or overnight. Serve with lots of freshly whipped cream.

Double-crusted Peach-Blueberry Pie {Serves 8 to 10}

Nothing beats this fabulous summertime treat. In August, we're lucky enough to get tree-ripened organic white peaches from our farmer friends. Each piece of fruit is a fragile perfumed jewel that lasts only a day or two, so we eat them out of hand, make them into sorbets and ice creams, freeze them for the winter, and bake them in this deep-dish pie along with plump, sweet blueberries from our neighboring state of New Jersey. Try serving this pie with hand-churned vanilla-strawberry ice cream.

1 pound, 12 ounces Basic Pie Dough (page 280), prepared through Step 3

6 cups peeled, pitted, sliced ripe peaches (about 3 pounds)

1 pint (2 cups) blueberries, rinsed and picked over

½ cup plus 1 tablespoon sugar

¼ cup plus 1½ teaspoons all-purpose flour

2 tablespoons grated orange zest

½ teaspoon ground cinnamon

Pinch of ground cloves

Heavy cream, for glazing the crust

1. On a lightly floured surface, roll out half of the dough in an even 12-inch circle ⅛- to ¼-inch thick. Fold the dough in half and carefully transfer to a 10-inch pie pan. Unfold the dough and gently press into the pan. Trim the edge to fit the pan.

2. Combine the peaches, blueberries, ½ cup of the sugar, the flour, zest, cinnamon, and cloves in a large bowl. Toss to combine well. Mound the filling in the pie shell.

3. On a lightly floured surface, roll out the remaining dough into an even 11-inch circle. Fold the dough in half and carefully transfer to the center of the pie. Unfold the dough over the fruit and press down on the edges to seal the crust. Crimp the edges of the top and bottom crust together with your thumbs in a decorative scallop pattern.

4. Cut a small steam hole in the center of the pie; cut four 1-inch slits around the steam hole. Refrigerate the pie for 30 minutes.

5. Meanwhile, preheat the oven to 450°F.

6. Brush the top of the pie with the cream. Sprinkle lightly with the remaining 1 tablespoon sugar. Place the pie on a baking sheet. Bake for 10 minutes.

7. Reduce the heat to 350°F and bake until the crust is golden and the filling is thick and bubbly, about 30 minutes more. Let cool on a rack for 1 hour before serving.

Lavender Biscuits with Mixed Summer Berries {Makes 12 biscuits; serves 6}

Serve these lavender-scented biscuits with mixed berries and whipped crème fraîche for a lovely summer dessert.

2 generous pints (about 4 cups) mixed ripe berries (blueberries, strawberries, raspberries, or blackberries)

⅓ cup plus 3 tablespoons sugar

2 cups all-purpose flour

1 tablespoon baking powder

2 teaspoons lavender flowers (available in specialty food stores)

1 teaspoon salt

¼ pound (1 stick) cold unsalted butter, cut into ¼-inch cubes

1 cup heavy cream, plus extra for glazing

2 cups Crème Fraîche (page 288), whipped, for serving

1. Place the berries in a large bowl and toss with ⅓ cup of the sugar. Use the back of a wooden spoon to crush some of the berries into the sugar. Let stand at room temperature until the berries begin to exude some of their juices, at least 30 minutes. Serve immediately, or cover and chill overnight.

2. Preheat the oven to 350°F. Butter a baking sheet.

3. Sift together the flour, 2 tablespoons of the sugar, the baking powder, lavender flowers, and salt in a large mixing bowl. Using a pastry blender or 2 knives, cut in the butter until the dough resembles coarse meal. Add 1 cup of the heavy cream and mix just to form a soft dough (it will be quite tacky).

4. Flour a work surface. Using your fingertips, pat out the dough to an even ¾-inch thickness. Cut the dough into rounds with a floured 3-inch biscuit cutter. Transfer the biscuits to the buttered baking sheet. Gather the scraps of dough, pat out again, and cut out the remaining biscuits; you should have enough dough for 12 biscuits. Brush the tops lightly with heavy cream and sprinkle with the remaining 1 tablespoon sugar. (The biscuits can be made to this point up to 24 hours in advance. Cover with plastic wrap and refrigerate until ready to bake).

5. Bake until the biscuits are cooked through and just beginning to brown, 18 to 20 minutes. Transfer to a rack and let cool for 5 minutes.

6. Cut the biscuits in half.

7. Place the bottom halves on serving plates. Generously spoon the berries over the biscuits, dividing evenly and spooning the juices over. Spoon on some of the crème fraîche; set the biscuit lids in place. Serve immediately.

Pumpkin and Walnut Shortbread Tart with Cranberry Coulis {Serves 8 to 10}

Here's the White Dog's version of the traditional Thanksgiving standby. The rich and tender walnut shortbread crust is good enough to eat on its own and is irresistible when matched with the spiced pumpkin filling and tangy cranberry sauce. The tart is best if eaten the day it is made; however, the crust can be made a day in advance.

CRANBERRY COULIS

3 cups fresh or thawed frozen cranberries

2 cups sugar

2 cups fresh orange juice

1 cup cold water

$1/4$ cup cornstarch

$1/2$ teaspoon ground cinnamon

$1/2$ teaspoon ground ginger

$1/4$ teaspoon ground cloves

WALNUT SHORTBREAD

12 tablespoons ($1^1/2$ sticks) unsalted butter, at room temperature

$1/4$ cup plus 2 tablespoons granulated sugar

$1/2$ teaspoon vanilla extract

$1/2$ cups all-purpose flour

$1/2$ cup ground toasted walnuts (see note, page 144)

FILLING

2 cups canned pumpkin purée

$1/2$ cup whole milk

2 eggs, whisked

$1/2$ cup packed light brown sugar

1 teaspoon ground cinnamon

$1/4$ teaspoon ground ginger

$1/4$ teaspoon ground cloves

$1/8$ teaspoon ground nutmeg

1. Prepare the Cranberry Coulis: Combine all of the ingredients in a large, nonreactive saucepan set over medium-low heat. Simmer, stirring occasionally, until the cranberries are soft and the sauce is thick, about 35 minutes. Let the coulis cool slightly and serve warm, or let cool to room temperature, cover, and refrigerate for up to 1 week. Rewarm before serving.

2. Preheat the oven to 350°F.

3. Prepare the shortbread: Cream the butter with the sugar and vanilla in the bowl of an electric mixer fitted with the paddle attachment. Beat for 2 minutes on low speed. Scrape down the sides of the bowl with a rubber spatula. Whip on high speed until light and airy, about 4 minutes more. Add the flour and ground walnuts and mix on low speed just to incorporate, about 15 seconds. Do not overmix. Gather the dough into a ball and remove to an 11-inch tart pan with a removable bottom.

4. Use your fingertips to gently press the dough into an even $1/4$-inch-thick layer on the bottom and up the side of the tart pan. Press aluminum foil over the shell. Fill with pastry weights or dried beans and bake 20 minutes. Reduce the oven temperature to 300°F and leave the oven on. Transfer the tart shell to a wire rack and let cool to room temperature. Remove the pie weights.

5. Prepare the filling: Combine the pumpkin, milk, eggs, brown sugar, cinnamon, ginger, cloves, and nutmeg in a large bowl. Whisk well to combine. Pour the mixture into the prepared crust.

6. Bake the tart on the middle rack of the oven until the filling is firm, about 45 minutes. Remove to a wire rack and let cool to room temperature. Serve with the warm Cranberry Coulis.

Lemon Curd and Almond Shortbread Tart {Serves 8 to 10}

This is an enchanting dessert of cool, airy lemon curd in a tender, almond shortbread crust. Although you can make this tart in a regular pie tin, it's far more attractive if you use a fluted tart pan with a removable or "false" bottom. The lemon curd can be made several days in advance.

LEMON CURD

6 egg yolks

3/4 cup sugar

6 tablespoons cold, unsalted cold butter

Juice and zest of 3 large lemons

3/4 cup heavy cream

ALMOND SHORTBREAD

12 tablespoons (1 1/2 sticks) unsalted butter, at room temperature

1/4 cup plus 2 tablespoons sugar

1/2 teaspoon pure vanilla extract

Grated zest of 3 large lemons

1 1/2 cups all-purpose flour

1/2 cup almond slivers, toasted (see note, page 144) and ground

Whipped cream, white chocolate curls, and fresh berries, for garnish (optional)

1. Prepare the curd: Combine the egg yolks, sugar, butter, and lemon juice and zest in a double boiler or stainless steel bowl set over simmering water. Whisk constantly until the yolks thicken, 10 to 15 minutes until it's about the texture of a loose jam.

2. Strain the curd through a fine sieve. Place plastic wrap directly on the surface to prevent a skin from forming. Set aside to cool to room temperature. Refrigerate until well chilled, at least 2 hours, or overnight.

3. Whip the cream until stiff. Gently incorporate one-fourth of the whipped cream into the chilled lemon curd, so when you add the remaining whipped cream it stays airy. Fold in the remaining whipped cream. Cover and refrigerate for at least 1 hour.

4. Preheat the oven to 350°F.

5. Prepare the shortbread: Cream the butter with the sugar, vanilla, and lemon zest in the bowl of an electric mixer fitted with the paddle attachment. Beat for 2 minutes on low speed. Scrape down the sides of the bowl with a rubber spatula. Whip on high speed until light and airy, about 4 minutes more. Add the flour and ground almonds and mix on low speed just until incorporated, about 15 seconds. Do not overmix. Gather the dough into a ball and remove to an 11-inch tart pan with a removable bottom.

6. Gently press the dough into an even 1/4-inch thick layer on the bottom and up the side of the tart pan. Press aluminum foil over the shell. Fill with pastry weights or dried beans and bake for 20 minutes. Remove the pie weights and foil and bake until golden brown, another 5 minutes or so. Let cool to room temperature on a wire rack. Remove the outer ring of the tart pan, and carefully transfer the tart shell to a platter.

7. Fill the cooled tart shell with the chilled lemon curd. Refrigerate until set, at least 2 hours or overnight. Cut into 8 to 10 wedges and serve cold. Garnish if desired.

Havana Banana Cake with Pineapple-Rum Compote {Serves 8 to 10}

Combining the flavors of this friendly but forbidden island, we marry ripe bananas and toasted peanuts, which are baked into a moist buttermilk-enriched cake topped with a rum-soaked pineapple compote.

BANANA CAKE

12 tablespoons (1½ sticks) unsalted butter, at room temperature

1½ cups sugar

2 eggs

3 cups mashed ripe bananas (about 4 whole)

½ cup buttermilk

1 tablespoon vanilla extract

2 cups cake flour (not self-rising)

1 teaspoon baking soda

1 teaspoon baking powder

1 teaspoon salt

¾ cup chopped peanuts, toasted (see note, page 144)

PINEAPPLE-RUM COMPOTE

¾ cup pineapple juice

¼ cup plus 1 tablespoon sugar

½ vanilla bean, split

1 ripe pineapple, peeled, cored, and cut into ¼-inch chunks

2 tablespoons fresh orange juice

1 tablespoon dark rum (or more to taste)

1. Prepare the cake: Preheat the oven to 350°F. Butter and lightly flour a 10-inch Bundt pan.

2. Cream the butter and the sugar in the bowl of an electric mixer fitted with the paddle attachment. Beat on medium speed until light and fluffy, 5 to 7 minutes. Add the eggs and mix to incorporate. Add the bananas, buttermilk, and vanilla and mix to combine. Sift together the cake flour, baking soda, baking powder, and salt. Add the dry ingredients to the batter and mix on low speed just to incorporate. (Do not overmix.) Gently stir in the peanuts.

3. Pour the batter into the prepared pan. Bake until a toothpick inserted in the center of the cake comes out clean, 50 to 60 minutes. Transfer to a wire rack and let cool to room temperature.

4. Prepare the compote: Combine the pineapple juice, sugar, and vanilla bean in a small, nonreactive saucepan set over high heat. Bring to a boil. Reduce the heat to a simmer and remove the vanilla bean. Add half of the pineapple chunks. Simmer until soft, about 10 minutes.

5. Remove the cooked pineapple mixture to a food processor or blender and purée. Remove to a bowl. Stir in the remaining pineapple, the orange juice, and the rum while the purée is still warm. Serve warm, or let cool to room temperature, cover, and refrigerate for up to 5 days. Bring to room temperature before serving.

6. Unmold the cake from the pan onto a cake plate. Cut into wedges and serve topped with the Pineapple-Rum Compote and Caramel Sauce (page 267).

FREEZING BANANAS

Over-ripe bananas freeze well and are great to have on hand for recipes like this one. To freeze them, simply peel the bananas and place them in a freezer bag. Squeeze any air out of the bag, seal tightly, and freeze for up to three months. For convenient portioning, freeze in small batches of three or four bananas each. Thaw overnight in the refrigerator before using.

Rose Geranium Pound Cake {Serves 8}

Rose-scented geranium is a bushy plant with heart-shaped leaves that feel like velvet. It belongs to the same family as the household geranium, but its leaves are spectacularly aromatic. Look for rose geranium leaves at your local farmers' market or grow your own; its correct species name is Pelargonium capitatum. We like to serve slices of this cake topped with sweetened berries and vanilla whipped cream, garnished with a geranium leaf. For a decadent breakfast, try toasting a few slices of this cake and spreading them with orange marmalade or strawberry jam.

½ pound (2 sticks) unsalted butter, cubed, at room temperature

1½ cups sugar

1 teaspoon vanilla extract

Grated zest of 1 lemon

4 eggs

½ cup sour cream

2 cups cake flour (not self-rising)

1 teaspoon baking powder

½ teaspoon salt

¼ cup minced rose geranium plus additional leaves for garnish

1. Preheat the oven to 350°F. Butter a 9 x 5-inch loaf pan.

2. Cream the butter, sugar, vanilla, and lemon zest in the bowl of an electric mixer fitted with the paddle attachment. Beat on medium speed until light and fluffy, 6 to 8 minutes.

3. In a separate bowl, whisk together the eggs and sour cream until smooth. Add to the butter mixture and mix.

4. Sift together the cake flour, baking powder, and salt in a bowl. Add the dry ingredients to the batter in 2 batches. Mix on low speed just to incorporate. (Do not overmix.) Fold in the minced rose geranium.

5. Pour the batter into the prepared loaf pan. Bake on the middle rack of the oven for 1 hour.

6. Reduce the oven temperature to 325°F. Bake until a tester inserted in the center of the cake comes out clean, about 20 minutes more. Transfer the cake to a rack and let cool to room temperature before serving. If tightly wrapped in plastic, the cake will keep for up to 2 days at room temperature and 3 months in the freezer.

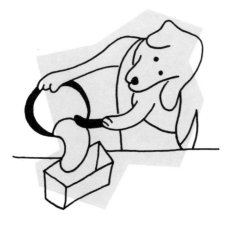

White Chocolate–Raspberry Cheesecake {Serves 10 to 12}

This is a seductive dessert of creamy white chocolate and fresh raspberries baked in a dark chocolate cookie crust.

CRUST

1 box (9 ounces) chocolate wafer cookies

¼ pound (1 stick) unsalted butter, melted

CHEESECAKE

2¼ pounds (four and a half 8-ounce packages) cream cheese, at room temperature

Grated zest of 1 lemon

½ cup sugar

8 ounces white chocolate, chopped, melted and cooled (see note below)

3 eggs

½ cup heavy cream

1 teaspoon vanilla extract

1½ cups fresh raspberries

1. Preheat the oven to 250°F. Place a shallow pan on the bottom rack of the oven and half-fill it with water. Line the bottom of a 10-inch springform pan with parchment paper.

2. In a food processor or blender, process the cookies to fine crumbs, about 1 minute. Remove to a bowl and add the melted butter. Mix until well combined. Press the crumb mixture evenly onto the bottom of the lined pan. Refrigerate for 15 minutes or until set.

3. Meanwhile, combine the cream cheese, lemon zest, and sugar in the bowl of an electric mixer fitted with the paddle attachment. Beat on medium speed, stopping to scrape down the sides and bottom of the bowl a few times, until smooth and creamy, about 8 minutes. Add the melted white chocolate and blend for 1 minute. Add the eggs, one at a time, and mix until well incorporated. Add the cream and vanilla. Remove the bowl from the mixer and fold in the raspberries by hand.

4. Pour the filling into the prepared crust. Set the cheesecake on a baking sheet and place on the middle rack of the oven. Bake until the cake is set and pulls away from the side of the pan, 45 to 60 minutes.

5. Turn off the heat (do not open the door). Leave the cheesecake in the oven for 1 hour.

6. Remove to a rack and let cool to room temperature. Cover and refrigerate for at least 2 hours or up to 2 days.

MELTING CHOCOLATE

Chocolate is tricky if you don't handle it properly: it will burn, seize up, or lump with seemingly no provocation. To ensure success, first chop it finely, then place it in a double boiler or stainless steel mixing bowl set over a gently simmering pot of water. Do not let any water get on the chocolate! After a few minutes, turn off the simmering water, stir the chocolate, and let the chocolate finish melting. The heat from the cooling water should be enough to finish melting it.

Creamy Chèvre Torte in Pine Nut Crust with Zinfandel-spiked Cherries {Serves 10 to 12}

If you have no penchant for sugary-sweet desserts, this elegant cheesecake is for you. Tangy goat cheese is combined with a modest amount of sugar and baked in a toasted pine nut crust. We serve the cake topped with Zinfandel-Spiked Cherries and Homemade Caramel and Hot Fudge sauces (page 267). The torte can be made up to two days in advance and kept refrigerated.

ZINFANDEL-SPIKED CHERRIES

1½ cups plus 1 tablespoon cocktail cranberry juice

1 cup red zinfandel or other hearty red wine

¾ cup sun-dried cherries

Juice of ½ lemon

¼ cup firmly packed light brown sugar

1 cinnamon stick

Pinch of freshly ground black pepper or to taste

2 teaspoons arrowroot powder

CRUST

1 cup pine nuts, toasted, (see note, page 144) and finely chopped

1 cup all-purpose flour

¼ cup sugar

¼ pound (1 stick) unsalted butter, at room temperature

FILLING

1 pound cream cheese, at room temperature

1 pound unaged chèvre, crumbled and at room temperature

1½ cups sugar

4 eggs

¼ pound unsalted butter, melted and cooled to room temperature

1. Prepare the cherries: Combine 1½ cups of the cranberry juice, the zinfandel, cherries, lemon juice, brown sugar, cinnamon stick, and pepper in a small, nonreactive saucepan set over medium heat. Simmer until the cherries are plump and the liquid is reduced by half, about 20 minutes.

2. Combine the remaining 1 tablespoon cranberry juice with the arrowroot in a small cup and stir until smooth. Stir the mixture into the cherry sauce; bring to a boil. Remove from the heat; discard the cinnamon stick. Serve warm. The sauce can be prepared up to 1 week ahead and refrigerated. Reheat before serving.

3. Preheat the oven to 325°F. Butter the sides of a 10-inch springform pan.

4. Make the crust: Combine the pine nuts, flour, sugar, and butter in the bowl of an electric mixer fitted with the paddle attachment. Mix on low speed until well combined, 2 to 3 minutes.

5. Pat the dough onto the bottom of the springform pan. Bake until lightly golden, about 20 minutes. Transfer to a rack, leaving the oven on.

6. Make the filling: Cream the cream cheese, chèvre, and sugar in the bowl of an electric mixer fitted with the paddle attachment. Beat on low speed until combined, about 1 minute. Add the eggs, one at a time, beating well after each addition. Add the melted butter, flour, cornstarch, and vanilla and mix thoroughly. Stir in the sour cream.

MAKING CHERRIES À LA MODE

For an extra-special sundae, omit the black pepper from the Zinfandel-Spiked Cherries and serve them warm your favorite ice cream—along with our Homemade Caramel and Hot Fudge sauces, of course.

{continued}

3 tablespoons all-purpose flour

3 tablespoons cornstarch

2¹/₂ teaspoons vanilla extract

2 cups sour cream

7. Pour the batter into the prepared crust. Bake for 1 hour; the cake will still be soft in the center.

8. Turn off the heat (do not open the door), and let the cake stand in the oven for 2 hours.

9. Remove the cake to a wire rack and let cool to room temperature. Loosely cover the cake with plastic wrap and refrigerate for at least 2 hours or overnight. Remove the sides of the pan and transfer the cake to a plate. Serve with the warm Zinfandel-Spiked Cherries.

White Dog Cafe Milk Chocolate Cream Pie {Serves 8 to 10}

Our most popular dessert, this star earned a permanent place on our menu years ago. Each layer is distinctly wonderful—starting with a dark chocolate cookie crust topped with chewy peanut caramel and finally smothered with an airy, milk-chocolate mousse. It's a dessert as rich and calorific as any could aspire to be, and worth every moment of penance in your jogging shoes.

MOUSSE

6 ounces milk chocolate, finely chopped

³/₄ cup heavy cream

3 tablespoons unsalted butter, at room temperature

2 eggs, separated

Pinch of cream of tartar

¹/₄ cup Crème Fraîche (page 288) or sour cream

PEANUT CARAMEL

3 tablespoons unsalted butter

¹/₄ cup plus 1 tablespoon sugar

¹/₄ vanilla bean, split

¹/₂ cup plus 2 tablespoons heavy cream

1 cup peanuts, toasted (see note, page 144)

CHOCOLATE COOKIE CRUST

1 box (9 ounces) chocolate cookie wafers, broken

¹/₄ pound (1 stick) unsalted butter, melted

1. Prepare the mousse: Combine the milk chocolate and ¹/₂ cup of the heavy cream in a double boiler or stainless steel mixing bowl set over gently simmering water. Cook, stirring occasionally, until the chocolate is melted and the mixture is smooth, about 2 minutes. Remove from the heat and let cool.

2. Place the butter in the bowl of an electric mixer fitted with the paddle attachment and cream until light and soft, about 2 minutes. Reserve.

3. Place the egg yolks in a double boiler or stainless steel bowl set over gently simmering water. Whisk until lemon-yellow and airy, 1 to 2 minutes. Add the yolks to the creamed butter and mix to incorporate. Add the melted chocolate mixture and mix until well incorporated. Remove the mixture to another bowl and reserve.

4. Place the egg whites and cream of tartar in a clean, dry bowl of the electric mixer. Beat on high speed until soft peaks form, about 2 minutes. Gently fold the egg whites into the chocolate base.

5. Combine the remaining ¹/₄ cup heavy cream with the crème fraîche in the bowl of an electric mixer. Whip on high speed until soft peaks form. Gently fold into the chocolate base to incorporate well. Cover the mousse, placing plastic wrap directly on the surface, and refrigerate for 6 hours or overnight.

6. Prepare the Peanut Caramel: Combine the butter, sugar, and vanilla bean in a small saucepan set over medium heat. Cook until the mixture caramelizes, 6 to 8 minutes. Reduce the heat to low and carefully add the heavy cream, slowly pouring it down the side of the pan. Simmer, stirring constantly, until thick, about 10 minutes. Remove the vanilla bean.

(continued)

7. Stir in the peanuts. Set the caramel aside to cool to room temperature.

8. Prepare the crust: Pulse the cookies in a food processor or blender until finely ground. Remove to a bowl, add the melted butter, and mix well. With your fingertips, press the crust onto the bottom and up the side of a 10-inch tart pan with a removable bottom. Chill until firm and well set, about 1 hour.

9. Assemble the pie: Spread the cooled peanut caramel in an even layer over the bottom of the cookie crust. Spread the chocolate mousse evenly over the caramel. Tent with foil, and refrigerate until set, about 4 hours.

10. Remove the tart from the sides of the pan and slice into wedges. For a dramatic presentation, we serve slices of this pie on plates drizzled with Hot Fudge Sauce (page 267) and hot Homemade Caramel Sauce (page 267), topped with vanilla whipped cream and a handful of chocolate curls. A sprig of mint and a dusting of cocoa send it on its way to the dining room.

Dense Bittersweet Chocolate Torte {Serves 10 to 12}

A keen affection for chocolate is requisite to enjoying this dense coffee-spiked torte. It employs only five ingredients, so the quality of chocolate used is crucial for success. The torte can be made up to two days in advance and kept refrigerated.

1 pound (4 sticks) unsalted butter

1 pound high-quality bittersweet chocolate, chopped

1 cup strong brewed coffee

8 eggs

1 cup sugar

1. Preheat the oven to 350°F. Butter the bottom and side of a 10-inch springform pan.

2. Combine the butter, chocolate, and coffee in a double boiler or stainless steel mixing bowl set over barely simmering water. Melt together slowly, stirring occasionally, until smooth, 6 to 8 minutes. Remove from the heat and let cool for 5 minutes.

3. In a separate bowl, whisk together the eggs and sugar. Add to the cooled chocolate mixture and whisk to combine.

4. Pour the batter into the prepared pan. Bake for 1 hour. Remove the pan to a wire rack and let cool to room temperature.

5. Remove the side of the pan. Cover the torte with plastic wrap and refrigerate for at least 6 hours or overnight.

6. Cut the torte into wedges and serve on plates. If you like, serve thin wedges of this torte with vanilla ice cream and Zinfandel-Spiked Cherries (page 000) or fresh raspberries and whipped cream.

Orange-Pistachio Biscotti {Makes 2 dozen}

This twice-baked cookie is intensely crunchy and is truly delicious when dipped in dessert wine, coffee, or sweet-ened mascarpone.

2³/₄ cups all-purpose flour

1²/₃ cups sugar

1 cup shelled pistachio nuts, toasted
(see note, page 144) and minced

1 teaspoon baking powder

¹/₂ teaspoon salt

Grated zest of 1 orange

3 whole eggs

3 egg yolks

1 teaspoon vanilla extract

1. Preheat the oven to 350°F. Line a baking sheet with parchment, or butter it well.

2. Combine the flour, sugar, pistachios, baking powder, salt, and orange zest in a large bowl and mix well.

3. In a separate bowl, whisk together the whole eggs, egg yolks, and vanilla.

4. Make a well in the center of the dry ingredients. Add the egg mixture to the well and mix gradually into the dry ingredients to form a loose dough. Using your hands, knead the dough a few times in the bowl to form a ball. Divide the dough in half. Shape each half into a log 2 to 3 inches in diameter and the length of the baking sheet.

5. Arrange the logs, a few inches apart, on the prepared baking sheet. Bake until the logs are lightly golden and firm to the touch, 20 to 25 minutes. Remove the pan to a wire rack. Leave the oven on.

6. Let the biscotti cool for 10 minutes.

7. Slice each log on a diagonal into ¹/₂-inch-thick rounds. Arrange the slices on the baking sheet. Return to the oven and bake for 5 minutes.

8. Turn the slices over and bake for 5 minutes more. Remove the biscotti and let cool on a rack. Store in a tightly covered container for up to 1 month.

Cappuccino Crème Brûlée {Serves 8}

This eye-catching dessert is a pun of sorts—cappuccino-infused crème brûlée baked into coffee cups and topped with cinnamon whipped cream—it has the appearance of cappuccino topped with frothed milk. In order for the custard to set, you must use shallow, wide-mouthed diner-style coffee cups—or custard cups.

3 cups heavy cream

1 cup half-and-half

2 cinnamon sticks

¼ vanilla bean, split

9 egg yolks

1 cup sugar

3 tablespoons coffee extract or very strong brewed espresso

Cinnamon whipped cream, for garnish

8 chocolate straws, for garnish (optional)

1. Combine the cream, half-and-half, cinnamon sticks, and vanilla bean in a nonreactive saucepan set over medium heat. Bring to a boil. Remove the pan from the heat and set aside to steep for 30 minutes.

2. Preheat the oven to 250°F.

3. Whisk together the egg yolks and ½ cup of the sugar in a small bowl until well combined.

4. Bring the cream mixture back to a boil over low heat. Remove from the heat. Pour one-fourth of the hot cream into the egg yolk mixture and whisk well. Return the mixture to the hot cream and whisk well for 1 minute. Stir in the coffee extract or espresso.

5. Strain the custard through a fine sieve; discard the solids.

6. Divide the custard among 8 shallow, wide-mouthed, oven-proof cups or custard cups. Set the cups in a baking dish. Add enough hot water to the dish to reach three-fourths of the way up the sides of the cups. Place on the middle rack of the oven and bake until set, about 1 hour. (Do not let the water boil.)

7. Remove the cups from the water to a wire rack and let cool to room temperature. Cover and refrigerate for at least 4 hours.

8. Preheat the broiler.

9. Sprinkle 1 tablespoon of the remaining sugar on top of each custard. Shake each gently to coat the entire surface evenly. Place the cups in a baking dish and surround them with ice water. Set the dish under the broiler and broil until the sugar caramelizes. Leave the door open and watch carefully so the sugar doesn't burn.

10. Serve the custards immediately, garnished with dollops of cinnamon whipped cream and chocolate straws, if desired.

Anne-Marie's Kitchen Cabinet Cookies {Makes about 4 dozen}

Anne-Marie Lasher, a sous-chef at the White Dog Cafe for many years, developed this recipe to blend all the tasty odds and ends from her kitchen cabinet into a cookie. The dough should be made as suggested, however the nuts, chips, chunks, and even dried fruits, can vary with your whim.

$^1/_2$ **pound (2 sticks) unsalted butter, at room temperature**

$^3/_4$ **cup packed light brown sugar**

$^3/_4$ **cup granulated sugar**

2 eggs

1 tablespoon instant coffee, dissolved in 1 tablespoon hot water

1 teaspoon vanilla extract

2 cups all-purpose flour

1 teaspoon baking powder

1 teaspoon salt

1 cup rolled oats

1 cup shredded coconut

1 cup semisweet chocolate chips

1 cup butterscotch chips

$^1/_2$ **cup coarsely chopped walnuts**

$^1/_2$ **cup coarsely chopped pecans**

1. Preheat the oven to 350°F. Lightly butter 2 baking sheets.

2. In the bowl of an electric mixer, cream the butter and both sugars on medium speed until light and fluffy, about 5 minutes. Add the eggs, dissolved coffee, and vanilla. Stir in the flour, baking powder, salt, oats, and coconut. Stir in the chocolate chips, butterscotch chips, walnuts, and pecans.

3. Drop rounded tablespoonfuls of dough, 2 inches apart, on the prepared baking sheets. Bake the cookies until lightly browned, 10 to 12 minutes.

4. Remove the baking sheets to a wire rack and let cool. Although they are best if eaten immediately, you can store the cookies tightly covered for 2 to 3 days.

James's Giant Oatmeal Cookies {Makes about 1½ dozen}

James Barrett, co-owner of Metropolitan Bakery in Philadelphia, shares these giant, not-too-sweet, healthy-tasting oatmeal cookies that fall somewhere between a granola bar and a cookie. They're perfect for picnics, camping trips, bike rides, or anytime you want a treat that's also a pick-me-up.

¾ **pound (3 sticks) unsalted butter, at room temperature**

¾ **cup granulated sugar**

1 cup packed light brown sugar

2 eggs

2 teaspoons vanilla extract

1 cup all-purpose flour

2 teaspoons ground cinnamon

1¼ **teaspoons baking soda**

½ **teaspoon salt**

4 cups rolled oats

1 cup oat bran

1¾ **cups dark raisins or currants**

1 cup pecan pieces, toasted (see note, page 144)

1. Preheat the oven to 350°F. Butter 2 baking sheets.

2. Combine the butter and both sugars in the bowl of an electric mixer fitted with the paddle attachment. Cream on low speed until light and airy, about 10 minutes.

3. Meanwhile, in a separate bowl, whisk together the eggs and vanilla until combined.

4. Continue beating the dough at low speed, adding the egg mixture to the butter in 3 additions, waiting until each portion is incorporated before adding more. Sift together the flour, cinnamon, baking soda, and salt. Add to the butter mixture and mix to incorporate. Add the oats and oat bran. Continue to mix on low speed until the dough just comes together. (Do not overmix.) Remove the bowl from the mixer and stir in the raisins and pecans by hand.

5. Drop the dough in scant ½-cup mounds, spacing them 4 to 5 inches apart, on the prepared baking sheets. Flatten the cookies slightly with the back of a spoon. Bake until golden and slightly firm to the touch, 15 to 18 minutes.

6. Remove the baking sheets to a wire rack and let cookies cool completely before serving. Although they are best if eaten immediately, the cookies can be stored, tightly covered, for 2 to 3 days.

Homemade Caramel Sauce {Makes about 1 quart}

This recipe makes a lot of caramel sauce, but it keeps well and is so delicious that you'll probably want to have a stash of it in your refrigerator. Serve with sundaes, slices of apple, or drizzle over Apple-Cranberry Deep-Dish Streusel Pie or pumpkin pie.

1 cup heavy cream

¼ pound (1 stick) unsalted butter

¼ vanilla bean, split

¼ cup light corn syrup

2 cups sugar

1. Combine the heavy cream, butter, and vanilla bean in a saucepan set over medium-high heat. Bring to a boil. Remove from the heat. Discard the vanilla bean.

2. Bring the corn syrup to a boil in a heavy saucepan set over medium-high heat. Gradually add the sugar, stirring with a wooden spoon, and cook until it dissolves and begins to caramelize, about 5 minutes. Cook a few more minutes until the caramel is deeply golden but not dark brown.

3. Remove the pan from the heat and very gradually whisk in the reserved cream mixture. Be very careful; the caramel will bubble and spit violently as you add the cream to it.

4. Return the pan to the heat and simmer for 2 minutes. Serve hot, or let cool to room temperature, cover, and refrigerate for up to 1 month.

Hot Fudge Sauce {Makes about 2½ cups}

Look how easy it is to have your own homemade chocolate sauce on hand whenever you have a craving for hot fudge sundaes and banana splits. Use it decadently to top fresh berries or angel food cake, or as a fondue for fruit chunks and marshmallows.

1 cup heavy cream

4 tablespoons unsalted butter

6 ounces high-quality bittersweet chocolate, minced

2 tablespoons unsweetened cocoa powder

¼ cup packed light brown sugar

1. Bring the cream and butter to a simmer in a saucepan. Remove from the heat.

2. Add the chocolate, cocoa powder, and brown sugar; whisk until smooth. Serve hot, or let cool to room temperature, cover, and refrigerate for up to 1 month. Reheat before serving.

CHAPTER EIGHT

BASICS

BASICS

The Coffee of Selva Negra: A Nicaraguan Tale 272

Pantry Essentials 276

Stocks

Chicken Stock 277

Vegetable Stock 277

Veal Stock 278

Veal Demi-Glace 279

Fish Stock 279

Pantry

Basic Pie Dough 280

Food Processor Pasta Dough 281

Garlic Crostini 281

Garlic Croutons 282

Thyme Croutons 282

Polenta Croutons 283

Spicy Pita Crisps 284

White Dog Cafe Curry Powder 284

White Dog Cafe Garam Masala 285

Gremolata 285

Herb Butter 286

Cumin Butter 286

Sun-dried Tomato—Olive Butter 287

Homemade Mayonnaise 287

BASICS

Crème Fraîche 288

Spicy Ginger-Lime Dressing 288

Spicy Asian Marinade 289

Sauces

Tartar Sauce 290

Rustic Tomato-Basil Sauce 290

Basic Aïoli 291

Lemon-Pepper Aïoli 291

Basil Pesto 292

Winter Herb Pesto 292

Creamy Basil Sauce 293

Green Goddess Sauce 293

Dips & Spreads

Black Olive Tapenade 294

Hummus 294

White Bean–Feta Brandade 295

Guacamole 296

Avocado Mousse 296

Condiments

Gingered Pear Chutney 296

Pepper Relish 297

Cucumber Raita 298

THE COFFEE OF SELVA NEGRA: A NICARAGUAN TALE

GRINDING SLOWLY UP A LONG DIRT ROAD, OUR BUS CUT BACK AND FORTH across a jungle-covered mountain in the central highlands of Nicaragua. It was 1987, a time of political upheaval and civil war, and I was on the first of many trips that would result in our international sister-restaurant project, Table for Six Billion, Please! Inspired by the concept of "sister cities" and concerned about United States support of the Contras, who were fighting to overthrow Nicaragua's Sandinista government, I had decided that establishing a relationship with another small business would be a way to understand the conflict and the effect of our foreign policy on the lives of Nicaraguans. As a teenager, I had at first been fooled into supporting the Vietnam War and was now determined that this wasn't going to happen again. This time I wanted to know the truth. What did the Nicaraguan people really think of the Sandinista government that the United States considered a communist threat? How did they view the U.S.-backed Contras, whom our president had dubbed "Freedom Fighters"?

Bouncing along on the long bus ride from Managua to the outskirts of the conflicted area, I thought about how I had at first been afraid to come here. Originally I had seen the sister-restaurant project as a pen-pal relationship to exchange recipes and opinions. I asked a friend, David Funkhouser, who traveled to Nicaragua to choose a restaurant for me. When he suggested that I come along, I replied, "Who me? Oh, no, I go upstairs to my house and downstairs to the Cafe, and sometimes I don't even leave the block for weeks at a time! I never travel anywhere, especially to countries having wars!" Yet here I was, convinced by David to join a fact-finding delegation to Nicaragua. I had checked on my life insurance and will, and said good-bye to my parents, husband, and two young children. I really thought that I might never come back. As I looked out the bus window at the green hills stretch-

Judy (left), with staff of Nicaraguan sister restaurant, Selva Negra, 1988

ing into the distance, I realized that I was not in the least afraid to be here. Rather than feeling threatened and vulnerable as a foreigner in a strange land, I had

White Dog Cafe patrons delivering medical supplies to a clinic in Nicaragua, 1989

a comforting sense of belonging, as though both the history and the future of our countries were inextricably linked, and that our presence here as U.S. citizens seeking friendship and understanding was as important to my own country as to theirs.

Our destination was an inn at the top of the mountain, centrally located for excursions into the countryside where villages were being attacked. When the bus stopped, I saw a beautiful little restaurant called Selva Negra, with bric-a-brac trim like a storybook house, nestled beside a small pond in a tropical forest. Paths led among flowering bushes and banana trees to a scattering of tiny guest cottages where our group would stay. After freshening up, we gathered for a dinner of beans, rice, and fried plantains with a very small portion of meat. Because of the war, food supplies were scarce and the only memorable part of our meal was the excellent coffee that I soon discovered was grown right there on the small family-owned organic coffee plantation that included the restaurant and inn. After dinner, Roger, the great-grandson of the plantation founder, spoke with our group. A history teacher as well as a wood carver, he was a strong supporter of the Sandinistas who had used Selva Negra as a headquarters during the 1979 revolution against the dictator Somoza.

Having heard from Contra supporters we had interviewed in Managua that all businesses, including restaurants, had been nationalized by the Sandinistas, I was interested to hear from Roger that this was not true. In visiting additional restaurants, I found only one that was owned by the state. It had been deserted after the revolution by the previous owners who were affiliated with Somoza's notorious national guard, most of whom had joined the Contras or fled to Miami. In talking with Roger about his business I learned that his obstacles to success were created by the Contra war, not the government. He had no objection to the minimum wage that the Sandinista-led legislature had passed. In fact, he paid above minimum to encourage production on the coffee plantation. He also had no problem with the price ceilings imposed to curb inflation; in his restaurant he charged below the maximum allowed markup. Yes, undoubtedly, mistakes were being made as the Sandinista government struggled to correct past injustices, and some of the large industries owned by the oligarchy had been nationalized, but this was clearly a mixed economy, not communist.

The next morning we traveled to a nearby village recently attacked by the Contras. Through a land-reform program, the Sandinistas had redistributed Somoza's property to landless peasants who had built private farm communities. The Sandinista government had placed a priority on education and health care, establishing schools and health clinics throughout the countryside, where no services had existed before the revolution. Avoiding direct confrontation with the Sandinista army, the Contras were targeting civilian communities in order to destroy the progress being made by the Sandinista government and force the people to accept a return to past conditions rather than death and destruction by the counter-revolutionaries. When we arrived at the village we learned that a recent attack had demolished a schoolhouse. The mother of a dead nine-year-old student met with our group and told us, "The United States is behind this war. Please go back and tell your people that we are suffering." I was horrified to feel that U.S. weapons were being used to kill innocent civilians. This was not the America I believed in.

Trip leader, David Funk-
houser, creates a make-
shift shower for White
Dog Cafe patron, Bill
Reiser, in Nicaragua, 1988

Back at my cottage at Selva Negra that night I wrote in my journal about the responsibility I felt to tell my fellow citizens at home what I had seen. Coming here had changed my perspective about what it meant to be an American citizen in the world community. I decided that I must come back and bring others to witness what I had seen. Being a pen-pal was not enough; we needed to have personal contact with the people whose lives we affect so dramatically by our choice of political leaders and the use of our tax dollars. I asked Roger if Selva Negra would be a sister restaurant to the White Dog Cafe as a way to establish dialogue between the people of our countries. Before we left the next morning, he brought me a necklace with a white dog he had carved from wood. On the back it said, *"Restaurantes hermanos para paz y la amistad"* (Sister Restaurants for Peace and Friendship).

I returned twice to Nicaragua during the war years and came to understand that the motive behind the U.S. support of the Contras and the previous Somoza dictatorship was purely economic. As an American patriot, it was hard for me to face the fact that my own government was actually undermining democracy in order to insure cheap labor and natural resources for U.S. corporations. It became part of our sister-restaurant program's mission to show that capitalism did not have to have such an ugly face—that free enterprise was a favorable alternative to socialism when practiced for the benefit of the common good.

After participating in a sister-restaurant trip to Selva Negra, a fellow traveler, Micky Simmons, started a coffee company, New Harmony, and eventually imported organic beans from the coffee plantation at Selva Negra. Now, every morning I sip coffee grown by our Nicaraguan sister restaurant and am reminded that we can build a world community through economic relationships that benefit all people without exploiting the less fortunate. Thinking back, I realize how that first trip changed my life forever. I will never again be afraid to travel to another country to represent the America I believe should be.

—JW

Pantry Essentials

Certain pantry essentials are needed to produce the recipes in this book. Having these items, which can be found in most supermarkets or specialty food stores, along with the freshest ingredients available, will allow you to make every recipe in this book.

ALCOHOL: Although the wine you cook with should be drinkable, it doesn't need to be special. We use four basic types of spirits in our cooking: dry white wine, dry red wine, dry sherry, and ruby port. Occasionally, we use vermouth, Marsala, Madeira, and Pernod.

BUTTER: All butter called for is unsalted.

CITRUS: We use the juices of lemons, limes, oranges, and grapefruits to add life and sparkle to food, and often we add the grated or minced zest of the fruit when a stronger flavor is desired.

COFFEE: Try to find good quality organic coffee from a purveyor who practices "fair trade," which promotes economic justice for third-world growers.

HERBS: Each year at the Cafe we use literally tons of fresh organic herbs to flavor and enhance everything we make. Fresh herbs are essential to good food. We do occasionally use dried herbs, however, when using fresh herbs isn't practical, for example, when roasting vegetables at high heat. Purchase dried herbs in small amounts and keep them tightly sealed as they tend to lose their essence quickly.

MUSTARD: We use both a high-quality, extra-strong Dijon and a country-style coarse-grain mustard.

OILS: Generally, we use three types of oil: a high-quality vegetable oil for frying and baking, a light-colored virgin olive oil for sautéing and roasting, and an extra-virgin olive oil as a flavorful ingredient. We also use more exotic oils to flavor dishes—white truffle oil, hazelnut oil, toasted peanut oil, sesame oil, and lemon oil to name a few.

PEPPER: At the Cafe we use lots of black peppercorns, which we grind each day in an electric coffee mill. Because the fragrance and flavor of freshly ground black pepper is lost in packaged, pre-ground pepper, a pepper mill is essential.

SALT: We use kosher salt or sea salt when cooking because their flavors are purer and less "salty" than ordinary table salt. We also use *nam pla* (Thai fish sauce), an Asian condiment made of the elixir pressed from fermented anchovies, instead of salt to season seafood dishes. Fish sauce is available in Asian markets and better supermarkets and is the "secret ingredient" in some of our best dishes.

STOCKS: One of the difficulties in translating restaurant food into recipes that can be made easily at home is the use of stocks. At the Cafe, we use veal, chicken, fish, and vegetable stocks in many of the foods we make. In developing recipes for this book, we have tried to stay away from complex sauces whenever possible, but some dishes simply can't be made without a flavorful, homemade stock—substituting canned beef broth in a glaze made from reduced veal stock just doesn't work. So, we encourage you to make your own stock. The effort is well worth it, and although time-consuming, it is not at all difficult. Once made, stock can be frozen for months and pulled out whenever you need it.

VINEGARS: There are dozens of exotic vinegars available today, however, I gravitate to six basic types: a good quality balsamic vinegar, sherry vinegar, red wine vinegar, Champagne vinegar, apple cider vinegar, and rice wine vinegar. Occasionally, we dabble in tarragon or raspberry vinegars, as well.

Chicken Stock {Makes 4 quarts}

8 pounds chicken bones, or 1 stewing hen (about 3 lbs), cut into 8 pieces, rinsed in cold water and patted dry

1 large white onion, peeled and cut into 1-inch chunks

2 carrots, scrubbed and cut into 1-inch chunks

2 celery ribs, cut into 1-inch chunks

1 bay leaf

10 black peppercorns

5 fresh parsley sprigs

6 quarts cold water

1. Combine the chicken bones, onion, carrots, celery, bay leaf, peppercorns, and parsley in a large stockpot. Add the water, place the pot over high heat, and bring to a boil. Reduce the heat to low and simmer for 4 to 6 hours. Skim off and discard any foam that rises to the surface.

2. Strain the stock through a fine mesh strainer or a double layer of dampened cheesecloth into a metal or heatproof glass container; discard the solids. Use immediately or let cool to room temperature. Skim off any fat that rises to the top. Cover and refrigerate for up to 5 days. Bring the stock to a rolling boil before using. To freeze the stock, divide among smaller containers, leaving about $1/2$ inch of headspace. Cover, label, and date the containers. The stock can be frozen for up to 2 months.

Vegetable Stock {Makes about 6 cups}

2 large carrots, scrubbed and cut into chunks

2 celery ribs, cut into chunks

1 leek (white and green parts), sliced lengthwise, rinsed of all grit, and cut into chunks

2 corn cobs (reserve the kernels for another use)

1 ripe tomato, cut into chunks

1 small onion, peeled and cut into chunks

1 cup halved white mushrooms

5 garlic cloves, peeled

4 fresh thyme sprigs

2 bay leaves

1 teaspoon salt

2$1/2$ quarts cold water

1. Combine all of the ingredients in a large, nonreactive stockpot set over high heat. Bring to a boil. Reduce the heat and simmer for $1/2$ hours.

2. Strain the stock through a fine mesh strainer or a double layer of dampened cheesecloth into a metal or heatproof glass container; discard the solids. Use immediately, or let cool to room temperature. Cover and refrigerate for up to 5 days. Bring the stock to a rolling boil before using. To freeze, divide among smaller containers, leaving about $1/2$ inch of headspace. Cover, label, and date the containers. The stock can be frozen for up to 2 months.

OTHER WAYS TO DO IT

This vegetable stock is rich and full flavored. The ingredients listed make a fantastic stock, but other vegetables can be substituted as long as the carrots, celery, garlic, and onion are included.

STOCKS

Veal Stock {Makes 4 quarts}

¼ cup vegetable oil

8 pounds veal bones, cut into 3-inch chunks, rinsed and patted dry

1 large white onion, peeled and cut into 1-inch chunks

2 large carrots, scrubbed and cut into 1-inch chunks

2 celery ribs, cut into 1-inch chunks

¼ cup tomato paste

6 quarts cold water

1 bay leaf

5 fresh parsley sprigs

10 black peppercorns

1 cup dry red wine

1. Preheat the oven to 450°F.

2. Heat the oil until it ripples in a large, nonreactive roasting pan set over high heat. Add the veal bones, onion, carrots, celery, and tomato paste and toss to combine. Roast in the oven, stirring occasionally, until the bones are golden brown on all sides, 45 to 60 minutes.

3. Transfer the bones and vegetables to a large, nonreactive stockpot. Add the water, bay leaf, parsley, and peppercorns. Pour off and discard any excess fat from the roasting pan; place the roasting pan over medium heat. Add the wine to the pan to deglaze it, scraping up any browned bits and drippings that stick to the bottom. Add the wine mixture to the stockpot.

4. Bring the stock to a boil over high heat. Reduce the heat to low and simmer gently until rich and flavorful, 4 to 6 hours. Skim off and discard any foam that rises to the surface during cooking. Check the pot occasionally to make sure the bones are always covered with water; add more water if necessary.

5. Strain the stock through a fine mesh strainer or a double layer of dampened cheesecloth into a metal or heatproof glass container; discard the solids. Use immediately or let cool to room temperature. Skim off any fat that rises to the top. Cover and refrigerate for up to 1 week. Bring the stock to a rolling boil before using. To freeze the stock, divide among smaller containers, leaving about ½ inch of headspace. Cover, label, and date the containers. The stock can be frozen for up to 2 months.

Veal Demi-Glace {Makes about 2 cups}

Veal demi-glace or glace de viande is simply veal stock that is slowly reduced to a syrupy consistency. It is the foundation of most of our meat sauces. Although the process is lengthy, it is neither laborious nor does it take any special skill or delicacy. However, there are no shortcuts to making glace de viande, and all commercially available substitutes are salty and lackluster. The good news is that it can be made in large quantities and frozen for several months. We suggest making a double batch of veal stock on Saturday, and reducing it on Sunday. Then pop it in the freezer and you'll have enough rich, meaty demi-glace to make sauces all winter long.

4 quarts veal stock (see opposite page)

1. Place the stock in a large stockpot set over medium heat. Bring the stock to a gentle simmer. Reduce the heat and simmer until the stock is reduced by half, 2 to 3 hours. From time to time, using a ladle, skim off any foam that appears on the top of the stock. This will prevent the demi-glace from becoming clouded.

2. Transfer the stock to a smaller saucepan and continue to simmer until the stock is reduced to a syrup, 1 to 2 hours longer.

3. Use immediately or let cool to room temperature. Divide the demi-glace into smaller portions (such as into an ice-cube tray). Cover with plastic wrap and freeze until solid. Remove the cubes and wrap individually, or place in a freezer bag. Cover, label, and date. Freeze for up to 6 months.

Fish Stock {Makes about 6 cups}

2 pounds fish bones from any nonoily, mild-flavored fish, such as red snapper, bass, or halibut (if you are using heads, make sure the gills are removed)

1 onion, peeled and cut into 1-inch pieces

1 carrot, scrubbed and cut in 1-inch pieces

1 celery rib, cut into 1-inch pieces

1 bay leaf

10 black peppercorns

5 fresh parsley sprigs

2 quarts cold water

1. Rinse the fish bones well. Combine the bones, onion, carrot, celery, bay leaf, peppercorns, parsley, and cold water in a large stockpot. Bring to a boil. Lower the heat and simmer gently for 45 minutes. Skim away any foam that rises to the top.

2. Strain the stock through a fine mesh strainer or a double layer of dampened cheesecloth into a metal or heatproof glass container; discard the solids. Use immediately or let cool to room temperature. Cover and refrigerate for up to 5 days. Bring the stock to a rolling boil before using. To freeze, divide among smaller containers, leaving about ½ inch of headspace. Cover, label, and date the containers. The stock can be frozen for up to 2 months.

Basic Pie Dough {Makes 1 pound, 12 ounces; enough for one 10-inch double-crust pie}

This dough yields a tender and exceptionally flaky crust.

3 cups all-purpose flour

Pinch of salt

2 tablespoons sugar

$^1/_2$ pound (2 sticks) cold unsalted butter, cut into $^1/_4$-inch cubes

3 to 4 tablespoons ice water

1. Combine the flour, salt, and sugar in the bowl of an electric mixer and mix well. Add the butter and mix on low speed until the dough resembles coarse meal, about 2 minutes.

2. Sprinkle 3 tablespoons of the ice water on the dough and mix just until it starts to come together, about 15 seconds. Press some of the dough together with your hands. If it holds together, it is ready. If it falls apart, sprinkle with a few more drops of water and mix just to incorporate. The amount of water needed will vary with the humidity and moisture level of the flour you are using. Monitor the amount of water you use carefully, as too much water will result in a soggy crust.

3. Gather the dough into 2 equal balls. Flatten each ball into a disk about 5 inches in diameter. Wrap with plastic and refrigerate for at least 30 minutes or up to 4 days. Frozen, it will keep for up to 3 months.

4. On a lightly floured surface with a floured rolling pin, roll out the dough into an even circle $^1/_8$ to $^1/_4$ inch thick. Fold the dough in half and carefully transfer to a pie pan. Unfold the dough and trim it to fit the pan. Refrigerate the pie shell until you are ready to fill or bake it.

5. To prebake the pie shell: Preheat the oven to 350°F. Prick the bottom of the pie shell all over with a fork. Place a piece of aluminum foil, parchment, or wax paper on top of the shell and add enough dried beans or baking weights two-thirds up the side of the shell. This prevents it from shrinking and helps to keep its shape while baking. Bake until lightly browned, 18 to 20 minutes. Let cool on a wire rack. Lift off the foil or paper with the beans inside and it's ready to fill.

Food Processor Pasta Dough {Makes about 1 pound}

Making pasta dough is very simple, particularly in this recipe where it is all whizzed up in the food processor. Of course if you want to give your arms a little workout, you can make it by hand. Simply mound the flour in a bowl or on a board and make a well in the center. Whisk together the eggs and water and add them to the well. Slowly stir the eggs into the flour and then knead the dough until it is smooth and elastic, 5 to 10 minutes.

2 cups all-purpose flour

2 eggs

1 tablespoon water, plus more if necessary

1. In a food processor, blend the flour and eggs for 15 seconds. With the motor running, add the water drop by drop until the dough forms a ball. Add only enough water to just bring the dough together.

2. Once a ball forms, process for about 15 seconds; the dough should be firm, elastic, and pliable, not sticky or wet. Wrap the dough with plastic and let rest at room temperature for 45 minutes before rolling out.

Garlic Crostini {Makes about 40}

Garlic crostini are a handy vehicle for all of your favorite spreads, dips, pâtés, and soft cheeses.

½ cup olive oil

½ tablespoons minced garlic

¼ teaspoon hot red pepper flakes

1 long (about 18 inches) baguette, cut diagonally into ⅓-inch slices

1. Preheat the oven to 350°F.

2. Combine the olive oil, garlic, and red pepper flakes in a small saucepan. Gently warm over low heat for 15 minutes; do not allow the garlic to brown.

3. Arrange the bread slices on a baking sheet. Liberally brush both sides with the warmed olive oil.

4. Toast the crostini in the oven until crisp and just beginning to brown, 8 to 10 minutes. Let cool to room temperature. Store in a tightly covered container for up to 1 week. Recrisp by toasting in a warm oven before serving.

Garlic Croutons {Makes 4 cups}

We serve these croutons sprinkled on our Romaine Salad with Egg-free Caesar Dressing (page 91); floating in hearty soups, or as stuffing for whole fish and roasted chicken.

¹⁄₄ cup olive oil

1 tablespoon minced garlic

1 teaspoon dried thyme

1 teaspoon dried basil

1 teaspoon dried oregano

¹⁄₂ teaspoon salt

¹⁄₄ teaspoon freshly ground black pepper

4 cups sourdough bread cubes (1¹⁄₂ inch)

1. Preheat the oven to 350°F.

2. Whisk together the olive oil, garlic, thyme, basil, oregano, salt, and pepper in a large mixing bowl.

3. Add the cubed bread and toss well to coat with the oil. Spread the bread cubes in a single, even layer on a nonstick baking sheet. Toast in the oven, stirring often, until golden brown, 18 to 20 minutes.

4. Let cool to room temperature. Tightly cover and store for up to 3 days. Recrisp, if needed, in a warm oven.

Thyme Croutons {Makes 1 cup}

These tiny herb-scented croutons are an addictive addition for your favorite soups and salads, or use them as stuffing for vegetables, poultry, and fish, or as a crunchy topping for casseroles.

2 tablespoons unsalted butter

1 teaspoon dried thyme

Pinch of salt

Pinch of freshly ground black pepper

1 cup crustless bread cubes (¹⁄₄ inch)

1. Preheat the oven to 350°F.

2. Melt the butter in a saucepan over low heat. Stir in the thyme, salt, and pepper. Add the bread cubes and toss well to coat.

3. Spread the croutons on a baking sheet and toast, stirring and tossing from time to time, until golden brown on all sides, about 5 minutes. Use immediately, or let cool to room temperature and store in an airtight container for up to 1 week. Recrisp in a warm oven if necessary.

Polenta Croutons {Makes about 4 cups}

These unusual croutons are a delight! They are crisp on the outside, creamy on the inside, and fragrant with exotic anise. We serve them atop soups and salads.

4 cups water

1$\frac{1}{2}$ teaspoons salt

1$\frac{1}{4}$ cups yellow cornmeal

$\frac{1}{3}$ cup freshly grated Parmesan cheese

1 tablespoon aniseeds, toasted
(see note, page 144)

$\frac{1}{2}$ teaspoon freshly ground black pepper

1. Bring the water and the salt to a gentle simmer in a saucepan set over medium-low heat.

2. Gradually sift some of the cornmeal into the simmering water, whisking constantly to prevent lumps. Continue to whisk and add the cornmeal slowly until incorporated. Reduce the heat to low and simmer, stirring occasionally, until thickened, about 20 minutes.

3. Meanwhile, butter 2 baking sheets. Remove the polenta from the heat and stir in the Parmesan, aniseeds, and pepper. Carefully pour the hot polenta onto 1 buttered baking sheet. Evenly spread it out into a $\frac{1}{2}$-inch layer; square off the edges. Set the baking sheet on a wire rack and let cool to room temperature.

4. Cover and refrigerate until firm and set, at least 30 minutes.

5. Meanwhile, preheat the oven to 400°F.

6. Trim any ragged edges from the sides of the polenta. Cut into 1-inch squares. Arrange the squares on the second buttered baking sheet. Toast in the oven, turning occasionally, until golden brown and crisp, about 20 minutes. Serve hot.

Spicy Pita Crisps {Makes 24}

Serve these pita crisps accompanied by any of our dips as a casual appetizer or hors d'oeuvre. Pita crisps also make a crunchy addition to leafy salads or a spicy cracker to accompany the Ratatouille Bisque (page 68). Make them a day in advance for easy entertaining.

$\frac{1}{2}$ **cup olive oil**

1 tablespoon chili powder

1 teaspoon salt

1 teaspoon ground cumin

1 teaspoon sweet paprika

Pinch of cayenne pepper

3 pita breads (6-inch), each cut into 8 wedges

1. Preheat the oven to 300°F.

2. Whisk together the olive oil, chili powder, salt, cumin, paprika, and cayenne in a shallow bowl.

3. Dunk each wedge of pita into the oil-and-spice mixture; scrape off the excess oil on the side of the bowl. Arrange the wedges in a single layer on a large baking sheet. Bake, turning once, until golden and quite crisp on both sides, about 20 minutes. Cool on paper towels. The crisps will keep in a tightly covered container for up to 4 days and can be recrisped in a 300°F. oven for a few minutes, if necessary.

White Dog Cafe Curry Powder {Makes about $\frac{1}{2}$ cup}

More distinctively flavored than store-bought and simple to make, our curry powder can be modified to your taste by adjusting the amount of your favorite spices. Make curry powder in small batches since it is best when used the day it is made. However, it will keep up to 1 month if stored in an airtight container.

$\frac{1}{2}$ **teaspoon hot red pepper flakes**

1 teaspoon black mustard seeds

1 tablespoon freshly ground black pepper

1 tablespoon ground cinnamon

1 tablespoon ground fennel seeds

1 tablespoon ground cumin

1 teaspoon ground cardamom

1 bay leaf, crumbled

1 tablespoon ground fenugreek seeds

1 tablespoon ground coriander

1 teaspoon turmeric

Combine all of the ingredients in a small bowl and mix well. Store tightly covered in an airtight container for up to 1 month.

White Dog Cafe Garam Masala {Makes about ½ cup}

An aromatic blend of warm Indian spices that lends an exotic taste to soups, stews, roasted lamb, or chicken.

1 tablespoon freshly ground black pepper

1 tablespoon ground cinnamon

1 tablespoon ground fennel seeds

1 tablespoon ground cumin

1 teaspoon ground cardamom

1 teaspoon ground cloves

1 bay leaf, crumbled

1 tablespoon ground fenugreek seeds

1 tablespoon ground coriander

Combine all of the ingredients in a small bowl and mix well. Store tightly covered in an airtight container for up to 1 month.

Gremolata

Gremolata is a simple garnish made from lemon zest, garlic, and parsley. When sprinkled over something hot, it releases a fantastic aroma and adds fresh sprightly flavor to the dish. We sprinkle it atop soups, pasta, grilled fish, and braised meat dishes.

1 tablespoon minced lemon zest

1 tablespoon minced garlic

1 tablespoon minced parsley

Combine lemon zest, garlic, and parsley in a small bowl. Use immediately.

VARIATIONS
For a different result, try using these ingredients:
- Equal parts minced orange zest, minced ginger, and minced cilantro leaves and stems
- Equal parts minced lemon thyme, minced parsley, and minced garlic chives
- Equal parts minced mint, minced lime zest, and minced garlic

Herb Butter {Makes ½ pound}

We make herb butter for red-letter meals when we want something special to spread on our bread. Try some with corn on the cob, steamed green beans, or grilled fish, too. The herbs listed in this recipe are just suggestions; feel free to use any fresh herbs that are available.

1 tablespoon chopped fresh sage leaves

1 tablespoon chopped fresh chervil leaves

1 tablespoon chopped fresh oregano leaves

1 tablespoon minced fresh chives

2 tablespoons chopped fresh basil leaves

½ pound (2 sticks) unsalted butter, at room temperature

¼ teaspoon salt

¼ teaspoon freshly ground black pepper

Combine all of the ingredients in a small bowl and mix well. Smooth the butter into a pretty serving dish and refrigerate until needed. Alternately, shape the butter into a log 2 inches in diameter on a piece of plastic wrap or parchment paper. Roll up the log in the plastic or paper wrap and refrigerate until firm for up to 1 week, or freeze for up to 2 months. When needed, slice the butter and serve.

Cumin Butter {Makes about ½ pound}

This cumin butter is terrific on grilled chicken, fish, or steak, but we like it best melted on grilled sweet corn. Some folks soak their corn in water before grilling them, but we place it straight on the grill. The smoldering outer husks give the sweet corn a smoky quality that is enhanced by the spicy lime-spiked cumin butter.

½ pound (2 sticks) unsalted butter, at room temperature

¼ cup minced red onion

1 teaspoon minced garlic

½ jalapeño pepper, seeded and minced

1 tablespoon ground cumin

⅓ whole lime, seeded and minced (about 2 teaspoons)

1 tablespoon minced fresh cilantro leaves (see note, page 158)

¾ teaspoon salt

1. Melt 2 tablespoons of the butter in a small sauté pan set over medium heat. Add the onion and cook until translucent, about 4 minutes. Add the garlic and jalapeño and cook for 2 minutes. Stir in the cumin and cook for 1 minute. Remove from the heat.

2. Combine the cumin mixture, the remaining butter, lime, cilantro, and salt in a bowl and mix well with a fork until the butter is smooth and all of the ingredients are incorporated. There should be no lumps of butter in the mixture.

3. Spoon the butter onto a piece of waxed paper or plastic wrap. Shape into a log 2 inches in diameter. Roll up tightly and refrigerate until firm. The butter will keep, refrigerated, for up to 1 week, or frozen, for up to 2 months.

Sun-dried Tomato–Olive Butter {Makes about ½ pound}

A rich compound butter with flecks of sun-dried tomatoes and kalamata olives makes a simple bowl of white bean soup luscious. It also adds moistness and sweet-tart flavor to chicken when placed under the skin before roasting or grilling. Use it for topping baked potatoes for an extra treat.

¼ pound (1 stick) unsalted butter, at room temperature

¼ cup minced rehydrated sun-dried tomatoes (see note, page 127)

¼ cup minced pitted kalamata olives

1 tablespoon minced seeded lemon (the peel and the pulp)

½ teaspoon freshly ground black pepper

1. Combine all of the ingredients in a small bowl and mix until no hard lumps of butter remain in the mixture.

2. Spoon the butter onto a piece of parchment or plastic wrap and shape into a log about 2 inches in diameter. Roll up tightly and refrigerate until firm. Slice into ¼-inch medallions. (The butter can be prepared in advance and frozen for up to 1 month.)

Homemade Mayonnaise {Makes about 4 cups}

We can't stand to see food go to waste, and so we developed this recipe for mayonnaise using whole eggs instead of just egg yolks. It's also more healthful since, cup per cup, whole-egg mayonnaise has about half the cholesterol as regular mayonnaise. We use it for making creamy salad dressings and aïolis and as a binder in crab cakes and stuffings. Your choice of oil for the mayonnaise will have a significant influence on its flavor. At the White Dog Cafe we use a blended oil (90 percent soybean oil and 10 percent olive oil) that gives the mayonnaise a neutral taste and allows us to flavor it for special purposes. If you like flavored mayonnaise, try replacing some of the light oil with a dash of a more flavorful oil, such as extra-virgin olive, walnut, hazelnut, avocado, white truffle, or an oil flavored with garlic, herbs, or spices.

3 eggs

1 tablespoon Dijon mustard

1 tablespoon fresh lemon juice

1 teaspoon salt

Pinch of cayenne pepper

3 cups light olive, vegetable, soybean, or canola oil

1. Process the eggs for 15 seconds in a food processor or blender.

2. With the machine running, add the mustard, lemon juice, salt, and cayenne. Add the oil in a slow, thin, steady stream. Process for 15 seconds.

3. Remove the cover and scrape down the inside of the bowl with a rubber spatula. Replace the lid and process for another 15 seconds. This mayonnaise will have a thinner consistency than the store-bought variety, but it will be easier to incorporate with other ingredients. Refrigerate in a tightly covered container for up to 5 days.

Crème Fraîche {Makes 4 cups}

Crème fraîche is available in some supermarkets at an inflated price; however, it seems silly to buy it when making your own is easy and inexpensive. Our crème fraîche has a slightly tangy flavor and rich velvety texture. We whip it and serve it over fresh fruits and other simple desserts. Because it can be boiled without curdling or breaking down, we add it to soups and sauces, and flavor it with everything from basil to wasabi.

3 cups heavy cream **1 cup buttermilk**	**1.** Combine both of the ingredients in a 1-quart plastic or glass container and mix thoroughly. **2.** Cover with a tight-fitting lid and let stand at room temperature for 12 to 24 hours, until thickened. Stir well to combine the solids and liquid. Cover and refrigerate for up to 10 days.

Spicy Ginger-Lime Dressing {Makes about 2 cups}

This dressing is our version of nuoc cham, a Vietnamese condiment based on fish sauce and lime juice. We use it to dress Asian-style salads, as a dipping sauce for spring rolls and salad rolls, and in any dish that needs an added spicy tang.

1/2 cup *nam pla* (Thai fish sauce, available in Asian markets and specialty food stores; see note, page 95) **1/2 cup fresh lime juice** **1/2 cup rice wine vinegar** **2 tablespoons packed light brown sugar** **2 teaspoons minced garlic** **2 teaspoons minced fresh ginger** **2 tablespoons chopped fresh basil leaves** **2 tablespoons chopped fresh mint leaves** **2 tablespoons chopped fresh cilantro leaves and stems (see note, page 158)** **1 teaspoon chili paste (available in Asian markets and specialty food stores)** **1 tablespoon vegetable oil**	Place all of the ingredients in a bowl and whisk to combine well. Use immediately or cover and refrigerate for up to 1 week.

Spicy Asian Marinade {Makes about 1 cup}

A teriyaki-style marinade that is fantastic for grilled pork, chicken, or any firm-fleshed fish such as tuna or swordfish.

¹⁄₄ cup soy sauce

¹⁄₄ cup dry sherry

¹⁄₄ cup water

1¹⁄₂ tablespoons grated fresh ginger

1¹⁄₂ teaspoons chopped garlic

1¹⁄₂ teaspoons chili paste (available in Asian markets and specialty food stores)

1 tablespoon packed light brown sugar

1 scallion, thinly sliced

1 tablespoon vegetable oil

Combine all of the ingredients in a bowl and mix well. Use immediately or cover and refrigerate for up to 1 week.

Tartar Sauce {Makes about 2 cups}

This is a zesty topping for our Salmon Burgers (page 109) that's great on any grilled, baked, broiled, or fried seafood.

1½ cups Homemade Mayonnaise (page 287) or store-bought

2 tablespoons sour cream

2 tablespoons coarse-grain mustard

1 tablespoon Dijon mustard

2 tablespoons chopped dill pickle

2 tablespoons drained capers, rinsed and chopped

1 scallion, minced

1 tablespoon chopped fresh parsley leaves

Zest of 1 lemon, minced or grated

Juice of ½ lemon

¼ teaspoon salt

¼ teaspoon freshly ground black pepper

Combine all of the ingredients in a bowl and whisk well. Chill for at least 30 minutes before serving. The tartar sauce will keep refrigerated in an airtight container for up to 4 days.

Rustic Tomato-Basil Sauce {Makes 4 cups}

This fresh tomato sauce should be made only with the finest tomatoes late summer brings to your garden.

½ cup extra-virgin olive oil

6 large ripe tomatoes (about 3 pounds), diced

1 tablespoon minced garlic

2 teaspoons salt, or to taste

½ teaspoon freshly ground black pepper

1 cup chopped fresh basil leaves

1. In a large, nonreactive sauté pan, heat the oil over medium heat until it ripples. Add the tomatoes, garlic, salt, and pepper.

2. Simmer gently for 10 to 15 minutes until the tomatoes soften and form a sauce. Stir in the basil and taste for seasoning. Serve immediately or let cool to toss into chilled pasta for a refreshing light supper or picnic dish.

Basic Aïoli {Makes 2 cups}

We are so happy someone invented this sauce! In its pure form it's a garlic-flavored mayonnaise originally made in a mortar with a pestle. We use the food processor and our homemade mayonnaise to accomplish the same task. It's an effortless, flavorful condiment with almost limitless variations. The basic recipe can be combined with fresh herbs and other ingredients, such as oil-packed sun-dried tomatoes, anchovies, or Black Olive Tapenade (page 294). When flavoring an aïoli, remember to use ingredients that can stand up to or enhance its bold garlic flavor. Aïolis are excellent with warm or chilled vegetables, shellfish soups or stews, grilled fish, chicken, or lamb, and sandwiches.

4 garlic cloves, peeled

2 cups Homemade Mayonnaise (page 287)

Salt

Place the garlic and mayonnaise in a food processor or blender and pulse until the garlic is fully incorporated. Depending upon how salty the mayonnaise is, you might need to add more salt. Use immediately or cover and refrigerate for up to 4 days.

Lemon-Pepper Aïoli {Makes 1 cup}

This sauce is terrific for topping fish. We especially like it atop our Leek-and-Caraway-braised Swordfish (page 163).

½ of a whole lemon, seeded

½ teaspoon freshly ground black pepper

1 cup Basic Aïoli (see recipe above)

Finely mince the peel and pulp of the lemon. Add the lemon and pepper to the Basic Aïoli and stir until well mixed. Use immediately or cover and refrigerate for up to 4 days.

Basil Pesto {Makes 2½ cups}

Originally, pesto (the classic green sauce from northern Italy) was made exclusively from basil, but nowadays it can be made with most any herb or combinations of herbs. Traditionally pounded in a mortar with a pestle, it is more easily made in a food processor.

1½ cups tightly packed fresh basil leaves

½ cup freshly grated Parmesan cheese

¼ cup pine nuts, toasted (see note, page 144)

¾ teaspoon minced garlic

¾ cup olive oil

1 teaspoon salt

½ teaspoon freshly ground black pepper

1. Rinse and dry the basil leaves well to remove any sand and extra water.

2. Combine the basil, Parmesan, pine nuts, and garlic in food processor or blender. Process with an on/off pulse action to a smooth paste, about 45 seconds.

3. With the motor running, slowly drizzle in the olive oil. Season with the salt and pepper. Pesto is best if used immediately; however, you can refrigerate it in an airtight container for up to 3 days.

Winter Herb Pesto {Makes about 2 cups}

In the winter months when the sweet herbs of summer are in short supply, there are plenty of green alternatives to make a tasty pesto.

1 cup tightly packed fresh parsley leaves

¼ cup tightly packed fresh sage leaves

¼ cup tightly packed fresh chervil leaves

¼ cup walnut pieces, toasted (see note, page 144)

½ cup freshly grated Parmesan cheese

½ teaspoon minced garlic

½ teaspoon salt

½ teaspoon fresh ground black pepper

1 cup olive oil

1. Rinse and dry the parsley, sage, and chervil.

2. Combine walnuts, Parmesan, garlic, salt, and pepper in a food processor or blender. Process until smooth, about 1 minute.

3. With the motor running, slowly pour in the oil to form a thick emulsion. Use immediately, or cover tightly and refrigerate for up to 4 days.

Creamy Basil Sauce {Makes about 2 cups}

This attractive sauce is more or less a basil mayonnaise that my friend and fantastic chef Nicole Routhier taught me. Its flavors are bold and its uses myriad. We serve it atop grilled fish or chicken, as a dip for crudite, a dressing for cold pasta salads, and over our Tuna Sandwich à la Niçoise (page 105).

1 cup tightly packed basil leaves, coarsely chopped

2 eggs

¼ cup rice wine vinegar

2 tablespoons Dijon mustard

2 garlic cloves, peeled

1 tablespoon sugar

1 teaspoon *nam pla* (Thai fish sauce, available in Asian markets and specialty food stores; see note, page 95)

1 teaspoon fresh lemon juice

Dash of Tabasco sauce

1 cup vegetable oil

1. Combine the basil, eggs, vinegar, mustard, garlic, sugar, *nam pla*, lemon juice, and Tabasco in a food processor or blender. Process to a smooth purée, about 1 minute.

2. With the motor running, add the oil in a slow steady stream and blend until well mixed. Cover and chill for at least 30 minutes before serving. The sauce will keep, covered and refrigerated, for up to 3 days.

Green Goddess Sauce {Makes about 2½ cups}

Not the bottled dressing you find in the supermarket or salad bar buffet, this fresh tangy sauce is an adaptation of the original Green Goddess Dressing conceived in the kitchen of the famous Palace Hotel in San Francisco. We love this sauce topped on our Mediterranean Shellfish Stew; the tarragon marries well with the saffron and fennel and complements the briny nature of the shellfish. But it's also great on any grilled fish.

2 cups Homemade Mayonnaise (page 287) or store-bought

6 oil-packed anchovy fillets

2 tablespoons chopped Italian parsley leaves

2 tablespoons chopped fresh tarragon leaves

2 scallions, thinly sliced

1 garlic clove, minced

1 tablespoon Worcestershire sauce

1 tablespoon fresh lemon juice

Pinch of cayenne pepper

Combine all of the ingredients in a food processor or blender; purée until smooth, about 45 seconds. Serve immediately, or cover and refrigerate for up to 3 days.

Black Olive Tapenade {Makes about 2 cups}

This is a racy, piquant spread of kalamata olives, capers, anchovies, and orange zest that we spread on crostini, stuff inside of cherry tomatoes for an hors d'oeuvre, toss with pasta, and devour on sandwiches. We also mix tapenade with Basic Aïoli (page 291) and add a dollop to grilled tuna or swordfish. If you love olives as much as we do, you'll find a way to sneak this tapenade into everything. Try it on a burger!

1½ cups kalamata, niçoise, or picholine olives, pitted and rinsed

2 tablespoons drained capers, rinsed

2 oil-packed anchovy fillets, rinsed

Minced zest of 1 orange

1 tablespoon fresh orange juice

¼ cup tightly packed fresh parsley leaves

3 garlic cloves, peeled

¾ teaspoon freshly ground black pepper

¼ cup extra-virgin olive oil

1. Combine the olives, capers, anchovies, orange zest, orange juice, parsley, garlic, and pepper in a food processor or blender. Blend to a smooth paste, about 30 seconds.

2. With the motor running, slowly drizzle in the olive oil. Use immediately, or cover and refrigerate for up to 2 weeks.

Hummus {Makes 4 cups}

This is our version of the traditional Middle Eastern sauce hummus bi tahina, a tangy dip of mashed chickpeas (garbanzo beans), tahini (sesame seed paste), lemon juice, cilantro, and spices.

3½ cups cooked chickpeas or 2 cans (14 ounces each) chickpeas, drained and rinsed

½ cup well-mixed tahini

Juice of 2 lemons

2 garlic cloves, peeled

2 tablespoons extra-virgin olive oil

¼ cup tightly packed fresh Italian parsley leaves

¼ cup fresh cilantro leaves and stems

½ teaspoon cayenne pepper

1¼ teaspoons salt

½ cup water

Combine all of the ingredients in a food processor or blender. Process until smooth, about 1 minute. Serve at room temperature with wedges of grilled pita bread and Cucumber Raita (page 298), or cover and refrigerate for up to 1 week.

DIPS & SPREADS

White Bean–Feta Brandade {Makes about 4 cups}

A creamy smooth spread of white beans and feta spiked with lemon and hot red pepper flakes, this dish has a multitude of uses—a topping for grilled vegetables or lamb, a sandwich spread, a dip for Spicy Pita Crisps (page 284), or an interesting addition to a tapas-style meal.

1 cup dried Great Northern beans, picked over for stones and rinsed well

1 garlic clove, peeled

1 bay leaf

1 teaspoon minced garlic

1 cup crumbled feta cheese

½ cup extra-virgin olive oil

1½ tablespoons fresh lemon juice

1 tablespoon red wine vinegar

½ teaspoon hot red pepper flakes

1 tablespoon chopped fresh oregano leaves

1. Combine the beans, garlic clove, and bay leaf in a saucepan; add water to cover by 2 inches. Bring to a boil over high heat. Reduce the heat and simmer gently, uncovered, until the beans are very tender, about 1 hour. Reserving the cooking liquid, drain the beans and discard the bay leaf. Let the beans cool to room temperature.

2. Combine the cooked beans, ¼ cup of the reserved cooking liquid, the minced garlic, feta, olive oil, lemon juice, vinegar, and hot pepper flakes in a food processor or blender. Process to a smooth paste, adding a bit more of the bean liquid if the brandade is too stiff.

3. Add the oregano and process for a few seconds to incorporate. Transfer to a bowl and serve immediately or cover and refrigerate for up to 3 days. Bring to room temperature before serving.

Guacamole {Makes about 4 cups}

We use the Haas variety of avocado for their smooth, buttery texture. Always use soft, ripe avocados for making guacamole. An avocado is ripe if it yields to gentle pressure from your thumb. To hasten ripening, store avocados at room temperature in a paper bag.

6 ripe Haas avocados, peeled and pitted

1 red onion, minced

1 large jalapeño pepper, seeded and minced

2½ tablespoons fresh lime juice

2 tablespoons chopped fresh cilantro leaves and stems (see note, page 158)

2 teaspoons ground cumin

1 teaspoon minced garlic

½ teaspoon salt

Tabasco sauce

1. In a large bowl, mash the flesh of the avocados with a fork until creamy smooth.

2. Stir in the onion, jalapeño, lime juice, cilantro, cumin, garlic, salt, and a dash of Tabasco. Taste and adjust the seasoning with more lime, salt, or Tabasco if you like.

3. Serve immediately, or place plastic wrap directly on the surface of the guacamole (this prevents browning) and refrigerate for up to 2 days.

Avocado Mousse {Makes about 2 cups}

This is a lush pastel-green topping that captures the richness of avocado. We serve it as a topping for our Sherried Lobster and Shrimp Crêpes (page 50) and our Southwestern Turkey Burgers (page 107).

2 ripe Haas avocados, peeled and pitted

1 tablespoon fresh lemon juice

⅓ cup créme fraîche or sour cream

½ teaspoon salt

¼ teaspoon Tabasco sauce

¼ cup cold water

Combine the avocado flesh, lemon juice, créme fraîche, salt, Tabasco and water in a food processor or blender. Process until smooth, about 1 minute. Serve immediately, or tightly cover and refrigerate for up to 1 day.

Gingered Pear Chutney {Makes about 8 cups}

This is a spiced pear chutney that we spread on Toasted Brioche with Ham and Brie (page 106), and serve along-side Center-cut Pork Chops with Gorgonzola-Walnut Stuffing and Ruby Port Glaze (page 144). It is also a superb addition to your Thanksgiving table.

10 ripe Bartlett pears, cored and cut into
  $\frac{1}{2}$-inch dice

1 yellow onion, minced

1 green bell pepper, cut into $\frac{1}{4}$-inch dice

1 red bell pepper, cut into $\frac{1}{4}$-inch dice

$\frac{1}{4}$ cup grated fresh ginger

1 jalapeño pepper, seeded and minced

1 tablespoon minced garlic

1 cup dried black currants

1 cup sugar

2 cups apple cider vinegar

1 tablespoon mustard seeds

1 teaspoon coriander seeds

8 allspice berries

2 bay leaves

1. Combine all of the ingredients in a large, nonreactive saucepan set over medium-high heat; bring to a boil. Reduce the heat to low and simmer gently, stirring occasionally, for 45 minutes, until thick and soft.

2. Remove from the heat and let cool to room temperature. Serve immediately or cover and refrigerate for up to 1 week.

Pepper Relish {Makes 2 cups}

The sweetness of slow-cooked peppers and aromatic spices make this an ideal condiment for sandwiches, especially grilled goat cheese or roasted lamb, beef or turkey burgers, or toppings for canapés or fillings for omelettes.

1 tablespoon olive oil

1 red bell pepper, thinly sliced

1 yellow bell pepper, thinly sliced

1 small red onion, thinly sliced

$\frac{1}{4}$ cup red wine vinegar

1 teaspoon fennel seeds

1 teaspoon coriander seeds

1 tablespoon sugar

Pinch of salt

Combine all of the ingredients in a small, nonreactive saucepan set over low heat. Cook slowly, stirring occasionally, until the vegetables are soft, about 20 minutes. Taste for seasoning. Serve warm, or let cool to room temperature, cover, and refrigerate for up to 1 week.

Cucumber Raita {Makes about 3 cups}

This cool and refreshing relish of cucumbers, yogurt, and fresh herbs is a delicious addition to Hummus (page 294) and wedges of grilled pita bread or Spicy Pita Crisps (page 284). We also serve it as a condiment with spicy dishes like Jamaican Curried Lamb Stew (page 150).

2 whole cucumbers, unpeeled

Salt

1 tablespoon olive oil

2 teaspoons minced garlic

1 teaspoon ground cumin

1 teaspoon black mustard seeds

³/₄ cup plain yogurt

1 tablespoon chopped fresh basil leaves

1 tablespoon chopped fresh mint leaves

1 tablespoon chopped fresh cilantro leaves and stems

1. Halve the cucumbers lengthwise. Scoop out the seeds; lightly sprinkle the exposed flesh with salt. Place the cucumbers, cut sides down, on a plate and set aside for 15 minutes.

2. Rinse the cucumbers under cold running water to remove all of the salt. Pat dry with a clean towel. Cut into ¼-inch dice. Reserve.

3. Heat the olive oil in a small sauté pan set over medium-low heat. Add the garlic and cook until soft but not browned, 3 to 4 minutes. Add the cumin and mustard seeds and cook for 1 minute longer to release their flavor.

4. Scrape the garlic mixture into a large bowl; add the yogurt, basil, mint, and cilantro. Mix well; cover and chill. Serve chilled. The raita is best when eaten the day it's made.

SALTING CUCUMBERS

When we combine cucumbers in a salad with a mayonnaise or yogurt base, we like to salt them first to draw out any excess moisture. That way the cucumbers won't weep in the salad and dilute the dressing. To salt a cucumber, slice it lengthwise in half, scoop out the seeds, and sprinkle the flesh lightly with salt. Place it, cut sides down, on a plate to drain for 20 minutes. Rinse the cucumber under cold running water for 30 seconds and pat dry.

CHAPTER NINE

SPECIAL OCCASION MENUS
& ANNUAL WHITE DOG CAFE EVENTS

NEW YEAR'S EVE FORMAL DINNER

Smoked Salmon "Party Hats" with Caviar Confetti

Artichoke Bisque

Grilled Beef Tenderloin with Roasted Red Pepper–Potato Cakes

Dense, Bittersweet Chocolate Torte with Grand Marnier Sauce

New Year's Eve is the grandest—and busiest—night of the year at the Cafe. Kevin creates a menu of so many delicacies that it's hard to choose among them, and we dress up the dining rooms to create an elegant look to fit the occasion. The blue-and-white checked tablecloths are replaced with white linens, our mâitre d' wears a tux, and strolling violinists circulate through the dining rooms.

Our most memorable New Year's Eve began with a complete electrical power failure at 4:00 P.M., leaving us with no lights, telephone system, computers, or stereo—nothing but the phone on the fax machine. I called the electric company in a panic and left the fax phone number for return calls. Because there wasn't a crew scheduled, repairmen had to be called in. I tried all the connections I could think of to speed things up: a city council person who called the president of the electric company, a former cook who's husband was on the company's repair crew. Then I sat in the office upstairs next to the fax machine, waiting for the phone to ring with good news. Nothing happened. I felt more and more dejected as the daylight faded and the walls grew darker around me.

Realizing that guests would be arriving soon, I was sure the evening would be ruined. There was nothing more I could do on the phone, so I went downstairs. To my surprise and delight, I found that the staff had all pitched in and used their ingenuity. The servers had raided our store next door and moved dozens of candles with candleholders into the dining rooms. It looked absolutely stunning! I went into the kitchen and the line crew had taped flashlights to their heads like miners' hats so that they could see the food they were preparing. Then the violinists arrived—who needed the stereo? It was 6:00 P.M. The guests began arriving and the show went on. Finally the repairmen arrived and restored the power—once they discovered the source of the problem: a squirrel had bitten the wires and blown out the transformer. In honor of that evening, we established "The Night of the Squirrel Award" to reward employees who rise to the occasion against the odds. Everyone won the award that night.

NEW YEAR'S DAY PAJAMA PARTY BRUNCH

Bloodhounds (WDC Bloody Marys)

Broiled Grapefruit with Star Anise

Scrambled Eggs with Smoked Salmon, Cream Cheese, and Dill

Roasted Red Pepper and Shrimp Grits

Brioche French Toast with Grand Marnier-Apricot Sauce and Vanilla Ice Cream

Getting up on New Year's Day morning is a difficult task. After all, we just partied in the new year decked out in our finest, and now we just want to relax in comfort. That's why we invite everyone to come to the White Dog for our annual New Year's Day Pajama Party Brunch without getting dressed. Just wake up, take two aspirin and pad on over in your slippers and robe! To emphasize the morning-after atmosphere we leave the confetti, streamers, crushed party hats and Champagne corks strewn across the floors.

One year I found to my dismay that the housekeeper had cleaned up all the mess. He was mighty surprised when I appeared in my pajamas and ran around dumping all the trash cans back out onto the floors. I always start off with one of our famous Bloodhounds, our version of the classic Bloody Mary, and then move on to my favorite brunch dish Roasted Red Pepper Grits Baked with Shrimp. I find a seat near the front door where I can easily hop up to take photos of our customers arriving in their pajamas. Over the years we've amassed quite a unique photo collection of pajama-clad customers, which is displayed on the wall in the bar, including a five-year series of a family of four who always wear a new set of matching flannel pajamas. I always wait for them to walk through the door, just to see what this year's style will be and how much the kids have grown.

"LADY & THE TRAMP" VALENTINE'S DAY DINNER

Oysters Stewed in Rich Thyme Cream
Roast Cornish Hens with White Truffle Jus
Sautéed Swiss Chard
White Chocolate–Raspberry Cheesecake

Valentine's Day is always a busy time in the restaurant business and our "Lady & The Tramp" Dinner, named after Hollywood's most famous dog couple, is one of our most popular events.

To make sure that our staff has a little fun of our own while working on a holiday, we've made a tradition of exchanging valentines at the end of the evening. Several weeks before, we encourage everyone to bring in a baby picture and then each is given a number. The idea is to make or buy funny valentines for each other and sign only with your number. After the customers have all gone home we relax with a big bowl of Love Potion Punch and then one of us, dressed up as Cupid, hands out the cards. The baby pictures are posted along with the numbers. The contest is to guess the identity of the baby pictures. The one who gets the most right, wins a bottle of Champagne, and a special Valentine's dessert like White Chocolate–Raspberry Cheesecake. I usually make my valentines with pictures of dogs sniffing each other and a caption such as, "You smell divine, Valentine, Love #9." Because I'm known as a dog lover, that might make my picture easier to guess—or maybe it's because my baby picture is the only one with that unique 1940s look!

A BIKE & TRAIN ADVENTURE PICNIC LUNCH

Prosciutto and Melon

Farm Stand Focaccia

Ann Marie's Kitchen Cabinet Cookies

Every summer we plan an outing to encourage biking as an alternative to commuting by car. We meet at the rail station on a Saturday morning and take the train out to a point in the local suburbs and then bike back into the city for lunch. It's quite a sight to see twenty to thirty bicyclists clambering up the stairs to the platform and onto a train. I'm always afraid we won't all fit, but we somehow manage to squeeze in. Our group is led by Bob Thomas, an architect who not only bikes to work regularly but also designs bikeways.

There are always a few tales to be told of the journey back into town, from a flat tire to a slip in the gravel but we all enjoy the beautiful countryside away from busy highways. At the end of our twenty-mile trip, we arrive at the Cafe eager for the lunch Kevin has waiting for us. While we dine on Farm Stand Focaccia made from fresh local tomatoes, Bob leads a discussion on the latest issues involving biking, such as the designation of bike lanes, the closing of streets for biking on weekends, and the environmental issues surrounding our dependence on gasoline. It's a great way to promote ecological living while having a wonderful time.

4TH OF JULY BUFFET

Sweet & Spicy Barbecued Chicken

Watermelon and Shrimp Salad with Jalapeño-Lime Dressing

Grilled Corn with Cumin Butter

Betty's Beef Kabobs

Summer Garden Vegetable Potato Salad

Tangy Six-Vegetable Slaw

Nana's Strawberry Pie

Every third of July, I begin to get labor pains in the morning. By evening, I'll be giving birth to the nation in the street on a bed draped in red, white, and blue at our annual Liberty and Justice for All Ball. Now in our twelfth year, the "All Ball" is held under tent top in the street in front of the Cafe. It begins with a buffet of all-American favorites, including some of my own family's summertime traditions, such as Mom's (Betty's) Kabobs that Dad used to grill out on the patio, and Nana's Strawberry Pie that she used to bring to our house in an old-fashioned wicker pie basket.

Just after we've finished off the last bite of pie, the annual pageant begins. A drummer in Revolutionary War garb leads the procession, followed by my midwife in colonial costume carrying a lantern, trailed by me in powdered wig and clown face, with a huge beach ball under my colonial dress and a sign on my back that reads, "George Washington Slept Here."

Assisted into bed by my midwife, who instructs the audience to yell, "Push!" I raise my knees in traditional birthing position and maneuver the beach ball down through a hidden hole in the bottom of the bed, from which the midwife delivers my twins, Liberty and Justice. (Oddly enough for twins, one is white and the other black.) They leap up onto the stage in sparkling red, white, and blue costumes, holding signs that read, "Liberty" and "Justice" and tap dancing to "Yankee Doodle Dandy," while the midwife and I hold up a big sign that reads, "For All." Next the Statue of Liberty steps onto the stage while we all sing "God Bless America" and light sparklers. What could be more patriotic?

BASTILLE DAY FRENCH SUMMER SUPPER

Sherried Seafood Crêpes with Avocado Mousse

Chilled Roasted Beef Tenderloin with Horseradish Crème Fraîche

Ratatouille Vinaigrette

Dijon Potato Salad

Lavender Biscuits with Mixed Summer Berries

Once a year on July 14th, we change our name to Café Chein Blanc, hang the French flag from the window, and celebrate the French Revolution. Tables seating two hundred guests fill the street, where an accordionist wearing a French beret plays Parisian cafe songs as he strolls among diners enjoying Sherried Seafood Crêpes with Avocado Mousse served with our private label wine, Chateau Chien Blanc. As soon as we finish off our blueberry pie, "La Marseillaise" booms forth and guests rise to sing the French national anthem while lighting sparklers. Towering over the tables is the Bastille, a stone fortress with locked door (reassembled each year from painted panels stored in our warehouse). As the last strains of "La Marseillaise" subside, the barking of dogs can be heard and from above the walls of the Bastille the heads of white poodles in red berets can be spotted. Suddenly a group of costumed French revolutionaries (whom we choose from among our most fun-loving customers) charge the Bastille with long plastic swords and axes and foam rubber boulders. The poodles are released from the Bastille and join the revolutionaries in the can-can. The next song is a French waltz and guests stream from the tables to the dance area where they whirl beneath strings of colored lights. On this magical night, Sansom Street could be in Paris.

Vive la Rèvolution!

NOCHE LATINA AND RUM & REGGAE CARIBBEAN BUFFET

Cuban-style Braised Tuna

Jamaican Curried Lamb Stew

Cool Island Cucumber Salad

Chiapas Pie

Black Beans and Rice

Golden Plantain Fritters

Havana Banana Cake with Pineapple Rum Compote and Coconut Whipped Cream

The best thing about living in the city is the great diversity of people, and for me music and food are two of the most enjoyable ways to appreciate different cultures. Among the many multicultural events during the year, my favorites are in the summer months when we can expand the Cafe out into the street with plenty of room for a live band and dancing. For twelve years, Rum & Reggae has livened up our August nights with a Jamaican Reggae band, Sons of Ace, and six years ago we started the tradition of Noche Latina, with a seven-piece Puerto Rican band, Edgardo Cintron y Tempo Noventa. Each event features an outdoor Caribbean-style buffet of island favorites. Dancing under the stars to tropical rhythms, all we need is a little sand to complete the island holiday!

Through our Philadelphia Sister-Restaurant Project we establish "sister" relationships with minority-owned restaurants in different ethnic neighborhoods where we encourage our clientele to visit. At our Puerto Rican sister restaurant, I first had Plantain Fritters and a coconut drink with rum that we now feature at the bar during Rum & Reggae. Relationships with our sister restaurants have led us to experience a real sense of city-wide community and helped build a diverse clientele for our events. When I'm out in the street dancing with folks from all different neighborhoods, I feel the joy and goodwill that I have only experienced through the sense of interconnectedness among diverse people. I am also reminded of how fun and interesting it is to live in a big city.

ROLLERBLADERS OVER-FORTY PICNIC

Desert Garden Vegetable Gazpacho with Crab and Jicama Slaw
Rolled Tortilla Sandwich
James's Giant Oatmeal Cookies

Exercise is one of those important activities I always put off. One way to make sure I get started is to put an athletic event on the White Dog calendar and then I'm locked in! Once I'm out and about, I have so much fun that I keep it up for the rest of the summer. In-line skating has become my favorite sport, and just to encourage my fellow baby boomers to prove that we're not old yet, I made this an "over-forty" event, which we schedule four times a year. Our typical crowd of twenty to forty skaters, along with two pros to help guide the beginners at the back of the pack, meets at the Philadelphia Art Museum and heads down to West River Drive in Fairmount Park, which is closed to auto traffic on weekends. Along the way we stop at one of the park's picnic pavilions for a healthy and refreshing gourmet picnic lunch the Cafe has waiting for us.

There's usually a few slowpokes who arrive just as we're finishing lunch, and they get a big applause from the rest of us just for making it. One time a worn-out beginner arrived holding on to the back of a police motorcycle, which pulled her along on her skates. That got the biggest hand yet! Although we'd rather have an afternoon nap in a hammock, the over-forty bunch always manages to get back up on our skates and head for home, with promises to meet again at the next skate, even when it's Bladers Over Sixty!

DANCE OF THE RIPE TOMATOES HARVEST BUFFET

Tangy Tian of Harvest Vegetables

Tomato-Potato Salad

Country Bread and Roasted Vegetable Salad

Lemon- and Herb-marinated Goat Cheese with Fresh Tomatoes

Barley and Corn Tabbouleh

Rosemary-roasted Leg of Lamb

Harvest Fruit Crisp

I had a dream one night in which giant tomatoes rose up from the fields and did a dance in celebration of the harvest. Of course, I had to make it come true. Each year on the last day of summer, we hold the Dance of the Ripe Tomatoes to give thanks for our bountiful harvest and raise awareness of the importance of organic agriculture and humane farming. Kevin creates a bountiful buffet using organic produce and meats from humanely raised livestock. It's not easy to find local humane farmers, and because we have to buy the whole pig, Kevin must find uses for all the cuts—not just the prime parts.

Once the eating is done and the music begins, the tomatoes appear, made of foam and red satin, and suspended from a long bamboo pole. We dangle them into the crowd, making sure everyone gets a chance to dance with a ripe tomato. Though not as dramatic nor as graceful as those in my original dream, they are definitely quite a sight and their dance is a spirited way to end our summer season.

HAPPY BIRTHDAY, GANDHI! VEGETARIAN DINNER

Tomato and Lentil Soup and Poppyseed Cracker Bread
Curry-roasted Vegetables with Indian Cheese Dumplings and Sautéed Greens and Garlic
Lemon Curd and Almond Shortbread Tart

How to honor heroes? Why not with food?

The two leaders whose work I admire the most are Dr. Martin Luther King, Jr. and Mahatma Gandhi. After researching their favorite foods, we held a birthday dinner in January in honor of Dr. King, featuring southern-style smothered chicken and black-eyed peas, and one in October for Gandhi, featuring vegetarian fare. On Dr. King's birthday we feature gospel music, dramatic readings, and a group discussion on how he influenced our lives. We've also begun a tradition of community service on King Day at Habitat for Humanity, which has now expanded to a Cafe-sponsored Community Service Day every month.

For Gandhi's Birthday, we recognize a group or individual who exemplifies Gandhi's method of non-violent resistance for social change. Now in our sixth year, past programs have honored Greenpeace, Harry Wu, the Dalai Lama, Witness for Peace, and American Friends Service Committee. It was Gandhi who pointed out that the fields of spirituality, politics, and economics are interrelated and it's logical, not inconsistent, to mix spirituality with politics and business, an example we've tried to follow.

NATIVE AMERICAN THANKSGIVING DINNER

Smoked Salmon and Corn Chowder

Thanksgiving Turkey with Native Grains and Sausage Stuffing, Maple-mashed Sweet Potatoes,

and Braised Brussels Sprouts with Thyme

Pumpkin and Walnut Shortbread Tart with Cranberry Compote

We often think of traditional Thanksgiving foods like turkey, cranberry, and pumpkin as those we inherited from Native Americans, but actually well over half the foods we enjoy today—including tomatoes, potatoes, wild rice, chiles, and beans—came from our country's original inhabitants. These foods were not just growing wild, but had been cultivated over many generations. A thousand years before Columbus, the Hopi and Zuni were harvesting large crops of vegetables in the Southwest. Our Native American Thanksgiving Dinner, which we first held in 1990, acknowledges these important contributions to our diet and provides a forum to hear a speaker on current Native American issues. Of course, we have not only learned about foods from Native Americans, we have also learned their philosophy of inclusiveness, which fostered the first Thanksgiving, and we've embraced their concept of the interconnectedness among all living things—ideas that continue to influence social and environmental movements today.

In addition to our Annual Multicultural Events, the White Dog Cafe organizes the following Community-Building Activities:

Community Service Days are held once a month to provide opportunities for White Dog Cafe patrons and staff to participate in volunteer projects such as rehabilitating houses or building community gardens.

Community Tours provide an opportunity for our clientele to have firsthand experience with different issues in Philadelphia neighborhoods. This expands our sense of community and interconnectedness and encourages active citizen engagement. These tours include the following:

Affordable Housing Led by the city's housing director, this annual tour began in 1993 and visits successful housing projects at different stages of development, highlighting cooperation between community, government, and the private sector.

Child Watch Visitation Program Conceived by the Children's Defense Fund and initiated locally by the Cafe, this tour provides an opportunity for citizens to experience firsthand the lives of inner-city children. The tours, which begin with breakfast and a speaker at the Cafe, are led by Philadelphia Citizens for Children and Youth and involve visits to child and family servicing facilities such as schools, public health centers, juvenile detention centers, shelters, and recreation centers.

Community Wall Murals and Community Garden Tour Begun in 1989, this annual tour demonstrates the importance of gardens and art to inner-city communities. It involves a neighborhood tour followed by a lunch with speakers from the communities.

Eco-tour provides firsthand experience with environmental issues such as recycling, energy conservation, and water purification.

Prison Garden Tour Customers drive to Graterford State Penitentiary for a tour of the organic garden project and dinner with the inmates prepared by the Cafe using vegetables from the garden. Following dinner is a discussion on the rehabilitative value of gardening and eating healthy food.

Mentoring Program Since 1992, this program with students from the Restaurant, Hotel, and Tourism Academy at West Philadelphia High School provides opportunities for workplace experience, community service participation, field trips to purveyors and family farms, and recreational and cultural activities. Students learn about the restaurant business and put on the Hip Hop, a special event in the spring with the help of our staff. Each year a Culinary Scholarship of $1000 is awarded to a graduate to attend restaurant management or culinary school.

Storytelling every Tuesday night provides the opportunity for guests to hear the life stories of prominent Philadelphians and gives voice to under-represented groups such as ex-offenders, senior citizens, gays, youth, immigrants, and homeless people. They also provide a forum to exchange perspectives on a personal level about experiences such as war, civil rights marches, parenting issues, and illness.

Table Talks: Serving Food With Thought are scheduled several times a month at breakfast and Monday dinners. Speakers talk on issues of public concern, followed by discussion. Topics have come

{continued}

from the areas of health care reform, crime and violence, the environment, foreign policy, cultural diversity, recreation, children and youth, and education. **New Visions in Business** is a Table Talk series given by leading socially responsible business people. **Saturday Rap** is a Table Talk at Saturday lunch that promotes intergenerational discussion.

"Table for Six Billion, Please!" is our international "sister" restaurant project begun in 1987, which envisions a world where everyone has a place at the table. Sister relationships are formed between the White Dog Cafe and restaurants in countries where poor dialogue exists with the United States. Through educational tours we gain an understanding of issues facing these countries and how the U.S. government policies and corporate interests affect the lives of others. We hope to demonstrate that world peace is achieved through communication, economic justice, and mutual concern for the natural environment, rather than through military domination and arms sales. Sister restaurants are located in Nicaragua, Cuba, Mexico, Brazil, Lithuania, Vietnam, Thailand, and Indonesia.

Take a Senior to Lunch Days are held every Saturday when the senior citizen's lunch is half price and opportunities are provided to match customers with seniors who would like to get out more often.

The Philadelphia Sister-Restaurant Project, begun in 1990, develops "sister" relationships with local minority-owned restaurants. Visits to our sister restaurants and nearby minority cultural attractions are promoted in our newsletter. The purpose of this project is to encourage our customers to visit neighborhoods they otherwise might not go to in order to increase understanding, build city-wide community, and support minority businesses and cultural institutions.

Urban Retrievers, our non-profit affiliate, currently focuses on youth, and sponsors the Philadelphia Student Union, which gives youth a voice in school reform and promotes youth activism, good citizenship, and communication between diverse groups of young people.

Whole World Products sold in our retail store, The Black Cat, feature products that support an inclusive and sustainable world economy including products made from recycled materials or products made by disadvantaged workers.

Contributions The Cafe contributes 10% of pre-tax profit, in the form of food, labor, and cash donations to non-profit projects and organizations. Approximately $10,000–15,000 a year is contributed in cash to organizations such as Action Aids, American Civil Liberties Union, Amnesty International, American Friend Service Committee, Bread & Roses Community Fund, Business Leaders for Sensible Priorities, Children's Defense Fund, Habitat for Humanity, Humane Society, NAACP Legal Defense Fund, Planned Parenthood Federation, People for the American Way, Witness for Peace, and Woman's Way. Food contributions are donated to numerous non-profit events and approximately $10,000 in gift certificates are contributed to fundraising events benefiting additional non-profit organizations.

Here's a listing of the organizations we work with to further our mission:

SOCIAL VENTURE NETWORK

P.O. Box 29221 · San Francisco, CA 94129-0221 · Tel 415-561-6501 · Fax 414-561-6435
e-mail svn@well.com · Website www.svn.org

A community of business and social entrepreneurs dedicated to using business as a vehicle for social change by integrating the values of a just and sustainable society into day-to-day business practices.

BUSINESS FOR SOCIAL RESPONSIBILITY

609 Mission St., 2nd Fl. · San Francisco, CA 94105 · 415-537-0888 · Website www.bsr.org

Assists companies seeking to implement policies and practices that contribute to the long-term success of their enterprise, and which balance the competing claims of key stakeholders, their investors, employees, customers, business partners, communities, and the environment. Programs focus on issues related to ethics, the workplace, the marketplace, the community, the environment, and the global economy. **REGIONAL OFFICES:** WASHINGTON, D.C: 1612 K St., NW, Washington, DC 20006, 202-463-9036 · BOSTON, MA: 160 2nd St., Cambridge, MA 02142, 617-576-7599 · COLORADO: PO Box 140411, Denver, CO 80214, 303-433-1020 · NEW YORK: 240 W. 75th ST., #4B, New York, NY 10023, 212-799-1381` · NORTH CAROLINA: 4613 Lancashire Dr., Raleigh, NC 27613, 919-510-9492 · NEW ENGLAND: 200 Domain Dr., Stratham, NH 03885, 603-773-1371 · SOUTHERN CALIFORNIA: 2961 Nichols Canyon Rd., Los Angeles, CA 90046, 213-845-4587

BUSINESS LEADERS FOR SENSIBLE PRIORITIES

130 William St. 7th Fl. · New York, NY 10038 · Tel 212-964-3534, ext. 28 · Fax 212-571-3332

Mobilizes and focuses the marketing and budgeting expertise of business leaders to redirect United States federal budget priorities away from Cold War military expenditure levels and toward meeting the basic human needs of our citizens, enhancing our economic competitiveness, and reducing the deficit.

BUSINESS ENTERPRISE TRUST

706 Cowper St. · Palo Alto, CA 94301 · Tel 650-321-5100 · Fax 650-321-5774 · Website www.betrust.org

Identifies and promotes business leadership that combines sound management with social conscience. Annual awards are presented and the stories of recipients are told through videos and case studies distributed to hundreds of business schools, universities and corporate training programs. Published *Aiming Higher: 25 Stories of How Companies Prosper by Combining Sound Management and Social Vision*, which includes the Cafe's story.

GLOBAL EXCHANGE

2017 Mission St. Rm. 303 · San Francisco, CA 94110 · Tel 415-255-7296 · Fax 415-255-7498

An educational and activist organization that leads groups to countries throughout the Third World, promoting fair trade and human rights. Has led White Dog Cafe tours to Havana, Cuba, and Chiapas, Mexico.

INTERNATIONAL VOLUNTARY SERVICES

c/o Don Luce · 185 Charter Oaks Dr. · Amherst, NY 14228 · Tel 716-689-9704

Runs educational tours to Vietnam and Cambodia. Led White Dog Cafe tours in 1991 and 1995.

CHEFS COALITION 2000

25 First St. · Cambridge, MA · Tel 617-621-3000 · Fax 617-621-1230

A network of over 1,000 chefs working collectively to advance sustainable food choices by strengthening farmer/chef connections, emphasizing locally-grown, seasonally fresh food in their restaurants, and educating young people about food issues.

CHEZ PANISSE FOUNDATION

1517 Shattuck Ave. · Berkeley, CA 96709 · Tel 510-843-3811 · Fax 510-548-0140

Supports youth and community programs that teach the vital connections between growing, cooking, and sharing food, and promotes projects that inspire young people to develop a sense of responsible stewardship of the land, and to respect and care for their communities and themselves.

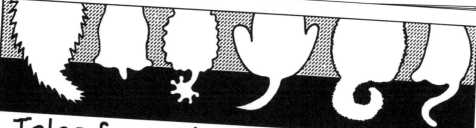

Tales from the White Dog Cafe

A Quarterly Newsletter 3420 Sansom St. Philadelphia

A Gift for All Seasons

Recently I was asked to speak to a group of young professionals on the subject of philanthropy. The first speaker was a prominent citizen and city councilman who told the group that he would pass on to them the sound advice his father once gave him. "Before you can do good," he told them, "you must do well." As I listened to the philosophy of Philadelphia's respected gentry and traditional philanthropists, I realized that I was about to give just the opposite advice.

It seemed to me that doing good should not be seen as a luxury, affordable only after being earned, but rather as a way of life which integrates our values with our work. I had looked up philanthropy in the dictionary, and in seeing it defined as "the effort to increase the well-being of mankind," had decided that making money by any means and then donating the excess change to charity did not truly fit the definition. Have we been improperly measuring philanthropy by how much money we give away at the end of the year or at the end of our careers, rather than considering how we earned that money in the first place? Do we take too much credit for the volunteer hours we may give once a month, rather than honestly examining how the work we do 40 or more hours a week actually benefits mankind? Should we not also consider how we spend our earnings and our tax dollars toward the best interests of the common good?

An acquaintance who works for the foundation of a major corporation recently confided in despair that all the money that would ever be given by her foundation could not begin to make up for the environmental and social damage caused by the funding corporation in the process of making that money in the first place. Doing well, or making a profit, should never be separated from doing good. Increasing profit while not increasing the well-being of mankind has led to most of society's major problems - from poverty, crime, and addiction, to ignorance, war, and environmental destruction. On the other hand, it's the combination of profit and goodness which is perhaps our most powerful tool for solving these very problems, while also providing livlihoods which bring fulfillment and happiness. In fact, is there really any other way that we can create a peaceful and healthy world where everyone can profit?

Looking at the concerned faces of these young professionals who were gathered here in their earnest desire to do the right thing, I wondered how many felt forced to compromise their own values in order to do well at their jobs. I gave them my advice: It's in your place of work, where you focus your full-time energy and attention, where you can most effectively be philanthropic by making business decisions which are profitable _and_ increase the well-being of mankind.

If your business mentor or boss tells you to leave your values at home when you start a business or go to work, tell them that your work must express what's important to you. If Madison Avenue tells you to buy products which harm you, the environment, or the workers who make them, tell them that you'll only spend what you've earned on products or causes you believe in. If Congress tells you to forget about those less fortunate and just look out for yourself, tell them that you'll gladly see your tax dollars used for teaching and healing, but not on weapons for killing and destroying. If someone advises you to do well before you do good, tell them that you'll do well _by_ doing good. Then you will be a true philanthropist and your gift will be the way you live your life every day of the year.

Judy Wicks

HOW TO REACH US

White Dog Cafe • 3420 Sansom Street • Philadelphia, PA 19104
(phone) 215-386-9224 • (fax) 215-368-1185
(on the web) www.whitedog.com • (via e-mail) info@whitedog.com

To receive our free (usually quarterly) newsletter, e-mail, fax, write, or call with your address.

INDEX

A

AÏOLI:
Basic, 291
Citrus, Tangy, Calamari, Chili- and
    Corn-Crusted, with, 52
Lemon-Pepper, 291
Saffron, Potatoes, Spicy Fried,
    with, 194

Alcoholic Beverages. *See* Beverages

**Almond Shortbread and Lemon
    Curd Tart, 254**

ANISE:
Balsamico, and Black Currant, Tuna,
    Seared, with, 161
star, about, 222
Star, Sugar, Grapefruit, Broiled,
    with, 222

**Anne Marie's Kitchen Cabinet
    Cookies, 265**

APPLE(S):
Bisque, Curried, with Minted Yogurt,
    73
Pie, -Cranberry Deep-Dish Streusel,
    248
Pork Tenderloin with Caramelized
    Shallots and, 146
"Sauce," Curried, Sea Scallops,
    Seared, with, 155
Waldorf-Style Chicken Salad, 99

APPLE CIDER:
Cabbage, -Braised, 200
Syrup, Pancakes, Six Grain-Pecan,
    with, 227

APRICOT:
Dipping Sauce, -Pickled Ginger,
    Shrimp and Pork Spring Rolls,
    Baked, with, 42–43
-Grand Marnier Sauce, with Brioche
    French Toast, 231

ARTICHOKE(S):
Bisque, 72
cleaning, 72
Salad, Chicken, Mediterranean Fried,
    with, 124

ARUGULA:
and Garlic, Sautéed, 202
using, 161

ASIAN:
Chicken Noodle Soup, 79
Marinade, Spicy, 289
Ribs, Barbecued, with Gingered Snow
    Pea Cabbage Slaw, 58
Vegetables and Shellfish, Warm, with
    Spicy Ginger-Lime Dressing, 53

ASPARAGUS:
Penne with, 175
Sesame-Roasted, 204
Strudel, Shrimp and Crab, Flaky,
    44–45

AVOCADO:
Guacamole, 296
Mousse, 296
Tortilla Roll Ups, Mexican, 110

B

BALSAMIC(O) (VINEGAR):
Anise and Black Currant, Tuna,
    Seared, with, 161
Chicken and Mushroom, Roasted,
    Salad, 98
Glaze, -Pancetta, Beef Tenderloin,
    Grilled, with, 134
Kale, -Braised, 203
-Pepper, Roasted, Dressing,
    Calamari, Lemon- and Pepper-
    Grilled, with, 54
Pork Medallions, Sautéed, with Basil
    and, 147
Portobello Mushrooms, -Roasted, 180
Vegetables, Roasted, 201

BANANA(S):
Cake, Havana, with Pineapple-Rum
    Compote, 255
freezing, 255
Muffins, -Nut, 236
Pancakes, -Buttermilk, with Honey
    Pecan Syrup, 228

BARBECUED:
Chicken, Sweet & Spicy, 121
Ribs, Asian, with Gingered Snow Pea-
    Cabbage Slaw, 58

BARLEY:
cooking, 215
Pilaf, Native Grains, 208
Risotto, -Wild Mushroom, 166
Tabbouleh, and Sweet Corn, 209

BASIL:
Melon and Prosciutto, -Dressed,
    with Black Pepper-Orange
    Mascarpone, 59

Pesto, 292
Pork Medallions, Sautéed, with
    Balsamic Vinegar and, 147
Sauce, Creamy, 293
-Tomato Sauce, Rustic, 290
Vegetable Tian, Tangy Summer, 181

Bass. *See* Sea Bass

BEAN(S):
BLACK:
    Refritos, 212
    and Rice, 211
    Soup, Cuban, 77
    Tortilla Floridita, 36
    dried, cooking, 215
Dried, flavoring cooking water, 169
Green, with Onions, 203
Salad, Firehouse Dalmatian, 205
Soup, Black, Cuban, 77
Soup, Minestrone, Garden Vegetable,
    75
WHITE:
    Brandade, -Feta, 295
    Fettuccine with Sun-Dried
    Tomatoes, Rosemary and, 169
    Zucchini with Mint and, 205

BEEF:
flank steak, identifying, 136
Kabobs, Betty's, 135
London Broil, Rosemary-Mustard,
    with Wild Mushroom Glaze,
    136–137
Philly Cheese Steak, White Dog
    Cafe's, 104
Shins, Braised, Nicaraguan, 139
Sirloin, Seared Peppered, with Red
    Wine- Chèvre Glaze, 138
Stew, Burgundy, 93
Tenderloin, Grilled, with Balsamic
    Pancetta Glaze, 134
Tenderloin, Roast, Chilled, with
    Horseradish Crème Fraîche, 133
See also Meats

**Beets, Roasted, and Gorgonzola
    with Orange-Rosemary
    Vinaigrette, 39**

BELL PEPPER(S):
Ratatouille Bisque, 68
Red, Roasted, Grits, and Shrimp, 223
Red, Roasted, -Potato Cake, 191
Relish, 298
Roasted, -Balsamic Dressing,
    Calamari, Lemon- and Pepper-
    Grilled, with, 54
roasting, 140

BERRIES:
Mixed Summer, with Lavender
    Biscuits, 252
See also names of berrries

Betty's Beef Kabobs, 135

BEVERAGES:
Bloodhounds, 233
Mint Julep, White Dog Cafe, 232
Rum Punch, White Dog Cafe, 233

BISCOTTI:
Orange-Pistachio, 263
Rosemary-Parmesan, 240

**Biscuits, Lavender, with Mixed
    Summer Berries, 252**

BISQUE:
Apple, Curried, with Minted Yogurt,
    73
Artichoke, 72
Ratatouille, 68

Black Bean(s). *See* Bean(s), Black

Black Currant(s). *See* Currant(s),
    Black

Black Olive(s). *See* Olive(s), Black

Black Pepper. *See* Pepper(ed)

Bloodhounds, 233

BLUEBERRY:
Muffins, 236
Pancakes, and Corn, with Maple-Pine
    Nut Butter, 229
Pie, -Peach, Double-Crusted, 251

**Blue Cheese Mayonnaise, with Cobb
    Salad Sandwich, 102**

Bok Choy and Garlic, Sautéed, 202

**Bourbon, Mint Julep, White Dog
    Cafe, 232**

**Bow-Tie Pasta, Chicken, Smoked, in
    Rosemary Cream with, 123**

**Brandied Fruits, Duck with Native
    Grains, Pistachio Stuffing and,
    Roasted, 131**

BREAD(S):
Biscotti, Rosemary-Parmesan, 240
Biscuits, Lavender, with Mixed
    Summer Berries, 252
Brioche, 238
Crackers, Poppy *See*d, Curried, 241
FOCACCIA:
    about, 111
    Farm Stand, 111
    Parmesan, 239
    Toasted, with Tomatoes, Roasted,
    Olives, and Feta, 112
    Salad, Country, and Roasted
    Vegetable, 94
    Scones, Orange and Black
    Currant, 235
See also Muffins; Toasts

**Brie, Brioche with Ham and,
    Toasted, 106**

BRIOCHE, 238:
French Toast, with Apricot-Grand
    Marnier Sauce, 231

with Ham and Brie, Toasted, 106
Rounds, Smoked Salmon "Party
Hats" with Caviar Confetti, 40

Broccoli, Risotto, 167

BROCCOLI RABE:
cooking with, 123
and Garlic, Sautéed, 202

**Buckwheat Pancakes, Cranberry-,
with Orange-Honey-Thyme
Butter, 230**

BURGER(S):
Lamb, Moroccan-Spiced, with Pepper
Relish, 108
Salmon, 109
Turkey, Southwestern, 107

BURGUNDY:
Beef Stew, 83
Butter, -Rosemary, Salmon, Pan-
Roasted, with, 164

BUTTER(S):
Burgundy-Rosemary, Salmon, Pan-
Roasted, with, 164
Cumin, 286
Herb, 286
making compound, 126
Maple-Pine Nut, Pancakes, Corn and
Blueberry, with, 229
Orange-Honey-Thyme, Pancakes,
Cranberry- Buckwheat, with,
230
Sun-Dried Tomato-Olive, 287

BUTTERMILK:
making homemade, 228
Pancakes, Banana, with Honey-Pecan
Syrup, 228

BUTTERNUT SQUASH:
Lavender and Honey-Roasted, 198
Ravioli, Curried, with Winter Herb
Pesto, 172–173

C

CABBAGE:
Cider-Braised, 200
Savoy, with Pancetta and Oyster
Mushrooms, 200
Slaw, Snow Pea-, Gingered, 214

**Caesar Dressing, Egg-Free, with
Romaine Salad, 91**

CAKE(S):
Banana, Havana, with Pineapple-Rum
Compote, 255
Cheesecake, White Chocolate-
Raspberry, 257
Chèvre Torte, Creamy, in Pine Nut
Crust with Zinfandel-Spiked
Cherries, 258–259
Chocolate Torte, Dense, Bittersweet,
262
Coffee, Sour Cream, 234
Pound, Rose Geranium, 256

Calamari. *See* Squid

CAPER(S):
about, 160
Cream Cheese, Smoked Salmon
"Party Hats" with Caviar Confetti,
40

Cappuccino Crème Brûlée, 264

**Caramelized Shallots, Pork
Tenderloin with Apples and,
146**

Caramel Sauce, Homemade, 267

**Caraway, Swordfish, -and Leek-
Braised, with Lemon-Pepper
Aïoli, 163**

**Caribbean Mahi Mahi, Grilled, with
Tropical Fruit Salsa, 157**

CAVIAR:
buying, 40
Confetti, Smoked Salmon "Party
Hats" with, 40

**Chanterelles, Tart of Swiss Chard,
Emmentaler and, Savory,
170–171**

Chard. *See* Swiss Chard

CHEDDAR:
Muffins, Corn, Sun-Dried Tomato and,
237
White, and Potato, Red-Skinned,
Gratin, 189

CHEESE:
Blue Cheese Mayonnaise, with Cobb
Salad Sandwich, 102
Brie, Brioche with Ham and, Toasted,
106
Cheddar, Muffins, Corn, Sun-Dried
Tomato and, 237
Cheddar, White, and Potato, Red-
Skinned, Gratin, 189
CREAM CHEESE:
Caper, Smoked Salmon "Party
Hats" with Caviar Confetti, 40
Chèvre Torte, in Pine Nut Crust
with Zinfandel-Spiked
Cherries, 258–259
Scrambled Eggs with Smoked
Salmon, Dill and, 224
White Chocolate-Raspberry
Cheesecake, 257
Dumplings, Indian, Vegetables, Curry-
Roasted, with, 179
Emmentaler, Tart of Chanterelles,
Swiss Chard and, Savory, 170–171
Feta, Brandade, White Bean-, 295
Feta, Focaccia, Toasted, with Roasted
Tomatoes, Olives, and, 112

Focaccia, Farm Stand, 111
Fontina, Black Mission Figs, Broiled, with Prosciutto, Sage Phyllo Flutes and, 57
Fontina, imported, about, 57
GOAT (CHÈVRE):
    Chicken Breasts, -Stuffed, Spicy, with Roasted Corn Salsa, 125
    -Eggplant, Roasted, Mousse, 38
    Glaze, Red Wine-, Sirloin, Seared Peppered, with, 138
    Greystone, about, 55
    Marinated, Lemon- and Herb-, with Fresh Tomatoes, 55
    Mashed Potatoes, -Rosemary-Garlic, 192
    Torte, Creamy, in Pine Nut Crust with Zinfandel-Spiked Cherries, 258
GORGONZOLA:
    about, 39
    and Beets, Roasted, with Orange-Rosemary Vinaigrette, 39
    Spinach and Fennel Salad with Curried Pears and, 93
    -Walnut Stuffing, Pork Chops, Center-Cut, with Ruby Port Glaze and, 144–145
    Mascarpone, Black Pepper-Orange, Melon and Prosciutto, Basil-Dressed, with, 59
    Mozzarella, Fresh, Fennel, Braised, with Sun-Dried Tomato Vinaigrette and, 56
PARMESAN:
    Biscotti, Rosemary-, 240
    Focaccia, 239
    Polenta, Herbed, 210
    Philly Steak, White Dog Cafe's, 104
    Potato Croquettes, Truffled, with, 190
    Ricotta and Spinach-Stuffed Chicken Breasts with Sun-Dried Tomato-Olive Butter, 126–127
    Stilton, Pear and Walnut Tart with Red Grape Compote and, 48–49

CHEESECAKE:
Chèvre Torte, Creamy, in Pine Nut Crust with Zinfandel-Spiked Cherries, 258–259
White Chocolate-Raspberry, 257

CHERRY(IES):
à la mode, making, 258
Sun-Dried, Glaze, Duck Breasts, Chili-Rubbed, with, 130
Zinfandel-Spiked, Chèvre Torte, Creamy, in Pine Nut Crust with, 258–259

Chèvre. See Goat Cheese

CHIAPAS:
Pie, 176–177
Tortilla Soup, 78

CHICKEN:
avoiding frozen, 121
Barbecued, Sweet & Spicy, 121
Braised with Tomatoes, Black Olives, and Pepperoni, 120
Chèvre-Stuffed Breasts, Spicy, with Roasted Corn Salsa, 125
Mediterranean Fried, with Artichoke Salad, 124
and Mushrooms, Sautéed, in Marsala-Sage Sauce, 122
poaching, 99
SALAD:
    and Mushroom, Roasted, Balsamico, 98
    Vietnamese, 97
    Waldorf-Style, 99
Sandwich, Cobb Salad, with Blue Cheese Mayonnaise, 102
Smoked, in Rosemary Cream with Bow-Tie Pasta, 122
smoking, 102
Soup, Noodle, Asian, 79
Soup, Tortilla, Chiapas, 78

Spinach and Ricotta-Stuffed Breasts with Sun-Dried Tomato-Olive Butter, 126–127
Stock, 277

Chickpeas. See Hummus

CHILI, CHILES:
Anaheim, buying and using, 176
Bean Salad, Firehouse Dalmatian, 205
Black Bean Refritos, 212
Calamari, -and Corn-Crusted with Tangy Citrus Aïoli, 52
Chipotle, flavoring with, 107
Duck Breasts, -Rubbed, with Sun-Dried Cherry Glaze, 130
Jalapeño-Lime Dressing, with Watermelon and Shrimp Salad, 100
New Mexican powder, about, 130
Pie, Chiapas, 176–177
Rellenos, Mushroom-Corn, with Mole, 178
Scotch Bonnet, working with, 36
Tortilla Floridita, 36

Chipotle Peppers, flavoring with, 107

Chips, Potato (or Sweet Potato), Fried, Spicy, 195

CHOCOLATE:
Cheesecake, White, -Raspberry, 257
Cream Pie, Milk, White Dog Cafe, 260–261
Mole, with Mushroom-Corn Rellenos, 178
Torte, Dense, Bittersweet, 262

CHOWDER:
Mussel, Creamy, with Sorrel, 81
Smoked Salmon and Corn, 80

CHUTNEY:
Gingered Pear, 297
Tomato-Mint, Lamb, Leg of, Derby Day, with, 148

Cider. *See* Apple Cider

Cilantro, fresh, using, 158

Citrus Aïoli, Tangy, Calamari, Chili- and Corn-Crusted, with, 52

CLAMS:
live, buying, 152
Shellfish Stew, Mediterranean, with Green Goddess Sauce, 152

Cobb Salad Sandwich with Blue Cheese Mayonnaise, 102

Coffee Cake, Sour Cream, 234

COMPOTE:
Pineapple-Rum, Banana Cake, Havana, with, 255
Red Grape, Pear and Walnut Tart with Stilton and, 48–49

CONDIMENTS:
Chutney, Gingered Pear, 297
Chutney, Tomato-Mint, Leg of Lamb, Derby Day, with, 148
nuoc cham, about, 53
Pickled Ginger, about, 71
Raita, Cucumber, 298
Relish, Pepper, 297
Relish, Tomato-Tarragon, Cucumber Soup, Chilled, with, 70

Contessa Lisa's, Grain Salad, Tuscan, 101

COOKIES:
Biscotti, Orange-Pistachio, 263
Kitchen Cabinet, Anne-Marie's, 265
Oatmeal, James's Giant, 266

Coriander, Lentil and Tomato Soup with Cumin and, 76

CORN:
Chowder, and Smoked Salmon, 80
Muffins, Cheddar, Sun-Dried Tomato and, 237
Pancakes, and Blueberry, with Maple-Pine Nut Butter, 229
Rellenos, Mushroom-, with Mole, 178
Salsa, Roasted, Chicken Breasts, Chèvre- Stuffed, Spicy, with, 125
Sweet, Risotto, and Tomato, 168
Sweet, Tabbouleh, and Barley, 209
See also Grits

Cornish Hens, Roast, with White Truffle Jus, 128–129

CORNMEAL:
Calamari, -and Chili-Crusted, with Tangy Citrus Aïoli, 52
Crab and Shrimp Cakes, -Crusted, with Summer Herbs Sauce, 154

Coulis, Cranberry, with Pumpkin and Walnut Shortbread Tart, 253

Couscous, Black Olive, 207

CRAB(S):
Cakes, and Shrimp, Corn-Crusted, with Summer Herbs Sauce, 154
Soft-Shell, with Thai Curried Vegetables, 153
Strudel, Shrimp and Asparagus, Flaky, 44–45

CRACKERS:
Biscotti, Rosemary-Parmesan, 240
Poppy Seed, Curried, 241

CRANBERRY(IES):
-Apple Pie, Deep-Dish Streusel, 248
Coulis, with Pumpkin and Walnut Shortbread Tart, 253

freezing fresh, 248
Pancakes, -Buckwheat, with Orange-Honey-Thyme Butter, 230

CREAM:
Crème Brûlée, Cappuccino, 264
Crème Fraîche, 288
Crème Fraîche, Horseradish, Roast Beef Tenderloin, Chilled, with, 133
Pie, Milk Chocolate, White Dog Cafe, 260–261
Rosemary, Chicken, Smoked, in, with Bow- Tie Pasta, 123
Sour Cream Coffee Cake, 234
Thyme, Oysters Stewed in, with Thyme Croutons, 41

CREAM CHEESE:
Caper, Smoked Salmon "Party Hats" with Caviar Confetti, 40
Chèvre Torte, in Pine Nut Crust with Zinfandel-Spiked Cherries, 258–259
Scrambled Eggs with Smoked Salmon, Dill and, 224
White Chocolate-Raspberry Cheesecake, 257

Crème Brûlée, Cappuccino, 264

CRÈME FRAÎCHE:
Crème Fraîche, 288
Horseradish, Roast Beef Tenderloin, Chilled, with, 133

Crêpes, Lobster and Shrimp, Sherried, 50–51

Crisp, Harvest Fruit, 249

Crisps, Pita, Spicy, 284

Croquettes, Potato, Truffled, with Chèvre, 190

Crostini, Garlic, 281

CROUTONS:
Garlic, 282
Polenta, 283
Thyme, 282

CRUST(ED):
Almond Shortbread and Lemon Curd
    Tart, 254
Chili- and Corn-, Calamari, with Tangy
    Citrus Aïoli, 52
Chocolate Cookie, Milk Chocolate
    Cream Pie, White Dog Cafe,
    260–261
Corn-, Crab and Shrimp Cakes, with
    Summer Herbs Sauce, 154
Pine Nut, Creamy Chèvre Torte in,
    with Zinfandel-Spiked Cherries,
    258–259
Walnut Shortbread and Pumpkin
    Tart with Cranberry Coulis,
    253

CUBAN(-STYLE):
Black Bean Soup, 77
Tuna, Braised, 160

CUCUMBER(S):
Raita, 298
Salad, Cool Island, 95
salting and draining, 298
Soup, Chilled, with Tomato-Tarragon
    Relish, 70

CUMIN:
Butter, 286
Lentil and Tomato Soup with
    Coriander and, 76

CURRANT(S), BLACK:
and Anise Balsamico, Tuna, Seared,
    with, 161
Scones, and Orange, 235

CURRY(IED):
Apple Bisque with Minted Yogurt, 73
Apple "Sauce," Sea Scallops, Seared,
    with, 155

Butternut Squash Ravioli with Winter
    Herb Pesto, 172–173
Lamb Stew, Jamaican, 150
Pears, Spinach and Fennel Salad
    with Gorgonzola and, 93
Poppy Seed Crackers, 241
Powder, White Dog Cafe, 284
Vegetable Salad, Chopped, with Pesto
    Pita Wedges, 96
Vegetables, -Roasted, with Indian
    Cheese Dumplings, 179
Vegetables, Thai, Crabs, Soft-Shell,
    with, 153

**Custard, Crème Brûlée,
Cappuccino, 264**

D

DEMI-GLACE:
making your own, 134
Veal, 279

DESSERT SAUCE(S):
Apricot-Grand Marnier, Brioche
    French Toast, with, 231
Caramel, Homemade, 267
Cranberry Coulis, with Pumpkin
    and Walnut Shortbread Tart,
    253
Hot Fudge, 267

Dijon Potato Salad, 195

**Dill, Scrambled Eggs with Smoked
Salmon, Cream Cheese, and, 224**

**Dipping Sauce, Apricot-Pickled
Ginger, Shrimp and Pork Spring
Rolls, Baked, with, 42–43**

DIPS AND SPREADS:
Avocado Mousse, 297
Black Olive Tapenade, 294
Guacamole, 296
Hummus, 294
White Bean-Feta Brandade, 295

DOUGH:
Pasta, Food Processor, 281
Pie, Basic, 280

DUCK:
Breasts, Chili-Rubbed, with Sun-Dried
    Cherry Glaze, 130
with Native Grains, Brandied Fruits
    and Pistachio Stuffing, Roasted,
    131

**Dumplings, Cheese, Indian,
Vegetables, Curry-Roasted,
with, 179**

E

EGG(S):
Baked, with Shepherd's Hash, 225
French Toast, Brioche, with Apricot-
    Grand Marnier Sauce, 231
Huevos Chihuahua, 226
Salad, Provençal, 224
Scrambled, with Smoked Salmon,
    Cream Cheese, and Dill, 224

EGGPLANT:
Ratatouille Bisque, 68
Roasted, -Chèvre Mousse, 38
Roasted, Marinara, 174
Tian, Summer Vegetable, Tangy, 181

**Emmentaler, Tart of Chanterelles,
Swiss Chard and, Savory,
170–171**

F

FENNEL:
about, 93
Braised, with Fresh Mozzarella and
    Sun- Dried Tomato Vinaigrette,
    56
Potatoes, Roasted, 193
Ratatouille Bisque, 68
Salad and Spinach, with Curried
    Pears and Gorgonzola, 93

FETA:
Focaccia, Toasted, with Roasted
    Tomatoes, Olives, and, 112
-White Bean Brandade, 295

**Fettuccine with White Beans, Sun-
Dried Tomatoes, and Rosemary,
169**

**Figs, Black Mission, Broiled, with
Prosciutto, Fontina and Sage
Phyllo Flutes, 57**

FISH:
fresh, buying, 109
Mahi Mahi, Grilled, with Tropical
    Fruit Salsa, Caribbean, 157
poaching, 99
Red Snapper, Crispy, with Shiitake
    Mushroom Glaze, 162
SALMON:
    Burgers, 109
    Pan-Roasted, with Burgundy-
        Rosemary Butter, 164
    See also Smoked Salmon
sauce *(nam pla)*, about, 95
Sea Bass, Rosemary- and Lime-
    Roasted, with Mediterranean
    Salsa, 165
skin, scoring, 162
SMOKED SALMON:
    and Corn Chowder, 80

"Party Hats" with Caviar Confetti,
    40
Scrambled Eggs with Cream
    Cheese, Dill and, 224
Stock, 279
stock, buying, 163
Swordfish, Leek- and Caraway-
    Braised, with Lemon-Pepper Aïoli,
    163
Trout, Roasted, with Potato-Shrimp
    Stuffing and Lemon-Thyme Sauce,
    158–159
Trout Tropicale, 156
TUNA:
    Braised, Cuban-Style, 160
    Sandwich à la Niçoise, 105
    Seared with Anise and Black
        Currant Balsamico, 161
See also Shellfish

FOCACCIA:
about, 111
Farm Stand, 111
Parmesan, 239
Toasted, with Tomatoes, Roasted,
    Olives, and Feta, 112

FONTINA:
Black Mission Figs, Broiled, with
    Prosciutto, Sage Phyllo Flutes
    and, 57
imported, about, 57

French Mushroom Soup, 74

**French Toast, Brioche, with Apricot-
Grand Marnier Sauce, 231**

Fritters, Plantain, Crispy, 213

FRUIT(S):
Berries, Mixed Summer, with
    Lavender Biscuits, 252
Brandied, Duck with Native Grains,
    Pistachio Stuffing and, Roasted,
    131

Crisp, Harvest, 249
Salsa, Tropical, Mahi Mahi, Grilled,
    with, Caribbean, 157
See also names of fruits and berries

Fudge Sauce, Hot, 267

G

GARAM MASALA:
about, 172
White Dog Cafe, 285

GARLIC:
Crostini, 281
Croutons, 282
and Greens, Sautéed, 202
Gremolata, 285
Mashed Potatoes, Chèvre-,
    Rosemary-, 192
Rice, Lemon-, 210
roasting, 38
See also Aïoli

GAZPACHO:
Desert Garden, with Margarita-
    Scallop Seviche, 69
Sauce, Huevos Chihuahua, 226

GINGER(ED):
Glaze, Pork Tenderloin, Sesame-
    Roasted, with, 143
-Lime Dressing, Spicy, 288
-Lime Dressing, Spicy, Shellfish and
    Asian Vegetables, Warm, with, 53
Pear Chutney, 296
Snow Pea-Cabbage Slaw, 214
See also Pickled Ginger

GLAZE(D):
Balsamic-Pancetta, Beef Tenderloin,
    Grilled, with, 134
Cherry, Sun-Dried, Duck Breasts,
    Chili- Rubbed, with, 130

Ginger, Pork Tenderloin, Sesame-Roasted, with, 143

Honey-, Turnips, 198

Red Wine-Chèvre, Sirloin, Seared Peppered, with, 138

Ruby Port, Pork, Chops, Center-Cut, with Gorgonzola-Walnut Stuffing and, 144–145

Shiitake Mushroom, Red Snapper, Crispy, with, 162

Wild Mushroom, London Broil, Rosemary- Mustard, with, 136–137

GOAT CHEESE (CHÈVRE):

Chicken Breasts, -Stuffed, Spicy, with Roasted Corn Salsa, 125

-Eggplant, Roasted, Mousse, 38

Glaze, Red Wine-, Sirloin, Seared Peppered, with, 138

Greystone, about, 55

Marinated, Lemon- and Herb-, with Fresh Tomatoes, 55

Mashed Potatoes, -Rosemary-Garlic, 192

Potato Croquettes, Truffled, with, 190

Torte, Creamy, in Pine Nut Crust with Zinfandel-Spiked Cherries, 258

GORGONZOLA:

about, 39

and Beets, Roasted, with Orange-Rosemary Vinaigrette, 39

Spinach and Fennel Salad with Curried Pears and, 93

-Walnut Stuffing, Pork Chops, Center-Cut, with Ruby Port Glaze and, 144–145

GRAIN(S):

cooking, 215

Granola, White Dog Cafe, 232

Native, Duck with Brandied Fruits, Pistachio Stuffing and, Roasted, 131

Native, Pilaf, 208

Salad, Tuscan, Contessa Lisa's, 101

See also names of grains

Grand Marnier-Apricot Sauce, Brioche French Toast with, 231

Granola, White Dog Cafe, 232

Grapefruit, Broiled, with Star Anise Sugar, 222

GRAPE(S):

Red, Compote, Pear and Walnut Tart with Stilton and, 48-49

Waldorf-Style Chicken Salad, 99

Gratin, Potato, Red-Skinned, and White Cheddar, 189

Green Beans with Onions, 203

Green Goddess Sauce, 293

Shellfish Stew, Mediterranean, with, 152

GREENS:

and Garlic, Sautéed, 202

See also Lettuces; names of greens

Gremolata, 285

Grinder, Italian Sausage, 103

GRITS:

identifying true, 223

Red Pepper, Roasted, and Shrimp, 223

Guacamole, 296

H

Ham, Brioche with Brie and, Toasted, 106

Hash, Shepherd's, with Baked Eggs, 225

Havana Banana Cake with Pineapple-Rum Compote, 255

HERB(S), HERBED:

Butter, 286

fresh, preserving flavor, 174

Goat Cheese, -Marinated, and Lemon, with Fresh Tomatoes, 55

Gremolata, 285

Pasta, -Printed, Mushrooms, Braised Wild, under, 46–47

Pesto, Winter, 292

Polenta, Parmesan, 210

Sauce, Summer, Crab and Shrimp Cakes, Corn-Crusted, with, 154

Tabbouleh, Barley and Sweet Corn, 209

See also names of herbs

HOMINY:

about, 208

cooking, 215

Duck with Native Grains, Brandied Fruits and Pistachio Stuffing, Roasted, 131

Pilaf, Native Grains, 208

HONEY:

Butter, -Orange-Thyme, Pancakes, Cranberry-Buckwheat, with, 230

Butternut Squash, and Lavender-Roasted, 198

Syrup, -Pecan, Pancakes, Banana-Buttermilk, with, 228

Turnips, -Glazed, 198

HORS D'OEUVRES:

Eggplant, Roasted, -Chèvre Mousse, 38

Smoked Salmon "Party Hats" with Caviar Confetti, 40

Strudel, Crab, Shrimp, and Asparagus, Flaky, 44–45

See also Dips and Spreads

HORSERADISH:
Crème Fraîche, Roast Beef Tenderloin, Chilled, with, 133
fresh, grating, 133

Hot Fudge Sauce, 267

Huevos Chihuahua, 226

HUMMUS, 294:
Mexican, Tortilla Roll Ups, 110

Indian Cheese Dumplings, Vegetables, Curry-Roasted, with, 179

Italian market in Philadelphia, visiting, 103

Italian Sausage Grinder, 103

J

Jalapeño-Lime Dressing, with Watermelon and Shrimp Salad, 100

Jamaican Lamb Stew, Curried, 150

James's Oatmeal Cookies, Giant, 266

K

Kabobs, Beef, Betty's, 135

KALE:
Balsamic-Braised, 203
and Garlic, Sautéed, 202

L

LAMB:
Burger, Moroccan-Spiced, with Pepper Relish, 108
LEG OF:
buying, 148
Derby Day, with Tomato-Mint Chutney, 148
Rosemary-Roasted, 149
Shanks, Tarragon-Braised, 151
Shepherd's Hash with Baked Eggs, 225
Stew, Curried, Jamaican, 150
See also Meats

LAVENDER:
Biscuits with Mixed Summer Berries, 252
Butternut Squash, and Honey-Roasted, 198

LEEK(S):
Crispy Fried, Sea Scallops, Seared, with Curried Apple "Sauce," 155
Swordfish, -and Caraway-Braised, with Lemon-Pepper Aïoli, 163

LEMON:
Aïoli, -Pepper, 291
Calamari, and Pepper-Grilled, with Roasted Pepper-Balsamic Dressing, 54
Curd and Almond Shortbread Tart, 254
Goat Cheese, -Marinated, and Herb, with Fresh Tomatoes, 55
Gremolata, 285
Rice, -Garlic, 210
rind, using whole, 209
Sauce, -Thyme, Trout, Roasted, with Potato-Shrimp Stuffing and, 158–159
Vinaigrette, -Olive Oil, with Mixed Salad of Many Lettuces, 90

Lemon Grass and Sweet Potato Soup with Peanut "Pesto," 67

LENTIL(S):
French, Warm, 206
Soup, and Tomato, with Coriander and Cumin, 76

LETTUCES:
cleaning, 91
Mixed Salad of Many, with Lemon-Olive Oil Vinaigrette, 90
Romaine Salad with Egg-Free Caesar Dressing, 91

LIME:
-Ginger Dressing, Spicy, 288
-Ginger Dressing, Spicy, Shellfish and Asian Vegetables, Warm, with, 53
-Jalapeño Dressing, with Watermelon and Shrimp Salad, 100
Sea Bass, -and Rosemary-Roasted, with Mediterranean Salsa, 165

LOBSTER(S):
Crêpes, and Shrimp, Sherried, 50–51
live, cooking, 50

London Broil, Rosemary-Mustard, with Wild Mushroom Glaze, 136–137

Mahi Mahi, Grilled, with Tropical Fruit Salsa, Caribbean, 157

MAPLE:
Butter, -Pine Nut, Pancakes, Corn and Blueberry, with, 229
Sweet Potatoes, -Mashed, 197

Margarita Scallop Seviche, Gazpacho, Desert Garden, with, 69

MARINADE, MARINATED:
Asian, Spicy, 289
Caribbean Mahi Mahi, Grilled, with Tropical Fruit Salsa, 157
Goat Cheese, Lemon- and Herb-, with Fresh Tomatoes, 55
Lemon- and Pepper, Calamari, -Grilled, with Roasted Pepper-Balsamic Dressing, 54
Rosemary-Mustard, London Broil with Wild Mushroom Glaze, 136–137

Marinara, Eggplant, Roasted, 174

Marsala Sauce, -Sage, Chicken and Mushrooms, Sautéed, in, 122

Mascarpone, Black Pepper-Orange, Melon and Prosciutto, Basil-Dressed, with, 59

MAYONNAISE:
Blue Cheese, with Cobb Salad Sandwich, 102
Homemade, 287
See also Aïoli

Meat Loaf, Layered, White Dog Cafe, 140–141

MEATS:
fatty, roasting, 149
poaching, 99
searing, 138
shanks, slow-cooking, 151

MEDITERRANEAN:
Chicken, Fried, with Artichoke Salad, 124
Salsa, Sea Bass, Rosemary- and Lime- Roasted, with Shellfish Stew with Green Goddess Sauce, 152

MELON:
and Prosciutto, Basil-Dressed, with Black Pepper-Orange Mascarpone, 59
Soup, Thai Three-, 71
Watermelon and Shrimp Salad with Jalapeño-Lime Dressing, 100

MEXICAN:
oregano, about, 78
Tortilla Roll Ups, 110
See also Chiapas

Minestrone, Garden Vegetable, 75

MINT(ED):
Chutney, Tomato-, Leg of Lamb, Derby Day, with, 148
Julep, White Dog Cafe, 232
Yogurt, Apple Bisque, Curried, with, 73
Zucchini with White Beans and, 205

Mole, with Mushroom-Corn Rellenos, 178

Moroccan-Spiced Lamb Burger with Pepper Relish, 108

MOUSSE:
Avocado, 296
Eggplant, Roasted, -Chèvre, 38

Mozzarella, Fresh, Fennel, Braised, with Sun-Dried Tomato Vinaigrette and, 56

MUFFINS:
Banana-Nut, 236
Blueberry, 236
Corn, Cheddar, and Sun-Dried Tomato, 237

MUSHROOM(S):
Chanterelles, Tart of Swiss Chard, Emmentaler and, Savory, 170–171
and Chicken, Roasted, Salad, Balsamico, 98
and Chicken, Sautéed, in Marsala-Sage Sauce, 122
Oyster, Savoy Cabbage with Pancetta and, 200
Portobello, about, 180
Portobello, Balsamic-Roasted, 180
Rellenos, -Corn, with Mole, 178
Shiitake, Glaze, Red Snapper, Crispy, with, 162
Soup, French, 74
-Spinach Salad, Warm, 92
Veal Chops Roasted with Pine Nuts and, 142
WILD:
    -Barley Risotto, 166
    Braised, under Herb-Printed Pasta, 46–47
    dried, about, 46
    Glaze, London Broil, Rosemary Mustard, with, 136–137

MUSSEL(S):
buying and cleaning, 82
Chowder, Creamy, with Sorrel, 81
Shellfish Stew, Mediterranean, with Green Goddess Sauce, 152
Stew, Portuguese-Style, 82

MUSTARD:
Dijon Potato Salad, 195
London Broil, Rosemary-, with Wild Mushroom Glaze, 136–137

N

Nam pla (fish sauce), about, 95

Nana's Strawberry Pie, 250

New Mexican chili powder, about, 130

Nicaraguan Beef Shins, Braised, 139

Niçoise, Tuna Sandwich à la, 105

NOODLE(S):
Chicken Salad, Vietnamese, 97
Chicken Soup, Asian, 79
somen, cooking, 79

NUOC CHAM:
about, 53
Ginger-Lime Dressing, Spicy, 288

NUT(S):
Almond Shortbread and Lemon Curd Tart, 254
Cookies, Kitchen Cabinet, Anne-Marie's, 265
Granola, White Dog Cafe, 232
Muffins, Banana-, 236
Peanut "Pesto," Sweet Potato-Lemon Grass Soup with, 67
Pecan Pancakes, Six Grain-, with Apple Cider Syrup, 227
Pecan Syrup, Honey-, Pancakes, Banana- Buttermilk, with, 228
PINE NUT(S):
    Butter, Maple-, Pancakes, Corn and Blueberry, with, 229
    Crust, Creamy Chèvre Torte in, with Zinfandel-Spiked Cherries, 258–259
    Veal Chops Roasted with Mushrooms and, 142
Pistachio Biscotti, Orange-, 263
Pistachio Stuffing, Duck with Native Grains, Brandied Fruits and, Roasted, 131
toasting, 144
Trout Tropicale, 156
WALNUT:
    Gorgonzola-Stuffing, Pork Chops, Center-Cut, with Ruby Port Glaze and, 144–145

and Pear Tart with Red Grape Compote and Stilton, 48–49
Shortbread and Pumpkin Tart with Cranberry Coulis, 253

Oatmeal Cookies, James's Giant, 266

OIL:
Olive, Vinaigrette, Lemon-, with Mixed Salad of Many Lettuces, 90
white truffle, buying, 128

OLIVE(S):
BLACK:
    Chicken Braised with Tomatoes, Pepperoni and, 120
    Couscous, 207
Butter, Sun-Dried Tomato-, 287
Focaccia, Toasted, with Roasted Tomatoes, Feta, and, 112
imported, buying, 112
Niçoise, Tuna Sandwich à la, 105
Tapenade, 294

Olive Oil Vinaigrette, Lemon-, with Mixed Salad of Many Lettuces, 90

ONIONS:
Green Beans with, 203
Pickled, Smoked Salmon "Party Hats" with Caviar Confetti, 40

ORANGE:
Biscotti, -Pistachio, 263
Butter, -Honey-Thyme, Pancakes, Cranberry-Buckwheat, with, 230
Mascarpone, Black Pepper-, Melon & Prosciutto, Basil-Dressed, with, 59

Scones, and Black Currant, 235
Vinaigrette, -Rosemary, Beets, Roasted, and Gorgonzola with, 39

Oregano, Mexican, about, 78

Oyster Mushrooms, Savoy Cabbage with Pancetta and, 200

OYSTERS:
buying, 41
Stewed in Thyme Cream with Thyme Croutons, 41

PANCAKES:
Banana-Buttermilk, with Honey-Pecan Syrup, 228
Corn and Blueberry, with Maple-Pine Nut Butter, 229
Cranberry-Buckwheat, with Orange-Honey- Thyme Butter, 230
Pecan, Six Grain-, with Apple Cider Syrup, 227

PANCETTA:
Glaze, Balsamic-, Beef Tenderloin, Grilled, with, 134
Rabbit with Tomatoes, Green Peppercorns and, Braised, 132
Savoy Cabbage with Oyster Mushrooms and, 200
substituting for bacon, 92

PARMESAN:
Biscotti, Rosemary-, 240
Focaccia, 239
Polenta, Herbed, 210

PARSLEY:
Green Goddess Sauce, 293
Gremolata, 285

PASTA:
Bow-Tie, Chicken, Smoked, in
    Rosemary Cream with, 123
Dough, Food Processor, 281
Fettuccine with White Beans, Sun-
    Dried Tomatoes, and Rosemary,
    169
Herb-Printed, Mushrooms, Braised
    Wild, under, 46-47
NOODLE(S):
    Chicken Salad, Vietnamese, 97
    Chicken Soup, Asian, 79
    somen, cooking, 79
Penne with Asparagus, 175
Ravioli, Butternut Squash, Curried,
    with Winter Herb Pesto, 172-173

Pastry(ies). *See* Phyllo; Pie(s);
    Tart(s)

PEA(S):
Snow Peas, Sesame-Steamed, 202
Snow Pea, Slaw, -Cabbage, Gingered,
    214
Sugar Snap, Sautéed with Scallions,
    201

**Peach-Blueberry Pie, Double-
Crusted, 251**

**Peanut "Pesto," Sweet Potato-
Lemon Grass Soup with, 67**

PEAR(S):
Chutney, Gingered, 297
Curried, Spinach and Fennel Salad
    with Gorgonzola and, 93
selecting, 49
Tart, and Walnut, with Red Grape
    Compote and Stilton, 48-49

PECAN:
Pancakes, Six Grain-, with Apple
    Cider Syrup, 227
Syrup, Honey-, Pancakes, Banana-
    Buttermilk, with, 228

Penne with Asparagus, 175

Pepper(s). *See* Bell Pepper(s);
    Chili, Chiles

PEPPER(ED):
Aïoli, Lemon-, 291
Calamari, and Lemon, -Grilled, with
    Roasted Pepper-Balsamic
    Dressing, 54
Mascarpone, -Orange, Melon and
    Prosciutto, Basil-Dressed, with, 59
Sirloin, Seared, with Red Wine-
    Chèvre Glaze, 138

PEPPERCORNS:
choosing by color, 132
Green, Rabbit with Tomatoes,
    Pancetta and, Braised, 132

**Pepperoni, Chicken Braised with
Tomatoes, Black Olives and,
120**

PESTO:
Basil, 292
Herb, Winter, 292
Peanut, Sweet Potato-Lemon Grass
    Soup with, 67
Pita Wedges, Vegetable Salad,
    Curried Chopped, with, 96

**Philadelphia, Italian market in,
visiting, 103**

**Philly Cheese Steak, White Dog
Cafe's, 104**

PHYLLO:
dough, using, 44
Flutes, Sage, Black Mission Figs,
    Broiled, with Prosciutto, Fontina
    and, 57
Spring Rolls, Shrimp and Pork,
    Baked, with Apricot-Pickled
    Ginger Dipping Sauce,
    42-43

Strudel, Crab, Shrimp, and
    Asparagus, Flaky, 44-45

Picadillo, Tortilla Floridita, 36

PICKLED GINGER:
buying, 71
Dipping Sauce, -Apricot, Shrimp and
    Pork Spring Rolls, Baked, with,
    42-43

**Pickled Onions, Smoked Salmon
"Party Hats" with Caviar
Confetti, 40**

PIE(S):
Apple-Cranberry Deep-Dish Streusel,
    248
Chiapas, 176-177
Chocolate Cream, Milk, White Dog
    Cafe, 260-261
Dough, Basic, 280
Peach-Blueberry, Double-Crusted,
    251
Strawberry, Nana's, 250
See also Tart(s)

Pilaf, Native Grains, 208

**Pineapple-Rum Compote, Banana
Cake, Havana, with, 255**

PINE NUT(S):
Butter, Maple-, Pancakes, Corn and
    Blueberry, with, 229
Crust, Creamy Chèvre Torte in, with
    Zinfandel-Spiked Cherries,
    258-259
Veal Chops Roasted with Mushrooms
    and, 142

PISTACHIO:
Biscotti, Orange-, 263
Stuffing, Duck with Native Grains,
    Brandied Fruits and, Roasted, 131

PITA:
Crisps, Spicy, 284
Wedges, Pesto, Vegetable Salad,
   Curried Chopped, with, 96

PLANTAIN(S):
Fritters, Crispy, 213
peeling, 213

POLENTA:
Croutons, 283
Parmesan, Herbed, 210

Poppy Seed Crackers, Curried, 241

PORK:
Chops, Center-Cut, with Gorgonzola-
   Walnut Stuffing and Ruby Port
   Glaze, 144–145
chops, butchering for stuffing, 145
Ham, Brioche with Brie and, Toasted,
   106
Medallions, Sautéed, with Basil and
   Balsamic Vinegar, 147
Ribs, Asian Barbecued, with Gingered
   Snow Pea Cabbage Slaw, 58
ribs, baby back, about, 58
Sausage, Italian, Grinder, 103
Spring Rolls, and Shrimp, Baked,
   with Apricot-Pickled Ginger
   Dipping Sauce, 42-43
Tenderloin with Caramelized Shallots
   and Apples, 146
Tenderloin, Sesame-Roasted, with
   Ginger Glaze, 143
See also Meats; Pancetta

PORT:
cooking with, 48
Ruby, Glaze, Pork, Chops, Center-Cut,
   with Gorgonzola-Walnut Stuffing
   and, 144–145

PORTOBELLO MUSHROOMS:
about, 180
Balsamic-Roasted, 180

Portuguese-Style Mussel Stew, 82

POTATO(ES):
Cake, -Roasted Red Pepper, 191
Chips, Fried, Spicy, 195
Country Style, 193
Croquettes, Truffled, with Chèvre,
   190
Fried, Spicy, 194
Gratin, Red-Skinned, and White
   Cheddar, 189
Mashed, Chèvre-Rosemary-Garlic,
   192
Roasted, Fennel, 193
Roasted, Rosemary-, 192
Salad, Dijon, 195
Salad, Vegetable, Summer Garden,
   196
-Shrimp Stuffing, Trout, Roasted,
   with Lemon-Thyme Sauce and,
   158–159

Pound Cake, Rose Geranium, 256

PROCEDURES:
Anaheim chiles, using, 176
artichokes, cleaning, 72
arugula, using, 161
bananas, freezing, 255
beans, dried, cooking, 215
beans, dried, flavoring, 169
bell peppers, roasting, 140
broccoli rabe, cooking with, 123
buttermilk, making homemade, 228
butters, making compound, 126
chicken, smoking, 102
chipotle peppers, flavoring with, 107
chops, butchering for stuffing, 145
cilantro, fresh, using, 158
crabs, soft-shell, cleaning, 153
cucumbers, salting and draining, 298
demi-glace, making, 134
fatty meats, roasting, 149
fish skin, scoring, 162
garlic, roasting, 38
grains, cooking, 215

horseradish, fresh, grating, 133
lemon rind, using whole, 209
lettuce, cleaning, 91
lobsters, live, cooking, 50
mussels, cleaning, 82
nuts and seeds, toasting, 144
phyllo dough, using, 44
plantains, peeling, 213
poaching fish and meat, 99
port wine, cooking with, 48
searing meat, 138
shank meats, slow-cooking, 151
shrimp, deveining, 51
spices, toasting, 73
squid, cleaning, 52
sun-dried tomatoes, rehydrating, 127
Swiss chard, cooking with, 170
tomato paste, cooking with, 120

PROSCIUTTO:
Black Mission Figs, Broiled, with
   Fontina, Sage Phyllo Flutes and,
   57
Melon and, Basil-Dressed, with Black
   Pepper-Orange Mascarpone, 59

Provençal Egg Salad, 224

**Pumpkin and Walnut Shortbread
Tart with Cranberry Coulis, 253**

Punch, Rum, White Dog Cafe, 233

R

**Rabbit with Tomatoes, Pancetta,
and Green Peppercorns,
Braised, 132**

Raita, Cucumber, 298

**Raspberry Cheesecake, White
Chocolate-, 257**

Ratatouille Bisque, 68

Ravioli, Butternut Squash, Curried, with Winter Herb Pesto, 172–173

Red Pepper(s). *See* Bell Pepper(s)

Red Snapper, Crispy, with Shiitake Mushroom Glaze, 162

Red Wine. *See* Wine

RELISH:
Pepper, 297
Raita, Cucumber, 298
Tomato-Tarragon, Cucumber Soup, Chilled, with, 70

RIBS:
baby back, using, 58
Barbecued, Asian, with Gingered Snow- Pea Cabbage Slaw, 58

RICE:
and Black Beans, 211
Lemon-Garlic, 210
Risotto, Broccoli, 167
Risotto, Tomato and Sweet Corn, 168
See also Wild Rice

Ricotta and Spinach-Stuffed Chicken Breasts with Sun-Dried Tomato-Olive Butter, 126–127

RISOTTO:
Barley-Wild Mushroom, 166
Broccoli, 167
Tomato and Sweet Corn, 168

Romaine Salad with Egg-Free Caesar Dressing, 91

Rose Geranium Pound Cake, 256

ROSEMARY:
Biscotti, -Parmesan, 240
Butter, -Burgundy, Salmon, Pan-Roasted, with, 164

Cream, Chicken, Smoked, in, with Bow-Tie Pasta, 123
Fettuccine with White Beans, Sun-Dried Tomatoes and, 169
Lamb, Leg of, -Roasted, 149
London Broil, -Mustard, with Wild Mushroom Glaze, 136–137
Mashed Potatoes, -Chèvre, -Garlic, 192
Potatoes, -Roasted, 192
Sea Bass, -and Lime-Roasted, with Mediterranean Salsa, 165
Vinaigrette, Orange-, Beets Roasted, and Gorgonzola with, 39

RUM:
Compote, Pineapple-, Banana Cake, Havana, with, 255
Punch, White Dog Cafe, 233

S

Saffron Aïoli, with Potatoes, Fried, Spicy, 194

SAGE:
-Marsala Sauce, Chicken and Mushrooms, Sautéed, in, 122
Phyllo Flutes, Black Mission Figs, Broiled, with Prosciutto, Fontina and, 57

SALAD(S):
Artichoke, Chicken, Mediterranean Fried, with, 124
Bean, Dalmatian, Firehouse, 205
Beets, Roasted, and Gorgonzola with Orange-Rosemary Vinaigrette, 39
Bread, Country, and Roasted Vegetable, 94
CHICKEN:
and Mushroom, Roasted, Balsamico, 98

Vietnamese, 97
Waldorf-Style, 99
Cobb, Sandwich, with Blue Cheese Mayonnaise, 102
Cucumber, Cool Island, 95
Egg, Provençal, 224
Goat Cheese, Lemon- and Herb-Marinated, with Fresh Tomatoes, 55
Grain, Tuscan, Contessa Lisa's, 101
Mixed, of Many Lettuces with Lemon-Olive Oil Vinaigrette, 90
Mushroom-Spinach, Warm, 92
Potato, Dijon, 195
Potato, Vegetable, Summer Garden, 196
Romaine, with Egg-Free Caesar Dressing, 91
Slaw, Snow Pea-Cabbage, Gingered, 214
Slaw, Vegetable, Six, Tangy, 214
Spinach and Fennel, with Curried Pears and Gorgonzola, 93
Tabbouleh, Barley and Sweet Corn, 209

SALAD DRESSING:
Basil-Dressed Melon and Prosciutto with Black Pepper-Orange Mascarpone, 59
Caesar, Egg-Free, with Romaine Salad, 91
Ginger-Lime, Spicy, 288
Jalapeño-Lime, with Watermelon and Shrimp Salad, 100
Mayonnaise, Blue Cheese, with Cobb Salad Sandwich, 102
Pepper, Roasted, -Balsamic, Calamari, Lemon- and Pepper-Grilled, with, 54
VINAIGRETTE:
Curried Chopped Vegetable Salad with Pesto Pita Wedges, 96
Lemon-Olive Oil, with Mixed Salad of Many Lettuces, 90

Orange-Rosemary, with Beets, Roasted, and Gorgonzola, 39
Sun-Dried Tomato, Fennel, Braised, with Fresh Mozzarella and, 56

SALMON:
Burgers, 109
Pan-Roasted, with Burgundy-Rosemary Butter, 164
SMOKED:
    Chowder, and Corn, 80
    "Party Hats" with Caviar Confetti, 40
    Scrambled Eggs with Cream Cheese, Dill and, 224

SALSA:
Corn, Roasted, Chicken Breasts, Chèvre- Stuffed, Spicy, with, 125
Fruit, Tropical, Mahi Mahi, Grilled, with, Caribbean, 157
Mediterranean, Sea Bass, Rosemary- and Lime-Roasted, with, 165

SANDWICH(ES):
Cobb Salad, with Blue Cheese Mayonnaise, 102
Focaccia, Farm Stand, 111
Focaccia, Toasted, with Tomatoes, Roasted, Olives, and Feta, 112
Ham and Brie, with Brioche, Toasted, 106
Italian Sausage Grinder, 103
Pesto Pita Wedges, Vegetable Salad, Curried Chopped, with, 96
Philly Cheese Steak, White Dog Cafe's, 104
Tortilla Roll Ups, Mexican, 110
Tuna à la Niçoise, 105
See also Burger(s)

SAUCE(S):
Apple, Curried, Sea Scallops, Seared, with, 155

Barbecued Chicken, Sweet & Spicy, 121
Basil, Creamy, 293
demi-glace, making your own, 134
Demi-Glace, Veal, 279
Dipping, Apricot-Pickled Ginger, Shrimp and Pork Spring Rolls, Baked, with, 42–43
fish (nam pla), about, 95
Gazpacho, Huevos Chihuahua, 226
Ginger-Lime Dressing, Spicy, Shellfish and Asian Vegetables, Warm, with, 53
Green Goddess, 293
Green Goddess, Shellfish Stew, Mediterranean, with, 152
Herbs, Summer, Crab and Shrimp Cakes, Corn-Crusted, with, 154
Lemon-Thyme, Trout, Roasted, with Potato- Shrimp Stuffing and, 158–159
Marinara, Roasted Eggplant, 174
Marsala-Sage, Chicken and Mushrooms, Sautéed, in, 122
Mole, with Mushroom-Corn Rellenos, 178
Tartar, 290
Tomato-Basil, Rustic, 290
White Truffle Jus, Cornish Hens, Roast, with, 128–129
See also Aïoli; Butter(s); Dessert Sauce(s); Glaze(d); Pesto; Salsa

Sausage, Italian, Grinder, 103

Savoy Cabbage with Pancetta and Oyster Mushrooms, 200

Scallions, Sugar Snap Peas Sautéed with, 201

SCALLOP(S):
Sea, Seared, with Curried Apple "Sauce," 155

Seviche, Margarita-, Gazpacho, Desert Garden, with, 69

Scones, Orange and Black Currant, 235

Scotch bonnet chiles, working with, 36

Sea Bass, Rosemary- and Lime-Roasted, with Mediterranean Salsa, 165

Seafood. See Fish; Shellfish; Squid

SEEDS:
Granola, White Dog Cafe, 232
toasting, 144
See also Sesame

SESAME:
Asparagus, -Roasted, 204
Pork Tenderloin, -Roasted, with Ginger Glaze, 143
Snow Peas, -Steamed, 202

SEVICHE:
Scallop, Margarita-, Gazpacho, Desert Garden, with, 69
Vegetable, Tortilla Roll Ups, Mexican, 110
Shallots, Caramelized, Pork Tenderloin with Apples and, 146

SHELLFISH:
and Asian Vegetables, Warm, with Spicy Ginger-Lime Dressing, 53
clams, live, buying, 152
Lobster, Crêpes, and Shrimp, Sherried, 50–51
oysters, buying, 41
Oysters Stewed in Thyme Cream with Thyme Croutons, 41
Scallop Seviche, Margarita-, Gazpacho, Desert Garden, with, 69
Scallops, Sea, Seared, with Curried Apple "Sauce," 155

Stew, Mediterranean, with Green
    Goddess Sauce, 152
See also Crab(s); Mussel(s);
    Shrimp

**Shepherd's Hash with Baked Eggs,
    225**

SHERRY(IED):
Lobster and Shrimp Crêpes, 50–51
vinegar, using, 108

**Shiitake Mushroom Glaze, Red
    Snapper, Crispy, with, 162**

SHORTBREAD:
Almond, and Lemon Curd Tart, 254
Walnut, and Pumpkin Tart with
    Cranberry Coulis, 253

SHRIMP:
Cakes, and Crab, Corn-Crusted, with
    Summer Herbs Sauce, 154
Crêpes, and Lobster, Sherried, 50–51
deveining, 51
Grits, Red Pepper, Roasted, and, 223
Potato-Stuffing, Trout, Roasted, with
    Lemon-Thyme Sauce and, 158–159
Salad, and Watermelon, with
    Jalapeño- Lime Dressing, 100
Spring Rolls, and Pork, Baked, with
    Apricot-Pickled Ginger Dipping
    Sauce, 42–43
Strudel, Crab and Asparagus, Flaky,
    44–45
Tortilla Floridita, 36
Sirloin, Seared Peppered, with Red
    Wine-Chèvre Glaze, 138

SLAW:
Snow Pea-Cabbage, Gingered, 214
Vegetable, Six, Tangy, 214

**Smoked Chicken in Rosemary
    Cream with Bow-Tie Pasta, 122**

SMOKED SALMON:
Chowder, and Corn, 80
"Party Hats" with Caviar Confetti, 40
Scrambled Eggs with Cream Cheese,
    Dill and, 224

**Snapper, Red, Crispy, with Shiitake
    Mushroom Glaze, 162**

SNOW PEA(S):
Sesame-Steamed, 202
Slaw, -Cabbage, Gingered, 214

Somen noodles, cooking, 79

SORREL:
fresh, buying, 81
Mussel Chowder, Creamy, with, 81

SOUP(S):
Apple Bisque, Curried, with Minted
    Yogurt, 73
Artichoke Bisque, 72
Beef Burgundy Stew, 93
Black Bean, Cuban, 77
Chicken Noodle, Asian, 79
Cucumber, Chilled, with Tomato-
    Tarragon Relish, 70
Gazpacho, Desert Garden, with
    Margarita- Scallop Seviche, 69
Lentil and Tomato, with Coriander
    and Cumin, 76
Melon, Thai Three-, 71
Minestrone, Garden Vegetable, 75
Mushroom, French, 74
Mussel Chowder, Creamy, with
    Sorrel, 81
Mussel Stew, Portuguese-Style, 82
Ratatouille Bisque, 68
Smoked Salmon and Corn Chowder,
    80
Sweet Potato and Lemon Grass, with
    Peanut "Pesto," 67
Tortilla, Chiapas, 78
See also Stock

Sour Cream Coffee Cake, 234

Southwestern Turkey Burger, 107

SPELT:
about, 101
Salad, Tuscan Grain, Contessa Lisa's,
    101

SPICE(D), SPICY:
Chicken, Barbecued, Sweet and, 121
Chicken Breasts, Chèvre-Stuffed, with
    Roasted Corn Salsa, 125
Garam Masala, about, 172
Garam Masala, White Dog Cafe, 285
Ginger-Lime Dressing, 288
Marinade, Asian, 289
Moroccan-, Lamb Burger with
    Pepper Relish, 108
Pita Crisps, 284
Potatoes, Fried, 194
Potato (or Sweet Potato) Chips,
    Fried, 195
tasting spices, 73
See also names of spices

SPINACH:
and Garlic, Sautéed, 202
and Ricotta-Stuffed Chicken Breasts,
    with Sun-Dried Tomato-Olive
    Butter, 126–127
Salad, and Fennel, with Curried
    Pears and Gorgonzola, 93
Salad, Mushroom-, Warm, 92

**Spring Rolls, Shrimp and Pork,
    Baked, with Apricot-Pickled
    Ginger Dipping Sauce, 42–43**

SQUASH:
Butternut, Lavender and Honey-
    Roasted, 198
Butternut, Ravioli, Curried, with
    Winter Herb Pesto, 172–173
Tian, Tangy Summer Vegetable, 181
See also Zucchini

SQUID (CALAMARI):
Chili- and Corn-Crusted, with Tangy
    Citrus Aïoli, 52
cleaning, 52
Lemon- and Pepper-Grilled, with
    Roasted Pepper-Balsamic
    Dressing, 54
Shellfish Stew, Mediterranean,
    with Green Goddess Sauce,
    152

STEAK:
flank, identifying, 136
London Broil, Rosemary-Mustard,
    with Wild Mushroom Glaze,
    136–137
Philly Cheese, White Dog Cafe's, 104
Sirloin, Seared Peppered, with Red
    Wine-Chèvre Glaze, 138

STEW:
Beef Burgundy, 83
Lamb, Curried, Jamaican, 150
Mussel, Portuguese-Style, 82
Oysters, in Thyme Cream with Thyme
    Croutons, 41
Shellfish, Mediterranean, with Green
    Goddess Sauce, 152

**Stilton, Pear and Walnut Tart with
    Red Grape Compote and, 48–49**

STOCK:
Chicken, 277
Fish, 279
Veal, 278
Vegetable, 277

Strawberry Pie, Nana's, 250

**Streusel Apple-Cranberry Pie,
    Deep-Dish, 248**

**Strudel, Crab, Shrimp, and
    Asparagus, Flaky, 44–45**

STUFFED, STUFFING:
Chèvre-, Chicken Breasts, Spicy, with
    Roasted Corn Salsa, 125
chops, butchering for, 145
Gorgonzola-Walnut, Pork Chops,
    Center-Cut, with Ruby Port Glaze
    and, 144–145
Mushroom-Corn Rellenos with Mole,
    178
Pistachio, Duck with Native Grains,
    Brandied Fruits and, Roasted, 131
Potato-Shrimp, Trout, Roasted,
    with Lemon-Thyme Sauce and,
    158–159
Spinach and Ricotta-, Chicken
    Breasts, with Sun-Dried Tomato-
    Olive Butter, 126

**Sugar, Star Anise, Grapefruit,
    Broiled, with, 222**

**Sugar Snap Peas Sautéed with
    Scallions, 201**

**Sun-Dried Cherry Glaze, Duck
    Breasts, Chili-Rubbed, with, 130**

SUN-DRIED TOMATO(ES):
Butter, -Olive, 287
Fettuccine with White Beans,
    Rosemary and, 169
Muffins, Corn, Cheddar and, 237
rehydrating, 127
Vinaigrette, Fennel, Braised, with
    Fresh Mozzarella and, 56

SWEET POTATO(ES):
Chips, Fried, Spicy, 195
Mashed, Maple, 197

Soup, -Lemon Grass, with Peanut
    "Pesto," 67
Tortilla Floridita, 36

SWISS CHARD:
cooking with, 170
and Garlic, Sautéed, 202

Tart of Chanterelles, Emmentaler
    and, Savory, 170–171

**Swordfish, Leek- and Caraway-
    Braised, with Lemon-Pepper
    Aïoli, 163**

SYRUP:
Apple Cider, Pancakes, Six Grain-
    Pecan, with, 227
Honey-Pecan, Pancakes, Banana-
    Buttermilk, with, 228

T

Tabbouleh, Barley and Sweet Corn,
    209

Tapenade, Black Olive, 294

TARRAGON:
Green Goddess Sauce, 293
Lamb Shanks, -Braised, 151
-Tomato Relish, Cucumber Soup,
    Chilled, with, 70

Tartar Sauce, 290

TART(S):
of Chanterelles, Swiss Chard, and
    Emmentaler, Savory, 170–171
Lemon Curd and Almond Shortbread,
    254
Pear and Walnut, with Red Grape
    Compote and Stilton, 48–49
Pumpkin and Walnut Shortbread,
    with Cranberry Coulis, 253
See also Pie(s)

THAI:
Melon Soup, Three-, 71
Vegetables, Curried, Crabs, Soft-
    Shell, with, 153

THYME:
Butter, Orange-Honey-, Pancakes, Cranberry-Buckwheat, with, 230
Cream, Oysters Stewed in, with Thyme Croutons, 41
Croutons, 282
-Lemon Sauce, Trout, Roasted, with Potato-Shrimp Stuffing and, 158–159

Tian, Summer Vegetable, Tangy, 181

TOASTS:
Brioche French Toast with Apricot-Grand Marnier Sauce, 231
Brioche Rounds, Smoked Salmon "Party Hats" with Caviar Confetti, 40
Crostini, Garlic, 281
Pita Crisps, Spicy, 284
See also Croutons

TOMATO(ES):
Bloodhounds, 233
canned, selecting, 76
Chicken Braised with Black Olives, Pepperoni and, 120
Chutney, -Mint, Leg of Lamb, Derby Day, with, 148
Fresh, Goat Cheese, Lemon- and Herb- Marinated, with, 55
Gazpacho, Desert Garden, with Margarita- Scallop Seviche, 69
Gazpacho Sauce, Huevos Chihuahua, 226
Marinara, Roasted Eggplant, 174
paste, cooking with, 120
Rabbit with Pancetta, Green Peppercorns and, Braised, 132
Relish, -Tarragon, Cucumber Soup, Chilled, with, 70
Risotto, and Sweet Corn, 168
Roasted, Focaccia, Toasted, with Olives, Feta, and, 112

Salsa, Mediterranean, Sea Bass, Rosemary- and Lime-Roasted, with, 165
Sauce, -Basil, Rustic, 290
Soup, and Lentil, with Coriander and Cumin, 76
Tian, Summer Vegetable, Tangy, 181
See also Sun-Dried Tomato(es)

TORTE:
Chèvre, Creamy, in Pine Nut Crust with Zinfandel-Spiked Cherries, 258
Chocolate, Dense, Bittersweet, 262

TORTILLA(S):
Floridita, 36
Huevos Chihuahua, 226
Pie, Chiapas, 176–177
Roll Ups, Mexican, 110
Soup, Chiapas, 78

TROUT:
Roasted, with Potato-Shrimp Stuffing and Lemon-Thyme Sauce, 158–159
Tropicale, 156

TRUFFLE(D):
Jus, White, Cornish Hens, Roast, with, 128–129
oil, white, buying, 128
Potato Croquettes with Chèvre, 190

TUNA:
Braised, Cuban-Style, 160
Sandwich à la Niçoise, 105
Seared with Anise and Black Currant Balsamico, 161

Turkey Burger, Southwestern, 107

Turnips, Honey-Glazed, 198

Tuscan Grain Salad, Contessa Lisa's, 101

V

VEAL:
Chops Roasted with Mushrooms and Pine Nuts, 142
Demi-Glace, 134, 279
Meat Loaf, Layered, White Dog Cafe, 140–141
Stock, 278
See also Meats

VEGETABLE(S):
Asian, and Shellfish, Warm, with Spicy Ginger-Lime Dressing, 53
CURRY(IED):
-Roasted, with Indian Cheese Dumplings, 179
Salad, Chopped, with Pesto Pita Wedges, 96
Thai, Crabs, Soft-Shell, with, 153
Focaccia, Farm Stand, 111
Gazpacho, Desert Garden, with Margarita- Scallop Seviche, 69
Minestrone, Garden, 75
Pie, Chiapas, 176–177
Potato Salad, Summer Garden, 196
Ratatouille Bisque, 68
ROASTED:
Balsamico, 201
Caraway-, 199
Curry-, with Indian Cheese Dumplings, 179
Salad, and Country Bread, 94
Seviche, Tortilla Roll Ups, Mexican, 110
Slaw, Six, Tangy, 214
Stock, 277
Tian, Summer, Tangy, 181
Tortilla Roll Ups, Mexican, 110
See also names of vegetables

VEGETARIAN MAIN DISHES:
Chiapas Pie, 176–177
Eggplant, Roasted, Marinara, 174

Fettuccine with White Beans, Sun-Dried Tomatoes, and Rosemary, 169

Penne with Asparagus, 175

Portobello Mushrooms, Balsamic-Roasted, 180

Ravioli, Butternut Squash, Curried, with Winter Herb Pesto, 172–173

Rellenos, Mushroom-Corn, with Mole, 178

RISOTTO:

    Broccoli, 167

    Tomato and Sweet Corn, 168

    Wild Mushroom-Barley, 166

Roundup, creating your own, 167

Tart of Chanterelles, Swiss Chard, and Emmentaler, Savory, 170–171

Vegetables, Curry-Roasted, with Indian Cheese Dumplings, 179

Vegetable Tian, Summer, Tangy, 180

Vietnamese Chicken Salad, 97

VINAIGRETTE:

Curried Chopped Vegetable Salad with Pesto Pita Wedges, 96

Lemon-Olive Oil, with Mixed Salad of Many Lettuces, 90

Orange-Rosemary, with Beets, Roasted, and Gorgonzola, 39

Sun-Dried Tomato, Fennel, Braised, with Fresh Mozzarella and, 56

VINEGAR:

sherry, using, 108

See also Balsamic(o) (Vinegar)

Vodka, Bloodhounds, 233

W

Waldorf-Style Chicken Salad, 99

WALNUT:

-Gorgonzola Stuffing, Pork Chops, Center-Cut, with Ruby Port Glaze and, 144–145

and Pear Tart with Red Grape Compote and Stilton, 48–49

Shortbread and Pumpkin Tart with Cranberry Coulis, 253

WATERMELON:

and Shrimp Salad with Jalapeño-Lime Dressing, 100

See also Melons

White Bean(s). *See* Bean(s), White

WILD RICE:

cooking, 215

Duck with Native Grains, Brandied Fruits and Pistachio Stuffing, Roasted, 131

Pilaf, Native Grains, 208

Stir-Fried, 204

WINE:

Burgundy Beef Stew, 83

Burgundy-Rosemary Butter, Salmon, Pan- Roasted, with, 164

Glaze, Red, -Chèvre, Sirloin, Seared Peppered, with, 138

Glaze, Ruby Port, Pork, Chops, Center-Cut, with Gorgonzola-Walnut Stuffing and, 144–145

Marsala Sauce, -Sage, Chicken and Mushrooms, Sautéed, in, 122

port, cooking with, 48

Zinfandel-Spiked Cherries, Chèvre Torte, Creamy, in Pine Nut Crust with, 258–259

Y

YOGURT:

Minted, Apple Bisque, Curried, with, 73

Raita, Cucumber, 298

Z

Zinfandel-Spiked Cherries, Chèvre Torte, Creamy, in Pine Nut Crust with, 258–259

ZUCCHINI:

Tian, Summer Vegetable, Tangy, 181

with White Beans and Mint, 205

ABOUT THE AUTHORS

Businesswoman, community leader, and activist, **Judy Wicks** has done a great deal to build community in Philadelphia, America, and the world. Combining her successful entrepreneurial skills with a passion for food and a commitment to social action, she opened the White Dog Cafe in 1983. Since then she's founded more than ten local and international sister-restaurant projects to promote city- and world-wide community. She also has received many awards and honors recognizing her business skills and community involvement. She was a 1995 recipient of the Business Enterprise Trust Award, the 1994 recipient of the Paradigm Award from the Greater Philadelphia Chamber of Commerce, a 1993 recipient of UNICEF's Mother-Friendly Business Award, and a 1991 recipient of the Human Rights Award from the Philadelphia Commission on Human Relations. She also has been named Delaware Valley Entrepreneur of the Year for Social Responsibility in 1994 and was one of four finalists for the national award from Ernst & Young, Merrill Lynch, and *Inc.* Magazine.

As a child in Texas, **Kevin von Klause** learned his mother's cooking secrets before going on to study and graduate from the Culinary Institute of America. A member of the International Association of Culinary Professionals and the James Beard Foundation, he has been executive chef at the White Dog Cafe since 1986.